P. 15

P. 281

P. 331

THE CHURCH IN CATHOLIC THEOLOGY:
DIALOGUE WITH KARL BARTH

Uniform with this volume

The Church in the Theology of Karl Barth

The Church in Catholic Theology:

Dialogue with Karl Barth

Colm O'Grady, M.S.C.

GEOFFREY CHAPMAN
LONDON   DUBLIN   MELBOURNE   1969

Geoffrey Chapman Ltd
18 High Street, Wimbledon, London SW 19

Geoffrey Chapman (Ireland) Ltd
5–7 Main Street, Blackrock, County Dublin

Geoffrey Chapman Pty Ltd
44 La Trobe Street, Melbourne, Vic 3000, Australia

First published 1969

© 1969, Colm O'Grady, M.S.C.

Nihil Obstat: Vidimus et approbamus ad normam
Statutorum Universitatis Romae,
ex Pontificia Universitate Gregoriana
die 3 mensis Iulii anni 1967
Ioannes Witte, S.J.
Franciscus Sullivan, S.J.

Imprimatur: † Josephus, Archiepiscopus Tuamensis
die 11 mense Iunio anno 1968.

Scripture quotations are taken from the Revised Standard Version. Quotations from Vatican II documents are taken from *The Documents of Vatican II*, edited by Walter M. Abbott, S.J., New York–London, 1966.

This book is set in 10 on 11pt. Lino Bookprint
Made and Printed in Great Britain by Butler and Tanner Ltd, Frome and London

Contents

Abbreviations

Introduction   1

CHAPTER ONE: FIDES QUAERENS INTELLECTUM: THE
    POSSIBILITY, NATURE AND METHOD OF THEOLOGY   5

Section One
The Church of the Father: The Eternal Basis of the Church in God's Election of Grace   21

CHAPTER TWO: THE ETERNAL ELECTION OF THE CHURCH   22

CHAPTER THREE: THE CHURCH ETERNALLY ELECTED—
    Apokatastasis   27

CHAPTER FOUR: THE CHURCH BEFORE AND AFTER CHRIST   35

CHAPTER FIVE: THE CHURCH AND JUDAISM   43

Section Two
The Church in the Son: The Objective Realization of Reconciliation   51

CHAPTER SIX: THE BEING AND WORK OF JESUS CHRIST IN
    CATHOLIC THEOLOGY   54

CHAPTER SEVEN: CONFRONTATION WITH THE DOCTRINE OF
    KARL BARTH   63

CHAPTER EIGHT: CHRISTOLOGY–ECCLESIOLOGY   71

CHAPTER NINE: CHRISTOLOGY–MARIOLOGY–ECCLESIOLOGY   79

Section Three

The Church through the Holy Spirit: The Fundamental Form of the Subjective Realization of Reconciliation   87

CHAPTER TEN: THE MESSIAH AND HIS PEOPLE   89

CHAPTER ELEVEN: THE NEW PEOPLE OF GOD AS THE UNIVERSAL SACRAMENT OF SALVATION   98

CHAPTER TWELVE: THE MISSION OF THE HOLY SPIRIT   123

CHAPTER THIRTEEN: THE MISSION OF THE PEOPLE OF GOD   143

CHAPTER FOURTEEN: THE MISSION AND MINISTRY OF THE LAITY   149
    I. The basis of the laity's mission and function   149
    II. A people of priests, kings and prophets   157

CHAPTER FIFTEEN: THE MISSION AND MINISTRY OF THE HIERARCHY   171
    I. The New Testament basis of the Church's Triple hierarchical ministry   171
    II. The theological understanding of the Church's triple hierarchical ministry   190

CHAPTER SIXTEEN: SCRIPTURE AND TRADITION   214
    I. Scripture   214
    II. Tradition   229

CHAPTER SEVENTEEN: THE JUSTIFICATION OF SINFUL MAN   238

CHAPTER EIGHTEEN: THE CHURCH IS EVENT AND INSTITUTION   251

CHAPTER NINETEEN: THE CHURCH IS VISIBLE AND INVISIBLE   263

CHAPTER TWENTY: THE CHURCH IS THE BODY OF CHRIST   267

CHAPTER TWENTY-ONE: I BELIEVE THE CHURCH   279

CHAPTER TWENTY-TWO: I BELIEVE THE CHURCH IS ONE   282

CHAPTER TWENTY-THREE: I BELIEVE THE CHURCH IS HOLY   289

CHAPTER TWENTY-FOUR: I BELIEVE THE CHURCH IS CATHOLIC   302

CHAPTER TWENTY-FIVE: I BELIEVE THE CHURCH IS APOSTOLIC   310

CHAPTER TWENTY-SIX: THE CHURCH IS ESCHATOLOGICAL	318
CONCLUSION	333
Bibliography	341
Index	379

To Maureen, Padraic, Liam, Michael, Thomas

Abbreviations

AAS	*Acta Apostolicae Sedis*
C.D.	Karl Barth, *Church Dogmatics*[1]
CR	Corpus Reformatorum
CTKB	*The Church in the Theology of Karl Barth* (uniform with this volume)
DBS	*Dictionnaire de la Bible, Supplément*
DCC	Dogmatic Constitution on the Church (Vatican II)
DS	Denzinger–Schönmetzer, *Enchiridion Symbolorum*
DTC	*Dictionnaire de théologie catholique*
ETL	*Ephemerides Theologicae Lovanienses*
Greg.	*Gregorianum*
ITQ	*The Irish Theological Quarterly*
IER	*The Irish Ecclesiastical Record*
K.D.	Karl Barth, *Kirchliche Dogmatik*[1]
LTK	*Lexikon für Theologie und Kirche*
NRT	*Nouvelle revue théologique*
PG	*Patrologia Graeca* (Migne)
PL	*Patrologia Latina* (Migne)
RGG	*Die Religion in Geschichte und Gegenwart*, third edition
RSR	*Revue des sciences religieuses*
RSV	Revised Standard Version of the Bible
Summa theol.	St Thomas Aquinas, *Summa theologiae*
Str.–Bill.	H. L. Strack–P. Billerbeck, *Kommentar zum Neuen Testament aus Talmud und Midrasch*
TS	*Theological Studies*
TWNT	*Theologisches Wörterbuch zum Neuen Testament*, ed. G. Kittel–G. Friedrich

---

[1] *C.D.* I/2, p. 126 (=S. 136) refers to page 126 of the Eng. trans. and to the corresponding *Seite* (page) of the original German of the second Part of Volume One of Barth's *Church Dogmatics*. When I make my own translation from the German (it will not occur very often as the authorized translation is excellent) I give the reference thus: *K.D.* 1/2, S. 136 ((=p. 126).

Introduction

THE news of Karl Barth's death reached me the very morning that an advance copy of my exposition of his doctrine on the Church arrived from the publishers.[1] The news saddened me as only the news of the passing of an esteemed friend can. While I knew him personally, my friendship and esteem was based above all on his theological and spiritual guidance. For if Karl Barth was anything he was a theologian. His faith in the mystery of God and his action issued in a whole life-time of unremitting search for understanding. His great contribution to theology has been his incessant reminder of the transcendency of the God of Christian revelation and of the freedom and gratuitousness of his salvific action.

At the beginning of the century this reminder constituted the salvation of Protestant theology which was then well on the way towards its own demise in liberalism, immanentism and pietism. It constituted a salutary reminder to Roman Catholic theology also. Through overentanglement with one particular philosophical thought-form, and counter to the Protestant Reformation of the sixteenth century, Catholic theology had developed onesidedly, and consequently exaggerated, the immutable and static aspect of Christianity, the created and intrinsic aspect of grace in man's justification, the visible, juridical and sociological aspect of the Church, the Church's traditions, hierarchical ministry, immutability, infallibility and so on. Karl Barth reminded it once more of the fact and essence of the sixteenth-century Reformation, namely, that in Christian theology the primary emphasis must always fall on the Trinity of divine persons and *their* role in the salvation of the world; on the divine origin, freedom and gratuitousness of man's justification; on the concreteness and event-character of every encounter between God and man; on the basic equality of all Christians before their one God and on the priority of the community over the individual; on the spiritual, functional and charismatic aspect of Christian existence, of the Christian Church, its ministries and sacraments; and on the essentially dynamic, missionary and eschatological character of all Christian life.

[1] *The Church in the Theology of Karl Barth*, London–Dublin–Melbourne, 1968.

The Catholic Church has listened to Karl Barth. Its recent ecumenical council can be viewed as an attempted implementation of legitimate demands such as his. Thus the conciliar documents and post-conciliar Catholicism emphasize the theological and spiritual aspect of the Church, the basic equality in dignity and activity of all as the one people of God, the priority of the community over the individual, the basic trinitarian aspect of the Church, that is, the primary and fundamental roles of the Father, Son and Holy Spirit, and the functional, dynamic, charismatic, historical, existential, missionary and eschatological character of its whole existence, life, ministry and structure.

But Catholic theology, for its part, has some legitimate questions for Karl Barth. It questions him basically on the reality of human participation in divine life and activity. It reminds him that it is as man that Christ redeemed and redeems the world, and consequently that his human life and existence shares in the saving power of God himself. It reminds him that Christ's human mother received a special grace from God on the basis of which she exercises a special role in the economy of salvation. It reminds him that through Christ's Spirit the Church shares in the life and ministry of Christ himself for the salvation of all men and the world. Finally, it reminds him that in the individual's justification by God he is empowered and enlivened to cooperate in his own salvation.

Barth has not listened to these legitimate demands. God's presence and activity remain for him so transcendent that, in all of the examples given, he never really becomes immanent as human life and action. God alone, he says, is salvifically operative. There is no such thing as real human participation in his life and salvific action. This is a denial of the very basis of what is distinctive to Catholicism. And this is why Barth has always presented such a challenge to Catholicism. Furthermore, Barth has repeatedly claimed that he presents the logical and consistent and consequent development of the principles of the Reformers, namely, of the *sola fide* of Luther and the *soli Deo gloria* of Calvin in the understanding of the relationship between God and man. Thus it would seem that the basic Protestant–Catholic dialogue is typified in the Barth–Catholic dialogue. Certainly, because of his radical interpretation of the Reformers, and because of the consistency and extensiveness of his theology, the discussion with him reveals in all its clarity and acuteness and breadth the basic Protestant–Catholic divergence.

From these few remarks the method, purpose and scope of this second volume of my study will be apparent. In the companion volume *The Church in the Theology of Karl Barth*, I tried to present faithfully Barth's doctrine on the Church. Here I will let *Catholic* ecclesiology be questioned by Barth's ecclesiology and try to develop and draw it out along lines suggested by Barth when this is considered to be in accordance with the Scriptures. On the other hand, I will let *Barth*'s ecclesiology be questioned by Catholic ecclesiology, and indicate the evangelical basis where I think the criticism of the former by the latter to be legitimate. Thus will appear the ecclesiological agreements and disagreements between Barth and Catholicism. Furthermore, I would like to indicate the basic theological reasons underlying these agreements and disagreements. These are not necessarily ecclesiological. In theologies so consistent and inter-connected as those of the Catholic Church and of Karl Barth it is necessary to view their respective ecclesiologies in the light of their doctrines on election, Jesus Christ and justification.

The understanding of both Catholic and Barthian theology is of course only my own. Consequently, it is entirely open to criticism and correction when this is shown to be needed. This applies in particular to my understanding of Barth. It would be a great pity if the Catholic reader limited himself to this second volume for an understanding of Barth. Barth speaks for himself in volume one. Because of his immense contribution to the recent renewal in Catholic theology he must be read for himself. In addition, the accurateness of my assessment must be judged from that source—better still, of course, from the works themselves of Barth there referred to. Finally, I present there the views of Barth on many points which are not raised here. My aim is a basic dialogue with Barth in the sense outlined in the preceding paragraph. I will follow, more or less, the basic divisions forced upon me by the matter itself in my exposition of Barth's ecclesiology. The principal source of my understanding of Catholic ecclesiology will be the Second Vatican Council's Dogmatic Constitution on the Church. The principal source and norm of my disagreements with Barth will be the Holy Scriptures—and in their Protestant Revised Standard Version. At the end of volume one I have given a select Barthian bibliography. At the end of the present volume the reader will find a list of overall reference works together with a select bibliography for each chapter. When these works are cited in the body of the book often only an abbreviated reference is given.

I would like to thank sincerely all who helped in any way in the preparation of these two volumes: my superiors for granting time and means; my teachers and moderators Frs J. L. Witte, S.J., and F. A. Sullivan, S.J., of the Gregorian University; my confrères for their interest and encouragement; Bob, John and Charles for their proofreading; Sandra and Roberta for their typing. In view of the current upheaval in our understanding of the Christian Church and of the faith in general my sole hope is that these two volumes may serve as a pointer, no matter how inadequate and imperfect, to that one Church of Jesus Christ for our time, whose realization is the common task of all Christians.

COLM O'GRADY, M.S.C.

Moyne Park, Christmas 1968

Chapter One

Fides Quaerens Intellectum:
The Possibility, Nature and Method of Theology

THESE introductory reflections are concerned with the corresponding introductory remarks to Karl Barth's method of theology, thought-form and conception of analogy, which I have given in the first volume of this study.[1] Like all else in this second volume, they are intended to be reflections on the christocentricism of his theology. For the moment I wish to consider his christocentricism from the point of view of the formal principle of theology. My reflections will bear principally on three points, which are intimately connected: i. Karl Barth's conception of the science of theology as *fides quaerens intellectum*; ii. his conception of analogy; iii. his actualist thought-form.

We must certainly admire Barth's concern for realism and objectivity in his search for a truly theological method. This whole concern sprang from his desire to safeguard God's sovereignty and transcendency—which has been his concern from the beginning. He did not think that it was safeguarded in Protestant liberal theology or in Roman Catholic theology—which he regarded as the two great adversaries, and between which he liked to consider his own theology a mean. Liberal theology denied it, he says, by subjecting the Word of God to history and subjective experience. Catholic theology denied it by objectifying the Word of God by means of a preconceived *analogia entis*. Barth endeavours to find a way between these two extremes. God must be the sovereign subject of theology because he is its sovereign object.[2] In his further development this is expressed in the phrase: Jesus Christ is the sole noetic principle because he is the sole ontic content of theology.

Has Barth been successful? Has he safeguarded God's transcendency and sovereignty? Has he safeguarded the objectivity of God's

[1] Cf *CTKB*, pp. 61f.   [2] Cf *ibid.*, pp. 62, 64–7.

Word and of theology? Was his criticism of Catholic theology just? These are the questions I must try to answer.

And first of all it must be acknowledged that he has safeguarded the transcendency and sovereignty of God. In his explanation God is really the subject of theology. He is the One who alone and always speaks his Word in the words of man. But has Barth safeguarded the objectivity of revelation, and therefore of theology? In his solution is there anything which can act as a criterion or control of what man, individually and subjectively, *thinks* is the Word of God? I do not think so. For according to him the origin of revelation is solely the Spirit speaking to his spirit in the Word. Certainly, the *Spirit* speaking to his spirit, but none the less *his* spirit is the norm of God's Word. The Holy Spirit speaking to his spirit in faith: this is the source of theology. This is a fact, and nothing more can be said either in proof or disproof.[3]

In his explanation is the humanity and human word of Jesus Christ, which for him is 'the basic sacramental reality', in some way in itself the Word of God? No, it is not.[4] Is the written word of Scripture in some way in itself the Word of God? No, it is not.[5] Does the human word of the Church proclaim the Word of God? No, it does not.[6] While theology, he says, as Church dogmatics is bound to the objective *Credo* of the Church, this obligation is relative and need only be provisional. All these forms of the Word of God never are in themselves the Word of God. They are the Word of God only in the ever new and direct act of God through his Spirit. Consequently, a direct appeal to them in so far as they are human words cannot settle any question. God uses this-worldly signs to speak to man but in all cases he and he alone remains the sole acting subject. 'The activity of the sign is, directly, the activity of God himself. . . . Whatever mediators or media God makes use of, in order to speak to man and to act on him, he always remains himself the subject (*immer selber das Subjekt*) of this speaking and acting.'[7] It is clear that whatever Barth may mean by 'creaturely mediation' he does not mean that human words and realities under the action of God effectively (in the sense that they really act) mediate revelation, and consequently that an appeal can be made to their objective authority.

---

[3] Barth has been accused of an 'as if' (*als ob*) theology—cf E. Peterson, *Was ist Theologie?*, Bonn, 1925, p. 7. The accusation is repeated by J. Hamer, *Karl Barth*, New York, 1962, pp. 101–2.

[4] *CTKB*, pp. 161f.

[5] Cf *ibid.*, pp. 193f.

[6] Cf *ibid.*, pp. 322f.

[7] *C.D.* I/2, p. 224(=S.245). Cf *CTKB*, pp. 87f, 162.

Barth's attempt at mediation between liberal Protestantism and Catholicism is not successful. I cannot see how he really safeguards the authority of Holy Scripture and of the Church. He *asserts* the objectivity of the Word of God, and the need for the authority of Scripture and of the Church. But if the Word of God is always God's direct act alone, in what does the authority of the Church consist? And how does what Barth says differ from liberal Protestant subjectivism? Again, he stresses the necessity of a secondary objectivity if God's Word is to reach us, for our knowledge is limited to creaturely reality.[8] But in what does this necessity consist if God's Word is not humanly objective in some way in this creaturely reality? Or, how can man know it if it is not expressed in some way *by* created reality to which his knowledge is limited?

I cannot see how Barth has really progressed beyond his original exegetical method.[9] He speaks now more in the line of a 'response theology'. But does the response of the authors of Holy Scripture really perceive and express in some way the Word to which they respond? Do they really hear and express it in some way? If not, in what does the authority of their response consist? What is to prevent my response from being different? We know from experience that it is not sufficient to say that the Holy Spirit guarantees the continuity of the response. Certainly, the Holy Spirit is the sole ultimate guarantee. But he is this *through* the written word of Scripture, and *through* the proclaimed word of the Church. I will show later that this in no way impugns God's absolute sovereignty and freedom.

If Barth's development on the question of *analogy* had really brought him to agree with Catholicism his method should have become more objective. There is undoubtedly a development in his anthropology, and consequently in his doctrine on analogy. From *C.D.* III/1 onwards he speaks of man's *existence* in God's image. As such man is God's 'good' creation. His goodness consists in his creation to be the 'theatre of grace'. That is, it consists in his existence over against and for God and his fellow man. It is hard to understand how Barth can say he exists over against (*gegen*) God and yet he enjoys no relatively autonomous existence. For he goes on to say that the *imago Dei* is not intrinsic to man but is the continual creation of God.[10]

In III/2 this position seems to be overcome. Barth speaks of man's adaptability to enter into covenant-partnership with God.[11]

[8] *CTKB*, pp. 86, 162f.
[9] Cf *ibid.*, pp. 38f.
[10] Cf *ibid.*, p. 91.   [11] *Ibid.*, p. 93.

Adaptability or susceptibility obviously presupposes a good being and activity proper to an already existing man. God can use man and his thoughts and words to express his Word. In this Barth does not seem to differ from the concept of 'analogy of being' expounded by certain Catholic authors, with whom he was in dialogue.[12] For these the analogy of being connotes, amongst other things, a certain autonomy of the human creature over against God, as well as man's *potentia obedientialis* towards God. Barth should be able to say that under the action of God man can think and speak God's Word, that is, that he can co-operate or sub-operate.

But immediately he goes on, in *C.D.* III/3, to speak of a sole subjectivity and a sole direct activity of God. This would seem to imply that man's existence and activity over against God as his image is not *ei proprium* after all, but can be predicated solely of the divine act. But if that is the case, what distinction can Barth place between nature and grace, reason and faith, creation and the Church? He accuses Catholicism of reducing all to nature by its doctrine of man's cooperation under grace. But is not the doctrine of cooperation, with its underlying implication of the value of human existence and action, necessary for the *distinction* between nature and grace? And is it not Barth himself who fails to distinguish them by reducing all to grace and to God's act? Similarly, Barth says that the grace of reconciliation is never given to man so that he can act in its power. He seems to emphasize always God's action to the detriment of its term, both in creation and reconciliation. Whatever development he accomplished seems to be vitiated by the recurrent *solo* of his theology: God alone, in Jesus Christ, through his Holy Spirit, is salvifically active.

When we turn now to a consideration of the reality and possibility of theology, as outlined by Barth, the same uni-divine activity meets us once more. It is refreshing to see Barth insist so much on faith as a perception of, and assent to, truth. This has been traditional Catholic teaching. But it is not easy to understand how, in Barth's view, faith is really *man's* act, and consequently how *man* really perceives God and can practise theology. For the *analogia fidei* which Barth says God creates between human thought and his truth in the event of his revelation is always and solely *his* act. The analogy is never grasped by man. Human knowing, in so far as man is its subject, never attains in any way to God. If it does, it is only in

---

[12] Cf the works of E. Przywara and G. Söhngen listed in the bibliography to *CTKB*. On the whole question, cf H. Bouillard, *Karl Barth*, vol. III, esp. pp. 190–217.

so far as God himself is its direct subject. At this point one particular claim of Barth's theology does break imperiously before us: God is known only by God.[13]

Barth rightly emphasizes that theology is *fides quaerens intellectum*, that it is the science of faith. This way of viewing theology was already present in Clement of Alexandria's concept of *Gnosis*,[14] and especially in Augustine whose formula *crede ut intelligas* or *nisi credideritis non intelligetis* (Is 7:9)[15] was repeated by, and influenced, the whole course of theology since then.[16] Faith is a movement into the world of eternal life which results in a penetration, apprehension, or in short, in an understanding (*intellectus*) by the human mind of the object of faith. Theology is thus *fides quaerens intellectum*. It owes its origin to God's special illumination through faith—through a pious and loving faith, as St Augustine insists. Knowledge of God's being therefore follows his activity through faith, or as Barth put it,[17] *esse sequitur operari*. Theology is a participation in God's own knowledge through self-communication in faith.[18] It is an illumination and participation *given to man*, and therefore a knowledge which is his. This participated knowledge then *quaerit intellectum* through its human receptacle, that is, through man's intelligence. It seeks to reproduce itself in human knowledge. Theology is this becoming incarnate of divine knowledge.

It is not simply the product of a light placed in the human mind. It is not simply the act of God knowing himself through human thoughts and words. It is the product of the human mind itself—'flooded by an infused light, but in accordance with its own abilities and structure'.[19] It is the act of man under the influence of God's act. As such, theology cannot of course be identified with God's knowledge of himself. Finite minds and concepts are incapable of adequately expressing the infinite. There will always be the element of symbolism (or analogy) in man's attempt to understand God and his revelation. His concepts and words will always point beyond

[13] Cf *CTKB*, p. 87.

[14] Cf Clement of Alexandria, *Stromateis*, VII, 20, 57, 55.

[15] Cf Augustine, *De lib. arb.*, l. II, c. 11, n. 6 (*PL* 32:1243); *Sermo*, 43 (*PL* 38:254–8).

[16] Cf, e.g., Anselm, *Proslogion*, c. I (*PL* 158:227); St Thomas Aquinas, *Summa theol.*, II–IIae, q. 4, art. 8, obj. 3; q. 8, art. 5, obj. 3. Cf Congar, *art. cit.*, in *DTC*, XV, col. 348 (Clement of Alexandria), 351 (Augustine and others).

[17] Cf *CTKB*, p. 87.

[18] St Thomas could describe it as 'velut quaedam impressio divinae scientiae, quae est una et simplex omnium' (*Summa theol.*, I, q. 1, art. 3, ad 2).

[19] M.-D. Chenu, *Is Theology a Science?*, p. 35.

themselves to the reality they indicate but do not adequately grasp or express.[20] Yet they can indicate him. While adequate knowledge is a promise for the future this does not deny the reality and truth of our present knowledge. 'For now we see in a mirror dimly, but then face to face. Now I know in part; then I shall understand fully, even as I have been fully understood' (I Cor 13:12). God's revelation is not so transcendent that man is unable to hear and obey it. 'For this commandment which I command you this day is not too hard for you, neither is it far off. It is not in heaven, that you should say, "Who will go up for us to heaven and bring it to us, that we may hear it and do it?" . . . But the word is very near you; it is in your mouth and in your heart, so that you can do it' (Deut 30:11-12, 14). Human words and thoughts, as spoken and thought by men, are able to express and grasp God's Word. Paul is in no doubt: 'And we also thank God constantly for this, that when you received the word of God which you heard from us, you accepted it not as the word of man but as what it really is, the word of God, which is at work in you believers' (I Thess 2:13). Human reason can become the sub-operative incarnational instrument of divine truth just as Christ's human nature became his sub-operative instrument in his once for all redemption and revelation as man (cf. I Tim 2:5-6). As Fr Mersch says:

> 'The admitting of human reason into divine truth, as is done in theology, is not an unnatural commingling or a sacrilegious intrusion, any more than the entrance of a believer into Church or the union of human nature with the Word is an intolerable profanation. Luther regarded [scholastic] theology as a monstrous hybrid, a sort of centaur: human reasonings coupled with divine truth. St Thomas spoke quite differently. Human reasoning is the act, the cooperation of an intellect divinized [I would prefer to say "elevated"] by living faith. Hence "they who employ philosophical demonstration in sacred science by bringing reason to the service of faith, do not mix water with wine but change water into wine".'[21]

[20] The same St Thomas who from one point of view could speak of theology as 'quaedam impressio divinae scientiae' could also say of earthly knowledge of God: 'tanto in hac vita deum perfectius cognoscimus quanto magis intelligimus eum excedere quidquid intellectu comprehenditur' (*Summa theol.*, II–IIae, q.8, art. 7).

[21] E. Mersch, *The Theology of the Mystical Body*, New York, 1958, p. 13, citing St Thomas, *In Boeth. de Trin.*, q. 2, art. 3, ad. 5; cf also *ibid.*, art. 2c.
Fr Mersch does not give any reference to the writings of Luther. He is

THE POSSIBILITY, NATURE AND METHOD OF THEOLOGY 11

And Fr Chenu:

'Theology is at one with the theandric mystery of the Word of God, the Word made flesh. There alone can it dare to find confidence in the coherence of faith and reason.'[22]

Did the man Jesus know and speak God's Word? And if he did was he the only man to do so? This is the perspective in which Barth's and the Catholic position should be confronted. Obviously, if Barth understands the 'theandric mystery' slightly differently, the 'coherence of faith and reason' will not be so conspicuous. This is, in fact, the case, as we shall see.[23] Even with regard to the man Jesus, Barth speaks of a solely divine act, of a solely divine subjectivity. He is consistent in saying the same with regard to all other men. His consideration of the human act of faith is very weak.[24] He reduces it practically to a continuation of his treatment of faith as God's creation.[25] He does not evaluate man sufficiently as God's good creation, and as the active and creative recipient of his grace. This is a constant failing of his theology. In the problem under consideration it appears in his denial of natural theology, of the value of philosophical reflection, of the elevation of man's knowing in faith, of the incarnation of faith through man's faculties.

He does allow a certain value to philosophy, and has some pertinent directions as regards the use of philosophical thought-forms in the understanding of Scripture.[26] But philosophy has only an 'immanental significance'. This seems to be identical with what he later called the 'relative validity' of man's truth.[27] No human thought-form, he says, is better than another for the service of God's truth. All can equally be used by God's Word, for all are equally unfitted

---

probably referring to such passages as *Dictata super Psalt.*, in ps. 73 (Weimar 3, 508–90); *in ps.* 84 (Weimar 4, 10–11); *in ps.* 68 (Weimar 3, 419); and especially Luther's *Disputatio contra scholasticam theologiam* (Weimar 1) where he affirms the absolute heterogeneity of philosophical knowledge and Christian doctrine, or the impossibility of utilizing philosophically acquired knowledge in theology—which rejected the very basis of the Church's traditional concept of theology (cf Congar, *DTC*, XV, col. 414f). Fr Congar says we can recognize in Luther 'le Pere de la "theologie dialectique", animée par le rejet de toute analogia entis et de tout "surnaturel" qui ne soit pas Dieu, l'Incréé, lui-meme' (*art. cit.*, col. 416).

[22] *Op. cit.*, p. 50.
[23] Cf below, Section Two, chapter seven.
[24] Cf *C.D.* IV/1, pp. 757–79 (=SS. 846–72).
[25] Cf *ibid.*, pp. 740–57 (=SS. 826–46).
[26] Cf *CTKB*, p. 73.
[27] Cf *ibid.*, p. 167.

to be made use of. Barth would seem to assert a double order of truth. There is a human order of truth, parallel to and reflecting, but in no way attaining, a divine order of truth. If the human attains or expresses the divine it is solely in so far as it is a divine act. Human thoughts and words are, as it were, taken out of man's hands. Man's participation in God's truth is always and solely God's own act.

The Catholic theologian's assessment of human reason is quite different.[28] He maintains that man's human faculties have value in themselves in the search for absolute truth and can consequently really serve faith in its incarnation in the human mind. Faith does not issue in theology independently of the human mind. As an illumination of the mind it attains its goal, namely, the *intelligere* of its object (what Clement of Alexandria called *Gnosis*), only *in* and *through* the human mind. Consequently every valid human philosophy can and should be used in this 'incarnation', in theology. This is why St Thomas could use Aristotelian metaphysics. He knew that theology would be simply impossible unless human reason could be brought into the service of divine faith. For otherwise theology, as the human science of the knowledge of God, would never be human knowledge but always remain God's own knowledge of himself. Everything would be reduced to grace, to the divine action, and no real distinction would be possible between faith and reason, grace and nature, in the economy of salvation. This basic validity of human reason is not solely a tenet of philosophy but is founded in revelation itself. According to Gen 1:24, 3f even in the natural order man owes his origin to God and is as such 'good'. Furthermore, since God the Creator and God the Redeemer are one (cf Heb 1:1f, John 1:1f) that which God created is not destroyed or nullified by his redemption but perfected. This was the truth the medieval scholastics expressed in the phrase *Gratia non tollit sed perficit naturam*, and which St Thomas explicitly adduces in explanation and defence of his theological method.[29] Creation is the outer basis of the covenant (to use Barth's own words[30]), created not only by but with a view to Jesus Christ. 'All things were created through him and for him' (Col 1:16). Finally, God's use of human and created media, and especially of his own human nature, as instruments of his revelation and redemption highlights the intrinsic possibility and validity of their use as instruments. It is only on the basis of this validity that

[28] Cf Vatican Council I, *De Fide et Ratione*, DS, 3015-20.
[29] *In Boethium de Trinitate*, q. II, ad 3, cited in Congar, *art. cit.*, *DTC*, XV, col. 390.
[30] Cf *CTKB*, pp. 81f, 89.

we can speak of theology at all, and also of a development of theology, and of the necessity of a continual renewal in theology.

The faith must become incarnate along the lines of the culture peculiar to each age and place. Barth says Catholicism subjects the Word of God to a foreign philosophical system and thus falsifies it. It has been 'hopelessly entangled with Aristotelianism from the Middle Ages onwards'.[31] He even considers the central task of protestant irenic and polemic to consist in its 'recall from this distraction to its proper business, the Christian theme'.[32] What I have already said should be comment enough on the word 'foreign'. True human philosophy, that is, that which presents a true assessment of anthropological, cosmological and even theological reality on the basis of human reflection, is never so foreign that it cannot be of service to divine revelation. That said, however, I cannot but agree with Barth in his accusation that Catholic theology has been, if not 'hopelessly', at least over-entangled with Aristotelianism. In more recent times this accusation has become the refrain of all the theological writers with regard to the past of Christianity in general, both Catholic and Protestant. But the recall they advocate is not so much from a 'distraction' but to a change of thought-form. The accusation is that the Christian theme has been perverted not because of the use of a philosophical thought-form but because of the over-protracted use of one particular thought-form. Christianity and God have become irrelevant and 'dead' to modern man because of the over-protracted use of an outdated socio-cultural framework. Barth's accusation is right therefore in the sense that Catholic theology has failed to acknowledge the value of other thought-forms and in its devotion to one thought-form even falsified revelation through one-sided emphasis. Often indeed the defence and preservation of the faith was identified with the defence and preservation of this one particular philosophy. Aristotelianism is not necessarily and perennially the best thought-form of theology.

On the other hand, I cannot agree with Barth when he says that the adoption of Aristotelianism by the medieval scholastics was a useless and falsifying distraction. Certainly, in later times Greek philosophy did seem to oust Scripture as the source and norm of theology. But who can doubt the insights gained to theological science through the employment of the Aristotelian categories of *nature* and *causality*? The medieval theologians never favoured Thomism because they wished to control the Word of God. Philosophy was always for them

[31] *C.D.* III/2, p. 9 (=S. 8.)
[32] *C.D.* II/2, p. 532 (=S. 591).

the *ancilla theologiae*. They did not subject the Word of God to any human philosophy. As Fr Congar points out,[33] the theological thought of St Thomas Aquinas and his time was essentially and profoundly biblical and traditional so that 'it is not Aristotle who commands but the Word of God itself'. This is illustrated in the fact that Thomas did not accept Aristotle *talis qualis* but corrected and changed his philosophy at many points. He used Aristotelian philosophy in the service of the Word in faith. To put it differently: the Word of God found Greek philosophy useful as an instrument for its incarnation in human minds of that time, while correcting it at certain points and therefore to that extent finding it a disservice, and issued in, and can even be said to have created to a certain extent, what became known as Thomistic theology. Apart altogether from the question of the relevancy of Thomism at this particular *kairos* of the world's socio-cultural evolution I think it did express better in its own way a certain aspect of revelation which forms precisely the basic bone of contention between Barth (and, as he himself claims, he seems to represent the logical position of the Protestantism of the Reformers) and Catholicism. This becomes clear when we consider Barth's actualist thought-form. No matter what the thought-form of the future will be, this aspect of revelation must find expression.

Barth says that the theme of theology, Jesus Christ, imposes an exclusively actualist thought-form on theology.[34] Jesus Christ is act, movement, history. There is nothing static about his person, states or time. His incarnation, death, resurrection, and glorification, that is, his reconciliation, is a once-for-all act. It is a history which takes place now as it did then. This is a basic element in Barthian theology. It offers, I think, a valuable insight for the elaboration of a theology of the history of salvation which is only just now being undertaken on the Catholic side. Later I will try to do it justice in an ecclesio-logico-sacramental context. The thought-form of a theology which is christology, Barth says, must think in terms of pure act and movement. To give but one example: the Church and Christian life, both here and hereafter, cannot be considered as a state of inactive introspection or enjoyment, but a mission in the service of the world.

This view of Barth's is very refreshing when compared with the static essentialism which has pervaded Catholic manuals of both philosophy and theology until quite recently. His actualism is far more suited to render evangelical theology understandable. How often, again to give but one example, I have found myself far more

[33] *Art. cit.* in *DTC*, XV, col. 391-2.
[34] Cf *CTKB*, pp. 75f.

at home and nearer to the sense of the *history of salvation* in reading the moving, dynamic, kerygmatic theology of Karl Barth than in reading about the 'state' of grace, and the 'state' of sin, and the 'states' of perfection, not to mention the 'state' or law of nature, in our own essentially static and dead manuals! For too long Catholic thought has been immersed in essentialism—not only as a thought-form but as a whole attitude towards the mysteries of our faith and towards human life.[35]

However, I do not accept Barth's thought-form unreservedly. He himself foresaw difficulties both as regards its legitimacy and possibility. And firstly I do not think it is *legitimate* in its *exclusivity*. The theme of the Bible certainly is a history. As the description or interpretation of this theme the language form of the Bible is above all that of narrative. Since the Bible is the source of theology the language form of theology must also be historical, actualist, moving. As the centre of the Bible and consequently of theology the person and the work of Jesus Christ is the description of a continual history between God and man, a continual upward and downward movement. And this centre is not merely the past centre of a past drama. Jesus Christ is the living centre of an ever present drama. The incarnation and resurrection of Christ, in so far as they are divine acts, cannot be measured by time. They are eternal and take place now as they did then. Theological thought- and language-form must be *actualist* to express this. But the incarnation, the hypostatic union, is an *unio* as well as an *unitio*, a gift as well as an act. Similarly, the union between the risen Christ and his Church through his Spirit is both an *unio* as well as an *unitio*, a gift as well as an act—one could say it is an 'institution' as well as an 'event'. An exclusive actualism is incapable of expressing the complete reality of the hypostatic union or of the union of the Holy Spirit and the Church. It must be complemented.

Secondly, I do not consider its exclusivity possible. Barth understands scholastic ontology (scholasticism, Thomistico-Aristotelianism) to mean static essentialism. In this he was undoubtedly misled by so-called 'scholastics' themselves, who had turned theology into a timeless and immovable science. Barth goes to the other

---

[35] Fr Schillebeeckx considers this essentialist versus existentialist attitude to be the fundamental source of the difference manifested by the participants in Vatican II. Cf his *A Struggle of Minds and other Essays*, pp. 10–32, for his illustration of this with regard to the questions of eirenism versus true ecumenism, diluted theology versus true pastoral theology, truth as possession and growing truth.

extreme. 'Being is act', he says.³⁶ For him the sole constituent of being is act or existence. But, one must ask him, how can existence be detached from essence? That is, how can I form a concept of existence without forming a concept of that which exists? The scholastic concept of being includes both the concepts of essence and existence. And, in fact, the true scholastic ontology is *centred*, not in essence, but in *existence*. Its thoroughly realist and existentialist nature is being brought more into light by recent thinkers.³⁷ Its object is first and foremost being as existence, or the consideration of that which exists in so far as it exists.

> 'Those who on the pretext that natures and intelligible structures and degrees of being exist for this philosophy, regard its conception of reality as "static", as they say, simply own that they do not know what they are talking about. Devoted to the mystery of the act of existing, this philosophy is by that very fact devoted to the mystery of action and the mystery of movement.'³⁸

Act cannot then be regarded as the sole constitutive principle of being. Being is not only act but that which acts or exists. It is of course primarily that which *exists*, and consequently every thought-form must be primarily existentialist or actualist. But being is also *that which* exists, and therefore every thought-form must be also essentialist. Barth may think that the Catholic understanding of Jesus Christ, the Church and Christian life, was determined by these philosophical principles. I believe they are simply a philosophical demonstration of the impossibility of an exclusive actualism and a corroboration of our understanding of these aspects of revelation. I believe they are principles which revelation in faith found useful in its incarnation in theology and that consequently no matter how differently they may find expression in the thought-forms of the future they must find expression.

From this point of view it may be well to point out that theological thought-form must become ecumenical too, like its content.³⁹ It must be able to express the totality of Christian truth. The thought-

---

³⁶ *C.D.* IV/2, p. 108 (=S. 120).

³⁷ The work of Blondel, Maréchal, Gilson, Maritain, de Finance, Coreth, K. Rahner, von Balthasar, De Petter, Schillebeeckx, Fabro, Nédoncelle, Lonergan, etc., comes to mind.

³⁸ J. Maritain, *Existence and the Existent*, p. 54. Cf pp. 40–1. Cf also F. McHenry, *art. cit.*, pp. 104, 217.

³⁹ Ecumenical theology for E. Schillebeeckx consists in a re-integration, through a return to the sources, of suppressed or overgrown truths, into the totality of a theological synthesis—cf *A Struggle of Minds*, pp. 18–19.

form reflected in the documents of Vatican II constitutes an immense progress in this respect. It overcomes that static essentialism which was so characteristic of former conciliar documents, but without falling into an exclusive existentialism. Many neo-Thomists or neo-scholastics would see in it a reflection of the repristination of true Thomistic metaphysics which is for them the form best suited to express the totality of Christian revelation—and it would be this because it is, and was, the human form of the incarnation of the faith of the *undivided Church*, of the *una, sancta, catholica et apostolica ecclesia*. It will be interesting to see if this repristination, and therefore the thought-form of Vatican II itself, has the power to achieve in all its extension that renewal for which our age clamours. Personally I think that while it provided the all-important and authoritative impetus in the right direction, it remained too introvert, too much centred on the Church itself as something distinct from the world, and consequently its thought-form remained also something understandable only to the initiated. Theology and Christianity are essentially historical. As the incarnation of the faith in the human mind theology is and must be the understanding and expression of that faith in the cultural, philosophical and sociological thought-forms of every place and time. This is being repeatedly emphasized by modern writers who are very much aware of the outdatedness, other-worldliness and irrelevancy of many of its present forms. Leslie Dewart, for instance, makes the point that Christian truth is essentially historical, that is, that its continuity is and can only be found in the factuality, contingency and temporality of its thought-forms.[40] As regards the Church Hans Küng, with characteristic realism, emphasizes that the essence of the Christian Church is to be found only in the contingency of its ever-changing forms and institutions.[41] Finally, Harvey Cox makes the quite legitimate demand that the socio-cultural setting of the contemporary technopolis must substitute those of the town and tribal eras, or at least be given full consideration and evaluation, in modern Christianity's self-understanding and self-expression in a secularized world.[42]

The *same* Christian religion must be understood and formulated in the historical *difference* of cultural, philosophical and sociological thought-patterns. To be realistically lived it must be re-thought and re-formulated in every age and in every culture. No one thought-form should be imposed. Theology is the incarnation in the human mind

[40] *The Future of Belief*, pp. 120–1.
[41] *The Church*, Part I, pp. 3–39: 'The Church as it is'.
[42] *The Secular City*, passim.

and therefore according to the socio-cultural background of that mind of the present action of the Holy Spirit in the word of Scripture read in the Church. Former expressions of the Church's understanding will have to be translated or transformed for later cultures, and formulations of the western world will be formulated differently in the eastern world. Only thus will Christianity, the Church and theology achieve relevancy and progress. Only thus can it prove itself the 'universal (or catholic) sacrament or sign and instrument of salvation'.[43] This is of course a tremendous task and responsibility. But it is a task which must face Christian theology in every age and culture. This is its mission. And it can carry it out with all the courage of its confidence in the promised presence of the Holy Spirit. Such a reformulation and transformation of our faith is just now particularly called for, and is indeed already under way. It may prove of immense benefit to the ecumenical movement for many of our differences may be shown to be based on traditional thought-forms rather than on the Word of God. There is, however, one thing we must always remember, and Karl Barth provides a timely reminder: the Word of God helps to provide its own thought-form. Philosophical and sociological study is not enough for the reformulation of the Christian faith. This must always be accompanied, and indeed preceded, by biblical and confessional study, for the Word of God in faith becomes incarnate and finds its understanding in the human mind only through the written word of Scripture as confessed and proclaimed in the Church.[44] This necessitates a study of the past which must then be concretely, realistically and meaningfully expressed and realized in the present. The future of the Church and faith really depends on its implementation in the present of its insight into its past. As H. Küng says of the Church: 'The Church must constantly reflect upon its real existence in the present with reference to its origins in the past in order to assure its existence in the future.'[45] I believe, therefore, that Karl Barth's basic observation that the thought-form of the Word of God is not taken solely from human philosophies but is to a certain extent imposed and created by the Word itself is a valid one, and timely, too, in the light of the hurried and even frantic searching that is currently being

[43] Vatican II, DCC, n. 1 and 48.
[44] B. Lonergan seems to intend some such self-formation of the Word of God in the human mind in theology when he writes: 'Since method is simply reason's explicit consciousness of the norms of its own procedures, the illumination of reason by faith implies an illumination of method by faith', *Collection*, Papers by B. Lonergan, ed. by F. E. Crowe, New York–London, 1967, p. 138. [45] *The Church*, p. 15. Cf pp. 414, 488.

done by Christian theologians for a new theological thought-form. At the same time I do not believe that his own solution of exclusive actualism does justice to ecumenical truth, that is, to the totality of Christian revelation. I think it is unduly restricted or limited by an unduly restricted or limited confessional pre-supposition.

What is the *ultimate basis* of the difference between Karl Barth and Catholicism with regard to the problems touched upon in this introduction, namely, the problem of analogy, of the method, nature, possibility and thought-form of theology? Karl Barth himself gives the answer, and I agree with him. The Reformers' retention of natural theology, he says, that is, their retention of man's possibility of knowing God apart from revelation and faith, as well as Protestant orthodoxy's assertion of an *analogia attributionis intrinsecae*, is incompatible and inconsistent with the Reformation doctrine of justification *sola fide, sola gratia*.[46]

From the beginning Karl Barth accepted the basic concern of Luther's theology, namely, justification by faith alone, but he radicalized it according to an ultra-Calvinistic *soli Deo gloria*. For him God *alone* is salvifically active in the relationship between God and man. This is the basis of his theology. It is the principle which determines his theological thought-form. Actualism is the sole thought-form which results from, and safeguards, God's sole subjectivity. God's sovereignty and freedom means *sola fide, sola gratia, solo Verbo, solo Spiritu, solo Christo, solo Deo*. Any talk of 'habitual grace', or of active human mediation of revelation or of reconciliation is a contradiction of the basic principle. This is the principle which determines his conception of analogy as well. Analogy is the act of God alone. It is never a possession of man. It is the principle which rules his conception of the possibility of theology. It is God who knows God in man's thoughts and words. Human reason does not actively cooperate or sub-operate in faith's incarnation in theology.

Barth concludes his treatment of the question of analogy and of man's knowledge of God with words which are very illuminating for the understanding of his whole theology and of the basic difference between him (and we should not forget his claim to represent the consistent Protestant view) and Catholicism:

'Warned by this precedent, we have therefore attempted to understand and form the doctrine of analogy otherwise than the older

[46] For the Reformers and natural theology, cf *C.D.* II/1, p. 127 (=S. 140). For Protestant orthodoxy and analogy, cf *ibid.*, p. 239 (=S. 270). Cf *CTKB*, pp. 88f.

orthodoxy did, and as in truth it must be understood and formed, *if we are already aware* that *Christology* really is and must remain the life-centre of theology, of all theology, *and if we are also aware that the correct interpretation of Christology,* as presented even by the older orthodoxy, *is to be found in the doctrine of the justification of the sinner by faith alone.*'[47]

I am fully in agreement with Karl Barth that theology must be christocentric and christofugal. But I cannot go along with him in claiming that christology must be interpreted according to another pre-conceived principle. This is what makes his christocentricism 'constricted', and this it is which ultimately forms my basic objection to his theology.

---

[47] *C.D.* II/1, p. 242 (=S. 274), emphasis mine. Cf also Barth's objections to Bultmann and von Balthasar cited in *CTKB*, pp. 78–9.

Section One

The Church of the Father:
The Eternal Basis of the Church in God's Election of Grace

WITH this first section I initiate my strictly ecclesiological dialogue with Karl Barth. The points to be discussed in this section are particularly difficult ones, and are very rarely considered in Catholic ecclesiological treatises. While wishing to present some basic elements of a Catholic position in their regard I do not intend to write a treatise on them. My aim is a dialogue with Karl Barth. The points considered are consequently limited to those raised by him, and indeed only to some of them. On the other hand, to him must go the merit of raising these points, which help so much towards the realization of that integral ecclesiology sketched and desired by the Second Vatican Council.

In the *first* chapter I will present briefly some Scriptural and patristic data bearing on the eternal pre-existence of the Church, or on its eternal predestination, and manifest in the process my basic agreement with Karl Barth's assertion of the *fact* of the Church's eternal, christological and eschatological election. In a *second* chapter I will try to probe in greater detail Paul's meaning with regard to the election of the Church and in the process I will have to disagree with Barth's detailed exposition because I believe it, and indeed his whole doctrine of election, and his whole theology, leads to the assertion of *apokatastasis*, that is, the final salvation of all. In a *third* chapter, while affirming my agreement with Barth as regards a Church from the beginning of time, I believe he fails to bring out sufficiently the historical substitution of one economy of salvation for the other. Finally, in a *fourth* chapter I will try to develop a positive theological evaluation of the relationship between the Church and Judaism, agreeing as much as possible with Karl Barth.

Chapter Two

The Eternal Election of the Church

ACCORDING to *St Paul* the people of God is not a chance product of man, history or creation. Its existence and nature is the result or realization of a divine plan which antedates and transcends all history and creation. As such it is an eternal mystery.[1] Furthermore the election of the Church is the goal of individual election. And its election is essentially christological and eschatological.

The object of the divine plan is 'spiritual Israel'.[2] The existence of spiritual Israel does not depend, the Apostle says in Rom 9:6-13, on membership of historical Israel, nor on human works, but on God's election and call: 'in order that God's *purpose* of *election* might continue, not because of works but because of his *call*'.[3]

The universal and historically perfect form of spiritual Israel takes place, according to God's eternal decree, only in and through *Jesus Christ*.

'Blessed be the God and Father of our Lord Jesus Christ, who has blessed us in Christ with every spiritual blessing in the heavenly places, even as he chose us in him before the foundation of the world, that we should be holy and blameless before him. He destined us in love to be his sons through Jesus Christ, according to the purpose of his will, to the praise of his glorious grace which he freely bestowed on us in the Beloved. In him we have redemption through his blood, the forgiveness of our trespasses, according to

---

[1] Paul himself may have been influenced by Jewish literature on this matter because in it a parallel pre-existence for Israel is claimed. Cf Str-Bill, III, 248, on Rom 8:20; III, 579, on Eph 1:4—references in Beumer, 'Die altchristliche Idee . . .' in *Wiss. und Weis.* 9 (1942) 16, n. 20, 21.

[2] St Paul distinguishes a 'spiritual' or 'ideal' Israel and a 'historical' Israel. The former denotes the people willed by God, or the people which corresponds to God's design. The latter denotes the Israel of flesh and blood. Cf Cerfaux, *La Théologie de l'Eglise* . . ., pp. 23-4, 40; E. Dinkler, in *The Journal of Religion*, 36 (1956), 114, 126, n. 22.

[3] . . . *eklogēn prothesis* . . . *kalountos*, Rom. 9:11b.

the riches of his grace which he lavished upon us. For he has made known to us in all wisdom and insight the *mystery of his will*, according to his purpose which he set forth in Christ as a plan for the fullness of time, to unite all things in him, things in heaven and things on earth.'[4]

This unification of all in Christ takes place through the participation of the *Gentiles* in the 'same body', in the same 'household of God', as the *Jews*. It takes place, that is, through the *Church*, which is the realization of the mystery of Christ.

'When you read this you can perceive my insight into the mystery of Christ, which was not made known to the sons of men in other generations as it has now been revealed to his holy apostles and prophets by the Spirit; that is, how the Gentiles are fellow heirs, members of the same body, and partakers of the promise in Christ Jesus through the gospel.'[5]

Thus Paul can further say to the Gentiles:

'So then you are no longer strangers and sojourners, but you are fellow citizens with the saints and members of the household of God, built upon the foundation of the apostles and prophets, Christ Jesus himself being the chief corner-stone, in whom the whole structure is joined together and grows into a holy temple in the Lord; in whom you also are built into it for a dwelling place of God in the Spirit.'[6]

'Some of the branches were broken off, and you, a wild olive shoot, were grafted in their place to share the richness of the olive tree.'[7]

This does not mean that hope is taken from the Jews. Salvation has come to the Gentiles to make them jealous (Rom 11:11). Once the predestined Gentiles have been saved the hardening of the Jews will cease and all Israel will be saved. 'Lest you be wise in your own conceits, I want you to understand this mystery, brethren: a hardening has come upon part of Israel, until the full number of the Gentiles come in, and so all Israel will be saved.'[8]

The idea of an eternally pre-existing or pre-temporal Church was well known to the *earliest Christian writers*. Some (Valentinian

[4] Eph 1:3–12.
[5] Eph 3:4–6.
[6] Eph 2:19–22.
[7] Rom 11:17.
[8] Rom 11:25–26a.

gnostics) even attributed to it a real pre-existence. They considered the Church as a pre-existing feminine aeon wedded substantially to the pre-existing masculine aeon Christ. Once the latter manifested himself for our redemption the former was also manifested. Generally, the idea of a pre-existing Church was bound up with the idea of the Church as the goal and purpose of creation. It would enjoy a precedence before the rest of creation in an ideal pre-existence in God's thought.

' "Who do you think that the ancient lady was from whom you received the little book?" I said, "The Sybil." "You are wrong," he said, "she is not." "Who is she then?" I said. "The Church," he said. I said to him, "Why then is she old?" "Because," he said, "she was created the first of all things. For this reason is she old; and for her sake was the world established".'[9]

'Thus brethren if we do the will of God our Father we shall be of the first Church, the spiritual, which was created before the sun and moon. . . . Therefore let us choose to belong to the Church of life, that we may be saved. But I do not think that you are ignorant that the living Church is the body of Christ. For the Scriptures say: "God made them male and female." The male is Christ, the female is the Church. And moreover the Books and the Apostles say that the Church is not of the present but has been from the beginning. For she was spiritual, as was also our Jesus but he was manifested in the last days that he might save us. Now the Church, being spiritual, was manifested in the flesh of Christ, thereby showing us that if any one of us shall guard her in the flesh and defile her not, he shall receive her back again in the Holy Spirit.'[10]

The idea was especially dear to Origen.

'For you must not think that she is called the bride of the Church only from the time when the Saviour came in flesh: she is so called from the beginning of the human race and from the very foundation of the world—indeed, if I may look for the origin of this high mystery under Paul's guidance, even before the foundation of the world. For this is what he says: ". . . as he chose us in him before the foundation of the world, that we should be holy and blameless before him. He destined us in love to be his sons through Jesus Christ, according to the purpose of his will . . ." (Eph. 1:4–5).

[9] *The Shepherd of Hermas*, Vis. II, IV, I (The Loeb Classical Library, *The Apostolic Fathers*, vol. I, p. 25).
[10] II Clement 14:2–3 (J. Quasten, *Patrology*, vol. I, pp. 55–6).

And in the Psalms too it is written: "Remember thy congregation, which thou hast gotten of old" (Ps 74:2). And indeed the first foundations of the congregation of the Church were laid at the very beginning; and for this reason the Apostle says that the Church is built on the foundation not of the Apostles only, but also of the Prophets (Eph 2:20). And among the prophets Adam too is reckoned, who prophesied the great mystery in Christ and in the Church, when he said: "Therefore a man leaves his father and mother and cleaves to his wife, and they become one flesh" (Gen 2:24). It is clearly with reference to these words of his that the Apostle says that "this is a great mystery, and I mean in reference to Christ and the Church" (Eph 5:32). When, however, the same Apostle says: "Christ loved the Church and gave himself up for her, that he might sanctify her, having cleansed her by the washing of water" (Eph 5:25-6), he is far from showing that she did not exist before. For how could he have loved her if she did not exist? Undoubtedly he loved her who did exist; she existed in all the saints who have been since time began.'[11]

From this general presentation of the scriptural and patristic data it will be clear that Karl Barth's insistence on the fact of the ecclesiological aspect of God's eternal predestination, together with its christological and eschatological nature, and its priority over the election of the individual, can only receive full concurrence.[12]

As I have already mentioned, one would look in vain in most Catholic ecclesiological treatises for a consideration of the Church *ab aeterno*, of its eternal basis in God's election. A remedy to this situation has been called for by the more integral understanding of the Church advocated but only barely outlined by Vatican II:

'All the elect, before time began, the Father "foreknew and predestined to become conformed to the image of his Son, that he should be the firstborn among many brethren" (Rom 8:29). He planned to assemble in the holy Church all those who would believe in Christ. Already from the beginning of the world the foreshadowing of the Church took place. She was prepared for in a remarkable way throughout the history of the people of Israel and by means of the Old Covenant. Established in the present era of time, the Church was made manifest by the outpouring of the Spirit. At the end of time she will achieve her glorious fulfillment. Then, as may be read

[11] Origen, *Commentary on the Canticle of Canticles*, Book Two, on Cant. of Cant. 1:11 (*Ancient Christian Writers*, 26, 149-50).
[12] Cf *CTKB*, pp. 100-1, 106f.

in the holy Fathers, all just men from the time of Adam, "from Abel, the just one, to the last of the elect", will be gathered together with the Father in the universal Church.'[13]

The merit of the renewal in modern Protestantism of the idea of the Church before the individual, and as the goal of the individual, belongs in great part to Karl Barth. Undoubtedly, it was a reaction on his part against the individualism, subjectivism and immanentism of the last century. But it was above all the fruit of his meditation on the Bible. Barth's reason for Calvin's neglect of the priority of the ecclesial aspect of predestination is that Calvin took as the starting-point and determining factor of his doctrine, not the self-revelation of the Word of God attested in Scripture, but, in its place, or in conjunction with it, a datum of experience, namely, the observation of the opposition by individuals to the Word of God and, secondarily, the observation of its positive acceptance by others. He presumed an eternal decree of God was at the back of these observed facts, and then asked the Bible to confirm his views. The problems themselves, Barth rejoins, must be posed by Scripture.[14]

[13] DCC, n. 2.
[14] Cf *CTKB*, pp. 100–2.

Chapter Three

The Church Eternally Elected—
apokatastasis

WHEN, however, we descend to the consideration of the nature of the election of the Church as expounded by Barth we must admit to some perplexities. He bases his exposition on chapters 9–11 of Paul's Epistle to the Romans. These are 'chapters of proverbial obscurity',[1] and there have been many different interpretations of them with no completely satisfying one. Barth's commentary is original, enlightening and profound. Yet he appears to overlook certain basic Pauline distinctions which are absolutely necessary for their interpretation. The absence of these distinctions can—and does in fact—have serious consequences. I will try to explain what I mean through a brief exegesis of these three Pauline chapters.

In 9:1–5a Paul presents the problem. On the one hand, his fellow Jews have been unfaithful, and he announces his sorrow and preoccupation (vv 1–3). On the other hand, God has given privileges and promises to Israel (vv 4–5). Has God therefore been unfaithful?[2] 'But it is not as though the Word of God had failed' (v 6a). From 9:6b to 11:36 Paul demonstrates that God, in spite of the infidelity of the Jews, remains faithful to his promises to Israel.

He begins (9:6b–18) with some precisions or distinctions. Those who inherit God's promises are not historical Israel, that is, the historical group of individuals called Jews. It is the Israel of God's design, the spiritual or eschatological Israel, that is, the people gratuitously elected by God, that inherit his promises.

This is clear already in the Old Testament. That the inheritance of the promise, or the constitution of the people of God, takes place

[1] F. Prat, *La Théologie de Saint Paul*, vol. I, p. 300.

[2] The seriousness of this problem for Paul becomes evident when it is realized that the solidity of his whole epistle depends on its answer: if God is not faithful then justification by faith (chapters 1–4), and the whole hope of salvation (chapters 5–8), are vain, because they are based on his promises. Cf Lyonnet, *Questiones in Ep. ad Rom.*, pp. 12f.

through a spiritual and not a carnal generation is clear from the examples of Israel and Ishmael (vv 7–10), Jacob and Esau (vv 10–13). Election depends solely on God's vocation and not on man's merits or demerits. It must be remembered that in adducing these examples from the Old Testament Paul is not thinking of the election of individuals, as was mistakenly understood from Augustine through the Middle Ages to Luther and Calvin. Following the context of his quotation he speaks solely of the election of peoples. 'And the Lord said to her, "Two nations are in your womb, and two peoples, born of you, shall be divided; the one shall be stronger than the other, the elder shall serve the younger." '[3] The problem Paul is dealing with concerns two peoples and not individuals.[4]

God is not unjust therefore (v 14). His action is completely gratuitous, yet not arbitrary, because it is ordained to the fulfilment of his promises. This is clear in the case of Moses and Pharaoh (vv 15–18). There is no question of Pharaoh's damnation or salvation, but of his instrumentality in God's service. He is no less an instrument in the fulfilment of God's promises than Moses.[5] In the following verses Paul applies to the case of Israel and the Gentiles what he has just said of Moses and Pharaoh. He will return to it in chapter 11. Already he has posed the problem clearly: it concerns peoples, not individuals, and it concerns a role in the economy of salvation, and not eternal damnation or salvation. At the end (11:25f) he will reveal God's wonderful design: everything, even the infidelity of historical Israel, is ordained by God to the salvation of all.[6]

Israel itself, and not God, is to blame for its own infidelity and rejection.[7] The majority of the Jews tried to attain justice by means of their own works and consequently did not attain to the justice which proceeds from faith.[8] They failed to posit an act of faith in Christ. And they are inexcusable. For not only was the justice of faith announced in the Old Testament so that they could have been taught it, but they were actually taught it. They heard and understood but rejected it because of the hardness of their hearts. 'All day long I

[3] Gen 25:23. Cf Mal 1:1–3.
[4] Cf Lyonnet, *op. cit.*, 30f; *id.*, in *Verbum Domini* 34 (1956), 195f; Dinkler, *art. cit.*, pp. 114, 126, n. 22; Cerfaux, *op. cit.*, 23–4, 40; Prat, *op. cit.*, pp. 304–5; Peterson, *Die Kirche aus Juden und Heiden*, pp. 23f; Demann, 'Israël et l'Eglise . . .' in *Cahiers Sioniens*, 3 (1950), 2, 11f.
[5] Cf Lyonnet, *op. cit.*, pp. 38–47; *id.*, *art. cit.*, pp. 196–201.
[6] Cf Lyonnet, *op. cit.*, pp. 48–70; *art. cit.*, pp. 257–71.
[7] Cf Rom 9:30–10:21; 11:20f; 3:3. Cf Bover, 'La Reprobacion . . .' in *Est. Eccles.* 25 (1951), 68; Cerfaux, *op. cit.*, pp. 61f.
[8] Cf Rom 2:1–3:20; 4:3.

have held out my hands to a disobedient and contrary people.'⁹ Their infidelity results in their rejection. 'Because of their unbelief' the Jews were 'broken off' (11:20), 'hardened' (11:7bf), 'rejected' (11:15).

Yet this does not mean that God has rejected his people. Firstly, because the infidelity of the Jews was not universal, but partial. Paul himself, the seven thousand and the remnant (11:1–6) remained faithful. The infidelity of some changes nothing. Israel remains the elected people of God. This, of course, does not take from the calamity which befalls unbelieving Jews. It is they and not Israel who fall (10:33; 11:11), who have fallen (11:22), who are enemies of God (11:28), who have been broken off, cut off, etc. (11:7–10, 17f).[10]

God has not rejected his people, secondly, because the infidelity of the Jews is temporary. It is ordained to the salvation of the Gentiles, which in turn is ordained to the final salvation of Israel itself (11:11–15). 'The hardening of Israel is not alone temporary but has a part in God's salvific plan, in so far as it is ordained to the salvation of the Gentiles, and ultimately to the salvation of Israel itself.'[11]

The Gentiles must not become proud (vv 16–24), thinking that 'branches were broken off so that I might be grafted in' (11:19). That is true. But they must remember that their own election, as well as the re-election of the rejected Jews, depends on their faith. 'They were broken off because of their unbelief, but you stand fast only through faith' (11:20). The rejection of the Jews is not absolute. 'If they do not persist in their unbelief' (v 23) they will be grafted back into the olive tree—and far more naturally than the Gentiles.

In 11:25f Paul sums up God's wondrous salvific plan which will end with a special act of God for the salvation of the unfaithful Israelite people then living. He closes with a protestation of praise and thanks.[12]

'Lest you be wise in your own conceits, I want you to understand this mystery, brethren: a hardening has come upon part of Israel, until the full number of the Gentiles come in, and so all Israel will be saved; as it is written, "The Deliverer will come from Zion, he will banish ungodliness from Jacob"; "and this will be my covenant with them when I take away their sins". As regards the gospel

---

⁹ Rom 10:21; Is 65:2.
¹⁰ Cf Jn 15:16; Heb 6:8.
¹¹ Lyonnet, *op. cit.*, p. 121; cf Cerfaux, *op. cit.*, p. 54.
¹² Rom 11:25–32 is the 'Ergebnis seines Denkens' which 'auf seinem Höhepunkt eigentlich ein Danken ist' (11:33–6), K. L. Schmidt, *Die Judenfrage* . . . , p. 35.

they are enemies of God, for your sake; but as regards election they are beloved for the sake of their forefathers. For the gifts and the call of God are irrevocable. Just as you were once disobedient to God but now have received mercy because of their disobedience, so they have now been disobedient in order that by the mercy shown to you they also may receive mercy. For God has consigned all men to disobedience, that he may have mercy upon all. O the depth of the riches and wisdom and knowledge of God! How unsearchable are his judgments and how inscrutable his ways! "For who has known the mind of the Lord, or who has been his counselor?" "Or who has given a gift to him that he might be repaid?" For from him and through him and to him are all things. To him be glory forever. Amen.'[13]

It is no wonder Fr Prat described these chapters of St Paul as 'chapters of proverbial difficulty'. The same words could be applied to Karl Barth's exposition. Yet his dialectical commentary has much to offer for a greater understanding of the present role of Judaism. None the less, while acknowledging the complexity of the problem itself and the difficulty of understanding, with its concomitant danger of misunderstanding,[14] and while not forgetting the merit due to him for bringing out the fact of the Church's eternal election, and its priority over the election of the individual, I think that his detailed understanding of this eternal election of the community, as well as his whole doctrine of election, and indeed the whole trend of his theology, lead inevitably to the doctrine of *apokatastasis*, and this of course brings to light the fact that our conceptions of the Church and of this salvation time between Christ's ascension and final coming differ fundamentally.

Karl Barth does not seem to distinguish between Israel's election as a *people* to a role in the economy of salvation and the election of *individuals* to salvation itself. Because of this it is not surprising that he 'worries' about the doctrine of *apokatastasis* at the end of his doctrine on the election of the community.[15]

The election of the individual has of course an ecclesiological aspect. As Barth correctly notes, the election of the individual is

[13] Rom 11:25-33.
[14] It is at points such as this that I am particularly glad to have given Barth the opportunity in a separate publication to speak for himself. He has much more to say than I comment upon, and he can correct any misunderstanding. Here then, as always in this volume, I presume the reader does not take my interpretation of Barth for granted but judges for himself. In this case cf *CTKB*, pp. 99–128.   [15] Cf *ibid.*, pp. 119f.

election through and to the Church. But it is not and must not be identified with the election of the community. In Rom 9–11 Paul is speaking of the election of peoples and not of individuals. Barth does not make this clear. For him the election of the individual takes place in the election of the community.[16] The election of the community witnesses to God's absolute grace and mercy in the election of man. Everything therefore that Paul says of the community Barth also says of the individual. God's election of the community to a role in the economy of salvation is unconditional. Consequently, God's election of the individual to salvation must be also unconditional. Just as nothing Israel posits or omits abrogates its election, so also nothing the Jew posits or omits can abrogate his election.

Barth himself does not explicitly teach the doctrine of *apokatastasis*. In fact, he rejects it. Everything must be left to God. Yet it follows logically from his teaching. Besides taking our point of departure from his identification of the election of the community and that of the individual, we could also take our point of departure from his concept of predestination. In basic agreement with Catholic teaching, against Augustine, Calvin and Jansenius, Barth affirms that God's decree is not a *decretum absolutum* to salvation or damnation but his election of all to reconciliation in Jesus Christ. The predestining God is the God revealed in Jesus Christ. He is solely a gracious God, and his decree is solely one of election. But for Barth there is nothing man can do to alter this decree of election. In his theology, and specifically in his doctrine of election, the Pauline statement that the Jews were 'broken off' (Rom 11:20), 'hardened' (11:7b), 'rejected' (11:15), '*because of their unbelief*' (11:20), does not seem to have any meaning. His doctrine of election says that everything has been decided beforehand, and that what has been decided upon is election and salvation for all. What can an appeal to the liberty of God mean?[17]

According to Barth, God's eternal election of grace precedes all else. Nothing human or historical can determine or nullify it. Barth does not deny the factual reality of disobedience to God's will, that is of sin. But he says that sin is 'ontologically impossible'. It is not a possibility of creation which God created good as the external basis of the covenant. It is not a possibility of man's freedom, which is

---

[16] Cf *ibid.*, pp. 107–8, 112f, 122f.
[17] 'There is no alternative to concluding that Barth's refusal to accept the *apokatastasis* cannot be harmonized with the fundamental structure of his doctrine of election'—Berkouwer, *The Triumph of Grace* ..., p. 116. Cf von Balthasar, *Karl Barth* ..., pp. 199f.

solely a freedom for God, and not a neutral capacity to choose for or against him. It exists, but it cannot annul the ontological reality established by God's eternal will in Jesus Christ. On the contrary, God's election of grace precedes and nullifies it. It takes place within the order of grace and so is ontologically impossible.[18]

Quite in line with this, and a further illustration of the intrinsic tendency of his doctrine towards *apokatastasis*, is Barth's conception of the necessity and urgency of faith and the danger of unbelief. The necessity of faith is not conditional for salvation. Later we shall see that for him the action of the Christian is neither a *conditio sine qua non* nor a cooperative factor in his own salvation. But does not this necessarily mean that redemption in *actu primo* is equivalent to redemption in *actu secundo*? That is: for Barth, God's eternal will is solely one of election. It was realized and manifested in Jesus Christ who died *for all*. If no condition is required on the part of the individual Christian for his subjective participation in this objective realization, or if he cannot annul it, then the objective reconciliation will necessarily be identical with subjective reconciliation—either here or hereafter. 'Regarded christologically and eschatologically the Church is always both *all* Israel—not only the seven thousand but also the hardened rest—and *all* the Gentile world, those who have already become believers and those who are yet to become so.'[19]

A human act of faith or anything else does not condition our election to salvation. Election cannot proceed from God and from man. The 'two-source' theory inevitably leads to synergism.

> 'There is no synergism of any kind in the history of Jesus Christ's election, for in this history neither the sin of man nor the prayer of man can play the part of an autonomous mystery, as man's decision complementary to God's. There can be no cooperation or reciprocal action of any kind between any such mystery in man and the mystery of the predestinating God. . . . The glory and the life of all this history are God's. Certainly it is a history between God and man. Certainly there takes place within it a twofold human decision. But this decision takes place in such a way as to form, not the second point in an ellipse, but the circumference around the one central point of which it is the repetition and confirmation.'[20]

For Barth there is no such thing as a 'possibility' of faith. Unbelief is ontologically impossible because it contradicts the faith decreed by

---

[18] Cf Berkouwer, *op. cit.*, pp. 234, 232, and his whole chapter IX.
[19] Cf *CTKB*, p. 120.
[20] *C.D.*II/2, p. 194 (=S. 214); cf *CTKB*, pp. 104f.

THE CHURCH ETERNALLY ELECTED—APOKATASTASIS   33

God for all. Barth's problem is therefore '*either* cooperation, synergism, synthesis between God's deed and ours, *or* the ontological impossibility of unbelief'.[21]

What then is the urgency of faith or the danger of unbelief? For Barth it is that *all* may *know* of their salvation in Jesus Christ. Otherwise people would go on 'dreaming dreams', 'blissfully unaware' of it. This communication of knowledge is the motive and problem of the Church's mission. 'This contrast between the church's and the world's terrible ignorance is the motive,' he says, 'and the bridging of the gap between them the problem, of the early Christian mission.'[22]

Finally, Barth's *apokatastasis* inclination and the absence of all urgency of faith or danger of unbelief is clear from his doctrine of rejection, death and judgment. Jesus Christ is the only rejected one. He was rejected in the place of all. After him there can be no rejection. 'Rejection cannot again become the portion or affair of man.'[23] Similarly, Jesus Christ has suffered death and judgment in our place.[24] Our death must be feared because it is ordained by God as a sign of judgment. But it is only a sign. It is 'even more so a sign of the setting aside of this judgment and therefore the defeat of death'.[25] We can no longer *really* stand under judgment. Jesus Christ was judged in our place. But in this conception of Barth's what urgency can the proclamation of the judgment have, or the danger of sin and unbelief, or what real fear of death and judgment can there be?

'This, then, is how the New Testament sees human death in the light of its centre. The centre of this insight is God's *judgment* accomplished in the crucifixion of Jesus Christ. No other man stands at this centre, and therefore no other *really* stands under the judgment of God.'[26]

Barth none the less has recourse to God's liberty to avoid the explicit avowal of the doctrine of *apokatastasis*. God's liberty must be respected, he says. But what can this mean if, on Barth's own primary

---

[21] Berkouwer, *op. cit.*, p. 268.

[22] *C.D.* III/2, p. 607 (=S. 738). 'The true impulse to go out into the world and address it can derive only from the fact that the community knows something which the world does not know,' *C.D.* III/4, p. 509 (=S. 583).

[23] *C.D.* II/2, p. 167 (=S. 182). 'That on the basis of this decree of His the only truly rejected man is His own Son; that God's rejection has taken its course and been fulfilled and reached its goal, with all that that involves, against this One, so that it can no longer fall on other men or be their concern.' *Ibid.*, p. 319 (=S. 348).   [24] Cf *C.D.* III/2, pp. 597f (=SS. 726f).

[25] *Ibid.*, p. 593 (=S. 721).   [26] *Ibid.*, pp. 605–6 (=SS. 736–7).

principle, Jesus Christ is the sole source of our knowledge of all God's works and ways, and this source tells us that he is the only rejected one, rejected for and in the place of all, so that after him there can be no real rejection? What can this recourse to the liberty of God mean in the light of Scripture's insistence on the conditioning necessity of faith for salvation;[27] in the light of its warning against sin and unbelief;[28] in the light of its teaching on the judgment of all according to their works;[29] and finally in the light of its teaching on the existence of eternal punishment?[30]

[27] Cf Rom 3:22, 26; Gal 3:22f; Jn 3:36; Heb 4:2.
[28] Cf Heb 10:26–31; 12:25; 4:11.
[29] Cf Rom 2:1–11; I Cor 3:13–15; II Cor 5:10; Gal 6:7f; Mt 25:31–46; Jn 5:29.
[30] Cf Mt 25:41, 46; 22:13; 25:30. Cf Vatican II, DCC, n. 48, par. 4.

Chapter Four
The Church Before and After Christ

BUT there is another aspect of Barth's doctrine of the election of the community which perplexes me. His main concern is to show the unity in duality, and duality in unity, of the community according to God's eternal election.[1] In correspondence to the election of Jesus Christ the election of the community is one, he says. Israel is not rejected and the Church elected. Both are elected. The bow of the one covenant arches over the whole. God's election takes one form in the case of Israel (Ishmael, Esau, Pharaoh, the synagogue) and another form in the case of the Church. This unity in duality of the community has been present from the beginning, and always will and must be present. The community has always been Israel and the Church, and always will be Israel and the Church. The Church already existed before Jesus Christ in Israel and performed its mediate and mediating function. Israel (whether believers or unbelievers) exists after Jesus as an essential elected form of the community, and performs its function according to God's plan. God's plan does not envisage the substitution of Israel by the Church, or a historical succession of the Church to Israel, but the permanent continuance of Israel and the Church in the one community. The New Testament Church already existed from the beginning of Israel's history. Israel continues its role, according to God's plan, in the New Testament economy of salvation. The duality is essential to the one people of God in all moments of its history.

In speaking of a temporal pre-existence of the Church in Israel Barth is repeating an idea which is as old as Christianity itself. The idea was probably first engendered by the anti-Jewish polemic, and by the triple reaction against Marcionism, Montanism and Manichaeism. The early Church Fathers insisted that the just, from Adam onwards, believed in Christ and thus belonged to him and his people,

[1] Cf *CTKB*, pp. 108f.

the Church.² In the various liturgies as well, the just of the Old Testament were often regarded and venerated as saints.³

With St Augustine the affirmation of the pre-existence of the Church achieved its prototypal form for the Latin West. Jesus Christ is the unique and universal mediator of grace. All believe in him and are saved solely through the grace of his mediation as man.⁴ He is the head of all and all belong to the one body the Church.⁵ Yes, to the one body.⁶ All are united by faith in one Jesus Christ. Faith is not changed

---

² Origen, *In Cant. Cant.*, lib. 2 (*PG*, 13, 134); Athanasius, *Contra Arianos*, IV, 29 (*PG*, 26, 513); Eusebius, *Hist. Eccl.*, lib. I, cap. 4; Greg. Naz., *Orat.* XV, 1 (*PG*, 35, 312–13); Chrysostomus, *In Eph.*, hom. 10 (*PG*, 62, 75); Ambrosiaster, *Quaest. ex Vet. Test.* 3 (*PL*, 35, 2219); Hieronymus, *In Gal.* lib. II, cap. IV, vers. 1, 2 (*PL*, 26, 370).

³ Cf J. Damarie, in *Bull. Cath. de la Quest. d'Israel*, 7 (1929), 1–11; H. I. Marrou, in *Memorial Chaine*, Lyon, 1950, pp. 282–90; B. Botte, in *Cahiers Sioniens*, 1950, 38–47. Devotion to Old Testament saints was a particular characteristic of old Irish Catholicism—cf J. Hennig, in *IER*, 104 (1965), 333–48. This point could be further studied as an illustration of Paul's expression of the continuity between the Churches of the Old and New Testaments precisely through his use of the term 'saints'—cf, e.g. Rom 1:7; 5:31; 15:25f; I Cor 1:2 with Ex 19:4; Num 16:3f, etc.

⁴ Cf, e.g., *De pecc. orig.*, cap. XXVI (*PL*, 44, 400–1); *Epist.* 179, 6 (*PL*, 33, 776).

⁵ *De Baptismo c. Donat.*, lib. I, cap. XVI (*PL*, 43, 123); *Enarr. in Ps.* LXI, 4 (*PL*, 36, 731). 'As the whole time before Christ is the pre-history of Christ so is it also the pre-history of the Church'—Schmaus, III/1, 60.

⁶ Authors differ with regard to the interpretation of this Augustinian 'body'. Fr Tromp maintains (*Corpus Christi quod est Eccl.*, I, 1946, 122–7) that Augustine and the whole Middle Ages spoke of the invisible and universal Church of those justified by faith in the Redeemer. There was a *periculum doctrinae*, consequently, in their ecclesiology, that is, a danger of regarding the visible organization willed by Christ as accidental. Fr Congar, on the contrary ('Ecclesia ab Abel' in *Festgabe für K. Adam*, 92, 97f; cf also his 'L'Idée de l'Eglise chez S. Thomas d'Aquin' in *Esquisses du Mystère de l'Eglise*, 59–91), says that Augustine and the medieval West were not thinking of some invisible and universal Church of the saints, but of the visible Church to which we also belong. There was no *periculum doctrinae*. He explains this by saying that from Augustine to Thomas a spiritual and personal notion of the Church predominated. To Fr Congar's explanation should be added the remarks of Fr Hamer (*The Church is a Communion*, 73f). He indicates Thomas' *corporeal* (and therefore not merely spiritual) conception of salvation (even in the beatific vision); his *sacramental* conception of the earthly economy of salvation (as the instrument of Christ's real body the sacrament of the eucharist is the proper cause of the mystical body; this applies also to the *Old Testament*; in the old economy there was a *manducatio spiritualis* of the sacrament of the eucharist *propter figuram* in the sacraments of the Old Law); and his theological demonstration from anthropology of the appropriateness of the present sacramental and hierarchical economy.

by the variation of sacraments.⁷ We are sons and members of the second Adam through a spiritual generation, and of the first Adam through a carnal generation.⁸ The distinction between the Old and New Testaments is spiritual and not historical. Those who live carnally in the New Testament Church belong to the Old Testament, and those who live spiritually in the Old Testament belong to the New. The change may even take place at any point of the economy in each individual soul.⁹ In the last twenty years of his life—at the time of the Pelagian controversy and especially when he was writing the *City of God* (A.D. 413–26)—Augustine expressed the distinction between carnal descendence from the first Adam and spiritual descendence from the second Adam, between the Old and the New Testaments, between Israel and the Church, between the city of the devil and the city of God, by the typology of Cain and Abel.¹⁰ In this may be seen an influence of the allegorical and spiritualizing exegesis of the school of Alexandria.¹¹

From the thirteenth century onwards ecclesiology became a tract separate from christology and soteriology. The Church began to be considered separately as an objective means of grace. This was made necessary by the need for theological elaboration and to stand up to heresies which denied precisely the institutional aspect of the Church. As a result, distinctions were introduced as regards the meaning of the word 'Church'. For example, the Church was distinguished from the synagogue as the collection of believers who are baptized and under Christ's vicar on earth. The idea of the 'Church before the Church' continued, however, up to the controversialists of the seventeenth and eighteenth centuries who, for polemical purposes, insisted solely on the institutional aspect.¹² It has been regained in modern times with the more precise use of the words 'preparation', 'prefigurement', 'foreshadowing'.

> 'For the Church of Christ acknowledges that, according to the mystery of God's saving design, the beginnings of her faith and her election are already found among the patriarchs, Moses, and the

---

⁷ 'Sed huius unius fidei pro significationis opportunitate per varia tempora sacramenta variata sunt': *De pecc. meritis et remiss.*, lib. 2, c. XXIX, 47 (*PL*, 44, 179); *De pecc. orig.*, cap. XXXII, 37 (*PL*, 44, 403).

⁸ *Sermo* 143, I (*PL*, 38, 784–5).

⁹ *De Bapt.*, lib. I, c. 15, 24 (*PL*, 43, 122–3); *Sermo* 4, XI–XII (*PL*, 38, 39); cf St Thomas, *Summa theol.*, I–IIae, q. 106, art. 1, ad 3; p. 107, art 1, ad 2 and 3.

¹⁰ *Enarr. in Ps.* LXI, 6 (*PL*, 36, 733).

¹¹ Congar, *art*. 'Ecclesia ab Abel', 86.

¹² For references cf *ibid.*, 93f, with notes.

prophets. She professes that all who believe in Christ, Abraham's sons according to faith (cf Gal 3:7), are included in the same patriarch's call, and likewise that the salvation of the Church was mystically foreshadowed by the chosen people's exodus from the land of bondage.'[13]

The resemblance between Augustine and Barth on this point is interesting. For the latter the one and same Church has always been in existence to witness to God's mercy in the election of man. While he says that the Old Testament Church was but the prefiguration of the Church which began at Pentecost,[14] it is difficult to understand what this beginning can mean. In the light of his doctrine on election the Church must always have existed. The 'beginning' at Pentecost is solely its revelation. It is not a historical substitution for an economy now outdated. Despite the laudable pro-Jewish bias of Barth's exposition I do not think it is fully based on the Bible. It denies the historical succession of one economy to another. Certainly the Church 'was prepared for in a remarkable way throughout the history of the people of Israel and by means of the Old Covenant', but she was only 'established in the present era of time, [and] was made manifest by the outpouring of the Spirit'.[15] Barth does not sufficiently allow for the difference between the Old and New Testaments. He does not allow for the newness introduced by the event of the incarnation or its abolition of the old economy. Closely connected with this is his misunderstanding of the Pauline antithesis between justice by faith and justice by law, as well as his misunderstanding of the gift of the Spirit in the new economy.[16]

Barth of course denies that the Church is an institution. In this sense his concept of the Church undoubtedly regulated his understanding of the Church's election.[17] The Fathers and scholastics, on the contrary, while affirming the continuity between the Churches of the Old and New Testaments, did not deny the institutional Church. There was as yet no specific ecclesiological tract in distinction to christology and soteriology. Hence they made no distinction between

[13] Vatican, II, *Declaration on non-Christian Religions*, n. 4, par. 2. Cf also DCC, nn. 2, 9, 16.
[14] Cf *CTKB*, p. 111.
[15] DCC, n. 2.
[16] Cf below Section Three, chapters twelve and seventeen. And cf H. Bouillard, *Karl Barth*, vol. II, pp. 92f, 190f.
[17] This is a remark which M. J.-Leuba made in his review of Mgr Journet's book on the Jews, and on behalf of Barth: 'The question is, in effect, to know with what conception of the Church one tackles the Jewish problem': *Judaica*, 2 (1946), 159.

the Church as means of salvation and as salvation, between *sacramentum* and *res*. The *sacramentum* was subordinate to the *res*. It existed in function of the *res*. The Church for them was primarily the body of believers, the body of those who, through grace, have Christ as head. But they did not deny the newness of the Church as institution. This is quite clear from their conception of sacrament and hierarchy.

St Thomas, for example, says that circumcision in the Old Law brought justification *quasi ex opere operato*, that is, circumcision really justified *ex opere operato* because its efficacy is the efficacy of Christ himself in his redemptive acts. It is *'quasi' ex opere operato* because it is not instrumentally imbued with the power of Christ. Baptism, because of Christ's foundation, is so imbued. Thus for Thomas there exists a visible institutional Church which did not exist before the incarnation.[18]

Both Augustine and Barth may have been influenced by the Alexandrian school of exegesis, with its tendency to allegorize and spiritualize. With regard to Augustine's expression of the distinction between carnal descendence from the first Adam and spiritual descendence from the second Adam, between the Old and New Testaments, between Israel and the Church, through the typology of Cain and Abel, Fr Congar writes:

> 'It is here that Augustine could have received inspiration from St Ambrose, and through him from the allegorical and spiritualizing type of exegesis of the Alexandrian school, itself inspired by Philo. In his *De Cain et Abel* (375) Ambrose has not the formula *Ecclesia ab Abel*, but he sees in Cain and Abel respectively the figures of the Jews and Christians, of the synagogue and the Church. The danger was that one could be led thus to substitute a truly *historical* perception or comprehension of the stages of the economy of God's gifts by a completely non-temporal consideration of spiritual types. That is, as is known, the at once great value and grave limitation of the Augustinian conception of history. It risks to see in this latter less a properly historical development than the destiny of two co-existent cities, not only in time but within each individual.'[19]

Whether he receives it from the same school of Alexandria through Augustine, or whether his doctrine of election naturally inclines him

[18] Cf E. Schillebeeckx, *Christ the Sacrament* . . ., p. 106, n. I, on St Thomas, *IV Sent.*, d. I, q. 2, a. 6, sol. I, ad 2. Cf also Congar, *Esquisses* . . ., pp. 84f.
[19] *Art.* 'Ecclesia ab Abel', 86.

that way, the same tendency to allegorize and spiritualize is noticeable in Barth. And I have already pointed to the danger of allegory present in his exegetical method.[20]

Discontinuity must be admitted between the Church of the Old Testament and that of the New, nor can the Church of the Old Testament be said to continue its role in the New. This has nothing to do, of course, with the assertion of a permanent rejection of the Jews by God in the New Testament because some proved unfaithful to the Gospel. What it means is that since the economy of salvation has been altered, the new economy succeeding the old, the Church which now exists and has a role in salvation history, is the one Church of Jews and Gentiles. Needless to say, the Church did not exist as an institution before Christ's incarnation. For as such it continues the function of Christ's own visible mediation as man (I Tim 2:5), and he had not yet become a man.[21] But even apart from its institutional aspect discontinuity must be admitted.

The Church of the New Testament 'holds together continuity and discontinuity, for the *"ecclesia"* is in a real sense a new creation'.[22] Just as Jesus Christ, as the end and plenitude of Scripture, constitutes the unity of the Old and New Testaments,[23] and the unity of the Church of the Old Testament and that of the New through his unique and universal mediation, so also he constitutes their discontinuity. He is something completely new. He is the new alliance, the new covenant, the kingdom of God in person, the fullness of revelation. He inaugurates the New Testament, the new economy. With the new the old ceases. 'The Law and the prophets were until John; since then the good news of the kingdom of God is preached.'[24] 'But now the righteousness of God has been manifested apart from law, although the law and the prophets bear witness to it, the righteousness of God through faith in Jesus Christ for all who believe.'[25] 'And they were all filled with the Holy Spirit.'[26]

As the creation of Jesus Christ, as the new people of the new covenant, the Church of the New Testament transfigures and replaces

[20] Cf *CTKB*, p. 42.
[21] Cf C. Journet, *The Church of the Word Incarnate*, vol. 1, p. 6. F. M. Braun, *Nuovi Aspetti del problema della Chiesa*, p. 73, n. 1.
[22] Johnston, 'The Church and Israel . . .' in *Journal of Religion* 34 (1954), 30; Dinkler, *art. cit.*, p. 116.
[23] Cf H. de lubac, 'L'unité des deux Testaments' in *Exégèse Médiévale*, vol. I, pp. 305–63.
[24] Lk 6:16.
[25] Rom 3:21–22.
[26] Acts 2:4. Cf I Cor 12:13; Col 1:12, 14.

that of the old.²⁷ As the goal and perfection of Israel the Church pre-existed in Israel. But precisely as such too it supplants Israel. Both the continuity and discontinuity between Israel and the Church come particularly to light in the theology of the Church of the Pauline Epistles, and in that of the first Epistle of St Peter. While it is expressed in terms taken from the Old Testament and from contemporary Judaism these terms 'are animated in Christianity by a new and conquering life, the creation of its founder, Jesus Christ'.²⁸

In the line of the more historical exegesis of the Antiochian school many pre-Augustinian Fathers emphasized the difference of spiritual gifts between the Old and New Testaments, and the preparatory character of everything preceding Christ.²⁹ St Isidore clearly distinguishes the Church and the synagogue and makes the former begin with Pentecost.³⁰ And Quodvultdeus says that with the perfection of the sacraments the synagogue has become useless.³¹

For Barth, unbelieving Israel continues to have a role in the New Testament economy according to God's plan of salvation. Its 'rejection' is but the confirmation of its election. We cannot find any basis in St Paul for such a statement. Certainly, God uses their infidelity for the implementation of his salvific plan of extending salvation to the Gentiles. But it is because of their unbelief that they were broken off (Rom 11:20). And their rejection must be taken seriously. Paul describes the historical succession of the spiritual Israel to the carnal Israel in God's economy of salvation. The unbelieving Jews who 'stumbled over the stumbling-stone' (Rom 9:32) have ceded their place to the Gentiles. They have been 'hardened'

---

²⁷ 'Sortie du flanc de Jésus au Calvaire, vivant de la foi en sa résurrection, animée de son Esprit reçu à la Pentecôte, l'Eglise tient désormais la place d'Israël': H. de Lubac, *op. cit.*, p. 328.

²⁸ L. Cerfaux, *La Théologie de l'Eglise*, p. 134. This continuity and discontinuity could be outlined from an examination of the way the privileges promised to Israel (Rom 9:4) were realized in historical Israel and are realized in the Church. Cf, e.g., Cerfaux, *op. cit.*, pp. 27–42, and whole first book: 'The theology of the People of God,' pp. 13–135.

²⁹ Cf Congar, *art. cit.*, 80f. St John Chrysostom, e.g.: 'Gloria enim major et honor ea sunt, quae fiunt in Novo Testamento, quando habet Christum caput, quando eius corput efficitur, quando fit frater et coheres, et conformis eius corpori, quando majorem quam Moyses accipit gloriam . . .' : *Exp. in Ps.* VIII, 7 (*PG*, 55, 117).

³⁰ 'Inchoavit autem Ecclesia a loco, ubi venit de coelo Spiritus sanctus, et implevit uno loco sedentes': *Etymol.* lib. VIII, cap I, n. 4f (*PL*, 82, 295).

³¹ 'Perfectis igitur universis sacramentis, quae aliis condita tegebantur in vellere, Judaeorum scilicet Synagogam inanem remansisse, omnis jam mundus agnoscit': *Liber de Promiss. et Predict. Dei*, Pars II, cap. XVIII, n. 33 (*PL*, 51, 787).

(Rom 11:7), 'rejected' (Rom 11:15), 'broken off' (Rom 11:17). 'Some of the branches were broken off, and you, a wild olive shoot, were grafted in their place to share the richness of the olive tree' (Rom 11:17). This historical succession of the Church to Israel is also abundantly clear in many parables of Jesus.[32]

Everything is decided in Jesus Christ. This is at once the merit and demerit of Karl Barth's doctrine of election. It is its merit because it illustrates its christological ontic and noetic aspect. It is its demerit because it detracts from the significance (both positive and negative) of man and history in the economy of salvation, and thus inevitably results in the doctrine of *apokatastasis*.

Everything is decided even 'before' Jesus Christ. Rather, Jesus Christ, as the electing God and the elected man, already exists *ab aeterno*. God's eternal election is the decision which precedes everything that takes place between God and man. This decision cannot be thwarted in the course of history—certainly not by a human historical decision. To speak of a historical replacement of Israel by the Church would be completely out of place in Barth's way of viewing things.

> 'His conception leaves the impression that everything has already been done, all the decisions have been taken, so that one can hardly say that the historical fall and the historical reconciliation are at issue, but only the revelation of redemption in history, the revelation of the definitive Yes of God's grace.'[33]

This severe judgment by G. C. Berkouwer is supported by another eminent Reformed theologian, E. Brunner.[34] Fr von Balthasar says much the same: 'In this theology of happening and history perhaps nothing happens because everything has already happened in eternity.'[35]

---

[32] Cf, e.g., Mt 20:1–16 and par.; Mt 22, 1–14. Cf also A. Feuillet, 'Les ouvriers de la Vigne et la théologie de l'Alliance' in *RSR*, 1947, 303–27.

[33] G. C. Berkouwer, *op. cit.*, p. 250 (although in a different context).

[34] Cf E. Brunner, *The Christian Doctrine of God* (vol. I of his Dogmatics), p. 351.

[35] '. . . die Ablehnung alles Redens von Wachstum, Fortschritt, aber ebenso von möglichem Abfall und Verlust der Gnade und des Glaubens, kurz von allem, was im Bereich des Relativen und Zeitlichen die immer bewegte Geschichte des Menschen mit dem ihn erlösenden Herrn und Gott ausmacht, das alles kann den Eindruck nur verstärken, dass in dieser Theologie des Geschehens und der Geschichte vielleichts doch nichts geschieht weil alles in der Ewigkeit schon immer geschehen ist'. H. Urs von Balthasar, *Karl Barth*, p. 380.

Chapter Five

The Church and Judaism

HAVING outlined some basic agreements and disagreements (or at least demands) with regard to Karl Barth's doctrine of election and in particular with his doctrine on the election of the Church I believe there is one area where we Catholics should be willing to learn from him: his love and concern for Jews as manifested in his attempt to provide a theological evaluation of their *present* role. We Catholics have tended to think of Jews only in the context of a historical substitution of one economy for the other. We have tended to forget their present here and now existence, and to bypass the evaluation of their present situation. Karl Barth wrote his main exposition of his understanding of the role of Israel at a time when history's greatest attempt at Jewish extinction was in full swing (*C.D.* II/2 appeared early in 1942), and this undoubtedly helped towards a sympathetic evaluation of their present reality. Still it was always a concern of his theology. In regard to the Jews the Catholic Church has many historical sins to atone for, but happily it has already begun its atonement. In its renewed self-understanding as the open Church it is ready and eager for dialogue with good no matter where it manifests itself, but especially 'it recalls the spiritual bond linking the people of the new covenant with Abraham's stock'.[1]

Because there is this intimate connection between the Church and the Jews there can be no question of *anti-semitism* on the part of the Church or the world.[2] Certainly, 'as Holy Scripture testifies, Jerusalem did not recognize the time of her visitation (cf Lk 19:44), nor did the Jews in large number accept the Gospel; indeed, not a few opposed the spreading of it (cf Rom 11:28)'.[3] It is also true that 'authorities of the Jews and those who followed their lead pressed for the death of

[1] Vatican II, *Declaration on the relationship of the Church to non-Christian religions*, n. 4, par. 1.
[2] Cf Barth in *CTKB*, pp. 112f, 116–20, 331; Vatican II, *Declaration* . . ., n. 4.
[3] Vatican II, *Declaration* . . ., n. 4, par. 4.

Christ (cf Jn 19:6)'.⁴ This was infidelity on the part of the Jews and because of it they were 'rejected', as Paul says (cf Rom 11:7f, 15, 20). 'They were broken off because of their unbelief' (Rom 11:20). However, this rejection, while it must be taken very seriously, forms no basis for any anti-semitism. First of all, not all the Jews were unbelievers nor were they consequently rejected. 'The Church recalls too that from the Jewish people sprang the apostles, her foundation stones and pillars, as well as most of the early disciples who proclaimed Christ to the world.'⁵ Secondly, while many do not believe in Jesus Christ and his Gospel not all Jews can be accused of what happened in his passion and death, nor should Jews alone be accused of what happened.

'What happened in his passion cannot be blamed upon all Jews then living, without distinction, nor upon the Jews of today. . . . Besides, as the Church has always held and continues to hold, Christ in his boundless love freely underwent his passion and death because of the sins of all men, so that all might attain salvation.'⁶

Thirdly, the rejection of unbelieving Jews was but a confirmation of their election to a role in God's plan of salvation, in the sense that God avails of their infidelity to bring the Gentiles to salvation and this in turn is ordained to the salvation of the Jews (cf Rom 11:11–15). Even though they proved and prove unfaithful to his election the Jews still remain God's chosen people. 'Nevertheless, according to the apostle, the Jews still remain most dear to God because of their fathers, for he does not repent of the gifts he makes nor of the calls he issues (cf Rom 11:28–29).'⁷ Thus fourthly, the origin and goal of the Church is so linked with the Jews that anti-semitism would present a total misunderstanding of the mystery of its own election. It is the Jews who are first and foremost and by right the 'saints and members of the household of God'. It is they who are the bearers of the promise. To them belong the sonship and glory and Christ according to the flesh. The Gentiles only share in Israel's inheritance. They are only 'built in', 'grafted on'.

'The Church cannot forget that she received the revelation of the Old Testament through the people with whom God in his inexpressible mercy deigned to establish the ancient covenant.

---

⁴ Vatican II, *Declaration* . . ., n. 4, par. 6.
⁵ *Ibid.*, n. 4, par. 3.
⁶ *Ibid.*, n. 4, par. 6 and 8.
⁷ *Ibid.*, n. 4, par. 5. Cf also DCC, n. 16.

Nor can she forget that she draws sustenance from the root of that good olive tree onto which have been grafted the wild olive branches of the Gentiles (cf Rom 11:17–24). . . . Also, the Church ever keeps in mind the words of the apostle about his kinsmen, "who have the adoption as sons, and the glory and the covenant and the legislation and the worship and the promises; who have the fathers, and from whom is Christ according to the flesh" (Rom 9:4–5), the son of the Virgin Mary. The Church recalls too that from the Jewish people sprang the apostles, her foundation stones and pillars, as well as most of the early disciples who proclaimed Christ to the world.'[8]

How can the Church and the Gentiles be anti-semitic when they owe their very salvation to the Jews? 'Remember it is not you that support the root, but the root that supports you' (Rom 11:18b). Similarly the Church's goal is ordained to include the Jews, for the salvation of the Gentiles is ordained to the salvation of the Jews (cf Rom 11:11–15). 'A hardening has come upon part of Israel, until the full number of Gentiles come in, and so all Israel will be saved' (Rom 11:25-6). 'In company with the prophets and the same Apostle, the Church awaits that day, known to God alone, on which all peoples will address the Lord in a single voice and "serve him with one accord" ' (Soph 3:9. Cf Is 66:23; Ps 65:4; Rom 11:11–32).[9] As Karl Barth sums up:

'God has so little forsaken them [the Jews] that it is for their sake that he has stretched out his hand to the Gentiles. . . . The Church can understand its own origin, and its own goal only as it understands its unity with Israel.'[10]

Fifthly and finally, there can be no anti-semitism on the Church's part because in the life, death and resurrection of Jesus Christ the reconciliation of all and the forgiveness of the sins of all has been accomplished, and the condition for salvation is the same for all: faith in Jesus Christ. And indeed the believing Jew will be grafted back into the olive tree far more naturally than the Gentile, for the root of the election of the Gentiles is the election of the Jews and not vice versa.

'Note then the kindness and the severity of God: severity toward those who have fallen, but God's kindness to you, provided you

[8] *Ibid.*, n. 4, par. 2–3.
[9] *Ibid.*, n. 4, par. 5.
[10] *CTKB*, pp. 117–18.

continue in his kindness; otherwise you too will be cut off. And even the others, if they do not persist in their unbelief, will be grafted in, for God has the power to graft them in again. For if you have been cut from what is by nature a wild olive tree, and grafted, contrary to nature, into a cultivated olive tree, how much more will these natural branches be grafted back into their own olive tree' (Rom 11:22–24).

'The Church believes that by his cross, Christ, our Peace, reconciled Jew and Gentile, making them both one in himself (cf Eph 2:14–16). . . . Besides, as the Church has always held and continues to hold, Christ in his boundless love freely underwent his passion and death because of the sins of all men, so that all might attain salvation. It is, therefore, the duty of the Church's preaching to proclaim the cross of Christ as the sign of God's all-embracing love and as the fountain from which every grace flows.'[11]

In the light of all this how could the Church be anti-semitic? Would such not be a total misunderstanding of the mystery of its own election? And must it not do all in its power to remedy the past (its own naturally included) and ensure for the future the elimination of even the faintest anti-Jewish sentiment? Vatican II, in what can be said to be one of its few approximations to the traditional conciliar 'anathema' or condemnation, speaks out very strongly on this point:

'Although the Church is the new people of God, the Jews should not be presented as repudiated or cursed by God, as if such views followed from the Holy Scriptures. All should take pains, then, lest in catechetical instruction and in the preaching of God's Word they teach anything out of harmony with the truth of the Gospel and the spirit of Christ. . . . Mindful of her common patrimony with the Jews, and motivated by the Gospel's spiritual love and by no political considerations, she deplores the hatred, persecutions, and displays of anti-semitism directed against the Jews at any time and from any source.'[12]

Not opposition or persecution should characterize the relationship of the Church and Jews but dialogue based on mutual understanding and respect. 'Since the spiritual patrimony common to Christians and Jews is thus so great, this sacred Synod wishes to foster and recommend that mutual understanding and respect which is the fruit

[11] Vatican II, *Declaration* . . . , n. 4, par. 2 and 8.
[12] *Ibid.*, n. 4, par. 6–7.

above all of biblical and theological studies, and of brotherly dialogues.'[13] As Barth again points out,[14] this dialogue from the Church's point of view cannot be described, strictly speaking, as a 'mission to the Jews'. The Gospel is not something alien to them. The Church cannot expect them to adopt another faith. This is true to a certain extent of course of all non-Christians. God is at work amongst all men so that very often there is an incipient faith present. The Church's mission cannot be understood as one of conversion and supplantation simply and solely but as a work of prudent and loving dialogue and collaboration in which the spiritual and moral goods found amongst all men, as well as the values in their religion, society and culture, are acknowledged, promoted and ennobled.[15] But first among these come the Jews to whom originally belong the promises and who still in a very special way are God's chosen people.

' In the first place there is the people to whom the covenants and the promises were given and from whom Christ was born according to the flesh (cf Rom 9:4–5). On account of their fathers, this people remains most dear to God, for God does not repent of the gifts he makes nor of the calls he issues (cf Rom 11:28–29).'[16]

What the Church must expect from the Jews is not a change of faith but a renewal of their faith. It must help and encourage them to become better Jews. For a Christian is but one who fulfils his Jewishness. The person who believes in the God who acted in Jesus Christ does not believe in a different God from the God of the Jews but in the same God who acted in Abraham, Moses and Jacob. In Jesus of Nazareth the same God acts once more for the salvation of Israel and the world. In believing in him the Jew is not abandoning his Jewish faith but becoming more fully Jew. Dialogue with Jews, as all its other dialogue, means first and foremost a self-examination and self-questioning for the Church. Can it honestly and credibly present itself as the fulfilment of Jewish longings? Paul says that the task of the Church in relation to the Jews is to make them 'jealous' of the salvation it has received and which belongs to them by right (Rom 11:11, 14). Or as Barth puts it: there is no question of a fanatical Jewish mission, but in its faith and hope and love the Church must make Jesus discernible as the Jewish Messiah.[17] Is the Jesus it

[13] *Ibid.*, par. 5.
[14] Cf *CTKB*, pp. 117, 331–2.
[15] Cf Vatican II, *Declaration* . . . , n. 2, par. 2–3; DCC, nn. 13, 16–17; *Decree on the Church's Missionary Activity*.
[16] Vatican II, DCC, n. 16.
[17] *CTKB*, pp. 117, 331–2.

proclaims discernible as the Jewish Messiah? Is the Church itself credible and discernible as the fulfilment of the promises to the people of the Old Testament? Is it credible and discernible as the representation and image of the kingdom of peace, justice, love, joy and salvation promised in the Old Testament? This must be the first and perennial question of the Church in its dialogue with the Jews. It must present itself credibly as the sacrament of their own promised salvation.

What exactly is the theological nature of Judaism or of the Jews in the time after Christ? Have they a positive role in the new economy of salvation? Of course they have. I have already disagreed with the Barthian basis for this role, namely, that they are elected from all eternity to a constitutive role in the one Church, irrespective of their obedience or disobedience. This fails to evaluate sufficiently the role of human action, human sin and human history in the history of salvation. It manifests of course a basic weakness in Barthian ecclesiology which says that 'Jesus Christ is the Church'.[18] Obviously such a Church requires an 'Israel' to witness to sin. According to St Paul God rejected the unbelieving Jews because of their unbelief (Rom 11:20). They do not form an essential and necessary part of the Church of the New Testament. Certainly God uses their infidelity to bring in the Gentiles, and does not definitively reject them because he ordains the salvation of the Gentiles to the salvation of the Jews. Barth is obviously spiritualizing, allegorizing and dialecticizing too much when he says that the Church 'is unable to bear witness to the saving passion of Jesus Christ' without Israel, i.e. that it knows and witnesses to man's misery as the reflection of the divine judgment executed in Jesus 'only in so far as Israel lives in it'.[19] God has inaugurated a new covenant with man on the basis of faith in Jesus Christ and this supersedes and outmodes the old covenant.

This does not mean of course that God does not use Judaism and the Jews or that the latter have no role in the new economy. All men of good will are in God's service, and especially sincere Jews. As regards the Church, do they not in their continuing disbelief serve as a reminder of the Church's own origin in God's free election of grace? This is of course a factual service which the believing Church must see in continuing Judaism. God wishes all to believe so that this role must be said to be a factual, rather than a necessary one (because of some eternal and irrevocable election). The rejectedness of the Jews reminds the believing Gentiles of the absolute grace and

[18] *CTKB*, pp. 258f.
[19] Cf *ibid.*, p. 110.

mercy of their own election, for they have only been grafted in to take their place. In this sense one can, I believe, agree with Barth's dialectics and say that the Jews constitute a witness to the divine judgment, to the sin, misery and death of man, to man's turning away from God, to his opposition to divine election, to his attempt at self-justification by works.[20] The rejection and infidelity of the Jews is used by God as a reminder to the believing Church of the very basis of Jewish rejection and of its own election: salvation through God's pure grace and not through works and law. 'If it is by grace it is no longer on the basis of works; otherwise grace would no longer be grace' (Rom 11:6). The presence of Jews reminds the Church of the transition from the old to the new covenant, and of the very basis of this new covenant. The Jews remind the Church of the basis of its existence in God's free election of grace and of the condition of his continuing election, namely, faith in Jesus Christ which is God's gift and not man's work (cf Rom 11:20f). Since they have the old Law, the prophets and the promises, the Jews also ensure the fidelity of the Church to her origins. In dialogue with her Jewish origins the Church must become more and more the people of God moving ever forwards and outwards in obedience to the free call and election of its one God, Father, Son and Spirit. For if there is one thing that the Old Testament Scriptures, as the objectification of the meaning of Israel's history, reveal, it is that the people of God which prefigures and prepares the Church and therefore foretells it to some degree is the people which owes its existence solely to God's salvific act and Word. The Church must never forsake this origin.

Just as with the Church, the Jews have also a positive role with regard to all other non-Christian religions. They must be a pointer on the way to Jesus and his Church by first of all pointing to God, to his grace and mercy, to his acts of salvation under the old covenant, to obedience and love for him, to his promise of a future redemptive Messiah, and to belief in his promises. While the history of salvation has taken place once and for all one can also say that in the life of the individual traveller on his return to God it takes place over and over again: the creation of man, his fundamental option for or against God, his call to and promise of salvation, his belief in Jesus Christ and incorporation into the Church. On this journey the Jew can have a decisive role. Here and now his very rejection can confirm his election to a role in the economy of salvation. This depends of course on his fidelity to his very Jewishness. The more Jewish he is the more he points the way to God and his promises. He can and must fulfil his

[20] Cf *ibid.*, pp. 108f.

prophetic and Old Testament role which, as prophetic and old, points to the 'coming' and 'new' man.

The Jew therefore must also recognize and acknowledge that his religion is only one of promise, of future fulfilment. For if the Scriptures which are the objectification of the meaning of Jewish history point to the origin of this history in God's free and gracious interventions they also unequivocally testify that the goal of this same history lies in the future and that Judaism exists solely as a pointer to that future and therefore to its own fulfilment and to that extent abolition. Once Judaism becomes a self-contained, independent and complete reality it forfeits its very nature. As Barth pointedly asks: 'Is an infinite waiting, such as is the result of an abstract Old Testament faith, a real waiting and not rather an eternal unrest?'[21] Judaism, for its part, must enter into dialogue too, therefore, and be ever open and willing to listen to the claim that its fulfilment has *taken place*, that its Scriptures have been *fulfilled* (cf Lk 24:27, 44f; Acts 8:26f), just as the Church for its part must consider it one of its greatest responsibilities and duties to present this claim to it. For Jesus Christ and his Church are the fulfilment of Judaism, the fulfilment of its promises and Scriptures. They are *par excellence* the 'universal sacrament of salvation'.[22] Israel must cease being Israel by becoming more truly Israel. Judaism is essentially a preparation, a pre-figuration, a prophecy. It lives for a future which will be its fulfilment. The Jew must fulfil his Jewishness by acknowledging that the God who acted in Abraham, Isaac and Jacob, acted and acts again also in Jesus Christ, and in and through his new people the Church. Only thus, that is, by not persisting in his unbelief, will he be grafted (and how much more naturally than the non-Jew!) back on to the root which is his by right of inheritance (cf Rom 11:17-24).

[21] *C.D.* I/2, p. 101 (=S. 110).
[22] Cf Vatican II, DCC, nn. 2, 48.

Section Two

The Church in the Son: The Objective Realization of Reconciliation

IN THIS ecclesiological dialogue with Karl Barth I am trying to follow the basic trinitarian scheme which I thought to be the most apt in my exposition of his ecclesiology in *The Church in the Theology of Karl Barth*. Accordingly, in this second section I intend to treat of the 'Church in the Son'. I think this is legitimate in Catholic theology also, in the sense that the Church has an objective realization in Jesus Christ. That is, the actually existing Church has an objective realization in the objective realization of the reconciliation of all men in Jesus Christ. Its objective realization is included in the objective realization of the reconciliation of all. In saying this, therefore, I do not wish to say that the subjective reality of reconciliation (which is the Church) is co-extensive with its objective reality. Karl Barth does not say this either, as is evidenced by his frequent description of the Church as the 'provisional representation' of the objective and eschatological salvation of all.[1] Neither do we wish to say that the salvific reality and effectiveness of the Church is absorbed in the mystery of its objective realization, that is, in Jesus Christ. I cannot see how Karl Barth avoids this. We should not misunderstand him, however. He does not say that the supernatural mystery of the Church is enclosed in a mystery (the mystery of Christ) which is past. The mystery of Christ is a supra-temporal reality, he says. It takes place now as it did then. He does not, therefore, deny every sense of a 'history of salvation' in the present. Christ is savingly active in the present through his Spirit. The point on which I would like to question him is: Is this history of salvation *solely* the history of Jesus Christ? Or is it *also* (in and under him) the history *of* the *community* and *of* the individual *Christian*?

[1] Cf *CTKB*, p. 340, for instance.

Does the community, and does the Christian, *participate* in this history of salvation? While we can accept Barth's general terminology we must beware of denying the Church's own distinct (not independent) supernatural and salvific activity.

My purpose in this section is a dialogue with Barth as regards the being and work of Jesus Christ (in whom is included the objective realization of the Church). It will be a dialogue within the Chalcedonian definition, for Barth affirms this ancient Church dogma no less than ourselves.[2] Our differences (and there are differences)[3] are, therefore, differences of interpretation, differences within the one Christian faith. In itself difference of interpretation is an excellent thing, for it but reveals the fervour of Christian life and leads to a better overall understanding of the mystery. All explanations must, however, safeguard the dogma. They cannot deny or omit any part. Of the particular dogma here in question there are many different explanations within the one Catholic Church. All safeguard the unity without compromising the duality, and vice versa. Does Barth's explanation do this? An unequivocal answer could only be given on the basis of a detailed study of the dogma itself and of Barth's doctrine. This I have not done, as it is outside my scope. I concentrate on those points which, in all consistent christocentric dogmatics, have repercussions in the doctrines of the Church, our Lady and justification. In doing so I seek to find the basis of our ecclesiological differences.

This is something which I think should receive greater stress in all Protestant–Catholic discussion: while our differences are most manifest in ecclesiology and mariology the basis of these differences does not usually lie in ecclesiology and mariology, but goes back to, and derives from, differences in justification and christology. Protestants should not criticize Catholic ecclesiology and mariology without considering the intimate connection which exists between its doctrine on these points and its doctrine on the role of the man Jesus in the accomplishment of the objective reconciliation.[4]

Karl Barth clearly perceives this intimate connection between christology, the doctrine of justification, ecclesiology and mariology. He explicitly admits the christological basis of our differences.[5] His

---

[2] Cf *CTKB*, pp. 133–4.
[3] Cf *ibid.*, for Barth's own understanding of these differences.
[4] Not all do this. 'The way I conceive Mary is intimately linked with the way I conceive the Church, the sacraments, and the incarnation itself': E. Reisner, in *Kirchenblatt für die reformierte Schweiz*, 1 March 1951, 69, from the German bi-monthly *Junge Kirche* (cited in Congar, *Le Christ, Marie et l'Eglise*, p. 26).   [5] Cf *C.D.* IV/1, pp. 500, 126 (=SS. 557, 137–8).

own theology is so centrally, exemplarily and consistently christology that his doctrine of the Church, the mother of God and justification are its direct consequences. As he so often repeats, Jesus Christ is the 'ontic and noetic centre' of all theology. Or, as he negatively puts it: 'A mistaken or deficient perception here would mean error or deficiency everywhere.'[6] In this, Catholic theology is in equally consistent agreement. Hence the necessity of this christological aspect of our ecclesiological dialogue. Because and as we differ in christology we differ in all the rest.[7]

In a first chapter I shall outline, very briefly, the Catholic understanding of the being and work of Jesus Christ; in a second I shall confront this view and that of Karl Barth; in a third chapter I shall consider the ecclesiological consequences of our Christological differences; and in a fourth I hope to illustrate how these christological differences are also the basis of our differences with regard to the person and work of the mother of God.

---

[6] *Ibid.*, p. 3 (=S. 1).
[7] I am not convinced that the difference between Barth and Catholic theology in christology is the original or fontal basis of our differences (cf below, Section Three, chapter sixteen). What I say here is valid in the sense that the one basic difference between us manifests itself here (as everywhere) and from here (at least factually) spreads to all the rest.

Chapter Six

The Being and Work of Jesus Christ in Catholic Theology

ACCORDING to Catholic theology Jesus Christ is *the fundamental* sacrament of universal salvation, that is, he is the culminating manifestation of God's salvific presence to the world and also the effective agent of that presence. He is the centre and apex of the whole history of salvation between God and man and the world, the apex towards which all salvific history tends and the centre from which that same history flows. Salvation history is essentially christocentric and christofugal. Why is Jesus Christ this foundation, centre and apex of salvation history? Because in him God assumes human existence through the power of his Holy Spirit. 'The Word became flesh and dwelt amongst us.'[1] Without ceasing to be God, yet shedding the glory of his divine form of existence, he took the form of human existence and existed as man. He 'emptied himself, taking the form of a servant', was 'born in the likeness of men', and was 'found in human form' (Phil 2:7–8). He began to exist as man. This human existence, as the human form of existence of God, is different from all other human existences. Yet it remains a truly human existence. It does not become a divine form of existence. It is different therefore in so far as it is more perfectly the same. It is exemplarily different, the very exemplar and revelation in fact of what true human life and existence should be. As such it is the goal towards which the history of salvation strives—from creation to prefiguration to realization. Whether one views the matter historically as a history proceeding from a creation in the past to a past pre-figuration in the history of Israel, or whether one views it as a history which takes place here and now in all times and places in each individual and in the world, the humanly perfect existence of Jesus Christ is the goal and culmination towards which it strives. He is the 'omega point' of all religious development. The basis of the change or perfection in his existence

[1] Jn 1:14. Cf Lk 1:26–38.

is not due originally to anything human existence did but is due solely to God's free and absolutely gracious act of assumption or incarnation. But given this assuming act, his human existence is the human existence or realization of divine holiness and power. And because of this it is not only the sign or manifestation but also the effective instrument of universal salvation. God became man to redeem and save the world (Jn 3:16f), and he accomplished this work in and through his human existence as 'the man Christ Jesus' (I Tim 2:5-6). Jesus Christ is thus the fundamental sacrament, that is, the sign and instrument, of universal salvation.

Traditional scholastic theology understood the hypostatic union as a *tractio* or *unitio* by which the second person of the Trinity assumes an integral human nature into substantial union with himself. It took place once and for all.[2] It is an act whose sole Subject is Pure Act itself, without cause or merit on the part of the creature.[3] In this act the Word gifts his own existence to a human nature, actuating it, while not being limited by it—what the same scholastics termed a *causa quasi-formalis*. It is an uncreated grace, supernatural, substantial, the most intimate of unions and the greatest of gifts.[4] The Word assumes a human nature in such a way that it exists solely with his existence.

Since this union is both *true* and *real*, a real change necessarily results in the assumed nature by which it is really related to the person who assumes it.[5] This change is completely the effect and consequence of the act of the Word and in no sense its principle or cause. Nevertheless it is the expression and demonstration of the truth and reality of the assuming act of the Word. God's will, or action or knowledge as regards existing things is not caused by existing things but is itself the cause of existing things. Just as in creation God remains unchanged and the creature enters into a real relation to him by the reception of its being, so also in the assumption by the Word of a human nature this human nature enters into a real relation of union with the Word through the reception of a perfection in itself. Otherwise Christ's

---

[2] Cf Jn 1:14; Lk 1:32, 33; Heb 13:8; the Council of Chalcedon, *indivise, inseparabiliter* (DS 302); the Council of Toledo, DS 534.

[3] Cf Lk 1:34-38; Jn 3:16.

[4] *Maxima unionum, maxima donorum*, St Thomas, *Summa theol.*, III, q. 2, art. 9, 10, 11.

[5] Cf *id., ibid.*, q. 1, art. 1, ad. 1; q. 2, art. 7 and 10; q. 6, art. 6; q. 7, art. 1, 9, 13; q. 8, art. 1-6; IaIIae, q. 110, art. 1. Cf also the commentaries of Franzelin, *Theses* 33 and 41; Galtier, Sectio 2, cap. 2, art. 2, and Sectio 3, cap. 2, art. 1; Boyer, *Theses* 8, 11, 12; Mersch, *The Theology of the Mystical Body*, especially pp. 206ff, 602ff; Lonergan, *Theses* 9 and 11.

c

incarnation is neither real nor true. The human nature alone suffers change, namely, the change from non-existence to existence in the Word. Strictly speaking, of course, this can hardly be termed a 'change', for a change presupposes the existence of the reality which is changed, and in this case nothing of the human nature pre-existed (*ex ouk autōn*). The human nature changes therefore in the sense that where before there was nothing there is now this perfected human existence. The scholastics often considered the hypostatic union as a ray of light which unites humanity with divinity by illumining and thereby changing the object, itself remaining unchanged.[6]

Because Christ's human existence is the form of existence of God it is the greatest earthly approximation to divine existence. It is perfect human existence. It is this, as St Thomas says, 'through a participation which is in the order of grace'.[7] It is in the order of grace because it is due solely to God's merciful and gratuitous action. And it is a participation because it is a gift from God, the gift of participation in his own existence. It remains human existence. The divine efficacious unifying action is received in the human nature and according to the capacity of that nature.[8]

What is this perfection received in the human nature, the *passio unitiva* corresponding to the *actio unitiva* of the assuming or incarnating Word, the *terminatio ad Filium*, by means of which it is, not the cause of the union, but the assumed nature of God? What is it, in the human nature, which renders it capable of a divinely-human or humanly-divine existence? For E. Mersch this is 'the great question in all theology'.[9]

The change in Christ's human nature, which constitutes the foundation of its real relation to the divine person who assumes it, and which is the expression and demonstration, resulting from

[6] Cf e.g., Alexander of Hales, *Summa* 3, q. 7; m. 3, a. 1; St Thomas, *Summa theol.*, III, q. 7, art. 13. The necessity of this change was often expressed in scholastic terminology by the phrase: 'Quae contingenter de Deo dicuntur, exigunt terminum ad extra contingentem et convenientem.' As Fr Mersch says: 'Unless we wish to reduce this union to nothing, to a logical juxtaposition, to a mechanical juncture, or to a juridical fiction, we have to admit something in the assumed humanity, something that is human because it pertains to Christ's humanity but that is also divine because it makes that humanity the humanity of God': *op. cit.*, p. 602.

[7] '... per participationem quae est secundum gratiam': *Summa theol.*, III, q. 7, art. 1.

[8] '... in duabus naturis *inconfuse, immutabiliter* ... *nusquam sublata differentia naturarum* propter unitionem magisque salva proprietate utriusque naturae': Chalcedon, DS 302.

[9] *Op. cit.*, pp. 207–8.

Christ's assuming act, of the truth and reality of that act and therefore of the incarnation, is, according to one of the more tenable of the scholastic positions, an absolutely supernatural substantial act which actuates the obediential potency of the assumed nature. 'Obediential potency', according to St Thomas, is the passive capacity of every creature before its Creator to be elevated to a higher form of activity while remaining essentially the same creature.[10] Christ's human existence is not some form of higher non-human existence but simply *is* human existence more perfectly. Pure Act actuates it in a special way. 'It makes the human nature exactly what a human nature is, but with an intensity of existence that reflects and expresses Being itself, through a transcendental human actuation.'[11]

Christ's human nature is different from ours—but in the sense that it *is more perfectly the same*. It is different, yet not different. It is changed, yet not changed. God is the ground of all being. Created being is the gift of participation in the being of God. The more the creature exists 'in God', or simply the more he 'exists', the more perfect he is. The man Jesus exists 'in God' in the most intimate and intensive, because personal, way conceivable. And in existing thus his human nature does not cease to be human nature. On the contrary, it is more perfectly human nature. For it is taken more into personal relationship with God, it exists more 'in God', which is the ground of the being of all reality. Every existing creature exists 'in God', albeit to a different degree and perfection. Human nature, by the fact that it is assumed into personal unity with God, by the fact that it exists with the sole personal existence of God, does not cease to be human nature, but 'is' more perfectly the same. That which in other men exists imperfectly 'in God' in Christ exists perfectly 'in God'. God the Father, who is the ground of being of all creation, is also the ground of being of the man Jesus in that he gives himself to be his personal existence. Here we have an analogical conception of being demanded by the mystery of the incarnation and the dogma of the Church. It does not contradict the dogma of Chalcedon which only forbids the *confusio* and *mutatio* of the natures, but on the contrary, explains it in some way.

Existing in personal unity with God the man Jesus does not cease

[10] 'Est autem considerandum quod in anima humana, sicut in qualibet creatura, consideratur duplex potentia passiva: una quidem per comparationem ad agens naturale; alia vero per comparationem ad agens primum, qui potest quamlibet creaturam reducere in actum aliquem altiorem, in quem non reducitur per agens naturale; et haec consuevit vocari potentia obedientiae in creatura': *Summa Theol.*, III, q. 11, art. 1.

[11] E. Mersch, *op cit.*, p. 220.

to be man. He is, more perfectly, *the same*. He took the form of a servant, and was in every respect like ourselves, except that he did not sin (cf Phil 2:7–8; Heb 4:15). He was subject to growth, change and history (cf Lk 2:52). While we can say that the Word became flesh once and for all in his mother's womb we can also say that his incarnation is a process which goes on all his life and even includes his death and resurrection. For only then did he become the man he set out to become: the head of the Church (cf Eph 4:13–16). Human life is an evolutionary process from birth to manhood to death. Christ's incarnation is the history of his becoming man. And this history, which is the history of his being, or becoming, is also the history of his work: his being is his work and also revelation. For in and through his becoming man, in his life, death and resurrection, he accomplished the mediation of revelation and redemption. The purpose of the incarnation or of Christ's mission from the Father was the salvation of mankind. 'For God sent the Son into the world, not to condemn the world, but that the world might be saved through him.'[12] It is as man he accomplished this mission: 'For there is one God, and there is one mediator between God and man, the man Christ Jesus' (1 Tim 2:5). He accomplished it in the whole history which is his incarnation, viz. in his life, death, resurrection and ascension.

His human existence was salvifically effective because it was the human existence of the incarnating God. It was the human existence or embodiment of divine life, power and holiness. Actuated substantially by uncreated act it was the efficacious instrument of salvation. Loved by the Father,[13] who gives Jesus his Holy Spirit,[14] the man Jesus is said to possess the Spirit,[15] to give and send the Holy Spirit,[16] to be full of grace and truth and the source of all grace.[17] The man Jesus forgave sins, cast out demons, worked miracles, that is, he accomplished what is properly and originally a divine prerogative.[18]

[12] Jn 3:17. Cf 5:36; 6:29.
[13] Cf Mt 17:5; Jn 3:35; Eph 1:6.
[14] Cf Is 11:1–3; Mt 12:18.
[15] Cf Mt 3:16, 17; Mk 1:10, 11; Lk 3:21–22; 4:18.
[16] Cf Jn 14:26; 15:26, 16:7, 12–15.
[17] Cf Jn 1:14, 16; Col 1:18–20; 2:2–3, 9–15; Eph 3:16–9.
[18] 'Christum in humanis actibus divina gesisse mysteria et in rebus visibilibus invisibilia exercuisse negotia lectio hodierna (Mt 9:1–8) monstravit': St Peter Chrysologus, *Sermo* 50. And as St Thomas says: 'Cuius humanitas ex hoc quod est Divinitati coniuncta habet virtutem iustificandi': *Summa theol.*, III, q. 8, art. 6. In another place he says that Christ as man causes grace both by meriting it and by effecting it: '. . . dare gratiam, aut Spiritum Sanctum convenit Christo, secundum quod est Deus, auctoritative; sed instrumentaliter convenit etiam ei, secundum quod est homo; inquantum scilicet eius humani-

Christ's human *acta et passa in carne* are salvific because they are the human acts of a divine person.[19]

Scholastic terminology explained this mediatory or salvific power and efficacy by saying that Christ's human nature was the conjoined and animated organ of his divinity.[20] By 'organ' it meant the means, instrument or ministry by which God reconciles the world to himself. By 'conjoined' and 'animated' it distinguished the instrumentality of Christ's human existence from all other created instrumentalities of divine grace. 'Conjoined' means that it is united in its very existence to the power which is active in and through it. It is joined in unity to the very person of God. It is not like all other human ministries and sacraments who work in the power of another, namely, God.[21] The power which is operative in Christ's human existence is not the power of another, of a separate (*disiunctum*) subject, but of Christ himself whose existence it is, and who is the only subject here active. The term 'conjoined', despite its inadequacy, does not wish to attenuate in any way the hypostatic union, but on the contrary wishes to affirm the greatest possible union. The term 'animated' means that the organ which is Christ's human existence is responsible for its own thoughts and actions. It is not an organ as the hand is an organ of the brain, or the pen of the hand. It possesses a spiritual intelligence and free will. Christ really wills and loves humanly in his accomplishment of salvation. For this reason the holiness and power which accomplished salvation are truly and properly the holiness and power of his human existence, and are not the holiness and power of a separate and inanimate organ which must receive them from outside by an ever new act. Commenting on a phrase which occurs in one of the documents of Vatican II, Fr Grillmeier says:

> 'The idea that the humanity of Christ serves the Logos as an "instrument of salvation inseparably joined to him" is found

tas instrumentum fuit divinitatis eius; et ita actiones ipsius ex virtute divinitatis fuerunt nobis salutiferae, utpote gratiam in nobis causantes, et per meritum, et per efficientiam quamdam': *Ibid.*, q. 8, art. 1, ad. 1.

[19] St Thomas, referring to Rev 1:5 and Rom 3:24–25, says that Christ's blood had the power of washing sins: *De Veritate*, q. 27, art. 4, resp.

[20] Cyril of Alexandria already spoke of *sarx zoopoios* and John Damascene of Christ's humanity as the 'organ' of his divinity—cf St Thomas, *De Ver.*, q. 27, art. 4, resp. For the development in St Thomas' christology, and consequently in his ecclesiology, on this point, under the influence of the Greek Fathers, cf Geiselmann, *art. cit.*, in *Theol. Quartalschrift*, who refers on p. 251 to the classical work of M. Grabmann, *Die Lehre des Heiligen Thomas von Aquin von der Kirke als Gotteswerk*, Ratisbona, 1903, p. 243.

[21] Cf St Thomas, *De Ver.*, q. 29, art. 4.

throughout the whole history of Christology. . . . The closer the union of Logos and human nature in Christ is seen—in the ultimate analysis of what hypostatic union implies—and the more fully on the other hand the human nature of Christ is seen to be taken up in its freedom, knowledge and truly human qualities, the greater the tension in the notion of organ of salvation, and the more correct its theological exploitation.'[22]

As man, then, Jesus is the *eminent* and *universal* cause of grace.[23] He is the first principle within the human species of the sanctification of that species. His humanity does not become divine. Yet as the organ joined in personal unity and existence to the divinity, it can perform any miraculous change which is in some way connected with the purpose of the incarnation.

'If we speak of Christ's soul from the point of view of its being the instrument of the Word united to it, it had an instrumental power to bring about all those miraculous changes which are in any way related to the purpose of the incarnation, which is to restore all things, in heaven and on earth. It does not possess the power of annihilation, which is the counterpart of creation out of nothing, and therefore the power of God alone.'[24]

Jesus accomplished as man this salvation of the world in his whole life, death and resurrection, in his whole threefold ministry as priest, king and prophet. As priest the man Jesus offered his life as a sacrifice for the expiation of sin. 'Therefore he had to be made like his brethren in every respect, so that he might become a merciful and faithful high priest in the service of God, to make expiation for the sins of the people.'[25] As king the man Jesus inaugurates the kingdom of God, lays down the law of the New Testament, rules all things by his will.[26] And as the prophet foretold in the Old Testament, the same Jesus preaches the Gospel of the kingdom, the good news of salvation. 'And he went about all Galilee, teaching in their synagogues and preaching the Gospel of the kingdom.'[27] As Jesus said, according to

---

[22] Commenting on DCC, n. 8, in *Commentary on the Documents of Vatican II*, ed. by H. Vorgrimler, vol. I, London–New York, 1967, p. 148.
[23] Cf St Thomas, *Summa theol.*, III, q. 8, art. 5; q. 7, art. 9 and 11.
[24] *Id., ibid.*, q. 13, art. 2, translated in Vonier, *op cit.*, pp. 131–2.
[25] Heb 2:17. Cf 5:5–10; 7:24–28; 9:11–15, 23–28. Cf also St Thomas, *Summa theol.*, III, q. 22, art. 1, ad 3.
[26] Cf Mt 12:28; 5; Mk 4: 39; 5.
[27] Mt 4:23. Cf Lk 4:16f.

the Gospel of John, 'I am the way, and the truth, and the life; no one comes to the Father, but by me' (14:6).

All of Christ's human acts were salvific. But this is especially true of his miracles, death and resurrection.[28] The resurrection of Jesus from the dead forms an absolutely essential part of Christ's work of salvation. St Paul says that Jesus Christ 'was put to death for our trespasses and raised for our justification' (Rom 4:25). Christ accomplished the reconciliation of the world especially in the one mystery of his death and resurrection. His death is the final consequence of his emptying of himself (*kenosis*), of his assumption of a human form (cf Phil 2:7). At the same time, it removes his state of *kenosis* by meriting his resurrection and glorification. The resurrection is the positive side of Christ's redeeming mystery. In it God justifies the man Jesus, and in and with him all mankind.

Through the fundamental grace of the hypostatic union, therefore, the man Jesus is the universal sacrament of salvation.[29] His visible human actions and sufferings signify and effect the objective salvation of all men and of the whole world. 'Designated Son of God in power according to the Spirit of holiness by his resurrection from the dead' (Rom 1:4) he then became the head of the Church. He is the fulfilment, the goal, the omega, the 'mature manhood', the 'measure and stature' of the world's history, the head towards which the whole world must strive and strives (cf Eph 4:10–16). And he is this because he is first of all the alpha, the source from which all salvific history springs. Risen and glorified he is full of grace and truth, and the source of all grace and truth through his life-giving Spirit.[30] In the subjective realization in all men and time and places of his objective salvation the risen Christ sends his Holy Spirit and his apostles.

'Being therefore exalted at the right hand of God, and having received from the Father the promise of the Holy Spirit, he has poured out this which you see and hear. . . . Peace be with you. As the Father has sent me, even so I send you. And when he had said this, he breathed on them, and said to them, "Receive the Holy Spirit. If you forgive the sins of any, they are forgiven; if you retain the sins of any, they are retained." . . . And Jesus

---

[28] Cf St Thomas, *Summa theol.*, III, q. 13, art. 2; q. 43, art. 2; q. 48, art. 6; q. 49, art. 1; q. 50, art. 6; q. 56, art. 1; q. 57, art. 6.

[29] Augustine (*Epistola* 187, n. 34) and Leo the Great (Sermo 22, 1; 25, 1) already spoke of Christ as sacrament of salvation.

[30] Cf Jn 1:14, 16; I Cor 15:45; Col 1:18–20; 2:2–3, 9–15; Eph 1:22–23; 3:16–19.

came and said to them, "All authority in heaven and on earth has been given to me. Go therefore and make disciples of all nations, baptizing them in the name of the Father and of the Son and of the Holy Spirit, teaching them to observe all that I have commanded you; and lo, I am with you always, to the close of the age." . . . We were buried therefore with him by baptism into death, so that as Christ was raised from the dead by the glory of the Father, we too might walk in newness of life.'[31]

In the uniqueness and totality of his whole salvific mystery the man Jesus is the fundamental and absolutely unique sacrament of salvation. In the power of his Holy Spirit the Church is the sacrament of the risen Christ.

---

[31] Acts 2:33; Jn 20:21-23; Mt 28:18-20; Rom 6:4.

Chapter Seven

Confrontation with the Doctrine of Karl Barth

IT WILL be seen that Karl Barth's conception of the being and work of Jesus Christ is not all that dissimilar to the one outlined. And yet there is a difference which has grave divisive consequences for our conceptions of the being and work of our Lady, justified man and the Church.

Both Barth and ourselves assert the absolute goodness, freedom and mercy of the divine initiative and act in becoming man. It was alone his act, unmerited and absolutely supernatural. Again we both agree in asserting a consequent change and perfection of the human nature, without changing it as human nature.[1] For Barth, however, the union is always an *unitio*. It is an event which never ceases to be an event. It is an ever-new act. It is always a union *in fieri*, and never *in facto esse*. The resultant change of the human nature is always a 'changing'. No perfection is *given* to it. It is perfected in the ever-new act of the second person of the Trinity uniting to himself this humanity. The perfection is not possessed by it. It is given—and yet not given. *We* can never assert the hypostatic union as true or real. Both its reality and truth always depend on God's ever-new act.

Following the obvious meaning of Scripture we say that Christ assumed a human nature to himself once and for all in the womb of the Virgin Mary. In that act his human nature entered into a real relation of union with him through a divine grace gifted to it. The hypostatic union simply has not taken place or does not exist unless the human nature receives in itself a perfection which is the foundation of its real relation of union with, or the foundation of the man Jesus' response to, the Word. With this gift Christ's human nature is elevated to be the human nature of God. It exists divinely, while remaining human nature.[2]

[1] Cf *CTKB*, pp. 141f, 148f, 152f.
[2] This difference in our conception of the hypostatic union, namely, as event and relation or as solely an event, is paralleled by a varying conception

We must acknowledge the value of Barth's actualist exposition. In a detailed study one could develop many points in agreement with him. For example, his saying that the incarnation is always a 'being which does not cease to be a becoming'³ can be understood in the sense that Jesus as man is subject to the process of development which is human life. He becomes ever more and more incarnate. His incarnation is a process which ends only with his final glorification. In an ecclesiological dialogue with him we can confront only those points which have a decisive bearing on our ecclesiologies. Barth's understanding of the incarnation as an event, that is, as an ever-new act of God, with no resulting perfection of his human nature as the expression and realization of its personal unity with God, is such a point, and *the* basic one. For him there is no such thing as the possession of grace by a human creature. It is always and solely a *divine act*. It can never be shared in or possessed by another. It is God's gift only in so far as it is and remains *God's* ever-new *act*.⁴

Barth divides his whole treatment of the being of Christ into a movement downwards from God to man, and a corresponding movement upwards from man to God. As such it is also a movement outwards, revealing himself to men. The limpidity of Barth's style and exposition are admirable. Since Christ's being is his work, the work of reconciliation also consists in this downward, upward and outward movement. Barth thus divides his christology into the threefold aspect of Christ's priestly, kingly and prophetic ministries. I have nothing against such a division. On the contrary, I think it should be developed much more in Catholic theology.⁵ In Barth's exposition,

---

of creation. For Barth, for whom Jesus Christ is the noetic basis of all theology, creation is an event. The common catholic conception, following St Thomas, is that creation is both event and the relation of dependence of the creature to the Creator. Indeed, strictly speaking, the hypostatic union and creation are relations and not events: the relation of union of a human nature to the assuming Word, and the relation of dependence of the creature to the Creator. For Barth's conception of creation cf *C.D.* III/1, pp. 42-94 (=SS. 44-103). An ample commentary will be found in the work of H. Bouillard, *Karl Barth* . . . , esp. vol. II, pp. 178-87.

³ Cf *CTKB*, pp. 141f.

⁴ Cf Barth's *C.D.* IV/1, pp. 84-8 (=SS. 89-94) where he spiritedly rejects the Catholic division of the one grace of Christ.

⁵ The systematization of Christ's three offices was only made after the sixteenth century, especially by Protestant theologians. The idea is, however, traditional. It is to be found in Heb 1:1-4; Justin, Eusebius of Caesarea, St Thomas, Calvin, and the *Catechismus Romanus* (cf J. Fuchs, *Magisterium, Ministerium, Regimen. Vom Ursprung einer ekklesiologischen Trilogie*, Bonn, 1941). Pastor J. Bosc sees in it 'an adequate formulation of scriptural truth'

in conformity with his basic mode of thought, there may be the danger of an over-functional conception of the existence of Jesus Christ. I shall have something to say later with regard to the functionalism of his ecclesiology.

Even though I would much prefer to enumerate all the points on which I agree with Barth's Christology I am constrained, both because of the scope of this study, and because of space, to list the points on which we are in basic disagreement. I am convinced that Barth does not develop sufficiently the scriptural assertions that Christ redeemed the world *as man*. In his human work as priest, king and prophet, Christ redeemed the world. For Barth, the work of reconciliation would seem to be solely a *divine act*.

He understands reconciliation as an exchange.[6] In this exchange God substitutes his divine action for human action. The cause of the atonement is a divine action alone. Christ's being and work consists in a continual descending of a divine act and in a continually corresponding ascending of a human act. God does not live out his divine life through his human life. In this sense the divinity seems to remain 'outside' the humanity. As it stands, Barth's interpretation of the Pauline *heauton ekenōsen* (Phil 2:7) is in agreement with the Catholic interpretation. Even after his incarnation Christ exists and works without human nature as well in his intra-trinitarian relationships. Nevertheless, we differ in our understanding of this text, which is of primary importance for the understanding of Pauline christology. Catholic doctrine insists that the work of reconciliation, for which Christ became incarnate, is not the work of his divinity alone. *ekenōsen* means that he really emptied himself, not of his divine existence, but of the glory to which as the Son of God he was entitled, and really put on the form of the servant with all its consequences. 'For Paul, the miracle of his humiliation is precisely that he did not simply put on the outward appearance of the servant's garb, but wore it in reality with all its consequences.'[7] The work of reconciliation takes place as the work of this *one through* his human nature. Barth

---

as regards the work of the Saviour (*L'Office royal du Seigneur Jésus-Christ*, Geneva, 1957, 22; cited in Dewailly, *Envoyés du Père*, Paris, 1960, p. 65, note I). This trilogy is basic to Vatican II's christology and ecclesiology. Cf, e.g., DCC, ch. I, nn. 3-6; ch. 2, nn. 9-13; ch. 3, nn. 21-5; ch. 4, nn. 31-5. I shall follow its (and Barth's) example in my later development of Catholic ecclesiology.

[6] Cf *CTKB*, p. 139.

[7] K. Adam, *The Christ of Faith*, p. 165. Cf *id.*, *ibid.*, pp. 163-6; J. L. Witte, in *Chalkedon*, III, pp. 500, 506-7, 517; P. Henry, 'Kenose' in *DBS*, 1950, pp. 7-161.

insists far more on the separate operation of the natures even after the incarnation. The work of reconciliation is caused exclusively by the divine nature. Such an *Extra Calvinisticum* is in danger of denying the *reality* of the incarnation and work of reconciliation.

In Barth's theology, God does not seem to redeem mankind in and through human nature and time. Christ's human activity is but a *consequens sine qua non*, serving, attesting and reflecting the divine. It does not cooperate. Thus for him, Christ's priestly action cannot be his *human* action. And in fact, in his exposition, Christ's priestly office is connected solely with God's judgment, with his movement 'into the far country', that is, with the divine action.

The divine act is the sole cause of the incarnate being of Christ. Barth identifies Christ's being with his work. The sole cause of reconciliation is also, therefore, for him, a divine act. He does not admit a truly ontological elevation of Christ's humanity in the incarnation. Consequently, it cannot possibly be a real, true, animated instrument, or efficacious sign, in the work of salvation. Human nature, he says, is the instrument in act of divine power.[8] It does not *acquire* or *exercise* divine power. But, we ask, if it neither acquires nor exercises it how can it possibly be said to be a truly joined and *animated* instrument of the divinity? It is hard to see how Barth avoids saying that the instrumentality of Christ's human nature is something inanimate. He does not say it is juxtaposition, or that the divine act takes place on the 'occasion' of the human act. The divine act takes place through the human, but in such a way that the human never participates in the power and life of the divine, and consequently never shares in the creation of the effect. The effect is attributable solely to God. Christ does not effect reconciliation through his human acts. In the work of reconciliation his truly human willing and loving have no *effective* part. In this sense, for Barth, his truly human acts seem to be non-existent in the work of reconciliation. From his identification of Christ's being as act with his work, and from his denial of a real ontological perfection of Christ's human nature, Barth is led to profess an 'economic' monophysitism as regards the work of salvation.

The Catholic conception of the incarnation is not as 'static' as Barth thinks.[9] While we assert that the second person of the Trinity joined human nature to himself once and for all in the womb of the Virgin Mary, we do not say that there was no development in his incarnation. To be a man is a process of becoming a man. His whole life was a

[8] Cf *CTKB*, pp. 150, 151f.
[9] Cf *ibid.*, pp. 152f, 134. And cf above, chapter six.

becoming incarnate. And this being (or becoming) was also his work. It does not consist in a succession of states, or in a transition from one state to another. It is the one continual process of glorification.

'But the incarnation of Christ is not something static. Christ's redeeming action, though a single reality, grows and develops so that, in the context of his whole human life, we can distinguish in it three principal elements: (a) His death and descent into hell. (b) The resurrection from the dead. (c) His glorification or his being established by the Father as Lord and thus sender of the Holy Spirit. St John sees this progressive action as all one process of glorification.'[10]

Moreover, we also speak of a downward and upward movement in Christ's incarnation and redemption. For us, however, the downward movement ontologically elevates or sanctifies the human nature. It becomes the human nature of God. God acts out his divine life in and through it. It is a complete, animated instrument of his divine life, joined to the existence of the Word. We also say, therefore, that it is the downward movement of God which accomplishes our reconciliation, but in and through human nature, and therefore in and through the upward movement, which is the supreme act of worship, the supreme realization of all religion. The cause of the atonement is both divine *and* human. Christ's human actions are theandric.

Catholic doctrine by no means denies that reconciliation is a divine act. Nor does Barth deny a human activity to Christ as man, and that this activity forms an integral part of reconciliation. What we assert and what he seems to deny is that reconciliation took place as a divine-human activity; that Christ accomplished our reconciliation *through* his human nature as an animated instrument joined in personal unity to the divinity. For him, terms like 'god-man, divine-human or divine-humanity' evade the historicity of the Subject, and especially the historicity of the relationship of his two predicates, and are, therefore, inadmissible.[11]

Because we admit the ontological sanctification of Christ's human nature, as the consequence and realization of its personal unity with God, and because we admit this human nature's instrumentality in the work of reconciliation, we also assert the legitimacy and necessity of rendering the homage of adoration to, for example, Christ's physical heart. Not to a physical heart in itself, in abstraction from the

---

[10] E. Schillebeeckx, *Christ the Sacrament of encounter with God*, p. 27. Cf the same author's quasi-Barthian statements *ibid.*, pp. 18–21.

[11] Cf *C.D.* IV/2, p. 115 (=S. 128).

divine person, but to the physical heart of the man Jesus of Nazareth, which never *is* in abstraction from him. God's divine love is manifested and bestowed in the human love of his physical heart. 'His human love is the human embodiment of the redeeming love of God.'[12] Karl Barth's rejection of devotion to the sacred heart[13] is a confirmation of his monophysite tendency in the explanation of Christ's work of reconciliation.[14] For him, the man Christ's human love is the embodiment of his divine love only as the ever-new direct act of God alone.

The difference which I have outlined lies also at the root of our varying conception of the prophetic role of Christ's humanity.[15] According to Barth, revelation becomes an event in history but never a predicate of history. This is but one of a series of irreversible statements which recur throughout Barth's theology.[16] It, and all the others, are due to his mono (divine)-actualist conception of the economy of salvation. Revelation is always an ever-new direct act of God.

Barth no longer speaks of revelation touching history as a tangent touches a circle, that is, without touching it. Revelation for him is an event in history. He also speaks of revelation as a sacramental reality, even if afterwards he 'demythologized' the general term sacrament.[17] For him, too, the first and basic sacrament of revelation is the human nature of Jesus Christ. He differs from us, however, both in his understanding of the term 'sacrament' and of the word 'first' or 'basic'. For him, Christ's humanity is the sacrament of the revelation of God, not in the sense that it effects what it signifies, but in the sense that God uses it, factually, as the instrument of his direct revelation, so that the resulting revelation is never contained in or attributable to Christ's human acts and words and life. Similarly, the man Jesus is the basic or first sacrament, not in the sense that his humanity is so sanctified in itself that it is the perfection of revelation, but in the sense (apparently) that God does through

[12] E. Schillebeeckx, *op. cit.*, p. 14.

[13] Cf *CTKB*, pp. 152–3.

[14] 'A cet égard, la moderne dévotion au Sacré-Coeur, si on la comprend bien, est comme une nouvelle condamnation, particulièrement efficace, de tout apollinarisme comme de tout monophysisme.' Congar, 'Dogme christologique et Ecclésiologie' in Grillmeier-Bacht, *Chalkedon*, III, p. 244.

[15] Cf *CTKB*, pp. 161–3.

[16] For example: God is this man, but we cannot say that this man is God (cf *ibid.*, pp. 152f); the kingdom is the Church, but the Church is not the kingdom (cf *ibid.*, p. 347).

[17] Cf *ibid.*, pp. 162f and 77f.

Christ's humanity first what he also does through his apostles. Thus he says that the secondary objectivity of Christ's human nature is repeated in the Apostles.[18] This would seem to be consequent if one says that revelation is always God's own direct act, or that human life, words and actions never in themselves reveal God.

Barth's divine actualism would seem to be very far from Paul's statement that Christ is 'the image (*eikōn*) of the invisible God',[19] and especially from the christology of St John, who regards Christ's human nature as the transparent of his divine.

'That which from the beginning, which we have heard, which we have seen with our eyes, which we have looked upon and touched with our hands, concerning the word of life—the life was made manifest, and we saw it, and testify to it, and proclaim to you the eternal life which was with the Father and was made manifest to us—that which we have seen and heard we proclaim also to you, so that you may have fellowship. . . . And the Word became flesh and dwelt among us, full of grace and truth; we have beheld his glory, glory as of the only Son from the Father.'[20]

The divine word became the human word of revelation.

For Barth the hypostatic union is always an *unitio*, that is, an evernew act of the Son of God. This act produces a corresponding but purely human reflection in Christ's humanity. His humanity is not sanctified in itself with the sanctity of God in order to be the humanity of God, and to exist as his organ, efficacious sign or sacrament in the accomplishment of the work of reconciliation.

Barth's doctrine on the being and work of Christ would seem to stand very close to Luther's concept of 'exchange', and to his assertion of the sole operation of God in salvation.[21] This would reveal a certain monophysite tendency as regards the work of salvation.[22]

---

[18] Cf *ibid.*, p. 162.
[19] Col 1:15. Cf II Cor 4:4.
[20] I Jn 1:1–3a; Jn 1:14. Cf Kittel, in *TWNT*, IV, 130f. 'Invisibilis in suis visibilis est factus in nostris': Leo the Great, DS 294.
[21] *Alleintätigkeit Gottes* would be a more Barthian rendering of Luther's *Alleinwirksamkeit Gottes*. H. Bouillard speaks of a 'mono-actualism' in relation to Barth: *op cit.*, vol. II, p. 122.
[22] For the monophysite tendency in Luther's christology, cf Congar, 'Regards et reflexions sur la christologie de Luther' in *Chalkedon*, III, pp. 463–9, 485–6; *id.*, *Le Christ, Marie et L'Eglise*, pp. 34–8; Ternus, *art. cit.* in *Chalkedon*, III, pp. 533f. This Lutheran idea of the sole activity of God in the work of salvation is very clearly expressed and adhered to by modern Swedish Protestant theologians, such as G. Aulén and A. Nygren. Cf Congar, *art. cit.*, in *Chalkedon*, III, pp. 515f.

On the other hand, he shows a certain Calvinistic-Nestorian tendency.[23] Not that he denies the unity of the person. Unlike Nestorius, he attributes to Mary the title *Theotokos*, and thus asserts unambiguously the unity of the person.[24] He also certainly attributes an activity to Christ as man. But he speaks of *two* acts, of a divine and then a human act, of an eternal and temporal act, of the *separated* activity of the two natures, with the result that he does not seem to do full justice to the profundity of the hypostatic union. Logically, he would have to assert either two persons or one impersonal nature.

Both the tendency to Nestorianism and the tendency to Monophysitism agree in this that they deny any cooperation of the man Jesus or of his human nature in salvation. It is not surprising that Barth differs from us in christology, and by a tendency to *both* Nestorianism and monophysitism. It may be observed that this Lutheran-monophysite, Calvinistic-Nestorian tension in Barth's christology would appear to be the logical christological application of his original adherence to the Calvinistic *soli Deo gloria* in the light of the Lutheran *sola gratia*, or of his doctrine of *sola fide* in justification.[25]

---

[23] For the Nestorian tendency in Calvin's christology, cf J. L. Witte, *art. cit.*, in *Chalkedon*, III, pp. 515f.
[24] Cf *C.D.* IV/2, p. 71 (=S. 77).
[25] Cf *CTKB*, pp. 36f, 38f, 43, 227f, 231f.

Chapter Eight
Christology–Ecclesiology

ACCORDING to God's economy of salvation the gift of grace, or man's encounter with God, is bound up with a personal encounter with the man Jesus.[1] For it is as man that his Son is the mediator of grace. He is mediator in his humanity and according to the ways of humanity. His human activity is, consequently, *sacramental*. A sacrament is a bestowal of salvation in historical visibility. Christ's human actions are salvific, that is, they possess a divine saving power, because they are the actions of a divine person. At the same time, this bestowal of salvation is visible, manifest and perceptible because Christ's actions are human and visible.

Christ as man is '*the* sacrament, the primordial sacrament', because he is in his humanity the unique mediator between God and man. 'For there is one God, and there is one mediator between God and men, the man Christ Jesus.'[2] Christ's human actions are the primary sacraments, the fundamental causes and signs of grace.[3] His humanity is the 'great sacrament', 'the sacrament *par excellence*',[4] 'the primal sacramental Word of God'.[5]

How does this encounter take place now that Christ has ascended to the right hand of the Father? He is no longer visible amongst us as man. A direct encounter with him in his bodily presence was the unique privilege of his contemporaries. Yet if God's constant economy of salvation is to be continued this encounter will also take place now in a visible way. It is not adequate to say that it takes place merely through a commemoration of his former bodily existence. Neither is it adequate to say that it takes place solely

[1] Cf E. Schillebeeckx, *Christ the Sacrament*, pp. 13–54.
[2] I Tim 2:5.
[3] St Thomas, following a universal patristic tradition, stresses this: *Summa theol.*, III, p. 62, art. 5, ad 1. Cf E. Schillebeeckx, *op. cit.*, pp. 16–17, note 3.
[4] Cf Mersch, *op cit.*, 66, 548–9; Congar, 'Dogme Christologique et Ecclésiologie' in *Chalkedon*, III, p. 267.
[5] K. Rahner, *The Church and the Sacraments*, Quaest. Disp. 9, pp. 15, 18.

through a faith, love or hope in him as now invisibly active among us. The encounter takes place also visibly. It takes place through the visible contact with the extension of his body, which is the Church. Christ himself instituted the Church as the visible extension or prolongation of the function of his humanity.

> 'Christ makes his presence among us actively visible and tangible too, not directly through his bodiliness, but by extending among us on earth in visible form the function of his bodily reality which is in heaven. This precisely is what the sacraments are: the earthly extension of the "body of the Lord". This is the Church.'[6]

Here we can observe the profound connection which exists between the teaching of the Catholic Church as regards the man Jesus as the one mediator, and its teaching as regards itself as the sacramental, institutional and unique Church.[7] The Church is the body of Christ. It is his body in so far as salvation is given to it only in dependence on Jesus Christ (the Church as communion). It is also his body as the means of salvation (the Church as institution), because in some mysterious way it puts us into contact with Jesus Christ himself who as man is the unique mediator. The Church as the means of salvation puts us into living, physical contact with Jesus Christ's *acta et passa in carne*, that is, with his humanity, which was the efficient and meritorious instrument of salvation. It is not Christ's original physical body, but it prolongs that body in its power and holiness. The apostolic succession prolongs the function of Christ's humanity.[8]

---

[6] Schillebeeckx, *op. cit.*, p. 49, referring to Eph 1:23; 4:12, etc.

[7] Cf the valuable article of Fr Congar: 'Dogme christologique et Ecclésiologie. Verité et limites d'un parallèle', *art. cit.*, in Grillmeier-Bacht, *Das Konzil von Chalkedon*, III, pp. 239–68.

[8] 'Toute l'institution ecclésiale prend ainsi son sens par rapport à l'incarnation': Congar, *art. cit.*, p. 475. Cf *ibid.*, pp. 474–6, with references. 'Quod conspicuum erat in Christo transivit in Ecclesiae sacramenta': Leo the Great, *Sermo* 74, 2 (*P.L.*, 54, 398) (cited in Schillebeeckx, *op. cit.*, p. 54, n. 1). Fr. Schillebeeckx tries to bring out the inner significance of the sacramental Church, which is but the continuation of God's constant way of offering us salvation. The whole meaning of the sacramental Church is to continue the personal encounter God initiated with us in his Son made flesh. As such it continues 'one of the profoundly human qualities of the incarnation'. It is the continued manifestation of 'God's sovereign respect for our earthbound humanity', because God continues to offer us salvation in terms of 'mutual human availability'. In the Church we encounter Christ. In it we encounter visibly Christ's heavenly and invisible saving activity. The sacraments are not things but encounters of men on earth with the glorified man

The Church also is the holy and sanctifying instrument, the sacrament, the efficacious sign, of God's redeeming mercy. It, too, is a 'conjoined and animated instrument of the divinity'. It is a *conjoined* instrument. It is not joined to the divinity in personal unity, in its existence, but mystically, in power and alliance. The law of the *communicatio idiomatum* does not apply. For the same reason, all the Church's human actions are not divine but only those which are either the instituted instruments or true charismatic subjects of a divine action. For it is only in this alliance of grace that an action can be said to proceed really and effectively from the Church and the Holy Spirit as one subject of action, of life or of right. Ontologically the subjects remain always distinct. This precision must be made in order to avoid any danger of identifying the Church and Jesus Christ—a danger to which an 'organicist' or 'romantic' conception of the Church, as well as the idea of a 'continuation of the incarnation', may possibly leave themselves open.

Similarly, the Church is an animated or living instrument. Its human action is not merely the veil or result of a divine action. The principle or cause of the divine and sanctifying action of the Church is primarily the Holy Spirit but also, albeit secondarily, these human words and actions. Thus it is the *human* words of the apostles, by reason of Christ's *gift* to them of the Holy Spirit, which forgive sins. 'As the Father has sent me, even so I send you. And when he had said this, he breathed on them, and said to them, "Receive the Holy Spirit. If you forgive the sins of any, they are forgiven; if you retain the sins of any, they are retained." '[9]

Strictly speaking, there is no parallelism between the being of Jesus Christ and the being of the Church. In the Church there are neither two natures nor one divine person. None the less, there is a profound functional parallelism between them. The general law of God's economy of salvation, manifested in the Old Testament and in Jesus Christ, is verified also in the Church. There is a human visible element in the service of a divine invisible element. The divine invisible element comes *through* the human visible element. There is, therefore, a functional or economic parallel or analogy between Jesus Christ and the Church, or between God's accomplishment of objective

---

Jesus who makes himself visible and available to us in historical form. 'This is precisely what the sacraments are: the face of redemption turned visibly towards us, so that in them we are truly able to encounter the living Christ. The heavenly saving activity, invisible to us, becomes visible in the Sacraments': Schillebeeckx, *op. cit.*, p. 52; cf *id. ibid.*, pp. 49–54.

[9] Jn 20:21–23.

reconciliation and his accomplishment of subjective reconciliation. In both there is an ontological unity of the divine and the human, with a resultant functional cooperation. The basis of the comparison lies in the fact that just as Jesus Christ was composed of a divine and a human, invisible and visible, heavenly and earthly element, with the human, visible and earthly serving the divine, invisible and heavenly as a salvific or effective or cooperative instrument, so also is the Church. Vatican II puts it succinctly:

> 'Christ the one mediator established and ceaselessly sustains here on earth his Holy Church, the community of faith, hope and charity, as a visible structure through which he communicates truth and grace to all. The society furnished with hierarchical agencies, however, and the Mystical Body of Christ, the visible assembly and the spiritual community, the earthly Church and the Church enriched with heavenly things, are not to be considered as two realities, but form one complex reality which is comprised of a divine and a human element. For this reason, by a not inconsiderable analogy (*ob non mediocrem analogiam*), this reality is compared to the mystery of the incarnate Word. Just as the assumed nature inseparably united to the divine Word serves him as a living instrument of salvation, so, in a similar way, does the communal structure of the Church serve Christ's Spirit who vivifies it by the way of building up the body (cf Eph 4:16).'[10]

Any attenuation of the *unity* would betray a certain ecclesiological Nestorianism, while any attenuation of the true human nature or *instrumentality* of the Church in the work of salvation would betray a certain ecclesiological Apollinarism or monophysitism or at least an economic monophysitism.

The comparison between christology and ecclesiology is particularly fruitful for the illustration of the difference between Barth and Catholicism, as well as for the understanding of Barth's own ecclesiology. Barth denies the very truth which we claim is the sole basis for a valid parallelism. The economy of salvation does not take place, he maintains, through the cooperation of a divine and human element, but through a divine and solely causal action and a corresponding witness of human action.

Christ ascends to heaven and exists now at the right hand of the Father as Son of God and Son of man. He transcends time.[11] He also

[10] DCC, n. 8.
[11] I am in agreement with Karl Barth as regards his insistence on the part of the resurrection in our reconciliation; on the fact that the risen Christ

exists here and now in the community, his body. The community is the second form of his own physical body, for it was contained in it. The human nature assumed by him was the human nature of all men. His existence here and now is not a prolongation or continuation of the incarnation. It *is* the incarnation. It is indirectly identical with it. It is the second form of his one existence. He has assumed a human nature which has two forms: individual and comprehensive, one and many. His existence in the first form is unique because his existence in the second form does not differ from it. Jesus Christ existed once and for all, that is, not just past but also present and future, in his human nature. Existing now in heaven in his first form he continues to exist on earth in a secondary form (the community) in the same way as he existed once in his human nature. The Church is not a mystery in itself which can be placed over against and compared with the mystery of the incarnation. It is both divine and human in exactly the same way as Jesus Christ is divine and human. For he himself directly is its invisible being, and the community fulfils the same function as his individual human nature. As Barth himself says: 'The being of Jesus Christ is the being of the Church. . . . He is the community', and 'The community of Jesus Christ can be that which the human nature of its Lord and head is.'[12]

One sees immediately the basic difference between Barth and Catholicism, and the basic deficiency of Barth's whole theology. Barth often accuses Catholicism of divinizing the Church by speaking of it as a 'continuation of the incarnation', or as 'Christ living on in the world', or as an *alter Christus*. In this he certainly had a point to the extent that there was a tendency amongst Catholics to exaggerate the changelessness, infallibility and holiness of the Church, that is, a tendency to make it like God. I will come back to this later. But the point is that it is Barth himself who falls into the very error he accuses Catholicism of: he identifies Jesus Christ and the Church, as we have just seen. For him the mystery of the incarnation literally continues in the Church. He accuses Catholicism of identifying the Church and Jesus Christ in the sense that according to it the Church would usurp the position of, and therefore oust, Christ. But by denying the Catholic position Barth is led to deny any reality, salvific reality that is, to a human Church and to reduce all to

---

transcends time and lives now as the eternal priest, prophet and king; on the fact that the head of the Church is this risen Christ (cf *CTKB*, chapter 11). In our later elaboration of Catholic ecclesiology I shall try to take all these extremely valuable reminders into account.

[12] Cf *ibid.*, pp. 259f, 143f.

Jesus Christ and his continuing mystery of incarnation. Thus, just as Barth, as I have already remarked (cf above, pp. 8f), through his failure to evaluate sufficiently human reason and activity and the indwelling presence and action of divine revelation and grace in and through that reason and activity, is unable to posit a *distinction* between nature and grace, reason and faith, creation and redemption, so also, through his failure to evaluate sufficiently the inherent presence and action of the Holy Spirit of the risen Christ in the human Church, the personal freedom and responsibility of individual members of the community, and the existence of the community as the distinct bride to its bridegroom, he is unable to posit a *distinction* between the Church as a holy and salvific reality and Jesus Christ. The Church as the mystery of salvation, or as the sacrament of salvation, is Jesus Christ. It is not a human mystery at all. This reveals his monophysite conception of the economy of salvation.

For Barth, the human Church is not created a saving reality in and under the action of Jesus Christ through his Spirit. It responds to the action of its heavenly head, but does not participate in the holiness of its head, nor share in his saving power. In itself it is neither a holy nor a sanctifying reality. Barth asserts the truth and reality of the visible Church, and therefore of two 'natures'. But there is that 'economic' monophytism whereby he refuses to grant an activity to the human 'nature' in the one salvific mystery which is the Church. The cause of grace is in no sense the human Church but solely the divine Church, that is, the direct act of Christ through his Spirit. The thoroughly unsatisfactory thing about his view is that we cannot even term this an *ecclesiological* mono-actualism. It is simply the same christological divine mono-actualism in a second form. This is practically a denial of all ecclesiology.

It is very hard to understand how Barth can explain Jesus Christ as the *pleroma* of the Church, and on the other hand, the Church as the *pleroma* of Jesus Christ. It is precisely because Catholic theology attributes to Christ's individual human nature an ontologically comprehensive character that it can also avoid the assertion of a continuation of the incarnation in the strict sense in the Church, while affirming a profound parallelism between Christ and the Church based on the 'economic' or functional continuation of the incarnation in the institutional Church and in the individual's cooperation with the gifts of the Holy Spirit. Christ's human nature possesses the plenitude of grace and is as such the principle of all grace. This is the ontological basis and reality of the inclusion of all in the one. As man he is both one and includes within himself a collectivity, the Church.

'He is the head of the body, the Church; he is the beginning, the first-born from the dead, that in everything he might be pre-eminent. For in him all the fulness of God was pleased to dwell, and through him to reconcile to himself all things, whether on earth or in heaven, making peace by the blood of his cross.'[13] Thus St Thomas can say that Christ plus the Church is no more than Christ alone.[14]

But while the reality of the Church is already present and accomplished in Jesus Christ it also remains to be accomplished. One of the dominant and decisive characteristics of the New Testament Church is that it is a reality already present in one while still remaining to be accomplished in many.[15] Christ still has to be built up. Thus the Church adds something to Christ. It is his fulness. 'He has put all things under his feet and has made him the head over all things for the Church, which is his body, the fulness of him who fills all in all. . . . Now I rejoice in my sufferings for your sake, and in my flesh I complete what is lacking in Christ's afflictions for the sake of his body, that is, the Church.'[16]

Christ's life is not merely communicated to the Church or repeated by it. Because he himself possesses the plenitude of grace as man and is consequently the principle of all grace we too may possess grace and be a principle of grace. There is no mere repetition of the incarnation in the Church. Christ as the one is not actually the many, but virtually. His life is offered to us by his own action through Word and sacrament, and accepted by us as new and freely acting subjects—as animated, living subjects, that is. The unity of the mystical body is then actualized. This actualization in the many adds something to its actualization in the one in that Christ's life is newly possessed and newly lived by autonomous and freely acting subjects. Jesus Christ is not the sole possessor and principle of supernatural life in the Mystical Body. Under him, and together with him, there are also instituted instruments and freely acting persons. Because Christ as man possesses the plenitude of grace there is no need to assert a continuance of the incarnation in the Church, or to assert the Church as a second temporal form of Christ's one eternal act of incarnation, in order to explain the inclusion of all in the one. Because the

---

[13] Col 1:18–20. Cf 2:9f; Eph 3:19; 4:12f.
[14] '. . . nec est aliquod maius ipse et alii quam ipse solus': *IV Sent.*, d. 49, q. 4, art. 3, ad 4. Cf Congar, *Esquisses du Mystère de l'Eglise* (Unam Sanctam 8), Paris, 1953, p. 72.
[15] This twofold truth Fr Congar terms the 'dialectique du "donné" et de l' "agi" ': *Esquisses* . . . , p. 26. Cf *id., ibid.*, pp. 11–57; *id.*, 'Dogme christol. et ecclés.' in *Chalkedon*, III, pp. 249–50. I shall return to this later. Cf below, Section Three, chapter twenty. [16] Eph 1:22–23; Col 1:24.

man Jesus possessed the plenitude of grace he is the principle of grace. Similarly grace can be possessed by others who become also principles of grace. They remain human and freely acting subjects of holy acts. Thus is affirmed and explained the profound parallelism between Christ and the Church. Thus also is explained how the Church is the *pleroma* of Christ.

The difference between Barth and Catholicism is always one of the denial or assertion of human nature as an ontologically united and animated instrument of divinity in the work of salvation. This is true with regard to our explanation of the being and work of Jesus Christ. And because and as it is true of him it is true of all else.[17]

---

[17] Cf above, p. 53, note 7.

Chapter Nine

Christology–Mariology–Ecclesiology

IN this fourth article I intend to confront Karl Barth's and the Catholic Church's doctrine with regard to the person and work of Mary, virgin-mother of God, in its relation to our christological and ecclesiological doctrines. I hope to illustrate the consistency of both our positions on this point with our basic differing principles.[1]

Karl Barth treats very briefly of the mother of God in a christological context.[2] He affirms unequivocally the dogma of the virgin birth—not because it is a dogma but because the Church's dogma is substantiated by revelation itself. While it is true that 'in dogma as such we hear merely the voice of the Church and not revelation itself', it is also true that 'no one can dispute the existence of a biblical testimony to the Virgin Birth'.[3]

The virgin birth, he says, is an expression, explanation and illumination of the mystery of revelation and reconciliation. On the one hand, it affirms the event of Jesus Christ to be a real event accomplished in space and time as history within history. On the other hand, it affirms it as an event whose subject is God alone. It is the first indication of the mystery of the incarnation, the first attestation of the divine sonship of the man Jesus of Nazareth. It is not a statement about the basis and condition of his divine sonship, but about how the Son of God became man. It is a miracle which indicates a mystery. It marks off this birth from all other births. It means that God himself, in the direct act of his creative omnipotence, is the basis and beginning of the human existence of Jesus Christ. It indicates that he himself has given to man, in the person of Mary, what man of himself could never possess—the capacity to be his mother. He makes his Son her Son.

The words of the Creed *conceptus de Spiritu Sancto, natus ex*

[1] Cf above, pp. 52f.
[2] Cf his *C.D.* I/2, pp. 172–202 (=SS. 187–221); *Credo*, pp. 62–72; IV/I, pp. 206–7 (=SS. 226–7).
[3] *C.D.* I/2, pp. 174, 176 (=SS. 190, 192).

Maria Virgine have a 'general and a special, an inner and an outer, a material and a significative sense'.[4] In both cases they point to the incarnation, but specifically to it as *miracle* and generally to it as *mystery*.

This is a real event in our space and time. But it can be properly understood only as the sign wrought by God himself to signify the freedom, immediacy and mystery of his action. As such it stands in analogy with the thing signified. It is a miraculous event. The dogma of the virgin birth 'describes this mystery by a miraculous event in analogy with the mystery'.[5] The miracles of the virgin birth and the empty tomb mark out the existence of Jesus Christ as that historical existence where God alone is directly the subject (mystery).

The *natus ex Maria virgine* describes *negatively* this mystery of God's sovereignty. It affirms of course the genuineness of the birth and humanity of Jesus Christ. But it affirms the discontinuity and 'supernaturalness' of this event, and so passes judgment on man. Grace is not imparted to human nature except through judgment. The *natus ex virgine* denies all human power, attributes and capacities for God. The man whom revelation and reconciliation reach is not just God's creature: he is the creature who, in the totality of his creatureliness, lives in disobedience to his Creator. A mystery must be wrought on this nature if it is to live in personal unity with God. A sign however is required to indicate that man actually is God's fellow-worker. This sign is the miracle of the virgin birth. It indicates a man bearing our sinful nature (*vere homo*), but not committing sin (*vere Deus*), that is, who possesses the *liberum arbitrium* of obedience to God and does not possess the *servum arbitrium* of disobedience.

The *conceptus de Spiritu Sancto* describes *positively* the same mystery. It states that the conception of Jesus Christ was the exclusive work of God the Holy Spirit. This is the ground and content of the miracle and sign indicating the mystery. It states from God's side what the *natus ex virgine* states from man's side regarding the sign of the mystery of the person of Jesus Christ, of the mystery of the free grace of God.

The Holy Spirit is named here because of his significance for the act of divine reconciliation or revelation: he is God himself in his freedom to be present to his creature, in his freedom to make man fit for communion with him, to make man capable of receiving his revelation, to make man the object of reconciliation. In the incarnation, therefore, we are concerned with the real basis of the Church, its

[4] *Credo*, p. 62.
[5] *C.D.* I/2, p. 184 (=S. 201).

original and proper ground. For in it the same Holy Spirit is at work, rendering Christ's human nature free to be assumed into unity with the Son of God, who also is at work in us rendering us free to receive God's revelation here and now. It is not through its own capacity, but through God's free grace, that human nature participates in reconciliation and revelation. As such the incarnation is the objective realization of reconciliation and revelation, the prototype of all subjective reconciliation and revelation, the real ground of the Church.[6]

The title 'mother of God' (*Theotokos*) ascribed to Mary at the Council of Ephesus, against Nestorius, elucidates the true humanity and unity of Jesus Christ. It makes a twofold assertion: (*a*) it explains the *vere homo* in that it asserts that *egeneto* means simply 'born', that Jesus belongs to the unity of the human race; and (*b*) it illumines and strengthens the unity of *vere Deus* and *vere homo* in that it asserts that he whom Mary bore is none other than God's eternal Son.[7]

It is heartening to hear these truths about the mother of God, which have always been stressed by the Roman Catholic Church, being so firmly asserted on the Protestant side. Unfortunately this seeming agreement between Barth and Catholicism as regards the mystery of Mary is merely material, and does not reduce one whit the ancient disagreement between Protestantism and Catholicism. In fact, our basic formal disunity lies hidden under this material unity.

For Barth, the description of Mary as the mother of God, as well as the dogma of the virgin birth, is a 'legitimate expression of christological truth', an 'illumination of revelation'.[8] As it stands this is a perfect Catholic statement. In Catholic teaching the description of Mary as mother of God (as well as all her other privileges) is a 'description of christological truth' and an 'illumination of revelation'.[9] Barth's and our understanding of these statements is, however, very different. And in this difference there appears the basic theological difference between us.

For Barth it is *exclusively* a christological statement. It is in no sense a description of mariological truth also. What is said is not

[6] Cf *C.D.* I/2, p. 199 (=SS. 217–18).
[7] Cf *ibid.*, pp. 138–9 (=SS. 151–3); IV/2, p. 71 (=SS. 77).
[8] For the following cf *C.D.* I/2, pp. 138–46 (=SS. 151–60).
[9] 'The Church has endorsed many forms of piety toward the Mother of God, provided that they were within the limits of sound and orthodox doctrine. . . . While honouring Christ's Mother, these devotions cause her Son to be rightly known, loved, and glorified, and all his commands observed. Through him all things have their being (cf Col 1:15–16) and in him "it has pleased [the eternal Father] that . . . all his fulness should dwell" (Col 1:19)': Vatican II, DCC, ch. 8, n. 66.

said to her honour at all. Mary's greatness consists in her low estate (Lk 1:48), in her humility and receptivity. It does not consist in her person but in the fact that she points away from herself to Christ. Lk 1:28 must be understood in the light of Lk 11:27f and of Mt 12:48f. The description of Mary as the mother of God does not grant to her person, Barth says, such an independent and emphatic position that she can become the *object of a theological doctrine, or even of a mariological dogma*. Roman Catholic mariology, he says, is an 'obscuring of revealed truth', 'an excrescence, i.e., a diseased construct of theological thought. Excrescences must be excised.'[10] Mary is an illumination of revelation in so far as in her passivity and pointing she is representative of man in his reception of God. 'She is simply man to whom the miracle of revelation happens.'[11] 'We reject mariology, (*i*) because it is an arbitrary innovation in the face of Scripture and the early Church, and (*ii*) because this inovation consists essentially in a falsification of Christian truth.'[12]

Roman Catholic doctrine, on the contrary, while retaining Mariology as a description of christological truth, also maintains that devotion to her in her own person is quite legitimate. Jesus Christ is the unique mediator between God and man. As the God-man he accomplished the redemption of all mankind. Grace is his gift, a participation in his being and power of action, by which man can cooperate with him in his own subjective redemption. God does not favour each one equally. To the degree of each one's union with God by grace there corresponds the degree of his cooperation in redemption. Because our Lady was predestined to be the mother of God she is united to Christ in a way which transcends the union of any other member of the Church. She is the 'favoured one' (Lk 1:28, 30). But she really *is* the favoured one, she really *is* blessed among women, she really *is* holy. God's grace is a *real gift* which she appropriates. As a consequence she can and does cooperate, and in a very special way, by her obedience, faith, hope and charity in the mystery of redemption. This cooperation does not add anything to, or take anything from, the unique mediation of Jesus Christ (I Tim 2:5–6). Just as the unique priesthood of Christ does not exclude its participation, and as the one goodness of God does not exclude its real diffusion, so also the unique mediation of the Redeemer does not exclude but stimulates among creatures a varied participated cooperation from the one source. Our Lady does possess, therefore, a mystery of her own, and

[10] *C.D.* I/2, p. 139 (=S. 153).
[11] *Ibid.*, p. 140 (=SS. 153–4).
[12] *Ibid.*, p. 143 (=S. 157).

she can and should become the object of both a devotion and a theological doctrine and dogma.[13]

This mystery of Mary is the symbol or type of the mystery of the Church. The typology of Mary and the Church is a frequently recurring theme in the commentaries of the Fathers of the Church on Scriptural texts such as Gen 3:15, the Canticle of Canticles, Sirach 1, Jn 19:25-27, Gal 4:26 and Rev 12—even though patristic thought in general was more centred in Christ and the Church, and Mary was only seen in relation to these.[14]

Mary the virgin mother is essentially the symbol of the Church our virgin mother. Motherhood and virginity provided the two main bases for the parallelism, which most often were united in the one concept of fruitful virginity or bridal motherhood. But the whole mystery of the Church is inseparably bound up with the mystery of Mary. 'We need to learn once more what was so treasured by the early Church; to learn to see the Church in our Lady, and our Lady in the Church.'[15]

It was an idea especially dear to St Augustine,[16] who summed up and gave definitive formulation to the wealth of material gone before.[17] As the mother of the living, the Church is the new Eve born from the side of the new Adam.[18] As life-bringer Mary stands opposed to Eve the bringer of death.[19] The Church is our mother *per fidem*,[20] *per sacramenta*,[21] per *'Spiritum Sanctum'*,[22] while remaining a virgin.[23] That is, her motherhood is the result of her total dedication to Christ through the faith which is an operation from above alone.[24] Finally, Mary's virginal maternity is a type of the Church's.[25]

---

[13] Cf Vatican II, DCC, ch. 8, nn. 55-9, 60-2, 66-7.
[14] Cf Congar, 'Marie et l'Eglise dans la pensée Patristique' in *Rev. de Sc. Phil. et Théol.*, 38 (1954), 4-5.
[15] H. Rahner, *Our Lady and the Church*, pp. 3, 5. Cf also H. de Lubac, *Méditations sur l'Eglise*, Aubier, 1953, p. 275.
[16] Cf F. Hofmann, 'Mariens Stellung in der Erlösungsordnung nach dem Hl. Augustinus' in *Alma Socia Christi*, vol. 5, p. 94.
[17] Cf A. Müller, *Ecclesia-Maria. Die Einheit Marias und der Kirche*, p. 179.
[18] St Augustine, *De Nupt. et Conc.* 2, 4, 12 (*PL*, 44, 443); *Enarr. in Ps.* 126, 7 (*PL*, 37, 1672).
[19] *Id., Sermo* 232, 2, 2 (*PL*, 38, 1108): 'Per feminam mors, per feminam vita.' Cf Mascall, *Christ, the Christian and the Church*, pp. 130-4, for other patristic texts.
[20] St Augustine, *Sermo* 214, 11 (*PL*, 38, 1071).
[21] *Id.*, Ep. 34, 3 (*PL*, 33, 132).
[22] *Id., Sermo* 359 (*PL*, 39, 1593).
[23] *Id., In Ev. Joh.*, tract. 13, 12 (*PL*, 35, 1499).
[24] Cf Congar, *art. cit.*, pp. 4-5; Müller, *op. cit.*, p. 207.
[25] St Augustine, *De Sancta Virgin.*, cap. 6 (*PL*, 40, 399): 'quia cooperata

From St Albert the Great to Scheeben this analogical relationship between Mary and the Church was little considered. It is only in the past forty years, in conjunction with the great interest and development in both ecclesiology and mariology, that it has been re-discovered and re-asserted in all its depth and beauty. This recent interest in a very old theme was climaxed by the whole Church's recognition and assertion of Mary as the type of the Church in the second Vatican Council.[26]

Barth himself noted this typology and the basis of its justification in Catholic theology—at least as regards the aspect which basically distinguishes the Roman Catholic concept of our Lady and the Church from all others.

'In the doctrine and worship of Mary there is disclosed the one heresy of the Roman Catholic Church which explains all the rest. The "mother of God" of Roman Catholic Marian dogma is quite simply the principle, type and essence of the human creature co-operating servant-like (*ministerialiter*) in its own redemption on the basis of prevenient grace, and to that extent the principle, type and essence of the Church.'[27]

As we have seen, Catholic theology itself recognizes this consistency between its mariological and ecclesiological doctrines. Liturgically, one can see it expressed very concisely in the antiphon to the third nocturn of the Roman breviary's common office of our Lady: 'Rejoice, Virgin Mary: by yourself you have crushed all heresies in the whole world.'[28] Our Lady, virgin mother of God, expresses the typically Catholic conception of the economy of salvation and refutes all opposing 'heresies'.

Obviously, Barth's own doctrine on Mary is a type or indication of his doctrine on the Church. The Church's essence for him also consists in pointing away from itself to Christ. It, too, is a 'description of christological truth', and in the same sense. The mystery of the Church is not its own but Jesus Christ's. 'Jesus Christ is the community.'[29] 'Jesus Christ is Mary the virgin mother' is the mariological

---

est charitate, ut fideles in Ecclesia nascerentur': *Sermo* 25, 7, 8 (edited by Morin); *Sermo* 195, 2 (*PL*, 38, 1018); *Sermo* 191, 2, 3 (*PL*, 38, 1010); *Sermo* 213, 7 (*PL*, 38, 1064).

[26] Cf DCC, nn. 53–4, 63–5.

[27] *C.D.* I/2, p. 143 (=S. 157).

[28] 'Gaude, Maria Virgo: cunctas haereses sola interemisti in universo mundo.'

[29] Cf *CTKB*, pp. 259f.

expression of 'Jesus Christ is the Church'. Both of course are exclusively christological statements.

This difference as regards our Lady illustrates and pinpoints, therefore, the decisive difference between Barth (and Protestantism in general) and Catholicism. In the work of salvation Protestants ascribe solely to God the role of subject. While Barth ascribes an active role to man in the subjective realization of reconciliation this is by no means a cooperative activity in his own reconciliation. Justification is *sola fide*, that is, *solo Christo*.[30] Catholics also ascribe solely to God an active role in the sense that all sanctifying activity owes its origin to him. But with and under the activity of God it also ascribes a subordinate but really conditional and effective activity to man. On the basis of a prevenient grace man truly cooperates in the work of redemption. He 'is not merely an object, but also a subject of the divine redemptive activity'.[31] This difference with regard to justification explains our difference in mariology, and explains also our differences with regard to Christ's human nature and the Church's ministry.

Barth understands the Catholic position. Why exactly does he reject it? What exactly has he against the idea of a Christian cooperating with Christ? Barth (and Protestants in general) maintain that the cooperation of the human and the divine in the work of salvation (as asserted in the Catholic doctrine of our Lady, grace and the Church) is a denial of Christ's unique mediation and lordship, whereas we maintain that his unique mediation and lordship are perfectly safeguarded in so far as it is he himself who enables creatures to cooperate. For Barth it involves a rivalry between the Christian and Christ, between the creature and the Creator. It involves attributing to the creature a role 'whose independence is only too insufficiently relative'.[32] It means that the creature is the original cause of his own salvation to some extent. It thus means placing the creature in the place of God.

'The Evangelical statement of faith which we must set against Marian dogma is thus the very same as must be maintained against the Roman Catholic doctrine of grace and the Church. Jesus Christ, the Word of God, exists, reigns and rules in as sovereign a way within the created world as He does from eternity with the Father,

---

[30] Cf *ibid.*, pp. 227-32.
[31] K. Adam, *The Spirit of Catholicism*, 1929, p. 108, cited in Barth, *C.D.* I/2, p. 145 (=S. 159).
[32] *C.D.* I/2, p. 146 (=S. 160).

no doubt over and in man, no doubt in His Church and by it, but in such a way that at every point He is always Himself the Lord, and man, like the Church, can give honour only to Him and never, however indirectly, to himself as well. There can be no thought of reciprocity or mutual efficacy even with the most careful precautions. Faith in particular is not an act of reciprocity, but the act of renouncing all reciprocity, the act of acknowledging the one Mediator, beside whom there is no other. Revelation and reconciliation are irreversibly, indivisibly and exclusively God's work. Thus the problem to which the Roman Catholic doctrine of grace and the Church, to which Mariology in particular is the so-called answer, that is, the problem of creaturely co-operation in God's revelation and reconciliation, is at once a spurious problem, the sole answer to which can be false doctrines. *"Quid est creaturam loco creatoris ponere, si hoc non est?"* With this question of early Protestant polemic (F. Turrettini, *De necessaria secessione nostra ab ecclesia Romana*, 1678, Disp. 2, 16) we too must protest against Mariology as such.'[33]

Why is it that Barth has always aroused such interest and provokes such a challenge to Catholicism? Is it not because he denies the *basic* positive insight which *distinguishes* Catholicism over against Protestantism, namely, the real, ontological sanctification and cooperation of man and the Church in and under God's action? He compels the Catholic theologian to sound anew this positive insight which is basic to Catholic theology. Not since the Reformation itself has Protestantism so deeply disturbed Catholicism—and this because Barth is essentially faithful to the principles of the Reformers. In dialogue with him one must show clearly that Catholic theology asserts and safeguards God's sovereignty, freedom and priority. At the same time one must insist on Scripture's unambiguous witness to man's participation in God's holiness and power. Only in this way can one do justice to the *whole* of revelation, to the catholicity of Scripture.

---

[33] *C.D.* 1/2, p. 146 (=S. 160). Cf *ibid.*, pp. 557, 566 (=S. 619–20, 630), where Barth repeats the same objection.

Section Three

The Church through the Holy Spirit: The Fundamental Form of the Subjective Realization of Reconciliation

FOLLOWING the main divisions of Karl Barth's essentially trinitarian ecclesiology I turn in this third section to a consideration of the Church's subjective reality and realization through the Holy Spirit, who is the Spirit of the risen Christ, and the third person of the Trinity. I will not cover all the points raised by Barth in his corresponding third section. My aim is to illustrate the basic agreements and disagreements between us through the examination of key concepts, and to draw out Catholic ecclesiology along lines suggested by Barth when this is possible.

In a first general but basic chapter of this section I immediately link up the Church with its origin in the intention, words and action of its founder, Jesus Christ. In a second and panoramic chapter, all the while in dialogue with Karl Barth, I treat of the Church as the new people of God, its priority over the individual, its necessity for salvation, its relationship to the Roman Catholic Church, to other Christian Churches, to non-Christian religions, and to the world—all under the title of 'The New People of God, the Universal Sacrament of Salvation'. A third chapter outlines the mission and role of the Holy Spirit in relation to the Church, which, as the title of this whole third section indicates, forms the very basis of all else that is said. Adopting Barth's basic dynamic and functional thought-form a fourth chapter treats of the whole Church in mission. A fifth illustrates what the Church's mission and function connotes from the point of view of the laity, while a sixth presents the biblical basis and theological understanding of the Church's hierarchical mission and ministry. A seventh chapter treats of the nature of Scripture and tradition, and the role and relationship of both in the transmission of revelation. An eighth chapter tackles, at what seems to be its factual source, namely, in the problem of justification, the overall and all-pervading basic difference between Barth and Catholicism. While intended to implement Barth's legitimate demand for an understanding of the Church as 'event' a ninth chapter is also intended to be a completion of his event-Church by the addition of the word 'institution'. In the following tenth chapter I illustrate the necessity and unity of the Church's twofold 'nature' as visible and invisible. The eleventh chapter, on the Church as the Body of Christ, really brings out Catholic theology's agreements and disagreements with Barth's 'christocentric' theology. The five succeeding chapters try to outline, as much as possible in agreement with Barth, the mystery of the one, holy, catholic and apostolic Church. Finally, having considered the mystery of the Church from its eternal predestination, through its objective realization in and historical foundation by Jesus Christ, to the various aspects of its subjective realization through the Holy Spirit, a final seventeenth chapter of this section rounds off the ecclesiological dialogue with Karl Barth with the consideration of the Church's eschatological nature and tension.

Chapter Ten

The Messiah and His People

AT THE end of the nineteenth century, and the beginning of the twentieth, there was general agreement amongst Protestant theologians that Jesus Christ did not found, nor had any intention of founding, a visible and universal Church. Such an attitude could have given very little promise of an ecumenical ecclesiological dialogue between Protestantism and Catholicism for the view is diametrically opposed to what the Catholic Church has always maintained. Karl Barth, however, is no less opposed to it. And when we consider the various reasons behind this former Protestant attitude and the reasons behind Barth's opposition to it, an extensive agreement between Barth's and Catholic thought on this point will become apparent.

Two reasons can be mentioned as underlying this denial of the possibility of the foundation of a visible universal Church by Jesus. The first was that of liberal Protestant thinkers of the last century. According to them the kingdom preached by Jesus was solely one of interior religion in spirit and truth. As Barth so often points out,[1] the whole Christian message was directed primarily and decisively to the individual. There was no necessity of a Church for the salvation of the individual. Its necessity was merely practical, arising as a consequence of living together. It was a creation of man, from below. As he did with so many other forms of Protestant liberal theology, Karl Barth, in agreement with Catholic thought, reacted vigorously against this view. The community, he says, is the primary and fundamental form of subjective reconciliation.[2] As such it is necessary, with a divine necessity, for the subjective reconciliation of the individual. It is a creation of God, from above. There is no specific reference in the New Testament, he says, to a foundation of the Church for the simple reason that this reference is everywhere. As an

[1] Cf *CTKB*, pp. 242–3, 277–8.
[2] Cf *ibid.*, p. 242f.

account of Jesus and of his salvation the whole of the Gospel narrative is necessarily an account of the community.

The second reason underlying the denial of the foundation of a Church by Jesus was that of 'consequent eschatologists'. In reaction against the preceding liberal theologians, who emphasized solely the present and internal aspect of the kingdom of God, these authors rediscovered the eschatological element in Christ's preaching. The kingdom of God is not to be achieved by the actions of men but by the other-worldly transcendental action of God. But they, too, were unilateral. They said that the preaching of Jesus was dominated by the expectation of the *parousia*, of the imminent end of the world 'consequent' on his death. Accordingly, there can be no question of his intending to found or of his foundation of a Church. Christ, they said, came to found the kingdom, not a Church.³ But these authors did not go the whole way. In the light of the fact that the *parousia* did not take place they explained the element of imminent expectation in Christ's preaching by saying that it was merely the thought-form of his time used by Jesus as the framework of his essentially moral doctrine.⁴

Karl Barth, and his dialectical friends, still in reaction to liberal Protestantism, went further. They restored the eschatological perspective to Christ's *message*. Christ's doctrine (not merely the framework) is eschatological. But again they were unilateral. Eschatological meant non-temporal. There is no such thing as a kingdom of God on earth or in history. Later Barth corrected this view.⁵ The incarnation, revelation, resurrection, the coming of the Spirit, all are historical events in the sense that they take place in history. He distinguishes forms or moments of the one kingdom of God. By the grace of God its last form does not coincide with its first. There is an intervening form and time in which it takes place. This time is the time of the Church. Hence Barth has nothing against the foundation of a Church by Christ from the point of view of his understanding of Christ's prediction of the kingdom. On the contrary, Christ's preaching of the event of the kingdom in three forms necessarily connotes his intention of founding a Church.⁶

³ In the words of Loisy: 'Jesus announced the kingdom and it was the Church which came': *L'Evangile et l'Eglise*, Bellevue ³1904, p. 155.

⁴ Whence the designation of this eschatology as *Zeitgeschichtlich*; cf F. M. Braun, *Nuovi aspetti* . . . , 112f, where he summarizes the study of F. Holmström, *Das eschatologische Denken der Gegenwart*, Gütersloh, 1936.

⁵ Cf *CTKB*, pp. 19, 86 (n. 100), 342.

⁶ I shall return later to Barth's conception of the relationship between kingdom and Church (chapter twenty-six). Some modern exponents of abso-

A particularly difficult and discussed question in this respect is that of the universalism of Jesus' awareness of his mission. Many authors[7] say that before his death and resurrection Jesus considered his mission as one to the Jews alone. The New Testament texts which would seem to intimate an awareness on Jesus' part of a universal mission, as well as a universal mission of his disciples, they explain either by saying that Jesus changed his mind during the course of his life (because of his failure to convert the Jews, or because of an evolution in his understanding of his mission), or by saying that such texts refer solely to an eschatological afflux of the Gentiles, and/or that they are additions by the evangelist. Thus J. Jeremias interprets Mk 14:9 and 13:10 as referring 'not to human proclamation, but to an apocalyptic event, namely, the angelic proclamation of God's final act' (cf Rev 14:6f). Moreover, he rejects all Matthaean texts before the resurrection which inculcate universality as 'interpretations or additions of the evangelist'.[8]

Such a conception in itself need not necessarily deny Jesus' intention of founding a universal Church. Some modern Catholic authors are in large agreement with Jeremias, and assert the intention of the historical Jesus of founding a universal Church. Anton Vögtle, for example, says that Jesus did not exercise a universal mission before his resurrection, and did not begin the construction of a universal Church then.[9] During his public life Jesus never founded nor expressed at large his intention of founding a separate congregation or 'holy remnant'.[10] Where Jesus does express such an intention, as for example in Mt 16:18 and at the last Supper, he is speaking exclusively to the *twelve*, and of a *future* occurrence.

The reason for his refusal to found a Church during his life was not that he expected an imminent *parousia*, but that he did not want

---

lute eschatology are E. Grässer, W. Schmithals, and G. Klein. W. G. Kümmel says Christ foresaw an interval (*Zwischenzeit*) between his ascension and *parousia* but made no preparation for it; cf his *Promise and Fulfilment*, pp. 47–8, 77.

[7] Despite the differences between them, von Harnack, Holtzmann, Goguel, Kümmel and J. Jeremias may be taken as examples.

[8] J. Jeremias, *Jesus' Promise to the Nations*, pp. 23–4.

[9] Cf the articles of A. Vögtle in: *Begegnung der Christen* (Festschrift für O. Karrer), pp. 54–81; *Sentire Ecclesiam* (Festschrift für H. Rahner), pp. 50–91; *Gott in Welt* (Festschrift für K. Rahner), vol. I, pp. 608–67. J. Schmid, *Das Evangelium nach Markus, ad loc.*, says Mk 13:10 and 14:9 are post-resurrection sayings.

[10] This is also the opinion of Kümmel, *op. cit.*, p. 139.

to give the impression of founding another Qumran sect or of being another rabbi, and especially because a condition of universal mission and salvation had first to be accomplished: his death and resurrection for all. To the same group of the twelve to whom he reveals the meaning of his death he speaks also of his future building of the Church. The Church is a new and post-Easter creation, but one whose nature he had already foretold. The undertaking of a universal mission by the early Church needed 'a special and express indication of the Holy Spirit'.[11]

For Karl Barth Jesus is the Son of man who arose in Israel and for Israel (for the lost sheep of the house of Israel). But as such, as the fulfilment of the covenant-promise of the Old Testament, 'in Israel and for Israel' means 'in the world and for the world'. Jesus' whole life and activity, in obedience to the will of his Father, and as a reflection of the way God himself went in his incarnation from those who have all things to those who have nothing, was a gradual turning from the mission to Israel (Mt 10:1f) to a world-wide mission (Mt 28:19). The decisive turning point occurred in his deliverance up to Pilate and the Gentiles by the representatives of Israel. The community, too, must address its witness first to the Jews, and then to all nations. This is but a reflection of his own way and action in fulfilment of the divine plan of salvation.[12]

The ontological basis of the universalism of the community's mission is 'the universalism of the Easter revelation itself'.[13] The universalism of Christ's objective reconciliation, and of the missionary command of the Church, both foretold in their presupposition, namely, in God's covenant with Israel, are amongst the most characteristic elements of Karl Barth's theology.[14] On this point, too, his understanding of the mission of Jesus not only has nothing against but necessitates the foundation of a Church.

Karl Barth was not, of course, alone in his reaction against the general Protestant position of the beginning of the century. The twentieth century, which already in 1926 was termed the 'century of the Church',[15] has produced various exegetes and theologians who have striven to return Christ and the Church to their traditional direct contact. In a work published in 1942 Fr Braun ascertained that the foundation of a visible, universal Church as an essential

[11] H. Schlier, *Die Zeit der Kirche*, 1956, p. 101.
[12] Cf *C.D.* IV/2, pp. 170–1, 769f (=SS. 189–91, 872f).
[13] Cf *CTKB*, pp. 253–4.
[14] Cf *ibid.*, pp. 187f.
[15] O. Dibelius, *Das Jahrhundert der Kirche*, Berlin, 1926.

part of Christ's messianic work was one of the chief tenets of a 'new consensus' amongst Protestant authors.[16]

Even though the basis of this consensus, namely, the understanding of the Son of man of Dan 7 as a 'collective' or 'corporate personality', has met with severe criticism,[17] the fact of the historical Christ's intention to found a Church must be retained.

The people of God before the death and resurrection of the Messiah was a people in covenant with God, ruled by his Old Testament. God promised to establish a covenant with Noah (Gen 6:18), and establishes it with him and 'with every living creature of all flesh that is upon the earth' (Gen 9:8–17). He calls Abraham and promises and establishes a particular covenant with him and all his descendants (Gen 12f). But even this particular covenant (as Barth points out, interpreting it christologically) has 'provisional representative significance'.[18] God's covenant is with all nations through Israel. He promises and establishes his covenant with Moses and the whole people of Israel (Ex 19:3–6; 24:7–8). As Barth again points out,[19] the covenant is not a bilateral contract. God does not simply offer a covenant. He establishes it. It is his gift to his people because he wishes to save them. It is the expression of his desire to save them, and the means he employs to do so. On the part of Israel it implies fidelity. They freely elect to obey it. 'All that the Lord has spoken we will do, and we will be obedient' (Ex 24:7). Israel's history is ruled by fidelity and infidelity to God's covenant.

God does not establish or announce his covenant with his people and its leaders once for all. He renews it throughout its history. He renews it, for example, with David, and with the Levitical priests who minister to him (Jer 33:20–22). And each time it is both a realization and a promise. A new and more perfect covenant is promised, and in and with it a new and more perfect relationship between God and his people.

[16] Cf F. M. Braun, *Nuovi aspetti* . . . (original French published in 1942), pp. 99f. The authors mentioned include Kattenbusch, Schlatter, Schmidt, Wendland, Gloege, Linton.

[17] The term 'corporate personality' was invented by H. Wheeler Robinson and its concept was first methodically investigated by him (cf his 'The Hebrew Conception of Corporate Personality' in *Zeitschrift für Alttestamentliche Wissenschaft*, Suppl. 66 (1936), 49–61). It was adopted by F. Kattenbusch and further developed especially by T. W. Manson, C. J. Cadoux and V. Taylor. Amongst its severest critics is A. Vögtle (cf his articles cited in the bibliography), while it has found a modern defender in J. de Fraine (cf. his *Adam and the Family of Man*, New York, 1965) who tries to show how much of the New Testament is determined by this way of thinking.

[18] Cf *CTKB*, p. 131.   [19] Cf *ibid.*, pp. 130f.

'Behold, the days are coming, says the Lord, when I will make a new covenant with the house of Israel and the house of Judah, not like the covenant which I made with their fathers when I took them by the hand to bring them out of the land of Egypt, my covenant which they broke, though I was their husband, says the Lord. But this is the covenant which I will make with the house of Israel after those days, says the Lord: I will put my law within them, and I will write it upon their hearts; and I will be their God, and they shall be my people. And no longer shall each man teach his neighbour and each his brother, saying, "Know the Lord," for they shall all know me, from the least of them to the greatest, says the Lord; for I will forgive their iniquity, and I will remember their sin no more.'[20]

The new covenant promised is the universal covenant of redemption in the promised Messiah. 'I have given you as a covenant to the people, a light to the nations. . . . It shall come to pass in the latter days that the mountains of the house of the Lord . . . shall be raised above the hills; and all the nations shall flow to it. . . . For out of Zion shall go forth the law, and the word of the Lord from Jerusalem. He shall judge between the nations. . . .'[21] In and with and by his servant God will create a new, universal people, a new, universal kingdom.[22] For the most part the universalism envisaged is conditioned by the fact that the nations must come to Israel, they must become members of the Jewish nation and religion.[23] The kingdom promised will be one of peace and plenitude, of joy and justice.[24]

Jesus Christ was conscious of being the promised Messiah of the Old Testament. He recognizes himself as the Son of man, as the Messiah to whom all nations would come.[25] As Son of David, as servant of Yahweh, he dies for 'the many'.[26] He instituted the new, universal covenant of redemption by his death on the cross. And he was fully aware of doing so. Offering bread and wine to his disciples at the Last Supper he said: This is my body which is given for you, this is my blood of the new covenant, which is poured out for many for the forgiveness of sins.[27] He is obviously referring to his future

---

[20] Jer 31:31–34. Cf Jer 32:37–44; 33:10–26.
[21] Is 42:6; Is 2:2f. Cf 19:18–25; 49:6f; 52:13–53:12.
[22] Cf Is 49:18; 66:23.   [23] Cf Is 55:5; 60:3–4; Zach 8:20–23.
[24] Cf Is 41:18–20; 52:7; Jer 31:12–14; Ps 98; Is 35.
[25] Mk 11:1–10 = Zach 9:9–10.
[26] Mk 10:45; 14:24 = Is 42; 52:13–53:12.
[27] Cf Mt 26:26f; Mk 14:22f; Lk 22:14f; I Cor 11:23f. 'For many' means 'for all'—cf J. Jeremias, *TWNT*, VI, 544.

death in fulfilment of the prophecy of Is 52:13-53:12 as regards the servant of Yahweh. 'The Son of Man came . . . to give his life as a ransom for many' (Mt 20:28). The 'blood' is obviously an allusion to the blood of the sacrifice in which the old covenant was sanctioned in Ex 24:4-8. And the 'new covenant' obviously refers to the fulfilment of the promised covenant of the Old Testament (Jer 31:31-4).

As the promised Messiah Jesus founds the new, universal covenant in his death and resurrection. In and with his covenant he found a newly covenanted people. Just as the effect of the old covenant was the selection and creation of a people as God's own possession;[28] and just as a new people is promised in and with the new covenant;[29] so the effect of the new covenant founded by Jesus is a new people of God, a people of the New Testament, worshipping 'in spirit and in truth' (Jn 4:24), 'a chosen race, a royal priesthood, a holy nation, God's own people, that you may declare the wonderful deeds of him who called you out of darkness into his marvellous light' (I Pet 2:9). For this reason he called and sent a group of followers to bear witness to all men of the new covenant: 'And you shall be my witnesses in Jerusalem and in all Judea and Samaria and to the end of the earth' (Acts 1:8). Because God is in covenant with this people it will never dissolve or be superseded nor will its God-given structure ever completely fail to fulfil the purpose for which it was given, namely, the sanctification and salvation of mankind. It owes both its existence and continuance solely to God's new covenant relationship with it in Jesus Christ through his Spirit.

This is the universal Church founded in the death and resurrection of Jesus Christ. It did not exist before then. But his intention of founding it was already apparent during his public life, especially towards the end. This is clear from his saying to Peter in Mt 16:18: 'And I tell you, you are Peter, and on this rock I will build my Church. . . .' The greatest arguments against the historicity of this text stem from the three reasons mentioned above in denial of the possibility of the foundation of a visible universal Church by Jesus, namely, that the kingdom of God preached by Jesus was solely internal and invisible, was completely eschatological, and was limited to the Jews alone. Once the onesidedness of these assertions is demonstrated the historicity of this text is beyond doubt, even though its time and circumstances are not recorded. As J. Schmid says: 'The fact that the Messianic consciousness of Jesus and universalism are already demonstrable from the Gospel tradition necessitates the

[28] Cf Ex 19:5-6; Dt 7:6-11; 26:16-19.
[29] Jer 32:37-44; 33:10-26.

assumption that a word corresponding to Mt 16:18 was spoken by him even if Matthew had not preserved this word for us.'[30] As I have mentioned, however, this is a promise. Jesus did not found a Church during his historical pre-Easter life. But his intention of doing so is clear from this text of Matthew once the above-mentioned objections to its authenticity are shown to be groundless.

Finally, Jesus' intention is revealed at the Last Supper. Just as the people of the old covenant received precise directions for cult (Ex 12:1–28), so also Jesus prescribes the celebration of his new sacrifice in his memory: 'Do this in remembrance of me.'[31] On the implications of the eucharist for the Church H. Riesenfeld has this to say: 'That Jesus reckoned with an intervening epoch between his death and the *parousia*, that is, with the epoch of the Church, appears to me a necessary consequence of the institution of the Lord's Supper.'[32] The early Christian community recognized this indispensable connection with the intention and founding acts of Jesus in its maintenance of the circle of the Twelve,[33] and in its recognition that its preaching and divine worship were inseparable from the original cell of the 'Church of God'.[34]

The New Testament community recognized itself as the new people of God. It recognized both its continuity with the people of God of the Old Testament,[35] its realization of the new people there promised,[36] as well as the newness of its relation to Jesus Christ.[37] This newness is apparent, for example, in its spiritualization and

[30] 'Lassen sich das Messiasbewusstsein Jesu und der Universalismus (vgl. zu 28:19f) aus der Evangelienüberlieferung sicher nachweisen, dann muss auch ein Mt 16:18 entsprechendes Wort als von ihm gesprochen angenommen werden, selbst wenn uns Matthäus dieses Wort nich erhalten hätte': *Das Evangelium nach Matthäus*, p. 252. Cf A. Feuillet in *Introd. à la Bible*, vol. II, p. 801. So also O. Cullmann, *Peter* . . . , p. 196, and J. Betz in *Theol. Quartals.*, 138 (1958) 160f, although they are too much influenced by the 'corporate personality' theory.

[31] Lk 22:19; I Cor 11:24–25. J. Jeremias judges it 'very probable' that this command goes back to Jesus himself: *The Eucharistic Words of Jesus*, London, 1966, p. 255. Cf *ibid.*, pp. 237–62, for his detailed arguments.

[32] *The Gospel Tradition and its Beginnings. A Study in the limits of Formgeschichte*, Oxford, 1957. Cf also R. Schnackenburg in *LTK*, 6, 169. Kümmel admits that Mk 14:25–28 inculcates a 'considerable interval' between the resurrection and the parousia: *Promise and Fulfilment*, p. 77.

[33] Cf Acts 1:13, 15–26; I Cor 15:3–5.

[34] Cf I Cor 15:3f; 11:23f. Cf R. Schnackenburg, *The Church in the New Testament*, pp. 13–14.

[35] Cf Ex 19:4–6a = I Pet 2:9.

[36] Cf Hos 2:3 = I Pet 2:10.

[37] Cf I Pet 2:5 'through Jesus Christ'.

therefore universalization. The universality of the new people of God surpasses that envisaged in the Old Testament. Participation in the new kingdom is not conditioned by membership of the Jewish race, nationality or religion. National, ethnic and social distinctions are transcended. What matters is the spiritual relationship from and to Jesus Christ through faith and baptism (cf Gal 3:26-29).

Vatican II sums up this basic covenantal relationship between Jesus and the new people of God thus: God

'chose the race of Israel as a people unto himself. With it he set up a covenant. Step by step he taught this people by manifesting in its history both himself and the decree of his will, and by making it holy unto himself. All these things, however, were done by way of preparation and as a figure of that new and perfect covenant which was to be ratified in Christ, and of that more luminous revelation which was to be given through God's very Word made flesh. "Behold the days are coming, says the Lord, when I will make a new covenant with the house of Israel and the house of Judah. . . . I will put my law within them, and I will write it upon their hearts; and I will be their God, and they shall be my people . . . for they shall all know me, from the least of them to the greatest, says the Lord" (Jer 31:31-34) Christ instituted this new covenant, that is to say, the new testament, in his blood (cf I Cor 11:25), by calling together a people made up of Jew and Gentile, making them one, not according to the flesh but in the Spirit. This was to be the new people of God. For, those who believe in Christ, who are reborn not from a perishable but from an imperishable seed through the Word of the living God (cf I Pet 1:23), not from the flesh but from water and the Holy Spirit (cf Jn 3:5-6), are finally established as "a chosen race, a royal priesthood, a holy nation, a purchased people. . . . You who in times past were not a people, but are now the people of God" (I Pet 2:9-10).'[38]

---

[38] DCC, n. 9.

Chapter Eleven

The New People of God as the Universal Sacrament of Salvation

As Karl Barth so aptly notes,[1] the new covenant is a relationship between Christ and a *people*, just as the old one was. There can be no question therefore of Jesus not intending to found, or not founding, a Church. Willing the communal salvation of the individual, he willed the foundation of the Church. Participation in the new covenant involves participation in a community. While the subjective realization of reconciliation takes place in a communitarian and an individual form the communitarian form is fundamental and primary. In saying this our author is conscious of inverting the traditional order of Protestant dogmatics which placed the individual first. He is quite justified in this reaction against the individualism prevalent in Protestant theology, especially in the last century. As he rightly notes, it is not the individual Christian but the *ecclesia una sancta catholica et apostolica* which stands (in close connection with the Holy Spirit) in the Creed. He was not, of course, alone in this reaction. 'For a generation now Protestant thought has refound the sense of the Church, of the religious community. The old individualism has lost ground; a return has been made to the primitive idea of the Church as a mystical reality, the body of Christ.'[2] Recent Catholic ecclesiology has re-emphasized too this fundamentally communal aspect of subjective reconciliation, mainly through its rediscovery of the oldest and most fundamental biblical concept for the Church, namely, the 'people of God'. Vatican II has crowned this development by devoting the whole of chapter two of its Dogmatic Constitution on the Church to this theme. And as it explicitly states: 'It has pleased God, however, to make men holy and save them not merely as individuals without any mutual bonds, but by

[1] *CTKB*, pp. 106f, 130f, 243f.
[2] M. Goguel, 'Unité et diversité du christianisme primitif' in *Rev. Hist. Phil. Rel.*, 19 (1939), 1 (cited in Cerfaux, *La théologie de l'Eglise* . . . , p. 7).

making them into a single people, a people which acknowledges him in truth and serves him in holiness.'³

This community aspect characterizes the Church in its whole life and structure. All members of the Church form a community equal in basic dignity and activity.⁴ The common dignity consists in the common participation in the one salvation, the one faith, hope and charity, and the one call to perfection. The common activity consists in the common participation in Christ's priestly, prophetic and kingly functions. And even where the activity of the Church is essentially unique, as for example in the instituted and charismatic lay or hierarchical ministries,⁵ or in its seven sacraments,⁶ it is primarily communitarian or ecclesial, directed first of all to the building up of the body of Christ (cf Eph 4:12), and only as such directed to the salvation of the individual.

This fundamental communal character of subjective reconciliation means that the Church is necessary for salvation. The individual will not be saved except in relation to the Church. As Barth notes,⁷ this is not a distinctively Roman Catholic but a biblical and therefore of necessity a universally Christian doctrine. He goes on to show from Scripture the factuality of the 'reality and clarity, the finality and exclusiveness with which the Church is the place in which God turns men into recipients of his revelation'. What is the basis of this factual necessity of the Church for Barth? The first impression is that he based it on God's Lordship and freedom: God is free to grant reconciliation where he will and he factually grants it only in the Church. When he wrote this he was speaking from within a theology of mediation,⁸ and it was undoubtedly causing him embarrassment. I think his thought on this point is intimately connected with his whole christological, pneumatological and ecclesiological development and can best be understood from the point of view of his later event or response theology.⁹ Certainly salvation is due to God's graciously free act. But this assertion can hardly explain why it invariably takes place in the Church. Whereas if we begin with the understanding of the Church as the human result or reflection of the direct act of the risen Christ through his Spirit pressing from within outwards we can far more easily understand its factual, as opposed to a mediatory,

³ DCC, n. 9.
⁴ Cf *ibid.*, n. 32.
⁵ Cf *ibid.*, ch. 2, nn. 10, 12; ch. 3 and 4.
⁶ Cf *ibid.*, n. 11.
⁷ Cf *CTKB*, p. 243.
⁸ *Vermittlungstheologie*, cf *ibid.*, p. 77.
⁹ As I have already tried to understand him, *ibid.*, pp. 246–9.

necessity. The Church is necessary for salvation because the Church takes place in some way there where this direct act of the risen Christ takes place. The act of the risen Christ creates the Church—and not only invisibly but visibly as well. Factually or consequentially then there is no salvation outside the Church because there is none outside Christ.

We can agree in many points with Barth. Jesus Christ, through his Spirit, certainly acts directly in the hearts and minds of men, and where this action takes place *there* the Church is in some way. The life created by the Spirit is an incipient form of the life of the Church for *he is* the one life of the Church. There is no salvation outside the Church because the Church is in some way there where the Spirit acts. The life of the individual is a life *in* and *with* a community. This applies to those who, without blame, have no explicit knowledge of God, Christ or the Church, yet strive to live a good life thanks to his grace.[10] While Barth strongly emphasizes the factuality and exclusivity of salvation in what is 'outwardly and visibly' the Church, in view of his reminder on the one hand that Scripture witnesses to some (even as an exception to prove the rule) who received salvation 'quite away from Israel and the Church', and on the other, that Christ's lordship is not confined to the Church,[11] I do not think that he would limit salvation to what is visibly accepted as the Church. All men receive God's grace and call to salvation. If they answer this call as best they can they are in some way 'related' to the Church.[12] Their life is a communal or ecclesial life. It is the life of the Church. The life of each is necessarily the life of all for it is a share in the life of the one Spirit who is the unique source and power of the subjective realization of reconciliation. Participating in the one communal life of the Father, Son and Holy Spirit, they are necessarily one in many, many in one. 'So we, though many, are one body in Christ, and individually members one of another' (Rom. 12:5). 'For all the faithful scattered throughout the world, are in communion with each other in the Holy Spirit, so that "he who occupies the See of Rome knows the people of India are his members".'[13]

The more a person lives under the impact of the Spirit of Christ the more he is united to Christ and therefore also to his body which is the Church. The basic fact is that Christian life, that is, the life created

[10] Cf DCC, n. 16.
[11] Cf *CTKB*, pp. 242f, 233, 322.
[12] Cf DCC, n. 16.
[13] *Ibid.*, n. 13, citing St John Chrysostom, *In Joan.*, Hom. 65, 1 (*PG*, 59:361).

by Jesus Christ through his Spirit, is communal or ecclesial. One's faith is a participation in the common *Credo* of the Church. As St Thomas points out,[14] the Church is the primary and fundamental subject which says 'I believe in God, Father, Son and Holy Spirit.' Similarly, Christian love is a participation in the life of the one Spirit of love who is the principle of the Church's life. 'God's love has been poured into your hearts through the Holy Spirit who has been given to us' (Rom 5:5). Faith and love issue in hope for that which is already seen and experienced but in its fulness and clarity is still to come. The life of each is necessarily the life of all. In this way Christians form a reflection of the fellowship or community of God's own one-in-threeness, and their communal life is a kind of *perichoresis* in analogy to that of the three divine persons. It is this internal participation in and reflection of the life of the Trinity which is of primary importance in the Church. While there will be distinction in office and ministry in the Church there is first and foremost this basic equality and community.[15] The external and visible Church, with its ministries and sacraments, exists in the service of this internal communal life and not vice versa.

Again, 'outside Christ no salvation' means 'outside the Church no salvation' because this one communal life created by the Spirit necessarily issues in the upbuilding of the Church. It is a life in and with and *for* the Church. This communal aspect has recently been given more emphasis in Roman Catholic understanding of Christian spirituality, life and action. God's plan of salvation certainly envisages the individual. But the actualization of the salvation of the individual takes place only in the upbuilding of the *community* of salvation. As St Paul says, the gifts of the Spirit are given 'for the work of ministry, for building up the body of Christ' (Eph 4:11–12). The relationship of the individual from and to God is not 'unidimensional'. One is not a Christian to 'save one's soul' or 'to get to heaven', but to serve Jesus Christ in the service of the community. This involves, as Barth indicates,[16] total dedication to the Church's commission and service to the world, concern for and solidarity with the Church, participation in its sacraments and witness, in its whole life and thought and action. Self-centredness and individualism have no place in the Christian life. Each one is responsible for the Church, for its growth and welfare. As Barth again says,[17] passivity in one's responsibility

---

[14] *Summa theol.*, II–II, q. 1, art. 9, ad 3.
[15] Cf DCC, n. 32.
[16] Cf *CTKB*, pp. 248–9.
[17] Cf *ibid.*, p. 247.

for the upbuilding of the Church means necessarily passivity in one's Christian life. This applies to the whole Church. All members of God's people, and not just those with a special hierarchical ministry, are responsible for the Church. As Vatican II puts it: 'Whoever they are, they are called upon, as living members, to expend all their energy for the growth of the Church and its continuous sanctification.'[18]

For all Christians then, that is, for all those who explicitly believe in God, Jesus Christ and the Church, this necessity of the visible Church must be asserted. I am thinking still within Barth's event and response type of ecclesiology. The visible Church is necessary in the sense that it is the communal incarnation of the grace of the Holy Spirit, the visible expression (and sacrament in that sense) of subjective reconciliation or salvation. This visible 'Church', depending on the extent of its faith, possesses an inner dynamism towards the fulness of catholic visibility, sacramentality and unity. Everything depends here of course on what we mean by 'Church'. As is well known the strict exclusive identification of the one, holy, catholic and apostolic Church with the Roman Catholic Church was modified by Vatican II. While it affirms the historical existence of the one true Church of Christ, and its recognizability as such in the Roman Catholic Church, it does not assert an exclusive identity of this one true Church and the Roman Catholic Church but says that it 'subsists' in the Roman Catholic Church, thus recognizing and allowing for 'the many ecclesial elements of sanctification and truth' to be found 'outside' the Roman Catholic Church.[19] While the Council is undoubtedly speaking from the point of view of a mediatory ecclesiology, that is, of the necessity of the Church as the effective sacrament or instrument of salvation, I believe these genuinely ecclesial elements need not necessarily be restricted to instituted *mediatory* means of salvation such as sacraments and ministries but can extend also to all communal external *expressions* of the grace of Christ (be they confessions of faith, Bible gatherings, prayer and liturgical assemblies, community meetings, etc.) welling out spontaneously from within. This is what I have been thinking of above in trying to draw out Barth's response—ecclesiological understanding of the necessity of the Church for salvation. Such communal expressions simply must

---

[18] DCC, n. 33. Cf n. 37.
[19] Cf DCC, nn. 8, 16; *Decree on Ecumenism*, n. 3. Cf also the commentaries of A. Grillmeier in *Commentary on the Documents of Vatican II*, ed. by H. Vorgrimler, vol. I, pp. 149–50, 177f; K. McNamara in *Vatican II: The Constitution on the Church*, pp. 101, 151f; *idem*, in *Vatican II on Ecumenism*, ed. by M. Adams, Dublin, 1966, pp. 76–9; Baum, *art. cit.* Bläser, *art. cit.*

take place because of the incarnational and ecclesial character of all grace.

But I believe a certain necessity of the *visible* Church must also be asserted for the salvation of *all men*, and not just of Christians. Can we not go on and say that the visible Church is necessary in some way for salvation for those who do not explicitly acknowledge Christ and his visible Church but strive to live a good life with God's help? I believe we can. Even in their case 'outside Christ no salvation' means 'outside the (visible) Church no salvation'. This brings particularly to mind the ambiguity of the phrase 'outside the Church no salvation'. Here again everything depends on what we mean by 'Church'. According to the Council, generally speaking, the Church is one complex reality comprising a divine and human, invisible and visible, earthly and heavenly element, an invisible community of life but also a visible social structure and means of life,[20] in short, it is the sacrament of salvation.[21] Vatican II might seem contradictory in asserting on the one hand that this Church is necessary for salvation,[22] and on the other, that there is salvation outside this Church.[23] The Church has always acknowledged that all people of goodwill, but with no explicit knowledge of Christ and his Church, can be saved. Even when there was the most rigorous interpretation of 'outside the Church no salvation' there was also this other stream of thought.[24] If one maintains that it is fundamental to the concept of Church to have an explicit profession of faith in Christ and acknowledgement of him then it would seem to follow that there is salvation outside the Church and also that there is no salvation outside the Church.[25] However, I do not think this is necessary, or I believe it is possible to speak of all non-Christians who are saved as 'pre-Church' in some way, so that the phrase 'outside the Church no salvation' is not only possible but necessary also in their regard. The Council speaks of their relatedness or orientation[26] to the Church, without explaining

---

[20] Cf DCC, n. 8.
[21] Cf *ibid.*, nn. 1, 9, 48.
[22] Cf *ibid.*, n. 14.
[23] Cf *ibid.*, n. 16.

[24] The most recent example of this was the letter of the then Holy Office to the Archbishop of Boston on 8 August, 1949 correcting the over-rigorous interpretation of Fr Feeney; cf *Amer. Eccl. Rev.*, 77 (1952), 307–11; DS 3866–73.

[25] And as Fr Küng rightly points out it would be better in such a case to substitute the phrase 'outside the Church no salvation' by some other, or at least omit it; cf his *The Church*, pp. 316–18.

[26] 'Ordinantur', DCC, nn. 13, 16.

what this relatedness exactly means. By Church I take it to mean the same complex of invisibility and visibility of which it has been speaking all along. We have already seen how all those who share in any way in the life of the Spirit are invisibly ordained to the life of the one community of the people of God whose life principle is the same Spirit. Now we must also say that they are ordained visibly to the visible Church. There is no such thing as a purely internal, spiritual and individual relationship with Christ. Relationship with the risen Christ through his Spirit is always a relationship to his Church, which is his sacrament, just as relationship with the Father is always a relationship with his incarnate Son, the fundamental sacrament of God's love, grace and truth. The necessity of the Church for salvation is the necessity of the communal and incarnational character of all Christian (that is, of the Man Christ) grace. The living of a good life in accordance with God's grace will necessarily issue in visible communal forms, whether they be the construction of a just society, a peaceful world, a harmonious secular city or various cultic and religious practices and communities. As incarnations or concrete realizations of the grace of Jesus Christ they are sign-posts to the Church or prefigurements of it. All those who dedicate themselves to the creation of a peaceful, just and truthful human community create a prefigurement or foreshadowing[27] of the Church. Outside this prefigurement there is no salvation, that is, outside this visible ordination or relation to the visible Church there is no salvation. The Church however is the fulness of sacramentality. All prefigurements tend of necessity towards it. Salvation is a progressive history or history of progress from a more or less total anonymity to full sacramentality and incorporation in the Church. In this regard the Church, that is, the sacramental fulness of salvation, must be termed, not the 'ordinary', but the 'extraordinary' way of salvation, in so far as the vast majority of mankind find salvation outside its fulness. It is however the vanguard of anonymous Christianity, the *signum levatum in nationes*. On the part of the Church this implies mission. The Church must be made 'fully present to all nations'[28] to point out the way ahead. Its role will be not to supplant but supplement, aid, advance and ennoble all true human, social, moral and religious values.[29]

Karl Barth should have nothing against what I have said so far with regard to the necessity of the Church, and of the visible Church,

[27] *'Prefiguratio'*, DCC, n. 2.
[28] Vatican II, *Decree on the Church's Missionary Activity*, n. 5.
[29] Cf DCC, nn. 13, 16–17.

for the salvation of all mankind. It is based on the response ecclesiology he advocates. He acknowledges, as we have seen, that Christ's lordship and salvation are not limited to the Church, and that his grace is essentially ecclesial and incarnational. However, he absolutely refuses to find any 'point of contact' between revelation and non-Christian religions, and considers the missionary task of the Church to consist, not in dialogue and supplementation, but in opposition and supplantation.[30] We must not misunderstand Barth. Here, as always, his thought must be understood in the light of his doctrine on justification—and he himself reminds us of this: 'The preceding expositions have established the fact that we can speak of "true" religion only in the sense in which we speak of a "justified sinner".'[31] And here too, as always, the main brunt of his attack is directed towards the anthropological theology of liberal Protestantism, where man and not God was placed as the centre and measure of all things,[32] but also towards the natural theology of Catholicism and the imputed Pelagianism of its doctrine of justification.

'Religion', including the Christian 'religion', means for Barth simply man's attempt at self-justification. It is 'man's reality and possibility'.[33] Revelation and reconciliation on the other hand are solely and exclusively the reality and possibility of the Holy Spirit. Whence religion and revelation must be opposed absolutely as unbelief and belief. 'We have here an exclusive contradiction.'[34] It is because religion attributes to man some part or subjectivity in his own salvation that it is unbelief: 'This stamps religion as unbelief.'[35] Belief says that God alone is the subject of revelation and reconciliation, and therefore the missionary activity of the Church cannot be conceived of as a supplementation of 'religion', that is, of man's own efforts at knowledge of God and justification, but as their complete and total abolition and replacement. This applies to all religions—the Christian included. Before the Word of God (that is, justification by God alone) *all* religions are relativized (just as all philosophies are)—even if they proclaim justification by God alone. Can any religion be said to be 'true' then? Yes, but only in so far as it lives by God's grace, and this is decided only by God.

'The fact that by the grace of God they live by His grace. . . . That is what makes their religion true. . . . Or, to put it concretely,

[30] Cf *CTKB*, p. 331 and the reference there to *C.D.* I/2: 'The Revelation of God as the Abolition of Religion'.
[31] *C.D.* I/2, p. 325. Cf also *CTKB*, pp. 20f.
[32] *Ibid.*, pp. 292f.   [33] *Ibid.*, p. 283.
[34] *Ibid.*, p. 303.   [35] *Ibid.*, p. 214.

through the name of Jesus Christ there are men who believe in His name and give thanks. To the extent that this is self-evident in the case of Christians and the Christian religion, we can and must say of it that it and it alone is the true religion.'[36]

The Church's knowledge and worship of God, its service in teaching, worship and life, are determined by the realization of the free kindness of God. The Christian religion is the illuminated earth reflecting the sun's (that is, Christ's) light, and is as such the 'true' religion, the sign and proclamation of God's salvation.[37]

In so far as Barth by all this wishes to emphasize that salvation is due to God's grace alone and not to man's works we must wholeheartedly agree with him in saying that 'revelation' is the abolition of 'religion' as belief is of unbelief. And certainly the Church in its dialogue with non-Christian religions will find many things which will be simply opposed to revelation and the grace of God. But why does Barth refuse to allow that the reconciling and revealing Lord of the Church is already operative in the world, and in non-Christian religions, so that their 'reflection' will also be some kind of sign and pointer to the Church and the Church's missionary task will not be solely one of demolition but also of supplementation? Because, he himself replies, together with the fact of God's freedom and inscrutability, revelation is factually tied to the name Jesus Christ, and therefore also to the Church which alone proclaims that name.

> 'And in answer to this question we have not only to point to the freedom and inscrutability of the divine judgment. We have also to bear in mind that this freedom and inscrutability is identical with the revealed fact of the name of Jesus Christ. . . . Beyond all dialectic and to the exclusion of all discussion the divine fact of the name of Jesus Christ confirms what no other fact does or can confirm: the creation and election of this religion to be the one and only true religion.'[38]

But surely the fact of the name of Jesus Christ does not exclude the possibility of salvation for all those who do not explicitly believe in this name?[39] How are they saved? How can Barth reconcile their salvation with his affirmation that 'outside the Church there is no salvation'? Or with his affirmation that non-Christian religions must

[36] *C.D.* I/2, pp. 345–6.
[37] Cf *ibid.*, p. 358.
[38] *Ibid.*, pp. 355–6.
[39] Cf Acts 17:25–28; I Tim. 2:4; DCC, n. 16. Cf H. Küng's scriptural demonstration in J. Neuner (ed.), *Christian Revelation* . . . , pp. 37–47.

be simply opposed by revelation? There are other questions one might like to pose to Barth at this point in the light of his exposition of the relationship between revelation and religion (for example, concerning the truth and reality of religion's reflection of divine salvation, and concerning his comparison of a free human being's reception of God's grace to the 'earth' reflecting the light of the sun) but these are the most pertinent at the moment. And as with many other Protestant theologians one looks in vain to Karl Barth for even an attempted answer. Catholic theology at least attempts a solution. And in its solution there is no question of subjecting revelation to the test of any natural reason or religion, as Barth seems to fear. All things are tested solely in the light of Jesus Christ and his Gospel. Neither is there question, in giving a positive assessment to non-Christian religions, of 'taking man apart from God, in a human *per se*'.[40] Man has never lived, nor ever lives, in a 'human *per se*', that is, in a purely natural order. Consequently, there never is in practice a purely natural knowledge of God nor a purely natural religion (even while we must claim the physical possibility of such natural knowledge and religion on man's part precisely as the necessary presupposition of any knowledge and religion by him). The human and non-Christian 'religions' we speak of therefore are already under the influence of the revealing and redeeming activity of God in Christ through his Spirit. Only as such do we say that they foreshadow the Church. They are the communal, social, religious bodying forth or expressions or reflections of the grace of the risen Christ and as such prefigurements of the Church. This prefigurement of the Church, and therewith the Church of which it is the prefigurement, is necessary for salvation as the necessary human response of reflection of Christ's incarnating grace.

But we must also assert a certain *mediatory* necessity of the Church. And here Barth not only refuses but cannot follow. While he does say the Church is necessary for salvation because salvation takes place in and *by* the Church[41] this is still a simple statement of *fact* and not the attribution of any real instrumentality to the Church. For him 'by' the Church means in fact by Christ alone. For him there is never any such thing as a gift of God to the Church whereby it is enabled to cooperate or sub-operate in the mediation or diffusion of his revelation and his reconciliation. His assertion of the 'factual' necessity of the Church is the expression of his all-pervading mono-actualist conception of the economy of salvation, which excludes any effective human mediation of salvation. This, however, constrains

[40] K. Barth, *C.D.* I/2, p. 297. [41] Cf *CTKB*, p. 246.

him to discern an 'intention' behind the utterances of the Fathers with their 'developing Roman Catholic concept of the Church'.[42] But, as we will see, the same conception is already present in the New Testament so that Barth will have to exercise some discernment there too. He denies that salvation ever comes through the Church in the sense of (under and in the Holy Spirit) from it, because he wishes to safeguard Christ's lordship and freedom. We assert it for the very same reason. The necessity of the Church for salvation is simply and solely the necessity of Jesus Christ for salvation—Jesus Christ who constituted his Church the prolongation of his own sacramental action. He himself acts in and through it, as his efficacious sign or organ or instrument, in his accomplishment of subjective reconciliation. He thus continues the same sacramental economy which is the gracious characteristic of his objective reconciliation. The risen Christ through his Spirit acts in, to and from the Church.

To understand the Catholic doctrine of the Church's necessity for salvation more completely, and to continue my dialogue with Barth on this point, I can begin again with the same notion of the Church as the 'people of God' with which we started. In terming the Church the 'people of God' we bring out not only the necessarily communal aspect of salvation, but we also place the Church in immediate relation and distinction to all other peoples and to the world, as Karl Barth also points out.[43] As a 'people' it is like all other peoples, composed of human beings, forming a visible community, in linguistic, structural and social affinity and dependency on its surroundings. But as the people 'of God' it is unlike all others as the people elected, called, sustained and directed by God. Visibly dependent, related and weak, invisibly it is independent, unrelated and strong. It is a complex reality comprised of a divine and human, earthly and heavenly, visible and invisible element.[44] It is the *sacrament* of salvation. Just as Jesus Christ, who was 'full of the Holy Spirit',[45] was the sacrament of objective reconciliation, so in a comparable way the Church, which is also 'filled with the Holy Spirit',[46] is the sacrament of subjective reconciliation.

As is known, this theme of the Church as sacrament is basic to the ecclesiology of Vatican II.

'By her relationship with Christ, the Church is a kind of sacrament or sign and instrument of intimate union with God and of the

---

[42] Cf *CTKB*, p. 245.   [43] Cf *ibid.*, pp. 311f.
[44] Cf DCC, n. 8.   [45] Cf Lk 4:1, 14, 31f; 5:24f.
[46] Cf Acts 2:4; 4:31; 8:14f.

unity of all mankind. . . . Christ, having been lifted up from the earth, is drawing all men to himself (Jn 12:32, Greek text). Rising from the dead (cf Rom 6:9), he sent his life-giving Spirit upon his disciples and through this Spirit has established his body, the Church, as the *universal sacrament of salvation*. Sitting at the right hand of the Father, he is continually active in the world, leading men to the Church, and through her joining them more closely to himself and making them partakers of his glorious life by nourishing them with his own body and blood.'[47]

By mentioning this theme right at the beginning of its Dogmatic Constitution on the Church the Council previews admirably the christological aspect of the Church and therewith also its missionary openness to the world, and reforming aspects—all of which form the leitmotifs of the whole Constitution, and indeed of the whole Council. The christological aspect is immediately apparent, for it is only 'by her relationship with Christ' that the Church is the sacrament of the unity and salvation of mankind. Apart from this relationship it is not this sacrament, it is not the Church. But also because this relationship is the basis of her sacramentality the unity and peace which it manifests and visibly represents is something deeper than mere human unity and peace. It is the unity and peace based on spiritual union with God in Christ through the Holy Spirit, and as such the goal and aim of all strivings towards unity and peace. That which the Church signals or signifies then is not originally its own light and message but the light and message of Jesus Christ. He is the light of all nations (*Lumen Gentium*, the opening words of the Constitution), and that which has to be shed on all men is '*His* radiance which brightens the countenance of the Church'.[48]

As the sacrament of this light of Christ the Church must of course shine. This implies continual internal renewal and reformation. It must concretely, existentially and truthfully *be* such a sign. It must be the one, holy, catholic and apostolic Church. It must continually re-form itself in the light of its renewed understanding of its origins in the Bible and of the world in which it lives. It must be the *ecclesia semper reformanda*, the Church of continuous renewal.[49] But as the sacrament of the light of Christ the Church must also be ever open and in mission towards the world and all men. It cannot exist in introverted complacency. It is essentially outward looking and moving.

[47] DCC, nn. 1 and 48. Cf also nn. 9, 26.
[48] DCC, n. 1.
[49] Cf *ibid.*, n. 15.

If it is the sign of salvation it must signify, it must exist in the service of that salvation to all men. As such it is Christ's instrument in the mediation of his salvation. And the way in which it accomplishes this service is comparable to the way in which Christ himself accomplished objective reconciliation. Just as Jesus Christ was composed of a visible and invisible, an earthly and a heavenly, a human and divine element, with the human, earthly and visible serving the divine, heavenly and invisible as an effective instrument, so also the Church. 'Just as the assumed nature inseparably united to the divine Word serves him as a living instrument of salvation, so, in a similar way, does the communal structure of the Church serve Christ's spirit, who vivifies it by way of building up the body (cf Eph 4:16).'[50]

While frequently using the theme 'Church sacrament' the Council did not define its exact meaning. The Church is the sacrament of salvation in so far as it is the sign and instrument in the divine plan of salvation for all mankind, the world and history. It is the salutary sign of intimate union with God and of the unity of all mankind. It is the indication, in human, communal and historically recognizable and accessible form, of divine salvation operative among us. The biblical background to this usage is connected with the term *mustērion* which the Bible uses to describe the mode of God's whole plan of salvation. In Latin translations this term was often rendered by *sacramentum*, and since God's plan was realized in Christ and through his Church it became customary in patristic theology to apply the term to Christ, the Church, Scripture, the liturgy, etc. The mystery of God's will is realized and set forth objectively in Jesus Christ and subjectively in and through the Church.[51] The general biblical basis for this term is to be found in the Bible's illustration of the reality of salvation in the Church and of the reality of the Church's mediation in word and action. As regards the Fathers Cyprian speaks of the Church as the 'indivisible sacrament of unity',[52] and Irenaeus speaks of Christ's recapitulation taking place in and through the Church and its unity.[53] The term sacrament was then narrowed and applied to concrete words and actions. In this sense the term has been in general use since the early days of scholasticism. Recently the term has been applied once more to the Church

[50] DCC, n. 8.
[51] Cf Eph 1:3–12; 3:4–6; 2:19–22.
[52] *Inseparabile sacramentum unitatis*, which for him meant the mystery of visible unity with the legitimate bishop and therefore does not exist for those 'outside the Church': *Ep.* 69:6 (*PL*, 3:1142b).
[53] *Adv. Haer.*, III, 16, 6 (*PG*, 7:926).

in general. It is thereby hoped to construct a synthesis of the invisible and visible elements of the Church. The Church is neither solely visible nor solely invisible but is the 'visible form of invisible grace',[54] the sign and instrument of salvation. The Church is sacramental in the totality of its acts, life and worship. It manifests, bodies forth, in human and earthly visibility and availability, the grace of the risen Jesus Christ. Karl Rahner says that this notion of the Church as fundamental sacrament was regained to theology from christology and not so much from current teaching on the sacraments. And he explains it thus:

> 'Therefore fundamental sacrament means for us the one abiding symbolic presence similar in structure to the incarnation, of the eschatological redemptive grace of Christ; a presence in which sign and what is signified are united inseparably but without confusion, the grace of God in the "flesh" of an historical and tangible ecclesiastical embodiment, which therefore cannot be emptied of what it signifies and renders present, because otherwise the grace of Christ (who always remains man), would also be something merely transitory and replaceable, and in the last resort we would still be under the old covenant.'[55]

As the 'universal sacrament of salvation' the people of God is essentially directed towards all other people and the whole world and all other peoples and the whole world are directed towards it. This messianic people has for its head the risen Christ, for its heritage the dignity and freedom of the sons of God because of the indwelling presence of the Spirit, for its law love, and for its goal the consummated kingdom of God.[56] As such it is the sign and instrument of universal salvation.

> 'So it is that this messianic people, although it does not actually include all men, and may more than once look like a small flock, is none the less a lasting and sure seed of unity, hope and salvation for the whole human race. Established by Christ as a fellowship of life, charity and truth, it is also used by him as an instrument for the redemption of all, and is sent forth into the whole world as the light of the world and the salt of the earth' (cf Mt 5:13–16).[57]

The whole of the council can be viewed as the development of this theme.

[54] Council of Trent, DS 1639.
[55] *The Church and the Sacraments*, pp. 23–4.
[56] DCC, n. 9.   [57] *Ibid.*

In its entirety the people of God is the sign and instrument of salvation. It is this in its whole priestly, prophetic and kingly ministry, both instituted and charismatic, lay and hierarchical, and in its seven sacraments.⁵⁸ Christ grants to his new people a participation, essentially differentiated as we shall see later, both charismatically and sacramentally, in his own unique priestly, prophetic and kingly ministry for the upbuilding of his body. All can and must effectively cooperate with him, because of this gift, in his subjective realization of reconciliation. They become his faithful instruments in leading all men and reality to him. Barth, as we shall also see, denies this real participation and consequently also all salvific mediation by the Church, and therefore its effective sacramentality.

But while every grace-giving ministry and event in the Church can be called 'sacramental' the Church is in a very special and proper sense sacramental in those seven actions of hers called precisely 'the seven sacraments'. 'For in them she herself attains the highest degree of actualization of what she always is: the presence of redemptive grace for men, historically visible and manifest as the sign of the eschatologically victorious grace of God in the world.'⁵⁹ The Council has little to say about the sacraments.⁶⁰ It speaks of them within the context of the *Church*, as the concrete actualizations of its general sacramentality. It emphasizes therefore their communal and ecclesial character. The few words it says, however, are important. In its very first sentence it brings out the fact that the sacraments are not something automatic or magical which confer grace without the exercise of the virtues of faith, charity and hope. The life and structure of the Church is not realized through the sacraments alone but through the sacraments and the virtues. The sacraments do infallibly offer grace (*ex opere operato*) and also infallibly confer grace in those who do not obstruct their efficacy (*non ponentibus obicem*). But the condition of not obstructing their efficacy is the mere negative

---

⁵⁸ Cf DCC, ch. 2, nn. 10–17; ch. 3–6. Also the Decrees on Ecumenism and on the Eastern Catholic Churches which develop DCC, ch. 2, n. 15; Decree on the Church's Missionary Activity, Declaration on the Relationship of the Church to Non-Christian Religions, and Pastoral Constitution on the Church in the Modern World, which develop DCC, ch. 2, nn. 16–17; Decrees on the Bishops' Pastoral Office in the Church and on the Ministry and Life of Priests which round off DCC, ch. 3; Decree on the Apostolate of the Laity which rounds off DCC ch. 4; and Decree on the Appropriate Renewal of Religious Life which rounds off DCC, ch. 6.

⁵⁹ K. Rahner, *The Church and the Sacraments*, p. 22.

⁶⁰ Cf DCC, n. 11 and the Commentary of K. McNamara, in *Vatican II: The Constitution on the Church*, pp. 121–32.

minimum requirement for a fruitful reception. Personal dispositions of faith and love are absolutely necessary for the fruitful reception of any sacrament and indeed are the measure of the grace conferred. The *ex opere operato* effect of the sacraments is but the crowning of a whole process of developing dispositions. The Council then goes on to treat of the individual seven sacraments precisely within an ecclesial context, that is, as the concrete actualizations of the Church's general sacramentality.

Through *baptism* the faithful are incorporated into the *Church*, are deputed or consecrated by a special seal or character to the exercise of the *Church's* cult, and, reborn as sons of God, are called upon to profess the faith before men which they have received from God through the *Church*. *Confirmation* continues what baptism begins. It binds more perfectly to the *Church*. It confers a special gift of strength from the Holy Spirit and obliges more strictly to spread and defend the faith of the *Church* both by word and deed. The *eucharist* is the fount and apex of the whole *Church*, manifesting the unity of God's people and wondrously effecting that same unity.[61] The sacrament of *penance* effects at once (*simul*) the forgiveness of God and reconciliation with the *Church* which was wounded by sin and which by charity, example and prayer seeks the conversion of the sinner. In the *anointing of the sick* the whole *Church* commends its sick members to the suffering and glorified Lord and at the same time reminds those same members of their responsibility to the *Church* precisely through their sufferings. The sacrament of *orders* grants a special power to feed the *Church* in Christ's name with the Word and grace of God. Finally, the sacrament of *matrimony* leads to the creation of a people of God in miniature, a domestic *Church*, a community related in intimate and indissoluble union with Christ and with one another.

In all these individual actions and words the Church fulfils and concretizes her sacramental existence. Karl Barth's ecclesiology is very weak with regard to the sacraments. We may recall that he considered it expedient to demythologize somewhat the general term sacrament in the course of his theological career.[62] He demythologized its mediatory connotation and retained it in its sense of response, witness and reflection of the Word and grace of God received directly. Baptism and the Lord's Supper (the only two sacraments he mentions of course) are for him part of the Church's witness and proclamation of salvation but in no sense 'a causative or generative means' of

[61] In addition to n. 11 of DCC cf also n. 3, and the *Constitution on the Sacred Liturgy*, n. 2.   [62] Cf *CTKB*, pp. 77f.

that salvation. Even when he says that baptism is necessary *necessitate praecepti* this means only that the individual is commanded to proclaim publicly his being in Jesus Christ and thereby also fulfil his ecclesial duty.⁶³ Certainly the sacraments are ecclesial expressions and proclamations of faith. But they are more. In no sense will Barth allow the phrase 'outside the Church no salvation' to mean that salvation comes through the Church in any way as its causal instrument (in and under God's grace and appointment) and is for this reason necessary for salvation. In denying it, however, he has the whole of tradition against him (including Luther and Calvin), for this was precisely the traditional understanding of Scripture's affirmation of the necessity of baptism (and therefore of the Church) for salvation.⁶⁴

The Church in its totality is the universal sacrament, that is, the sign and instrument, of salvation. Whence 'all men are called to belong to the new people of God', and this new people 'is to be spread throughout the whole world and must exist in all ages, so that the purpose of God's will may be fulfilled, namely, the unification of all mankind in the Church through Christ and his Holy Spirit.⁶⁵ The unity which is realized in the Church is a spiritual unity, a union with God through his Spirit and therefore with all men. Consequently, there is only one people of God, and in its unity it is universal, for it transcends the national, cultural and racial differences of all peoples. It takes its citizens from all nations, cultures, classes and colours and yet remains one, for its citizenship is not based on these distinctions but on the transcending spiritual union with Jesus Christ through his Spirit. Since the kingdom of Christ is not of this world the Church or people of God takes nothing away from any nation, class or race. On the contrary, recognizing that it 'must harvest with the king to whom the nations were given for an inheritance (cf Ps 2:8), and into whose city they bring gifts and presents (cf Ps 71(72):10; Is 60:4-7; Rev 21:24)', that is, recognizing that the Lord who is its Lord and operative in it is also the Lord of the world and operative in the world, it fosters, develops and makes its own whatever good it finds, no matter where it finds it.⁶⁶

In virtue of this unity and universality the Church must strive to unify humanity, and all humanity is called to its unity.

'This characteristic of universality which adorns the people of God is a gift from the Lord himself. By reason of it, the Catholic

⁶³ Cf *CTKB*, pp. 232–4, 248, 337.   ⁶⁴ Cf Mk 16:16; Jn 3:5.
⁶⁵ DCC, n. 13, par. 1   ⁶⁶ *Ibid.*, par. 2.

Church strives energetically and constantly to bring all humanity with all its riches back to Christ its head in the unity of his Spirit. . . . All men are called to be part of this catholic unity of the people of God, a unity which is harbinger of the universal peace it promotes. And there belong to it or are related to it in various ways, the Catholic faithful as well as all who believe in Christ, and indeed the whole of mankind. For all men are called to salvation by the grace of God.'[67]

This is equivalent to saying that the Church, as the universal sign and instrument of salvation, is necessary for salvation. It is necessary both as sign, expression or response and as instrument or means. I have already explained what I mean by 'Church'. Thus the Catholic faithful who internally possess the Spirit of Christ in faith, hope and charity and externally exist in communion with their brothers and leaders in faith, sacrament and obedience, are fully incorporated into this sacrament of unity.[68] For these (and of course not all Catholics fulfil all these requirements) the Church is necessary for salvation *necessitate medii* so that outside the Church (the one true visible and invisible Church of Christ which subsists in the Catholic Church) there is no salvation for them. The Church as Christ's body is the means of his presence to them and the means of their response to his presence. They are related to the Church by full incorporation, by the fulness of the Church's sacramentality both as means and expression, as instrument and sign. The incorporation decreases according as the union with the invisible life of the Church and with its visible structure decreases. But some relationship is necessary for all, and not only invisible but visible, and not only as orientated expression but as means as well.

Catechumens come close to full incorporation through their expressed desire for baptism.[69] Non-Catholic Christians are neither fully incorporated nor yet merely orientated or related to the Church. They are both *separati* (separated) because they do not profess the faith and communion in their entirety, and *coniuncti* (brethren) because they possess many visible and invisible ecclesial elements.[70] For them the Church is both the instrument and sign of salvation, the instrument in so far as they possess many ecclesial elements which really mediate sanctification and truth, and the sign in so far as these elements manifest their faith and sanctity.

What about non-Christians? How can we say that the Church is

[67] *Ibid.*, par. 2–4.   [68] Cf DCC, n. 14.   [69] Cf *ibid.*
[70] Cf *ibid.*, n. 15, and the Decrees on Ecumenism and the Eastern Catholic Churches.

necessary for salvation for them and that they are visibly related to the Church? They are related invisibly because all grace is the one grace of Jesus Christ through his Spirit and unites invisibly all who receive it. But they are also related visibly to it. Their human communities, institutions and religions, as the creations of man under the influence of divine grace, are prefigurements or foreshadowings of the Church, and are in their own way signs and instruments of salvation. We can, as Karl Rahner has suggested, assume a certain stratification in the reality of the Church as the visible sacrament of salvation. Thus at one level we can speak of what Rahner calls a 'quasi-sacramental visible aspect', a 'people of God', a 'Church as humanity consecrated by the incarnation', and at another level of the established juridical organization.[71] When an individual person totally accepts his concrete human nature he automatically consents to his membership of a 'people of God' based on the natural unity of the human race and on the reality of the incarnation of Jesus Christ who thereby calls all men to salvation and *eo ipso* to membership in the socially and juridically organized Church. This basic human community is the necessary means and expression of this individual's salvation.

> 'Thus the proposition about the Church as necessary means for salvation suffers no exception through the possibility of justification by the *votum ecclesiae*, in so far as the necessity of the Church for salvation always does and must mean—by "Church"—*at least* what we have called "people of God"—and, indeed, can always mean this.'[72]

Schillebeeckx assumes a similar stratification to that of Rahner when he speaks of a 'pre-Church', an 'anonymous Church', an 'implicit Church' on the one hand, and the visible socially organized Church on the other. Since creation takes place only in view of Christ, he says, all mankind bears within itself an anonymous ecclesial orientation as a grace to be accepted or rejected. Every free human act works to perdition or to salvation (that is, the Church). 'The human community in so far as it is created with this orientation towards Christ is an early rough-draft of the Church.'[73] The creation

---

[71] Cf his articles 'Membership of the Church according to the Teaching of Pius XII's Encyclical *Mystici Corporis Christi*' in *Theological Investigations*, II, pp. 1–88, esp. 76–88; 'The Christian Among Unbelieving Relations, *ibid.*, III, pp. 355–72; 'Christianity and the Non-Christian Religions', *ibid.*, V, pp. 115–34.   [72] K. Rahner, 'Membership . . .', *ibid.*, II, p. 85.

[73] E. Schillebeeckx, 'The Church and Mankind' in *Concilium*, vol. I, n. 1 (1965) 45.

of this human community is therefore a true *votum ecclesiae*, however implicit, and 'outside Christ no salvation' means 'outside the Church no salvation'. The characteristic of this true human community, and therefore of anonymous Christianity, as of all Christianity, is *love*. Love is the core of the Church's being. The Church takes place there where the human community is built up out of pure unselfish love for one's fellow men. And the visible Church itself will appear as the sign of salvation amongst men, actually drawing and inviting them, only when the love of its members for humankind becomes concretely and historically visible here and now.

Piet Fransen is in implicit agreement with Rahner and Shillebeeckx, even though he, together with Hans Küng, would prefer to speak of a *votum implicitum Christi* rather than a *votum implicitum Ecclesiae* in order to avoid giving offence to non-Christians (and non-Catholics) and to get away from an ecclesiocentric view of the Church's necessity for salvation to a theocentric or christocentric one.[74] God's universal call to salvation, Fransen says, affects every one internally. The response to this call for the person who has attained the use of reason consists in what St Thomas termed his fundamental theoretical and practical (moral) option for God as his final end, or in what St Augustine before him termed his choice between the two cities of love of self unto the contempt of God or love of God unto the contempt of self. That is, it consists in an implicit act of faith and charity. And in this fundamental option man is justified. Moreover, this act of faith leads to a personal and corporate or ecclesial creed and community, and this can be and is the expression and instrument of salvation. Thus all the human communities and structures created under the influence of Christ's salvific grace are both the expression and means of grace in an essential relationship of prefiguration to the Church.[75] This is especially true of non-Christian religions, as H. Küng brings out in his essay. In his salvation of non-Christians God sanctions and uses in part the socio-religious structures in which he finds them. These are for the vast majority of mankind the 'ordinary way of salvation'. Despite their error they are not entirely opposed to Christ and his revelation and

---

[74] Cf H. Küng, 'The World Religions in God's Plan of Salvation' in J. Neuner (ed.), *Christian Revelation and World Religions*, pp. 25–66; P. Fransen, 'How can Non-Christians find Salvation in their own Religions?', *ibid.*, pp. 67–122.

[75] In n. 2 of its DCC Vatican II speaks of a certain 'prefiguration of the Church from the beginning of the world'.

should be termed pre-Christian rather than non-Christian. To say therefore that there is no salvation outside Christ means there is no salvation outside the Church, or that the Church is necessary for salvation. For in all the human and religious communities created under the influence of Christ's grace it is present in prefiguration as the instrument and sign of salvation. It is thus the universal sacrament of salvation.

The Church of course as the fulness of sacramentality must continually engage in missionary activity. First of all to serve and bring out more clearly the goodness and truth which are everywhere present as the sign and fruit of the Lord's kingship of the world. The aim of missionary activity is not so much therefore the saving of that which is lost, nor the implanting of the faith or of the Church, nor the supplanting of existing cultures and religions, but the service of Jesus Christ in the world and in all men and their societies and religions. What is good and true must be understood, fostered, strengthened, purified and ennobled.[76] Not everything of course will be a *preparatio evangelica*. Non-Christian religions, like the world in general, will be found to contain much that is evil and untrue and therefore a hindrance to the Gospel. The aim of missionary work must be the correction and elimination of this evil and untruth so that all men may be liberated for the full knowledge and service of Jesus Christ.[77] Finally, the Church engages and must engage in missionary activity because it is *essentially* and totally a missionary Church, that is, a people *sent*, an *apostolic* Church.

> 'Mindful of the command of the Lord, "Preach the Gospel to every creature" (Mk 16:16), the Church painstakingly fosters her missionary work. Just as the Son was sent by the Father, so he too sent the apostles (cf Jn 20:21), saying: "Go, therefore, and make disciples of all nations, baptizing them in the name of the Father and of the Son and of the Holy Spirit, teaching them to observe all that I have commanded you; and behold, I am with you all days even unto the consummation of the world" (Mt 28:18-20). The Church has received from the apostles as a task to be discharged even to the ends of the earth this solemn mandate of Christ to proclaim the saving truth (cf Acts 1:8). Hence she makes the words of the Apostle her own: "Woe to me, if I do not preach the gospel" (I Cor 9:16), and continues unceasingly to send heralds of the Gospel until such time as the infant churches are fully

---

[76] Cf DCC, nn. 13, 16, 17.
[77] Cf DCC, n. 16.

established and can themselves carry on the work of evangelizing.'⁷⁸

Because the Church is the sacrament or sign and instrument of salvation it is essentially outward looking and moving in the service of Jesus Christ, the world and mankind. It is the sign which must shine forth, the instrument of Christ's universal call. As Karl Barth points out it is and must be to the world and all mankind the provisional representation of the world's own salvation which has already taken place in Jesus Christ.⁷⁹ It is 'provisional' because it is not yet what it will be either in extension or intension. But it is none the less a 'representation' for in it salvation is a real subjective reality. I will have to put a question later to Barth about the reality and nature of this subjective reconciliation as well as about the nature of the Church's ministerial role. Salvation is a true, real and intrinsic if anticipatory reality in the present time, and the Church really and effectively cooperates in its mediation. The Church does not thereby take the place of Jesus Christ, as Barth so often accuses.⁸⁰ It does not take the place of his Holy Spirit. On the contrary, it is only on the presupposition of the action of Christ and his Holy Spirit that it can be at all the effective instrument of salvation. On the presupposition of Christ's own alliance with his Church and on the presupposition of the internal action of the Holy Spirit in the minds and hearts of men and their consent, it effects salvation. It does more than merely announce the salvation of the world in Jesus Christ.⁸¹

'The Church is compelled by the Holy Spirit to do her part towards the full realization of the will of God, who has established Christ as the source of salvation for the whole world. By the proclamation of the Gospel, she prepares her hearers to receive and profess the faith, disposes them for baptism, snatches them from the slavery of error, and incorporates them into Christ so that through charity they may grow up into full maturity in Christ.'⁸²

The world can and must be able to see in the Church the unity, truth, justice and peace towards which it strives. This is the gift but also the task of the Church. Recent accusations of injustice, untruthfulness, impersonalness, outdatedness, of even being the grave of

---

⁷⁸ *Ibid.*, nn. 16–17.
⁷⁹ Cf *CTKB*, pp. 307f.
⁸⁰ Cf *ibid.*, pp. 322–3 and *passim.*
⁸¹ Cf *ibid.*, pp. 307f, and *passim.*
⁸² DCC, n. 17.

God,[83] would indicate that it is not fulfilling its role too admirably. It must concretely, existentially and credibly actualize and represent the unity, peace, love and justice the world is striving for. As H. de Lubac says: 'If she is not the sacrament, the effective sign, of Christ, then she is nothing.'[84] This alone is its splendour. If it is the sign it must signal and signify. This demands of course a continuous reforming and renewing programme on its part in the light of its renewed understanding of its biblical origins and of the world it lives in. In total submission to its head Jesus Christ, and to him alone, it must really reflect the light of Christ to the nations,[85] really be the visible sacrament of saving unity,[86] never cease to 'purify and renew [itself] so that the sign of Christ may shine more brightly over the face of the Church'.[87] If, as will always be the case to some degree because of human sin and error, and more at some times than others, it does not shine forth so luminously, the individual's road does not lie out of it but further into its mystery, as Barth also notes.[88] The individual is saved only in and through the Church. As the universal sacrament it is necessary for salvation. It alone, under Christ, is the hope for the world.

The Church or people of God must bear witness to the world's own past and objective reality in Jesus Christ, to its present becoming through his Spirit, and to its future in the *eschaton,* and so be the provisional representation of its salvation. It must existentially actualize its peace, unity and justice so that the world may know that Christ has sent it (cf Jn 17:21–23). God became man in Jesus Christ for the salvation of the whole world and not just of the Church (cf Jn 3:16; Mk 10:45). In his service the Church is essentially also in the service of the world. As Barth notes, there has been at this point a certain 'holy egoism' in the classical doctrine of the Church.[89] It has been directed in upon itself. One can notice in all the fields of spirituality, theology, liturgy, missions, etc, this introverted attitude. How embedded it is can be judged from the fact, as has already been pointed out by many commentators, that even such an open and outward looking council as Vatican II never really achieved a *rap-*

---

[83] Cf, e.g., C. Davis, *A Question of Conscience,* London, 1967; R. Adolfs, *The Grave of God. Has the Church a Future?,* London, 1967; J. A. Kavanaugh, *A Modern Priest Looks at his Outdated Church,* London, 1968.
[84] *The Splendour of the Church,* p. 161.
[85] Cf DCC, n. 1.
[86] Cf *ibid.,* nn. 1, 9, 48.
[87] *Ibid.,* n. 15.
[88] Cf *CTKB,* pp. 247f, 30f.
[89] Cf *ibid.,* pp. 315f.

prochement between the Church and the modern world, but remained essentially a 'churchy' affair.[90] The Church will never really achieve this until it realizes that the Holy Spirit which is its Spirit is active in the world too, that what it regards as an enemy is in fact a friend, that the world is the Church in some way, that the Church and mankind cannot be opposed as Church and non-Church, and consequently that its task is not withdrawal to any ivory tower (in doctrine, thought-form, liturgy, language, art, architecture, etc.) but full knowledge of, full immersion in and full service of the secular world where Jesus Christ the man for others is continually leading men to come of age.[91]

The Church cannot exist for itself but only for the God who in Jesus became man and therefore also for the world. This applies to its whole existence—even to its most solemn liturgical functions or most contemplative religious order. Barth points out three basic factors which should characterize this total and genuine existence for the world: realistic knowledge, total solidarity and active responsibility.[92] Realistic knowledge can only be gained by intimate contact both with Jesus Christ and the reconciliation accomplished in him and being accomplished by him and with the world itself. The world, its history and peoples will then be seen as an admixture of *Dei providentia* and *hominum confusione,* of the providence of God and the confusion of men. Accordingly, the Church will not underestimate the world as something entirely evil, to be rejected and contradicted at all costs. But neither will it ingenuously overestimate it, presuming that everything worldly is good and to be aped. In the light of this knowledge the Church can and must exist in total solidarity with the world. For it itself is world, and is also governed by divine providence and human sin. It must not pharisaically nor platonically separate itself from the world as a sinless or purely spiritual reality. It must demonstrate that it is in itself in the same boat with man and the world, and not hesitate to go down to hell in a very secular fashion to get its message across. Finally, on the basis of this knowledge and solidarity it must exist in active responsibility for the world. It will endeavour to erect signs in radical dissimilarity to its evil practice. But above all

---

[90] Cf E. Schillebeeckx, *Vatican II: The Real Achievement,* 1967, p. 20; M. Novak, *The Open Church,* London, 1964, p. 130; D. Fisher, *The Church in Transition,* London, 1966, p. 129. P. Hebblethwaite in his book *Understanding the Synod,* Dublin–Sydney, 1968, has a similar comment to make with regard to the first synod of bishops.

[91] Cf H. Cox, *The Secular City,* pp. 103–63, where he sums up the Church's role in the world under the headings 'kerygmatic', 'koinoniac', 'diakonic'.

[92] Cf *CTKB,* pp. 317f, 308f.

it will exist in absolute confidence, resolute decision and definite hope for the world.[93] It will exist in absolute confidence because it knows that God in Jesus Christ through his Spirit is for the world and that this action is pressing outwards from the world itself towards the Church. It must resolutely decide to aid these outward-pressing forms and signs and so fulfil its active responsibility. It will not be for ever condemning the world. To be sure, it must resolutely fight evil and nothingness. But above all it must exist *for* the world, just as God exists for it in the man Jesus. Its message will not be for ever one of damnation and condemnation but one of salvation and hope. It knows that Jesus Christ is active in the world apart from the Church and that he is leading it towards the Church.[94] For this reason it must really and realistically immerse itself in the world in order to discern and foster the signs of the kingdom of God already breaking forth in the world under the influence of Christ's universal lordship through his Spirit. This is particularly relevant at the present time because of the leeway to be made up due to the past mainly negative attitude with regard to the world and its values and because of the tremendous changes and upheavals taking place in the world. Because the Church is in the service of its one God, Father, Son and Holy Spirit, it must exist in the service of the world, proclaiming to it the good news of salvation, preparing, disposing and incorporating it into Christ, leading the world along the path of peace, unity, justice and brotherhood it has already begun, and especially by existing itself in all truth and clarity as the embodiment of that which it proclaims and strives to effect and perfect—as the universal sacrament of salvation.

---

[93] Cf *CTKB*, pp. 310f.
[94] Cf DCC, n. 48.

Chapter Twelve

The Mission of the Holy Spirit

THE more one speaks of the Church as the sign and instrument of salvation the more one realizes that one is speaking all along ultimately of the Holy Spirit, the third person of the divine Trinity, who is the in-dwelling and in-operative principle of the Church's whole life and action. Consequently, having outlined the historical origin of the Church in the intention and will of Jesus Christ, and having presented a panoramic view of the mission and nature of the 'people of God in world-occurrence',[1] I must go on immediately, always in dialogue with Karl Barth, to speak of this Spirit and of his presence and action in the Church.[2]

The Church is essentially 'after Pentecost'.[3] This means that were it not for the event of Pentecost, that is, the mission and coming of the Holy Spirit, the Church would not be what it is. It means that the Church is essentially the Church of the Holy Spirit. While the whole economy of salvation must be attributed jointly to all three persons of the divine Trinity, aspects or moments of this economy are and can be attributed to one or other of the three persons: eternal predestination and creation to the Father, objective reconciliation to the Son, subjective reconciliation to the Holy Spirit. In the risen and glorified Christ the predestined reconciliation of the world is already a reality. In him 'we have redemption, the forgiveness of sins ... he is the head of the body, the Church. ... For in him all the fulness of God was pleased to dwell and through him to reconcile to himself all things,

[1] As Karl Barth entitles the preliminary subsection to the third aspect of his treatment of the Church. Cf *CTKB*, pp. 307f.
[2] Vatican II touched upon this theme especially in DCC, nn. 4, 7 and 48 but did not clarify or develop it to any great extent. At the same time, implicitly, it constitutes one of the great gains of the Council.
[3] If we had let the liturgy be the theological guide it is capable of being we would never have minimized this basic insight. The liturgy depicts the time between Christ's ascension and his parousia, that is, the time of the Church, as the *Pentecostal* cycle, and all the Sundays of this cycle accordingly bear the appendage 'after Pentecost'.

whether on earth or in heaven, making peace by the blood of his cross.'⁴ What we are in him we must become in ourselves. We must be and live ourselves (subjectively) what he is and lives himself (objectively) for us. For this, time has been given us, namely, the time between Christ's ascension and final coming, that is, the time of the Church. The purpose of the Church's time is this subjective realization of reconciliation. This involves immediately, as Barth points out,⁵ a problem of mediation, a problem of the reality and possibility of subjective salvation. How does the reconciliation which was effected at a particular point of time and space in the past (*illic et tunc*) have effects at the present moment of time and space (*hic et nunc*)? But the problem must be framed more exactly. The spatio-temporal gulf, as Barth rightly notes, can obscure the real issue. And the real problem consists in the bridging of a gap between above and below, between the transcendent and the immanent. For the world's objective reconciliation is not merely a reality of the past: it is a present but transcendent reality in the risen Lord Jesus. The real problem concerns therefore the mediation and subjective realization of the reconciliation which is a transcendent reality in him. And as Barth once more rightly says, the answer to the problem lies with this transcendent reality itself. Just as Jesus Christ is the unique objective reconciler or mediator so also he is the supreme and ultimately unique subjective reconciler or mediator. He is this through his Holy Spirit and his apostles, both of whom he sends for this purpose.

The problem of mediation, therefore, and of the subjective realization of reconciliation, is answered basically and ultimately by the mission of the Holy Spirit. He is the Spirit of the risen Christ operative in the world for its subjective salvation. This does not mean, however, that the answer to the problem, or the problem itself, is *purely spiritual*. In this sense I must disagree with Barth when he says that the spatio-temporal is 'a blind for the real problem'.⁶ The mediation of reconciliation is spatio-temporal or sacramental as well as spiritual. Jesus Christ accomplishes subjective reconciliation through his Spirit and his apostles. I agree with Barth entirely when he says that this mediation cannot consist in a mere historical bridging of the time and space gap.⁷ This would indeed be a 'very disturbing fact'. But Christ's direct and spiritual action to each one in each time and place

---

⁴ Cf Col I : 14:18-20.
⁵ Cf *CTKB*, pp. 172f.
⁶ *Ibid.*, p. 172.
⁷ Cf *ibid.*, p. 173.

is not the only remaining possibility of mediation. For Barth it is the only remaining possibility because he excludes all cooperation or sub-operation of the human and earthly with the divine. Christ could have accomplished subjective reconciliation directly, of course. But factually this is not the way he determined. He determined to use visible means by sending human apostles and using their words and actions. This, too, is in understandable conformity with the way in which he accomplished reconciliation objectively, and with his love and consideration for the psychosomatic man to whom it is destined. Christ chose to mediate and accomplish reconciliation in this time between the times through the conjunction of a divine and human element, namely, through his divine Spirit and his human apostles. These together, in intimate union and collaboration, are the answer to the problem of mediation and of the reality and possibility of subjective reconciliation.

The primary factor is of course the Holy Spirit. He it is and he alone who creates the Church on earth the body of Christ, that is, the visible and earthly reflection of the peace and reconciliation which is a reality in the risen Christ. He it is and he alone who creates the Church the sign and instrument of reconciliation. The Church is the sign to all peoples and the world of the peace, justice, freedom and love of Christ solely because the Holy Spirit is present and operative within it. And the Church is the effective instrument of the extension or mediation of the same peace, justice, freedom and love solely because the Holy Spirit is present and operative in and through it. It is simply impossible to treat of the Church without treating of the Holy Spirit, for he is the ultimate principle of its unity and catholicity, sanctity and apostolicity, freedom and joy, peace and justice, renewal and growth. Everything good and holy that we can say about the Church is said basically about the Holy Spirit. Without him the Church can do no good. Without him it is no good. Without him the Church would not exist. It would not be what it is, viz. the sign and instrument of Christian salvation. Without him the Church would be a merely human and sinful reality. Certainly it is human and sinful. But it is more. It is the holy and salvific community, the *communitas sancta et sanctificans*. And it is this solely because of the Holy Spirit's indwelling presence and action.

The Holy Spirit is not of course the Church, nor is the Church the Holy Spirit. On the one hand, the Spirit is the third divine person of the Trinity, absolutely sinless and free, who creates the Church. On the other hand, the Church is not divine, but a created, human, sinful and erring reality.

'The Church is and remains something created. It is not something omniscient, and omnipotent, not self-sufficient and autonomous, not eternal and sinless. It is not the source of grace and truth, it is not Lord, redeemer and judge, and there can be no question of idolizing it.'[8]

The danger of idolizing or idealizing the Church is a constant one. Past Catholic triumphalistic theology and life have not been entirely free from it, and there is still one school of thinking within the Church which inclines very forcibly towards it. This is characterized by the attribution of immutability, infallibility and perfection to every manifestation of the Church, and also by the claim that persons and institutions within the Church are sinless, faultless, and have only the duty to speak but never to listen.

However, I disagree with Barth when he says that the Church is a purely human reflection, and when he repeatedly maintains that the Catholic explanation of the mystery of Scripture and tradition, the papacy, the Church's teaching authority, the sacraments, the Mystical Body, etc., leads of necessity to this idolization and divinization of the Church, or to the usurpation of Christ's unique Lordship.[9] While the Church is not divine, neither can it be said to be purely human. There can be exaggeration on this side too.

'At the same time we may not forget that the light of eternal glory is already breaking through in the Church, and that Christ already dwells in the Church, which is his body. A balanced view of the Church includes both aspects, the glory and the shadows, and enables us to distinguish that which is worthy of veneration and grateful praise from that which is the cause of sorrow and shame. One can err here by defect as well as by excess. For the Church is not merely the *ecclesia crucis*, it already shares in a measure in the glory of the resurrection and the final kingdom is not something that simply comes after the Church, as a new reality, but is a divine gift which perfects and brings to full fruition the kingdom as

---

[8] H. Küng, *The Church*, pp. 32-3. J. A. Möhler's saying (repeated frequently in various ways by later Catholic ecclesiologists) that the Mystical Body is the 'continuation of the incarnation' (*Symbolism*, London, 1906, sect. 36, p. 259) certainly leaves itself open to the interpretation that it transgresses this upper limit, To this extent, at least, we can agree with Barth's criticism; cf *The Church in the Theology of Karl Barth*, pp. 199f. Cf also H. Küng, *op. cit.*, p. 240, and the reference there to a W. Kasper, *Die Lehre von der Tradition in der römischen Schule*, Freiburg, 1962, pp. 141f.

[9] Cf *CTKB*, pp. 181, 198f.

already present. Failure to do justice to this principle probably goes far to explain the rejection by many Christians of infallibility, and therefore of dogma, or of the inviolability of the divinely instituted structure of the Church, or of holiness as a stable, interior, dynamic, and permanent quality of the Church and not simply a precarious gift which the Church does not truly make her own.'[10]

The Church is the intimate union in life and action of the divine Spirit and human and earthly people and realities. It is the union of opposites, of grace and sin, life and death. It is only when one begins with the supposition that such a union is impossible that one must speak of a purely human and a purely divine Church, and of apostolic and sacramental mediation as a usurpation and therefore abolition of divine lordship. The Church 'is one complex reality which comprises a divine and a human element'.[11] The divine element consists in the gifts, graces, assistances of the Holy Spirit who informs and indwells this particular people. The human element consists in the people, things and structures so informed. Both together form one mysterious reality. Neither of these constitutive elements can be exaggerated or attenuated if we wish to speak of the Church of Jesus Christ. In christological terms such an exaggeration or attenuation would be an ecclesiological monophysitism, manifesting itself on the one hand in an absolute divinization of the Church, issuing in Churchworship, Church idolization, triumphalism, immutability, *theologia gloriae*, pride, arrogance, Pelagianism, and on the other hand in an absolute humanization of the Church, issuing in relativism, indifference and historicism. Barth, I am convinced, speaks of a divine *and* a human Church as two distinct realities, and attributes salvific mediation solely to the divine Church, that is, to the Holy Spirit. Thus just as he is Nestorian and monophysite in his explanation of the mystery of the being and work of Jesus Christ so also he is Nestorian and monophysite in his explanation of the being and work of the Church of Jesus Christ.[12] And for the very same reason, namely, that any union or co-operation between God and man in the work of salvation would be a denial of God's sole subjectivity as affirmed basically in the doctrine of justification. It is precisely because he denies the possibility of intimate union and co-operation between the Holy Spirit and this particular people that Barth is led to absorb

---

[10] K. McNamara in *Vatican II: The Constitution on the Church*, p. 28.
[11] DCC, n. 8.
[12] Cf above, Section Two, chapters seven and eight, esp. pp. 69–70, 74f.

all salvific activity and reality into the divine: Jesus Christ (or the Spirit of Jesus Christ) is the Church.[13] It is precisely because Catholic ecclesiology affirms the intimate union and co-operation of the Holy Spirit and this people in one salvific reality that it is neither Nestorian nor monophysite in ecclesiology.

The presence and action of the divine Spirit in and through the Church must be emphasized by Catholic theologians and preachers in their presentation of the mystery of the Church and of Christian life. Paradoxical though it may seem, this is the basic answer of the Roman Catholic Church to the usual Protestant accusation of triumphalism, pride, arrogance, Pelagianism. It corresponds to the emphasis required in the doctrine of justification on the divine origin of all grace and salvation. The *solo Spiritu* is the ecclesiological correspondence to *sola gratia*. To judge from some pre-conciliar ecclesiological treatises, the Church is predominantly an external, visible, juridical society, much like any other human society. Historically, this way of viewing the Church arose as a counter to Protestant insistence on the interior, invisible and spiritual side of the Church. Unfortunately, it became exaggerated in the counter-Reformation. Not that this explicitly denied what the Protestant Reformers insisted upon; it presupposed and then passed over it. Protestant ecclesiology, on the other hand, has very often explicitly denied what Catholics liked to insist upon. In practice, however, Catholic ecclesiology has been just as one-sided as Protestant. It insisted so much on one aspect that it easily gave the impression of denying any other. Thus in so far as we neglected the divine origin and spiritual nature of the life of the Church and passed over it in silence it is easy to understand how Protestants could accuse us of human arrogance and pride. For if (apparently) we speak of the Church as only a historical reality like any other then it is the height of pride and arrogance to say that it is holy with the holiness of God, confers grace, is infallible, etc. These are divine prerogatives and are prerogatives of the Church solely because the latter is not a purely human reality but is the dwelling-place and instrument of the divine Holy Spirit.

The lack of mention of the Holy Spirit in recent Catholic theology, especially in its ecclesiology, and on the other hand, its strong emphasis on our Lady, precisely in relation to the Church, can explain the Protestant theologian's frustrated remark that the Catholic Trinity consists of Father, Son and Virgin Mary. Or again, the same failure to bring out the role of the Spirit in the Church, especially in relation to the eucharist, makes it very difficult for the

[13] Cf *CTKB*, pp. 259f.

Eastern Orthodox, with their liturgical and theological emphasis on the *epiclesis*, to recognize the Roman as really the *catholic* Church.[14] The name 'Pentecostal Church' conjures up immediately and solely an image of a Protestant sect whereas it is the basic description of the Catholic Church—as indeed of every Christian Church. Theology and preaching must remedy the false impression we have created in the past. It is necessary to counterbalance our former onesidedness by emphasizing the Church's pneumatological aspect. Significantly, this was the way of the great pre-Reformation (and therefore also pre-counter-Reformation!) scholastic theologians such as Alexander of Hales, Bonaventure and Thomas Aquinas. They centred their attention on the internal, invisible life of the Church, and on the author of this life, the Holy Spirit.[15] Even in its most visible function the Church is never merely human. It is a mystery, the mystery of the Holy Spirit. As R. Schnackenburg has so well said:

'The Church is not understood if it is only regarded as an institution, even as one founded by Jesus, or as an association of Christian believers, in the sense of an establishment or society willed by God. It is necessary to realize in addition to this that the Church owes to the divine Spirit of life and holiness its origin and existence, form and continuance, to that Spirit which since and through Jesus's glorification comprises and fills, unites and directs all who believe and are newly begotten in baptism. Through the Spirit of Christ the society of those who believe in him becomes the Church of Christ; through the Spirit, Christ becomes the Lord of his Church.'[16]

Christ's mission of the Spirit is clearly portrayed for us in the New Testament. During his pre-resurrection earthly life Jesus promised to send his Spirit. 'And I will pray the Father, and he will give you another Counsellor, to be with you for ever, even the Spirit of truth.'[17]

---

[14] This failure of the Western Church has received an initial but decided correction with the publication of the three new eucharistic prayers or canons of the Mass as possible alternatives in the Latin rite to the existing one Roman canon. The texts may be found in *The New Eucharistic Prayers and Prefaces*, London, 1969; see also *Notitiae*, May–June 1968, pp. 168f, and *The Furrow*, July 1968, pp. 415f. All three emphasize the role of the Holy Spirit in the eucharist.

[15] Cf Congar, *Esquisses* . . . , pp. 65–9, and note 2, p. 68 (Engl. translation *The Mystery of the Church*, pp. 56–9, where the note is not given).

[16] *The Church in the New Testament*, p. 160. Cf also H. de Lubac, *The Splendour of the Church*, p. 158.

[17] Jn 14:16–17. Cf 14:26; 15:25; 16:7f.

This was a promise and therefore concerned the future. Jesus had first to be glorified and exalted. 'As yet the Spirit had not been given, because Jesus was not yet glorified. . . . It is to your advantage that I go away, for if I do not go away, the Counsellor will not come to you; but if I go, I will send him to you.'[18] The sending of the Spirit depended on his own glorification and exaltation. This glorification and exaltation began at his resurrection. His sending of the Spirit of life, holiness and power depended on his installation as the living Lord, and his definitive constitution in the holiness and power of God. And he was 'constituted Son of God in power according to the Spirit of holiness by his resurrection from the dead, Jesus Christ our Lord'.[19] Accordingly it is the *risen* Christ who fulfils the promise to send the Holy Spirit. Only then did he become the head of the Church, only then was the reconciliation of all accomplished. The resurrection is as much part of Christ's redemption as his pre-resurrection life and death, as Barth so admirably reminds us in the footsteps of St Paul: Christ was 'put to death for our trespasses and raised for our justification. . . . If Christ had not been raised, your faith is futile and you are still in your sins.'[20] It was only with the completion of his redemption in his resurrection that Christ became the life-giving and spiritualizing principle of all.

According to John the sending of the Spirit took place on the day of the resurrection itself.

> 'On the evening of that day, the first day of the week . . . Jesus came and stood among them and said to them . . . "Peace be with you. As the Father has sent me, even so I send you." And when he had said this, he breathed on them, and said to them, "Receive the Holy Spirit. If you forgive the sins of any, they are forgiven; if you retain the sins of any, they are retained".'[21]

Luke however places the event of the Spirit's coming in the context of an Israelite end of the harvest feast of fruit offering to Yahweh which took place fifty days (*pentekostē*) after the feast of the unleavened bread.[22] In the second century before Christ this feast was celebrated as the liturgical anniversary of the giving of the Law to Moses on Sinai which had been set as having taken place fifty days after the

[18] Jn 7:39 and 16:7.
[19] Rom 1:4. For further elucidation of the connection between the resurrection and the sending of the Spirit, cf F. X. Durrwell, *The Resurrection. A Biblical Study*, London–New York, 1960, pp. 78–107.
[20] Rom. 4:25 and I Cor. 15:17. Cf *CTKB*, pp. 175f.
[21] Jn 20:21–23.
[22] Cf Collins, *art. cit.*, in *Scripture*, 20 (1968), 74f.

departure from Egypt (cf Ex 19:1-6). The theophanies presented by Luke in his narration of the coming of the Spirit resemble strongly the old covenant events at Sinai (cf Ex 19:16-20). He thus presents the coming of the Spirit in the context of the new covenant inaugurated by the Messiah. The coming of the Messiah was often associated with the coming of the Spirit (cf Lk 3:16 and par; 4:18). What Luke emphasizes is the reality, definitiveness and universality of the new covenant, of the messianic times, of the presence of the Spirit in the Church.

'When the day of Pentecost had come, they were all together in one place. And suddenly a sound came from heaven like the rush of a mighty wind, and it *filled all* the house where they were sitting. And there appeared to them tongues as of fire, distributed and *resting on each* one of them. And they were *all filled* with the Holy Spirit and began to speak in other tongues, as the Spirit gave them utterance. Now there were dwelling in Jerusalem Jews, devout men from *every nation* under heaven. And at this sound the multitude came together, and they were bewildered, because *each one* heard them speaking in his own language. . . . Being therefore exalted at the right hand of God, and having received from the Father the promise of the Holy Spirit, he has *poured out* this which you see and hear.'[23]

As it is clear from this Lucan account the presence of the Holy Spirit in the Church is both real and permanent. It is basically on this point of the reality and permanency of the Holy Spirit's presence in, union with and action through the Church that I must disagree with Barth's otherwise instructive doctrine of the Holy Spirit. Christ's presence through his Spirit does not take place exclusively by means of an ever-new direct act from heaven. Risen and glorified he sent his Spirit definitively and permanently to indwell his Church. Christ really gifts himself to his Church and his followers participate in his life and power. 'Pentecost reveals . . . that this communication of the Spirit is no longer a sporadic breathing, as it was for the prophets, but has happened definitively and irrevocably.'[24] The apostles are told that they know the Spirit 'for he dwells with you, and will be in you' (Jn 14:17). They are given a participation in the Spirit's power

[23] Acts 2:1-6, 33.
[24] K. Rahner and H. Vorgrimler, *Concise Theological Dictionary*, Freiburg–London, 1965, p. 211. As E. Schweizer puts it: 'That means that the Spirit is given to all members of the community, and that he is given lastingly': *TWNT*, VI, 408, 4-5.

to forgive sins (Jn 20:22–23). They are given a participation in the Spirit's power to witness faithfully to Christ (Acts 1:8). St Paul asks: 'Do you not know that your body is a temple of the Holy Spirit within you, which you have from God?' (I Cor 6:19). The Holy Spirit really dwells in the Church. And his indwelling is a permanent reality. There is only one mission of the Spirit spoken of. Christ prays the Father to send another Counsellor 'to be with you for ever'.[25] He is not merely present in momentary acts and manifestations; he 'fills the whole house' and 'dwells' amongst them (Mt 28:20).

This real and permanent indwelling and possession of the Spirit is the distinctive trait of the New Testament. Long before, it was foretold by the prophet Ezekiel. The house of Israel is like a valley of bones, he says. But the advent and action of the Spirit will be comparable to the action of God in the creation of man: he will breathe into it the breath of life and it will become a living reality.[26] The Lord promises that in the last days he will sanctify the house of Israel again as his people through his Spirit (cf. Ezek 37: 14, 28). Peter and Luke are aware that Pentecost is the fulfilment of the Old Testament prophecy as regards the eschatological people of God. 'But Peter lifted up his voice and addressed them: This is what was spoken by the prophet Joel: "And in the last days it shall be, God declares, that I will pour out my Spirit upon all flesh, and your sons and your daughters shall prophesy . . . and I will show wonders in the heavens above and signs on the earth beneath." '[27] Pentecost, or the outpouring of the Spirit, is the inauguration of the 'last time' of salvation, the time of the Church. Because of this outpouring the Church already possesses an anticipated participation in its final full possession of the Spirit. Even now on earth it is marked with a genuine if imperfect holiness, is signed with the Spirit 'who is the guarantee of our inheritance' (Eph 1:14), and its members are truly sons and heirs of God (Gal 4:6–7; I Jn 3:1). But precisely because it possesses the first fruits of the Spirit it realizes its exile from the Lord (II Cor 5:6), and groans within itself (Rom 8:19–23) desiring to be with him (Phil 1:23).[28] The present outpouring of the Spirit is not the final consummation. The Church is essentially a pilgrim Church, a Church on the way, a Church impelled ever forwards and upwards by its very foretaste of what it will be.

The Church is not a vacuum therefore with regard to the presence

[25] *hina ē meth' humōn eis ton aiōna*: Jn 14:16. Cf 16:7. There is one coming of the Spirit as there is one going of the Lord.
[26] Cf Ezek 37:1f and Gen 2:7.
[27] Acts 2:16f; Jl 2:28–32; Num 11:29. [28] Cf DCC, n. 48.

of its heavenly head, Jesus through his Spirit, as Barth notes.[29] He lives in it through his Spirit guiding, teaching and sanctifying 'to the close of the age' (Mt 28:20). St Paul depicts this Holy Spirit as the mode of presence and activity of the risen Christ in this time between his ascension and final coming. He is the way in which Christ is present in the time of the Church. The time of the Church is, consequently, the time of the Spirit. Barth would seem to be right in his description of the Spirit as a mode of being of God.[30] The Spirit is the mode of the risen Christ's presence and action in this time between the times. He is the presence of Jesus in power. We must beware, however, of identifying Jesus Christ and the Spirit. Ecclesiology must be equally theocentric, christocentric and pneumatocentric. The mission of the Spirit is not simply a continuation of that of Christ. It is a new mission 'from the Father' of 'another Counsellor'.[31]

Admittedly II Cor 3:17 would seem to demand an identification of Christ and the Spirit: 'Now the Lord is the Spirit. . . .' However, the interpretation of this passage in the light of the Palestinian Targum on which it depends throws some light on the old exegetical crux. In II Cor 3:16 Paul says that whenever an Israelite turns in repentance to the Lord the veil is taken away. He is probably dependent here on the Palestinian Targum of Pseudo-Jonathan on Ex 33:7. The 'Lord' is consequently the Lord referred to in the book of Exodus, although a reference to Christ is naturally not excluded. The identification of the Lord and the Spirit in the following verse (II Cor 3:17) is also found in the same Targum (on Num 7:89). In the Targum the Lord is the Spirit in so far as he reveals God's will to Israel.

'For Paul this same Lord who is the Spirit will now fulfil the same function each time one turns to him by conversion. The Spirit will show him the true place of the Mosaic dispensation in God's plan; he will likewise give him the power to live according to God's will because he is a lifegiving Spirit (3:6, 8), and where this Spirit is there is liberty (3:17), a liberty that the letter of the law excludes rather than bestows.'[32]

The Lord of II Cor 3:17 indicates directly, therefore, the Lord of Moses and Israel. This Lord is the Spirit in as much as he will give an understanding of the place of the Mosaic dispensation, and the power of life and liberty, to those who turn to him by conversion.

[29] Cf *CTKB*, pp. 181f. [30] Cf *ibid.*, pp. 182f.
[31] *allon paraklēton . . . para tou patros*: Jn 14:16 and 15:26.
[32] M. McNamara, *The New Testament and Palestinian Targum to the Pentateuch* (Analecta Biblica 27), Rome, 1966, pp. 187–8, cf pp. 182–8.

The Spirit is not Christ. He is the distinct third person of the Trinity. Nor is his mission simply a continuation of that of Christ; he has his own specific role in the history of salvation. Jesus prays the Father to send 'another counsellor', who will 'bear witness to me' (Jn 14:16 and 15:26). But while the mission and work of the Spirit is distinct from that of Christ it is closely related to it. Its object is not the accomplishment of a new work in relation to that of Christ but the realization or accomplishment in men of all times and places of the reconciliation accomplished once and for all in and by *Jesus Christ*. This is particularly emphasized in the Gospel of St John. The function of the Spirit is directly related to that of Christ. He is to bear witness to Christ, to bring to remembrance all that he said. No less than the ministry of the community the witness of the Spirit is not its own origin, content or goal. It is completely christocentric. Hence, as Barth also forcibly puts it,[33] the work of the Spirit will never be a completely new revelation, subjective illumination, inspiration or enthusiasm, unrelated to the objective word and work of Jesus Christ, and therefore also to the objective side of the Church.

This relationship of the subjective to the objective, of the Spirit to Christ, can be regarded as the basis of all ecclesiological differences between the Christian Churches and sects. It excludes all 'pentecostalism' in the sense of all material additions in the time of the Church, in the form of immediate spiritual inspirations, to the objective signgiving. The Holy Spirit brings the work of Christ to accomplishment in all men and space and time, just as Christ brought the work of the Father to accomplishment. Christ is sent to do the will of the Father; the Spirit is sent to do the will of Christ. For this reason the mission of the Spirit is portrayed in the New Testament as a mission not only by the Father (cf Jn 14:26, 16) but also by the Son (cf Jn 15:26; 16:7; Acts 2:33). And this dependence of the Spirit on the Father and the Son in the economy of salvation presupposes a dependence in the eternal procession of the three divine persons—that which is described by the Council of Constantinople as the Spirit's procession from the Father and the Son.[34] The denial of the eternal procession of the Spirit from the Son (*Filioque*) can lead, and has in fact led in the case of Eastern Orthodoxy, to a certain predominance and independence of subjective inspiration in the Church over against objective authority. St Thomas expressed it thus:

'To say that the Vicar of Christ, the Roman pontiff, does not hold the primacy in the universal Church is an error analogous to that

[33] *CTKB*, pp. 187-8.   [34] 'Qui ex Patre Filioque procedit', DS 150.

which denies that the Holy Spirit proceeds from the Son. For Christ, the Son of God, consecrates his Church and consecrates it to himself by the Holy Spirit as by his seal or stamp. In a similar way, the Vicar of Christ, by his primacy and government like a good servant preserves the universal Church subject to Christ.'[35]

For this reason then also the Spirit's function is described in the New Testament as one in which he will bear witness to Christ (cf Jn 15:26; 4:1f), bring to remembrance all that Christ has said (Jn 14:26), guide the Church into the truth of Christ (Jn 16:14f). During the Church's initial expansion and formation he completes and perfects the revelation and institutions of Jesus (cf Jn 16:12f).

It is important to remember this intervening activity of the Spirit if we are to reconcile, say, the forms of ministry of the early Christian community as witnessed to in writings such as the Acts of the Apostles and the Pastoral Epistles with the original intention of Jesus himself as witnessed to by the synoptic Gospels. It is something which is often overlooked by Protestant writers (and Catholic, too, and by C. Davis) who cannot see, for instance, how the New Testament attributes to *Jesus* the foundation of a hierarchical Church. The forms of ministry which arose are not simply to be brushed aside with the comment of 'developing Catholicism' (E. Käsemann), but are to be understood as the concretizations of the actual influence of the Holy Spirit. Thus the hierarchical mission and succession which took place in the early community, as witnessed to by passages such as I Cor 4:17; I Thess 3:2-6; I Tim 1:3; Tit 1:5; Acts 14:23 and II Tim 2:2, is obviously the result of the understanding granted by the Holy Spirit into Jesus' intention with regard to the Church as outlined, for instance, in passages of the Gospels such as John 14:26 and Matthew 28:18-20.

The Church is not without its heavenly head in its earthly historical journey towards eternity. He is present within it through his Spirit,

---

[35] *Contra Errores Graecorum*, Parma ed., 15:256; Paris Ed., Vivès, 29:369 (=lib. 2, prol.), cited in Congar, *Esquisses* . . . , pp. 136f. (the English translation, p. 111, diminishes slightly the complete christocentricity of Congar's translation). Eastern theology and liturgy have always emphasized the position and role of the Holy Spirit in the Church. Western theology has emphasized more the position and role of Christ. And having noted the danger in the Eastern emphasis it is only fair and much more relevant to note also how this traditional Western insistence on and development of the christological dimensions of the Church has led to a predominant insistence on objective authority and law over against, and to the detriment of, the aspects of communion of life, inspiration, freedom and charismata. Both points of view must complement each other.

in the sacraments, especially in the eucharist, but also in the Church's instituted and charismatic ministry. This is a reassuring thought, as well as a warning, in an age of transition and upheaval such as our own. It is a reassurance and warning to all who are inclined to view the Church as a given, static reality and therefore are wary of change and innovation. The coming and presence of the Spirit always means growth, movement, renewal.[36] And it is a warning and reassurance to those who are inclined to regard the Church as a completely new creation of the Spirit in every age and culture. The Spirit maintains an essential identity of the Church of all ages, and speaks through its instituted structures (in the variety of its historical forms), for he is the Spirit of Christ who founded the Church. This 'institutionalized' activity of the Spirit will, however, be rendered more apparent if it is not always restricted to judging, rebuking and commanding (cf I Tim 5:29, 20, 7 and II Tim 4:2), but also '*guides* into all truth', and 'declares the things that are *to come*' (Jn 16:13).

The Church is the eschatological abode of the Spirit of the risen Christ. It is not easy to understand and explain the exact nature of this indwelling presence and union of the Spirit. It is not hypostatic as is the union of God and man in Jesus Christ. The Spirit fills and dwells in the Church but not in the sense that the resulting actions of the Church are personally the actions of the Spirit alone. He is the ultimate vital principle of everything good and holy that takes place in the Church. But he is not the only subject of attribution. Human beings, in and under his influence, are also subjects of these actions. The union therefore is not personal in so far as the distinction of persons is not eliminated. None the less it is a very intimate union. It is so intimate that Christ can say to the persecutor of the community: 'Saul, Saul, why do you persecute *me*?' (Acts 9:4), and of that which is done, or not done, to the least of his brethren: 'You did it (or did it not) to *me*' (Mt 25:40, 45). It is so intimate that the book of the Acts of the Apostles can be, and often has been, termed the Acts of the Holy Spirit. Fr Congar terms it a union of alliance based on God's decree and promise.[37] 'Then after fasting and praying they laid their hands on them and sent them off. So, being sent out by the Holy Spirit. . . . For it has seemed good to the Holy Spirit and to us. . . .'[38]

Two comparisons may throw some light on this union. Firstly,

[36] Cf Acts 2:4; 4:3; DCC, n. 4. We may recall that Pope John prayed that Vatican II might be a 'new Pentecost'.
[37] Cf *Esquisses* . . . , pp. 160f (Engl. transl., pp. 129f).
[38] Acts 13:3–4 and 15:28.

the union of Christ, through his spirit, and the Church can be compared to that of the human soul and body. The Spirit fulfils a function in the Church comparable to that of the soul in the human constitution. He is the principle of life and unity; he 'vivifies, unifies and moves the whole body in such a way that his work could be compared by the holy Fathers with the function which the principle of life or soul fulfils in the human body'.[39] However, the Spirit is not united to the Church exactly as the soul is to the body. The Spirit and the Church do not constitute one divine-human being. Furthermore, the comparison cannot be extended so far as to mean that the Church limits the activity of the Holy Spirit, as the body undoubtedly is a limiting factor with regard to the soul. The Holy Spirit is the Spirit of the risen and victorious Christ and hence is free and all-powerful with regard to the Church and the world. The Spirit controls the Church and not vice versa. Too much use of the parallel would result in a closed Church, and a static institutionalism which would leave no room for freedom, growth and diversity. The Spirit blows when and where he wills, and not solely nor always when and where the body wills. Therefore, while this first comparison does help us, it has severe limitations.

The second comparison is with the hypostatic union of the two natures in Christ. In the incarnation the human nature of Christ was thoroughly and permanently sanctified and exalted to personal union with God, and to the service of his redemptive work. At Pentecost the Holy Spirit fills and indwells the Church so that it is intrinsically sanctified and exalted to the service of his vivifying action. There is therefore a functional comparison, but only a comparison and by no means an identity, between the mystery of the incarnate Word and the mystery of the Church. The Church is the intimate union of a divine and human element: one theandric mystery.

'Christ the one mediator established and ceaselessly sustains here on earth his holy Church, the community of faith, hope and charity, as a visible structure through which he communicates truth and grace to all. The society furnished with hierarchical agencies, however, and the Mystical Body of Christ, the visible assembly and the spiritual community, the earthly Church and the Church enriched with heavenly things, are not to be considered as two realities, but form one complex reality which is comprised of a divine and a human element. For this reason, by a not inconsiderable analogy (*ob non mediocrem analogiam*), this reality is

[39] DCC, n. 7.

compared to the mystery of the incarnate Word. Just as the assumed nature inseparably united to the divine Word serves him as a living instrument of salvation, so, in a similar way, does the communal structure of the Church serve Christ's Spirit, who vivifies it by way of building up the body (cf Eph. 4:16).'[40]

The activity of the Spirit in the Church takes place in various ways. He acts through the mediation of the *external ministry* of the Church, that is, through the instituted ecclesial structure. We say the same thing when we say that the ministry of the Church and its instituted structure acts in his power. This applies to the *hierarchical ministry* within the Church of teaching, guiding and sanctifying (cf Mt 28:18b–20a). It applies to the sacraments, especially the eucharist. These create the community as the communion (*koinōnia*) of life with the Father in the Son by conferring the 'first fruits of the Spirit' (Rom 8:23). 'For by one Spirit we were all baptized into one body—Jews or Greeks, slaves or free—and all were made to drink of the one Spirit' (I Cor 12–13). The Spirit is conferred, or confers himself, through the laying on of hands: 'Then after fasting and praying they laid their hands on them and sent them off. So, being sent out by the Holy Spirit they went. . . [and] proclaimed the Word of God.'[41] The equivalence of the action of the Spirit and that of the Church's ministers and sacraments brings out the priority of the spiritual side of the Church. The Church is above all the reality and presence of the Spirit in the hearts of men, and the hierarchy and sacraments are in the service of this trinitarian life of the people of God.

It applies to the *ministry common* to the whole people of God, and in particular to that of the laity. The Spirit acts through their ministry, or they act in the power of the Spirit. All members of the people of God share, through baptism and confirmation, in the Church's one mission and function which is also that of the Holy Spirit. 'But you are a chosen race, a royal priesthood, a holy nation, God's own people, that you may declare the wonderful deeds of him who called you out of darkness into his marvellous light' (I Pet 2:9). The recognition and practical (i.e. canonical) provision for the implementation of this divine right and duty of the laity to service of the Spirit in the Church and the world is probably the most urgent need pressing on the Catholic Church today, and at the same time the one which promises most salutary consequences for the life of the Church.

[40] DCC, n. 8.
[41] Acts 13:3–5. Cf also 8:17–19; II Tim. 1:6–7

Besides acting through the Church's permanent structure the Spirit acts *internally* in the minds and hearts of those who hear and believe. He is not only the force in which the Word of God is preached (Acts 4:31 and 33); he is also the force in which it is heard and lived. 'No one can say "Jesus is Lord" except by the Holy Spirit. . . . No one comprehends the thoughts of God except the Spirit of God. Now we have received . . . the Spirit which is from God, that we might understand the gifts bestowed on us by God.'[42] This is clear from the fact that the sacraments are sacraments of faith, that is, they owe their fruitfulness not only to the action of the Spirit through the external rite but also to the action of the Spirit preparing and disposing their *faithful* reception.

Finally, the Spirit also acts *directly* and spiritually for the building up of the Church. While indwelling in the Church he remains transcendent over it. The Spirit blows where he wills. 'It is not only through the sacraments and Church ministers that the same Holy Spirit sanctifies and leads the people of God and enriches it with virtues. Allotting his gifts "to every one according as he will" (I Cor 12:11), he distributes special graces among the faithful of every rank. By these gifts he makes them fit and ready to undertake the various tasks advantageous for the renewal and upbuilding of the Church, according to the words of the Apostle: "The manifestation of the Spirit is given to everyone for the common good" (I Cor 12:7).'[43] These charismatic gifts are not an extraordinary phenomenon of the Church's life. The ones enumerated by Paul may sound strange but, on reflection, it is amazing how many are found in this present-day conciliar and post-conciliar Church, and more besides. It is the duty of the institutional Church to judge the 'genuineness and proper use' of charismata, but it is also its duty 'not indeed to extinguish the Spirit, but to test all things and hold fast to that which is good'.[44]

A consideration of the Church as the Church of the Spirit does not mean a purely charismatic Church, nor even a watering down of the institutional aspect. The institutional Church, too, has its ultimate meaning solely in the Spirit. That said, it is true that such a view of the Church does bring out the equal importance of the charismata. What it brings out above all is that the Church cannot be reduced to an external, static institution, with fixed laws and ordinances. The external serves the internal, and so must allow for

[42] Cf I Cor 12:3; 2:10f; Rom 8:12–17, 26–27; Gal 4:6–7.
[43] DCC, n. 12.
[44] Cf I Thess 5:12, 19–21 and DCC, n. 12.

freedom, diversity and growth of the Spirit of the risen and glorious Christ. Barth is right in insisting on the aspect of the Church as the event of the direct intervention of the Spirit. The Church is both an institution and an event, as we shall see later. His theology of response and of reflection finds here too its full justification. But even here one wonders if the charism is really bestowed on man. Event for Barth is a repeated giving, and never a gift. The response does not participate in the divine life and power, but remains a purely human reflection.

In all these ways the Holy Spirit forms the earthly-historical body of the risen Christ. He creates a fellowship (*koinōnia*) of saints on earth (cf II Cor 13:13). Undoubtedly, this appropriated role of the Holy Spirit corresponds to his role in the inner life of the Trinity of persons. Because he is the source of fellowship in unity in the eternal life of the Trinity he is also the source of fellowship in the unity of Christ's Mystical Body. Barth has some profound reflections on this point.[45]

There is one final aspect of the Church viewed as the Church of the Holy Spirit which is demanded by the dialogue with Karl Barth and which also lies at the root of recent trends in Christian spirituality and general Christian morale. As the Church of the Spirit the Church is the sacrament of the *risen* Christ. As Abbot Vonier said: 'It is the extension of the mystery of the resurrection.'[46] The Spirit who is its principle of life and action is the Spirit of the risen Lord Jesus. Consequently the Church of the Holy Spirit must be a Church of freedom and joy.[47] Christian life is a participation in the life of the risen Christ who reigns victorious over death and evil. 'For the law of the Spirit of life in Christ Jesus has set me free from the law of sin and death . . . [and] made us alive together with Christ . . . and raised us up with him, and made us sit with him in the heavenly places in Christ Jesus.'[48] The life of the Church cannot consist solely in an imitation of Christ in his mortal life of humiliation, sacrifice and death. As Barth repeats after St Paul: 'Death is swallowed up in victory.'[49] The Church cannot be the sign or sacrament of the suffering and dead Jesus, but of the risen Christ. The object of its devotion and imitation must be above all the risen Lord. This should have important consequences for its understanding of such things as the Mass, devotion to the eucharistic Christ, to the sacred heart, etc. If we must 'do' the

[45] Cf *CTKB*, pp. 188–91.
[46] *L'Esprit et L'Epouse*, p. 85. Cf *ibid.*, pp. 72–5.
[47] Cf *CTKB*, pp. 72, n. 57, and pp. 182–5.
[48] Rom 8:2 and Eph 2:5–6.   [49] Cf I Cor 15:54 and *CTKB*, p. 177.

stations of the cross, for instance, let us remember that the last station alone points to the existing Lord, the head of the Church.

The Church must really and credibly become the sign of the risen Christ. Christian life is life, not death. It is a life which has conquered death, and must continue to manifest itself in victory over death and its sting, sin (Rom 6:4). We are not yet, of course, in full possession of the Spirit, or the Spirit has not yet full possession of us. The reality and possibility of sin remains. To walk by the Spirit then, or in this newness of life, entails mortification of the flesh, that is, of the love and service of self, which is 'from below', and is opposed to the Spirit, which is 'from above' (cf Gal 5:16f). In this our great exemplar is the Jesus who lived and died on earth (cf I Peter 2:21). But unlike Jesus, and thanks to him, we live lives that are not towards death but from death towards further life. We live with the life of the risen Christ. It is something positive, free and joyous.[50] It is a celebration of victory; a life to be lived; a power over death, evil and suffering; a mission of peace and justice to be accomplished. Many regard the recent more cheerful and activist attitude which has arisen in the Church simply as a manifestation of an over-optimistic naturalism. It is due far more to the renewed perception of the Spirit of the risen Lord as the source of the Christian life. This will have filtered through to the Church in general through renewed biblical, patristic, theological and liturgical studies, especially of the paschal mystery and its relation to the Church. And in this Karl Barth has made a valuable contribution.

The Christian life is basically one of joy. 'If we live by the Spirit, let us also walk by the Spirit . . . [and the] fruit of the Spirit is love, joy, peace . . .' (Gal 2:25, 22). Even from prison Paul's charge is: 'Rejoice in the Lord always; again I will say, Rejoice' (Phil 4:4). St Augustine has told us: We are men of the resurrection and alleluia is our song. The christian life is also one of freedom. 'Where the Spirit of the Lord is, there is freedom' (II Cor 3:17). Not arbitrary freedom to sin, but freedom from the old law and freedom to serve God which really makes us free. 'For the law of the Spirit of life in Christ Jesus has set me free from the law of sin and death. . . . Live as free men, yet without using your freedom as a pretext for evil; but live as God's servants' (Rom 8:2; I Peter 2:16). Human persons, laws and institutions must be at the service of this free and joyous life, and never crush, thwart, de-personalize or frustrate it, for its very existence depends on its freedom and joy. In Charles Davis' experience the Church he left was a 'sea of unhappiness and frustrations'

[50] The word 'joy' occurs eleven times in Philippians.

due to cramping institutions.⁵¹ Was not Nietzsche right in reproving Christians for regarding themselves as 'saved' but behaving in a manner not in keeping with their faith? Are our Christian lives full of that deep joy and humble thanksgiving befitting a people living gratuitously the life of its risen Lord? Certainly, the defeatism and pessimism so characteristic of modern novelists, as well as the predominant emphasis on death, suffering and mortification by spiritual writers and preachers, and in everyday Christian life, devotions and practices, ill accords with the spirit of the Church of Pentecost, that is, with the awareness of the presence and action of the Spirit of the risen Lord Jesus in the midst of humanity in this time between the times.

---

⁵¹ Cf his *A Question of Conscience*, London, 1967, pp. 21–2.

Chapter Thirteen

The Mission of the People of God

IN Karl Barth's understanding the Church is essentially *apostolic* or *missionary*. This can be said to be *the* great merit of his ecclesiology. For this reason I choose it as a type of *leitmotif* of my dialogue with him. I will try to give it the importance it deserves, and which Barth rightly demands. At the same time, within the framework of this dynamic ecclesiology, I will have to express reservations as regards Barth's conception.

At the close of his historical earthly life Jesus was aware of having accomplished his mission. 'I glorified thee on earth, having accomplished the work which thou gavest me to do' (Jn 17:4). In him the whole world is reconciled to God. And yet in itself the world remains to be reconciled. That which Jesus did perfectly and completely in himself for all men has to encounter man in other times and places and find each one's willing and loving acknowledgement. Jesus must become subjectively the light, the truth and way for all men. He himself effects this encounter. He does so through the conjoined operation of his Spirit and his apostles. Analogous to the way in which he accomplished the objective redemption he now accomplishes the subjective, that is, sacramentally, through the conjunction of a divine and human element.

The mission of Jesus by the Father is the starting point of the Church, for he was sent to become its head. 'He has made known to us in all wisdom and insight the mystery of his will, according to his purpose which he set forth in Christ as a plan for the fulness of time, to unite all things in him, things in heaven and things on earth.'[1] His task accomplished, Jesus sent his disciples as the Father had sent him. 'Go therefore and make disciples of all nations . . .' (Mt 28:19). The idea of mission is particularly strong in the Gospel of John: 'As the

[1] Eph 1:9–10. The Gk. text reads *anakephalaiōsasthai ta panta en Christō* and means 'to give all things their head in Christ'.

Father has sent me, even so I send you. . . . As thou didst send me into the world, so I have sent them into the world.'² And echoing St John, St Clement of Rome writes: 'Christ was sent from God, the apostles were sent from Christ.'³

The Church is essentially missionary or apostolic. Both these adjectives simply mean that the Church is a group of people who are *sent*. The Church is a people sent by Jesus Christ into the world for a definite purpose, with a definite task to perform. It is in mission. As Karl Barth notes,⁴ it is essentially apostolic, ec-centric, ec-static. Such a conception of the Church is typical of his christocentric, self-decentred and dynamic theology. It is also typical of the theology of Vatican II. It highlights excellently the *christological* and *functional* nature of the Church. The Church is unintelligible apart from its relation to, or rather from, Jesus Christ. He is its unique and permanent sender. This is the origin of, and sole reason for, its existence. It is unintelligible also apart from its relation to those to whom it is sent, or to that which it is sent to do. Mission implies movement from and towards. The Church is a dynamic movement from and for and towards.

This means that the Church is essentially a service. In imitation of its head, the aim of its mission is the unequivocal service of the one who has sent it, and the faithful accomplishment of the work it is sent to do. 'My food is to do the will of him who sent me, and to accomplish his work.'⁵ As a French writer correctly says: 'The privilege of the apostles can in no way be conceived as a benefit for those who hold it. It is a twofold service, completely related to their mission.'⁶ Existence in the Church, Christian existence, is essentially an existence in service. It is directed away from itself. This applies both to life and action and office. For example, it is not the external office and action which count, but the internal reality they are intended to transmit. Those members with a special mission, office or commission in the Church are completely in the service of the community and of the life they transmit. Similarly, the sacraments of the Church are completely orientated towards the life (*res*) they transmit. This was strongly emphasized in the ecclesiology of the Fathers preserved in the great scholastics. The Church is above all the reality and presence of the Spirit in the hearts of men, and the sacraments and hierarchy

---

² Jn 20:21 and 17:18.
³ I Clem 1–2.
⁴ Cf *CTKB*, pp. 122f, 315f.
⁵ Jn 4:34. Cf 12:28; 20:21; 7:16; 8:42; 3:17; I Cor 4:7.
⁶ L. M. Dewailly, *Envoyés du Père. Mission et apostolicité*, p. 70.

are in the service of this trinitarian life of the people of God.[7] This was brought out in Vatican II by its very designation of the hierarchy as 'ministry'. And specifically it says: 'That task, which the Lord committed to the shepherds of his people, is a true service, and in sacred Scripture is significantly called *diakonia* or ministry (cf Acts 1:17, 25; 21:19; Rom 11:13; I Tim 1:12).'[8] Bishops and priests exist in and for the service of God and his people, in imitation of the one who came not to be ministered unto but to minister, and to lay down his life for his sheep.[9]

But bishops and priests alone do not constitute the Church. They are not the only apostles. They are not the only ones sent by Jesus Christ. They are not the only ones in the service of the Lord. As Vatican II says:

> 'Pastors know that they themselves were not meant by Christ to shoulder alone the entire saving mission of the Church toward the world, but that it is their noble duty so to shepherd the faithful and recognize their services and charismatic gifts that all in their own way may cooperate in this common undertaking with one heart.'[10]

Every member of God's people is sent by Jesus Christ for a certain task. Every Christian shares in the Church's one basic mission and service. While all do not have the same function all do have a function. And even though there is an essential difference between the function of some and that of others there is a basic equality between all. 'If by the will of Christ some are made teachers, dispensers of mysteries, and shepherds on behalf of others, yet all share a true equality with regard to the dignity and to the activity common to all the faithful for the building up of the body of Christ.'[11] The equality in dignity of all, which in the Church enjoys priority of importance over all differentiation by position and function, is the common participation in the one grace, the one salvation, the one faith, hope and charity, the one call to perfection. The equality in activity of all is the common participation in Christ's priestly, kingly and prophetical functions.

We must be grateful to Barth for bringing out so forcibly the concept of the Church as an apostolic service, as a people 'in service'

---

[7] As Augustine said: 'For you I am a bishop; but with you I am a Christian. The former is a title of duty; the latter, one of grace. The former is a danger; the latter salvation', *Sermo* 340:1 (*PL*, 38:1483); cited also in DCC, n. 32. Cf also St Thomas, I–II, q. 106, art. 1.
[8] DCC, n. 24.
[9] Cf Mt 20:28; Mk 10:45; Jn 10:1.
[10] DCC, n. 30.
[11] DCC, n. 32.

because 'sent'. I am convinced that the presence of this conception in modern Catholic ecclesiology and in the documents of Vatican II is not entirely without his influence. We must be grateful to him, too, for his emphasis on the fact that this apostolicity and service applies to the *whole* Church. There is only one mission of the Church, just as there is only one Church. There is only one goal of the Church's mission. There is only one ministry of the Church. It is a differentiated ministry, where each has his own function to perform in the accomplishment of the one mission, in the service of the one Christ to the world. The whole Church, all Christians, are sent in this service. All are apostles. With its affirmation of the basic common dignity, function, mission and responsibility of all members of the people of God, Vatican II has righted the Catholic Church's former onesided insistence on the dignity and function of the hierarchy, and has come a long way towards meeting the legitimate demands in this respect made by Protestant ecclesiology in general and by Karl Barth in particular. Certainly, the members of the hierarchy have a special mission and a special function essentially different from that of others. But all Christians have a special mission and a special function. The whole people of God is essentially and totally missionary and apostolic. All Christians are apostles. All are in mission. All are responsible for the Church. 'Whoever they are', the Council once more reminds us, 'they are called upon, as living members, to expend all their energy for the growth of the Church and its continuous sanctification.'[12] There is no place in the Church for idleness or complacency. Christian existence depends on the fulfilment of mission. Neither is there place for selfishness or self-centredness. The Church is not its own end, just as it is not its own origin. The primary concern should be the task to be accomplished and not one's own salvation or the treasures one is storing up in heaven. Christian existence is essentially an existence in service. It can be centred only in God, the neighbour and the world.

This is the dynamic conception of the Church and of Christian existence which is so characteristic of the theology of Karl Barth and of Vatican II. The Church cannot be an introverted, self-complacent, stagnant reality. It is the people of God—the whole of God's people— *moving* ever outwards and forwards, and therefore upwards, through human history in fulfilment of its *mission*. I am not, however, completely satisfied with Barth's conception of the 'apostolic Church'.[13]

[12] DCC, n. 33.
[13] The following remarks are directed in particular to Barth's doctrine as expounded in *CTKB*, p. 315f, 284, 125, 232; and above, pp. 120f.

There is a tendency in his ecclesiology to an over- and uni-functionalism, which becomes quite apparent in the thought of some of his followers. The following three points should clarify what I mean.

Firstly, the Church is not a *pure function*. It is also a fellowship. It is a 'diakonia' *and* 'koinōnia', a 'diakonia' *in* 'koinōnia'. This more balanced concept of the Church was expressed by the second Vatican Council in the following terms: 'Established by Christ as a *fellowship (communio)* of life, charity and truth, it is *also used* by him as an instrument for the redemption of all, and is sent forth into the whole world as the light of the world and the salt of the earth (cf Mt 5:13–16).'[14]

Secondly, while one of the primary tasks of the Church's mission is witness to the world, this is only *one* of its tasks, or only one of the aspects of its task. The Church exists in the service of Jesus Christ and therefore of the world. It fulfils this service in its triple ministry of priesthood, kingship and prophecy. One should not let the three aspects of Christ's ministry run into the one aspect of prophecy in this time between the times,[15] nor should one treat of the Church's ministry solely under the aspect of prophetic witness.[16] In this respect, too, the ecclesiology of Vatican II is far more balanced:

> 'Just as Christ was sent by the Father, so also he sent the apostles, filled with the Holy Spirit. This he did so that, by preaching the Gospel to every creature (cf Mk 16:15), they might proclaim that the Son of God, by his death and resurrection, had freed us from the power of Satan (cf Acts 26:18) and from death, and brought us into the kingdom of his father. His purpose was also that they might exercise the work of salvation which they were proclaiming, by means of sacrifice and sacraments, around which the entire liturgical life revolves.'[17]

Undoubtedly Barth exaggerated the aspect of witness in order to restore the sense of mission to the Church. On the other hand, his exaggeration is quite in line with his doctrine of the subjective 'realization' (in the form of knowledge), of reconciliation; with his ecclesiology of 'reflection' and 'pointing'—one could say: with his John the

---

[14] DCC, n. 9 (emphasis mine).

[15] Cf *CTKB*, pp. 178, 192.

[16] Barth treats of it solely in his *C.D.* IV/3, whose title is: 'Jesus Christ, the True Witness'.

[17] Vatican II, *Constitution on the Sacred Liturgy*, n. 6. The Church does not merely communicate an idea. It accomplishes what it communicates. 'Christianity has a mission, not a message. . . . As news it is the report of an event that happens': L. Dewart, *The Future of Belief*, p. 8.

Baptist ecclesiology (that is, according to his understanding of Grünewald's painting), in which the precursor points to Christ on the cross; at bottom it is quite in line with his christocentricism.

Thirdly, the Church's ministry of witness is really a function *of the Church*. The proclamation of the Word of God is not always Christ's direct act through his Spirit. He does proclaim his word directly. But he also proclaims it through his apostles. In the Spirit of his power, or in the power of his Spirit, they too witness to him and proclaim his word.

One can see in Barth's theology the root from which a statement such as the following sprang:

> 'The *nature* of the Church can be sufficiently defined by its *function*, i.e., its participation in Christ's apostolic ministry. To proclaim the gospel of the kingdom throughout the *oikumene* is the Church's *opus proprium*, in fact, it is not her work at all but *ergon Kyriou*.'[18]

The understanding of the Church as a Church 'in mission' leads naturally to the question of its ministry. Sent by Jesus Christ the Church exists for a certain purpose, a certain service. Generally speaking this ministry can be described as a service of Jesus Christ, and therefore of the Church and the world, in the subjective realization of reconciliation. Now we must examine it more in detail. It is one, yet differentiated. First of all, it is differentiated as a threefold ministry of priesthood, kingship and prophecy. Secondly, it is differentiated as an essentially different participation in the one priesthood, kingship and prophecy of Jesus Christ. In dialogue with Karl Barth I would like: (i) to meet his demands as regards a christological and functional conception of the Church's ministry as service; (ii) to meet his demands as regards the diversity in equality of the Church's ministry; (iii) to question him as regards his denial of an essential differentiation in the Church's ministry.

---

[18] J. C. Hoekendijk, in *The International Review of Missions*, 41 (1952), 334.

Chapter Fourteen

The Mission and Ministry of the Laity

EVERY Christian is apostolic, that is, 'one sent'. This is his very essence. He is not a Christian if he does not accomplish the task and function for which he is sent. All the members of the Church participate in the Church's one basic mission and commission by its Lord. We can distinguish a triple aspect of this mission and commission, namely, a priestly, kingly and prophetic, in correspondence to the triple aspect of Christ's ministry. Jesus Christ continues to exercise his priestly, kingly and prophetic tasks here on earth through his Church. The laity, too,

> 'are by baptism made one body with Christ and are established among the people of God. They are in their own way made sharers in the priestly, prophetic and kingly functions of Christ. They carry out their own part in the mission of the whole Christian people with respect to the Church and the world.'[1]

I. THE BASIS OF THE LAITY'S MISSION AND FUNCTION

Traditionally, the anointing of the Christian to these three functions has been associated with baptism and confirmation. These sacraments, together with the sacrament of order, confer a certain seal or 'character'. This character has been explained as a spiritual

---

[1] DCC, n. 31. Usually, and also in the texts of Vatican II, the word 'ministry' is used only of the hierarchical ministry in the Church. The apostolate of the whole Church is also, however, a ministry, a service, a function (cf DCC, n. 34). Here I will use the word 'ministry' of all functions in the Church. The Council also speaks of a dignity and activity common to all the faithful (cf DCC, n. 32). In practice, however, there is no such thing as a 'common' ministry. I disagree with the terminology which speaks of the ministry of the hierarchy as a 'special' ministry and that of the laity as a 'common' ministry. The ministry of the laity, as of religious, is no less special and specific than that of the hierarchy.

instrumental power,² a participation in Christ's messianic functions of priesthood, kingship and prophecy. It is a spiritual power gifted to the Christian by the risen Christ through the sacrament.

Even as regards the ministry of the laity there is a great difference between the thought of Karl Barth and that of Catholic tradition. Firstly, with regard to its mode of transmission. In Catholic theology the sacraments are causes (only secondary and instrumental) of the risen Christ's anointing of the Christian to a participation in his triple ministry. Secondly, with regard to the participation of the Christian in Christ's ministry. Jesus Christ does not 'use' Christians as his instruments in the sense that he remains alone the effective subject. Through the sacrament he grants a participation in his own spiritual power to the Christian so that the latter can act in his power. Barth's doctrine appears to be no less opposed to the general Protestant affirmation of the priesthood of all believers (that is, that there is no essential differentiation in the Church's ministry, but all have the same power) than Catholic doctrine, even if for exactly opposite reasons. Barth says that all have an equal ministry to perform, but in the sense that *no one* has a sacred power. Catholic doctrine recognizes a true ministry of all, in which all have sacred power. But it recognizes an *essential diffentiation* in ministry and power. Barth's understanding of the Church and christology in the light of his principles in justification lead him quite consistently to this doctrine on the ministry.

Traditionally, also, the character conferred in baptism was closely connected with the priestly ministry, while that conferred in confirmation was closely linked with the prophetical ministry or the confession of faith.³ It would seem better, however, to say that both sacraments confer the power of exercising all three functions. The present preface to the chrism Mass on Holy Thursday speaks of the conferring of all three: 'That those who in the sacrament which thou hast established are anointed to the dignity of *kings, of priests and of prophets* may be clothed truly in the incorruptible robe of their state.'⁴ Vatican II

---

² Cf St Thomas, *Summa theol.*, III, q. 63, art. 1–3. Cf T. Marsh in *Sacraments*, ed. by D. O'Callaghan, Dublin, 1964, pp. 136f.

³ Cf St Thomas, *ibid.*, q. 63, art. 2–3; q. 72, art. 5–6; IV *Sent.*, d. 7, q. 1, art. 2. In confirmation he says the power of publicly professing the faith is received *quasi ex officio*. Journet says it gives a 'public, exterior and liturgical' value to one's confession of faith, *The Church of the Word Incarnate*, vol. I, p. 74.

⁴ 'Ut, secundum constitutionis tuae sacramentum, regio, et sacerdotali, propheticoque honore perfusi, vestimento incorrupti muneris induantur.' Cf J. Rogues, 'La préface consécratoire du Chrême' in *La Maison Dieu*, 49 (1957) 35–49, esp. pp. 45–6.

would seem to confirm this. The sacrament of baptism, it says, incorporates the faithful into the Church, consecrates them by a special seal or character to the exercise of the Church's cult, regenerates them as sons of God, and obliges them to confess before men the faith they have received from God through the Church. In baptism therefore the faithful are made priests of the Christian cult, are constituted kings in royal freedom over sin and self for the service of God and the world, and are sent as prophets to proclaim the faith that is in them. Confirmation continues what baptism has begun. It binds the faithful more perfectly to Christ and his Church and therefore strengthens their priestly, kingly and prophetic roles. Besides its general greater incorporation of the Christian into the Church it grants a special gift of the strength of the Holy Spirit and obliges more strictly to spread and defend the faith.[5]

Later on in its chapter on the laity the same Council document says that the lay apostolate is a participation in the saving mission of the Church itself (and therefore in its triple function), and the commission to this apostolate is received through both baptism and confirmation. 'The lay apostolate is a participation in the saving mission of the Church itself. Through their baptism and confirmation all are commissioned to this apostolate by the Lord himself.'[6] Participation in the Church's saving mission includes, as the Council had already pointed out, and as we have already seen, participation in its priestly, prophetic and kingly functions. Therefore baptism and confirmation basically depute one to the exercise of all three functions.[7] Besides being commissioned through the sacraments the laity also receive sacramentally the life of charity which is the soul of the apostolate. The Council continues: 'Moreover, through the sacraments, especially the holy eucharist, there is communicated and nourished that charity toward God and man which is the soul of the entire apostolate.'[8] The

---

[5] Cf DCC, n. 11, and the patristic references given there in note 35 (*The Documents of Vatican II*, p. 28).

[6] DCC, n. 33.

[7] Cf the commentary of F. Klostermann on n. 33 of DCC in *Commentary on the Documents of Vatican II*, ed. by H. Vorgrimler, pp. 240–1. It would seem that the Council sees a parallel, therefore, between the conferring of the episcopal ministry and the basic initiation of all the faithful to the Christian ministry. Just as the fulness of the episcopal ministry (in its threefold priestly, kingly and prophetical aspects) is sacramentally conferred in the sacrament of orders (cf DCC, n. 21) so the fulness of the initiation to the Christian ministry (in its threefold priestly, kingly and prophetical aspects) is sacramentally conferred in the sacraments of baptism and confirmation (cf DCC, n. 33).

[8] DCC, n. 33.

lay apostolate, or the transmission of the laity's mission, is effected by baptism, confirmation and the motive force of charity.

The mission and commission of the whole Church takes place, therefore, sacramentally. This has an important consequence. According to traditional Catholic theology the Church in her priestly and sacramental acts is not a principal cause but solely an instrumental cause completely and permanently dependent on the power of the First Cause. Their sole principal cause is God.[9] All the people of God receive their mission and commission from God himself, therefore, through the sacraments of baptism and confirmation. Thus the Council can say, in the words already cited: 'Through their baptism and confirmation all are commissioned to this apostolate *by the Lord himself.*'[10] This means that the laity and all the faithful by their very Christian and ecclesial existence are apostles. There is an apostolate incumbent on all on the sole basis of the reception of these sacraments. There is also an apostolate of more direct cooperation with the hierarchy to which some may be called.

> 'Besides this apostolate, which pertains to absolutely every Christian, the laity can also be called in various ways to a more direct form of cooperation in the apostolate of the hierarchy. . . . Further, laymen have the capacity to be deputed by the hierarchy to exercise certain Church functions for a spiritual purpose.'[11]

This opens a further immense field of possibilities in which the layman can exercise his responsibility. Needless to say, there must be cooperation between the laity and the hierarchy in every form of apostolate. While their functions are different both have the same origin and goal and are engaged in the same mission. Moreover, since authority in the Church belongs to the hierarchy, and the laity are a constitutive element of the Church, the latter must be submissive to the former.

However, the fact that the laity need the authorization of the hierarchy for a special type of apostolate, and must be submissive to the hierarchy in every type of apostolate, in no way detracts from their essentially divine apostolic right and duty. They receive their mission and commission sacramentally, and therefore from the Lord him-

---

[9] Cf e.g., St Thomas, IV *Sent.*, dist. 13, q. 1, art. 1, quaest. 3; disp. 15, q.1, art. 3, sol. 2; disp. 5, q. 2, art. 2, quaest. 3, ob. 1 and sol. St Augustine, *In Joh.*, tract V, n. 18 (*PL*, 35:1423) and tract VI (*PL*, 35:1428). Cf also E. Schillebeeckx, *Christ the Sacrament of Encounter with God*, pp. 103–4.

[10] DCC, n. 33.

[11] DCC, n. 33.

self (just as bishops receive their mission and commission sacramentally, and therefore from the Lord himself and not from the pope). They are essentially apostles, prior to any hierarchical delegation. It is not the mandate of the hierarchy (as, for example, in the movement known as 'Catholic Action') which makes some Christians apostles. All Christians are essentially apostles. 'The mandate of Catholic Action renders official, by endorsing it, a duty which is incumbent on every Christian in virtue of the sacraments he has received.'[12] The hierarchy has the duty of encouraging by every possible means the exercise of the divine commission of the laity.

Besides being sent and empowered through the sacramental action of the Holy Spirit the whole people of God are also sent to perform special tasks on the basis of the Holy Spirit's direct charismatic action (cf I Cor 12:7–11, 28).

'It is not only through the sacraments and Church ministries that the same Holy Spirit sanctifies and leads the people of God and enriches it with virtues. Allotting his gifts "to everyone as he will" (I Cor 12:11), he distributes special graces among the faithful of every rank. By these gifts he makes them fit and ready to undertake the various tasks or offices advantageous for the renewal and upbuilding of the Church, according to the words of the Apostle: "The manifestation of the Spirit is given to everyone for the common good" (I Cor 12:7).'[13]

These charismatic gifts are not an extraordinary aspect of the Church's life. Whether they are 'the most outstanding or the more simple and widely diffused'[14] they are an ordinary and essential aspect. This is emphasized by St Paul when he says that the greatest charisma is the most ordinary: love. 'But earnestly desire the higher gifts. And I will show you a still more excellent way. If I speak in the tongues of men and of angels, but have not love, I am a noisy gong or a clanging cymbal. . . . Love never ends; as for prophecies, they will pass away. . . . Make love your aim.'[15] Charisms are not proper to any one group in the Church. Where they occur they must be treated with the utmost respect. In particular it is the strict duty of the hierarchy to discern and further the responsible action of the laity

---

[12] J. Hamer, *The Church is a Communion*, p. 146, note 1. Cf the article by C. Koser, 'Cooperazione dei laici con la gerarchia nell' apostolato' in *La Chiesa del Vaticano II*, ed. by G. Barauna, pp. 994–1011, esp. 1005f.
[13] DCC, n. 12.
[14] *Ibid.*
[15] I Cor. 12:31; 13:1, 8; 14: 1.

on the basis of 'special graces' directly received. The Holy Spirit does not work solely through the hierarchy. He works also directly without them. The hierarchy has no monopoly of the Spirit but is completely in his service. It is their duty to judge the 'genuineness and proper use' of charismata but it is also their duty 'not indeed to extinguish the Spirit, but to test all things and hold fast to that which is good (cf I Thess 5:12, 19–21)'.[16]

Catholic ecclesiological theory has been developed onesidedly on the question of the Church's ministry since the Reformation. It has insisted upon and developed theoretically the Church's hierarchical ministry, as a counter to its denial by the Reformers. Relatively little was said of the role of the laity, or of the basic initiation of all the faithful to the ministry of the Church through baptism and confirmation. Not that it denied this aspect. Its onesidedness was more in theory than in practice. In practice it has always nourished and acknowledged the apostolate of the laity. Unlike Protestantism, which has theoretically and practically denied the Church's hierarchical ministry, it has not *denied* any essential aspect of the Church. It has neglected to develop, at least in theory, the concept of the Church in all its fulness. The recent Catholic 'ecumenical' movement has striven to develop this fulness.[17] The 'ecclesial'[18] position of the laity has begun to be developed also in theory, even if many points remain to be clarified. The constitutions and decrees of Vatican II present the result of the Catholic Church's recent attempt to overcome its former onesidedness as well as a stimulus for further reflection. For the first time in history the laity received explicit treatment in an ecumenical council. The hierarchy has been brought back from a position 'above' the Church, and the laity from a position 'outside' it.

The recognition and practical implementation of the mission and

---

[16] DCC, n. 12.

[17] I have already referred to this restoration of fulness as the essence of ecumenical theology, cf above, pp. 16f. 'None of the valuable precisions that theology has brought to the Church's structure and institution are denied; what people do want to do is to get beyond onesidedness, in so far as it may exist. Cannot all today's efforts be described as a search for completion and integration?'—Congar, *Lay People* . . ., p. 51.

[18] Fr Congar sees this development reflected in this word 'ecclesial'. Before the war, he says, the only derivative of the word *ecclesia* in use was 'ecclesiastical', with its obvious clerical overtones. 'Ecclesial' means 'belonging to the people of God or body of Christ', *op. cit.*, p. 50. For the above-mentioned onesidedness in Catholic ecclesiological theory since the Reformation, cf *ibid.*, pp. 36–52.

responsibility of all in the Church, and particularly of the laity, is one of the greatest needs, and also one of the greatest hopes, confronting the postconciliar Roman Catholic Church. It is a right and a duty, a privilege and an obligation, incumbent on all. On the part of the hierarchy it means the provision of at least the possibility for the active exercise of the laity's divine mission. Otherwise any talk of the responsibility of all in the Church's mission and function is pure deception or empty talk.[19] The provision of this possibility is a duty of the hierarchy and a *divine right* of the laity. It is not the hierarchy which confers responsibility on the laity, and hence it should not take it from them. The laity have a divine mission and no human being should prevent its exercise.

The practical and canonical implementation of the responsibility recognized by the Council as belonging to the laity in the mission and function of the Church will require much dialogue and mutual esteem between the hierarchy and the laity. This, however, ought to be the least one could expect in the Church of Christ. There will be no opposition or strife if each fulfils the mission assigned to it. There is only one basic task to be performed. All are responsible for its accomplishment. All gifts, graces and ministries in the Church have but one aim: 'The building up of the body of Christ.'[20] All therefore should exist in mutual acknowledgment and esteem, in mutual co-operative assistance, in the service of the one Lord, in the fulfilment

---

[19] The gradual but definite erection of universal, national, diocesan and parochial lay councils, in implementation of the strong recommendation of Vatican II (cf its Decree on the Bishops' Pastoral Office in the Church, n. 27), as well as the increasing requisition of the service of laymen in areas traditionally monopolized by the clergy, is a concrete proof of the hierarchy's sincerity on this point. (In his apostolic letter 'Catholicam Christi Ecclesiam' on 6 January 1967 (cf AAS, 59 (1967), 25–8) Pope Paul VI set out the norms for the two universal councils 'for the laity' and 'for studies' (or 'Justice and Peace'); and on Saturday, 6 April 1968, he named 27 lay people consultants to the Vatican in the fields of law, medicine, art and communications). Yet one still finds outbursts from the old order of things, where the responsibility for the Church is conceived to be the exclusive duty and right of the hierarchy. It is from this methodological and ecclesiological point of view, for instance, that many theologians bemoaned the encyclical *Humanae vitae*. If one is serious about the activity of the Holy Spirit in and through all believers, and if one is serious about the divine mission and responsibility of all the baptized, surely one would expect the laity to be consulted in a matter touching the very fibre of their existence? Why is the emphasis always on the divine right of the hierarchy and so very, very seldom on the divine right of the laity? Obviously because of an over-clericalized and onesided conception of the Church.

[20] DCC, n. 32, cf *ibid.*, n. 12.

of the one task. It would be illegitimate, and would inevitably lead to strife or separation, if the hierarchy were to assume all responsibility for the Church's mission. It would be illegitimate if the laity ignored their pastors and assumed all responsibility themselves. The laity has always the duty of living in communion with those who have been divinely constituted their teachers, priests and pastors. But the hierarchy have also a duty before the laity's divine right. They must see to it that the laity have the possibility of acting responsibly in the Church. And at this particular *kairos* of the Church's historical and theological journey the latter point needs the greater emphasis.

This would mean, amongst other things, that the laity's opinion on certain matters be requested. Very few would question the beneficial consequences such a procedure would have with regard to, for example, the subject matter and tone of pastoral letters and Church sermons, the opportuneness of a definite stand by the hierarchy on social and educational and other problems, the efficiency of financial and other types of administration, etc.

> 'Let sacred pastors recognize and promote the dignity as well as the responsibility of the layman in the Church. Let them willingly make use of his prudent advice. Let them confidently assign duties to him in the service of the Church, allowing him freedom and room for action. Further, let them encourage the layman so that he may undertake tasks on his own initiative. Attentively in Christ, let them consider with fatherly love the projects, suggestions, and desires proposed by the laity. Furthermore, let pastors respectfully acknowledge that just freedom which belongs to everyone in this earthly city. A great many benefits are to be hoped for from this familiar dialogue between the laity and their pastors . . .'[21]

Recognition of the mission of every member of the people of God implies, on the part of the laity, the joy but also the courage, the privilege but also the obligation, of assuming faithfully their divinely commissioned responsibility. They must eradicate once and for all the all too prevalent notion that the hierarchy is the Church. The Church is not simply bishops and priests, and bishops and priests are not alone responsible for the Church. The laity constitutes the Church just as much as bishops and priests, and all together are equally responsible for the Church. Recognition of this fact would also of course remind the faithful that in criticizing the Church they are in fact criticizing themselves, as Karl Barth also points out.[22] All the

[21] DCC, n. 37.
[22] Cf *CTKB*, p. 247.

members of the Church are in mission. All should carry out their mission in mutual respect and cooperation, animated by the one love of the one Christ, for the building up of his body.

II. A PEOPLE OF PRIESTS, KINGS AND PROPHETS

Through the sacramental and direct action of the Holy Spirit the laity participate in Christ's own priestly, kingly and prophetical functions, that is, in the one basic mission and commission of the Church. The fundamental biblical concept of priesthood is that of mediation. Israel was from the beginning a priestly nation, enjoying an intimate relationship with Yahweh and therefore able to mediate between God and all mankind. Priesthood means mediation between God and man which is naturally based on intimacy with God. Israel fulfilled its mediatory role in both an ascending and a descending manner. On the one hand, as the people of the Law, the chosen bearers of God's Word, it mediated the divine blessings of salvation to men, for it is through his word that God addresses man, revealing and giving himself in love, and on the other, by the offering of sacrifice, it gave expression to man's adoration and filial submission to God.[23] The idea of priesthood is closely connected with kingship and prophecy, as is clearly brought out in the classical text of I Pet 2:9 (cf Ex 19:6): 'But you are a chosen race, a *royal priesthood*, a holy nation, God's own people, *that you may declare* the wonderful deeds of him who called you out of darkness into his marvellous light.' The new people of God is in its entirety a priestly people as the mediator between God and the world, that is, as the universal sacrament of salvation.

Every member of the Church, that is, of the people of God of the New Testament, is in a true sense a *priest*, and has a priestly task. 'Like living stones be yourselves built into a spiritual house, to be a holy priesthood, to offer spiritual sacrifices acceptable to God through Jesus Christ.'[24] St Peter goes on to apply to the people of the New Testament the words spoken by God to his people of old: 'And you shall be to me a kingdom of priests and a holy nation.'[25] This priestly character and task of the whole people of God of messianic times was already foretold by Isaiah: 'But you shall be called the priests of the Lord, men shall speak of you as the ministers of our God' (Is 61:6). What is the nature and object of this priesthood of all? St Peter has already told us. It consists in the 'offering of spiritual sacrifices

[23] Cf K. McNamara in *Vatican II: The Constitution of the Church*, pp. 115f.
[24] I Pet 2:5. Cf Rev 1:6, 9; 5:10; Eph 2:19–22.
[25] Ex 19:6 = I Pet 2:9.

acceptable to God through Jesus Christ' (I Pet 2:5). These sacrifices are primarily spiritual (in contrast to the material sacrifices of the Old Law, cf Phil 3:4), internal and personal. They include *prayer* (cf Rev 8:4), *praise* (cf Heb 13:15), good works and suffering (cf I Pet 2:20b–21), goodness, and especially love towards others (cf Heb 13:16 and I Peter 4:8).[26] The whole personal and profane life of the Christian must be offered in worship to God. 'I appeal to you therefore, brethren, by the mercies of God, to present your bodies as a living sacrifice, holy and acceptable to God, which is your spiritual worship. Do not be conformed to this world but be transformed by the renewal of your mind, that you may prove what is the will of God, what is good and acceptable and perfect.'[27]

The specific object of the laity's priesthood is the world in which they live. 'They live in the world, that is, in all of the secular professions and occupations, in the ordinary circumstances of family and social life, from which the very web of their existence is woven.'[28] The laity are not, of course, so secular that they have to limit themselves to functions in the world. This could lead to a destruction of their religious and even Christian expression of life. They take their part 'in the mission of the whole Christian people *both* in the Church and in the world'.[29] On the other hand, those in holy orders are not so non-secular that they cannot 'at times engage in secular activities, and even have a secular profession'.[30] None the less 'a secular quality is proper and special to laymen. . . . By their very vocation they seek the kingdom of God by engaging in temporal affairs and by ordering them according to the plan of God'.[31] The special priestly mission, vocation and function of the laity is, consequently, 'the sanctification of the world from within, in the manner of leaven',[32] its offering to God as a sacrifice of praise.

> 'For all their works, prayers, and apostolic endeavours, their ordinary married and family life, their daily labour, their mental and physical relaxation, if carried out in the Spirit, and even the hardships of life, if patiently borne—all these become spiritual sacrifices acceptable to God through Jesus Christ (cf I Pet 2:5). . . . Thus, as worshippers whose every deed is holy, the laity consecrate the world itself to God.'[33]

[26] Contrast the forms of ministry mentioned by Barth, in *CTKB*, pp. 328–9, 332–3.
[27] Rom 12:1–2.
[28] DCC, n. 31.   [29] *Ibid.*
[30] *Ibid.*   [31] *Ibid.*
[32] *Ibid.*   [33] *Ibid.*, n. 34.

The priestly actions of the laity are not, however, solely spiritual, internal and personal. In the New Testament there seem to be also at least implicit references to the sacraments of baptism and the eucharist (cf 10:19–22). The Christian ethic is presented against a cultural background. In I Pet 2:5 we find all the ingredients: temple, priesthood, sacrifice. Although all exegetes would not agree, the Protestant exegete E. G. Selwyn says that for St Paul there was a connection between the spiritual priesthood of the people of God and the eucharist.

'The "spiritual sacrifices" of which Peter speaks have been correctly interpreted as consisting in righteousness, self-oblation, deeds of kindness and brotherly love, prayer and praise and penitence. But the background against which our author thought of these sacrifices, and out of which they arose, was the worshipping community gathered for the celebration of the eucharist and in particular, perhaps, for the baptismal eucharist, of which we have evidence in later days.'[34]

St Augustine speaks of a priesthood through incorporation in Christ.[35] He also associates priesthood with a special liturgical anointing, and with the sacrament of baptism.[36] St Thomas, too, speaks of an inward, spiritual priesthood,[37] and of a liturgical priesthood conferred by a special 'character' in certain sacraments.[38] In explanation Congar cites the following text of Thomas: 'In his passion [Christ] ushered in the *rite* or worship of the Christian religion by offering *himself* up as an oblation and sacrifice to God.'[39] Both the words 'rite' and 'himself' must be underlined. In place of the legal and material worship of the Old Testament Christ introduced a personal and spiritual worship of man himself. But the worship introduced by him is not something purely personal, private and altogether interior. It is an organized, social and institutional religion. To ensure the prolongation on earth of his own worship in the social and communal worship of the Church (and Christ remains its supreme author, its *verus sacerdos*) he gives to certain men a share in his priesthood. Journet points to the double consecration of Christ's humanity

[34] *The First Epistle of St Peter*, London, 1955, p. 297, cited in J. Hamer, *The Church is a Communion*, p. 104.
[35] Cf *Civ. Dei*, 20:10.
[36] Cf *Quaest. Evang.*, 40 (*PL*, 35:1355–6); *Enarr. in Ps.* 26, 2 (*PL*, 36:199–200).
[37] *IV Sent.*, *Dist* 13, q. I, art. 1, quaestiuncula 5; *Summa theol.*, III, q. 82, art 1, ad 2.   [38] *Summa theol.*, III, q. 63.
[39] *Ibid.*, q. 62, art 5, quoting Eph 5:2. In Congar, *Lay People* . . ., pp. 133f.

at the moment of the incarnation: he was consecrated the high priest of a supreme *cultus* and the source of all grace. Both of these consecrations overflow from him to his body, the Church. Only three sacraments confer a share in his priesthood.

> 'Something of the inalienable spiritual power which made of Christ the unique priest will pass into them along with the sacramental power or character of baptism, confirmation and order, spiritualizing them, making them ministers, the instruments, the cooperators of the one sole eternal priest.'[40]

The priestly actions of the laity have also a public, cultic and social aspect. The eucharist in particular is both the origin and goal of their spiritual priesthood. For, on the one hand, it is 'through the sacraments, especially the eucharist, that there is communicated and nourished that charity toward God and man which is the soul of the entire apostolate',[41] and, on the other, it is 'during the celebration of the eucharist that these sacrifices are most lovingly offered to the Father along with the Lord's body'.[42] In baptism and the eucharist there is especially created and manifested to the world the *fellowship* of God's people. Baptism is the sacrament of incorporation into the Church, the door through which the individual becomes a member of the community. Through it Christ establishes fellowship between God and man, and therefore between man and man. The same is true of the eucharist. 'Strengthened anew at the holy table by the body of Christ, they manifest in a practical way that unity of God's people which is suitably signified and wondrously brought about by this most awesome sacrament.'[43] By means of these sacraments that magnificent unity of God's people, which transcends all national, social, racial and cultural differences, is both effected and exemplarily proclaimed to the world.[44]

Jesus Christ, the unique high priest, wills to continue his own public worship in the social and communal worship of the Church. Through the sacraments of baptism and confirmation he grants to all a share in his own priesthood, enabling them to participate, not only passively and receptively, but actively, in the sacraments and

[40] *The Church of the Word Incarnate*, vol. I, p. 59.
[41] DCC, n. 33.
[42] *Ibid.*, n. 34.
[43] *Ibid.*, n. 11.
[44] Cf *ibid.*, n. 32. Cf Barth, in *CTKB*, p. 337. The provision of just such a community is one of the legitimate demands of the 'Slant' group of modern Catholic intellectuals. Cf, e.g., T. Eagleton, *The New Left Church*, London, 1966, and L. Bright (ed.), *The Committed Church*, London, 1966.

sacrifice of the Church's liturgy. Every time a Christian actively participates in the sacraments, for example in the eucharist, penance, and especially matrimony where the minister of the sacrament is not the ordained priest but the bridegroom and bride themselves, he is performing a priestly act. This is especially true of his active offering of the sacrifice of the Mass. Jesus Christ remains the supreme offerer. He offered his sacrifice once and for all. He offers it now as he did then, but in an unbloody and sacramental manner. He is now glorified in heaven. He offers it on earth through ministers. The power in which they act is his power. In this sense he remains the sole subject. But they also offer his sacrifice in his power. They also are subjects in his power. They offer through and with the specially appointed hierarchical minister, and through and with the supreme offerer, Jesus Christ himself.[45] This active power of offering the Mass is quite clear in the prayers of the Mass itself. 'Brethren, pray that my sacrifice and yours may be acceptable to God the Father Almighty.'[46] 'We, your ministers, as also your holy people, offer to your supreme majesty, of the gifts bestowed upon us, the pure victim, the holy victim, the all-perfect victim.'[47]

This priestly ministry is common to all baptized Christians. The officiating ordained priest should not be the only one who offers Mass. On the contrary, through a proper appreciation of the rites and prayers all of Christ's faithful who are present 'should participate knowingly, devoutly and actively . . . ; by offering the immaculate victim, not only through the hands of the priest but also with him, they should learn to offer themselves too'.[48] There is an essential difference between the hierarchical priesthood and the priesthood of the laity. The ordained priest alone, 'acting in the person of Christ, brings about (*conficit*) the eucharistic sacrifice, and offers it to God in the name of all the people'. None the less, all the laity really 'participate in the one priesthood of Christ', and therefore 'join in the offering of the eucharist'.[49] The primary aim of the restoration and promotion of the liturgy is the 'full and active participation by all the people',[50] and therefore precisely the full and active exercise of their ecclesial and Christian priesthood.

[45] Cf Pius XII, Encycl. *Mediator Dei*, in *AAS*, 39 (1947) 555–6=CTS transl. pp. 40–1; Vatican II, Constitution on the Liturgy, nn. 14, 48.
[46] 'Orate fratres' prayer from the ordinary of the Roman Mass.
[47] First prayer after the consecration.
[48] Vatican II, Constitution on the Liturgy, n. 48.
[49] DCC, n. 10.
[50] Constitution on the Liturgy, n. 14.

Secondly, all Christians are also in a true sense *kings*, with a kingly task. That this character and task is closely linked with that of priesthood is indicated by St Peter's use of the phrase 'royal priesthood' (I Pet 2:9). *Basileion* means, in fidelity to the sense of the Septuagint, belonging to the king. In so far as the holy priesthood belongs to the king it also shares in his glory. 'The priesthood serves the king, and in that it belongs to him it has a part in his kingship (*Herrlichkeit*).'[51]

True Christian kingship and authority has nothing to do with a dominion, control or tyranny over Christ or his Church, but is a spiritual freedom for their service. The risen Christ reigns over all created reality (cf I Cor 15:27). He communicates his kingly power to all Christians. Firstly, in order that they might be established in royal freedom as regards themselves. 'Now, Christ has communicated this power of subjection to his disciples that they might be established in royal freedom and that by self-denial and a holy life they might conquer the reign of sin in themselves (cf Rom 6:12).'[52] The kingship of Christians is first of all their spiritual power of self-control, of freedom from the reign of sin in themselves. Life in the Spirit of the risen Christ means freedom from sin and death (Rom 8:2), freedom as sons and heirs from slavery and bondage (Rom 8:15; Gal 4:1-11, 21f; 5:1).

Christ communicates his kingly power to all Christians, secondly, in order that they may be instruments of the extension of his kingdom to other men.

'Further, he has shared this power so that by serving him in their fellow men they might through humility and patience lead their brother men to that King whom to serve is to reign. For the Lord wishes to spread his kingdom by means of the laity also, a kingdom of truth, and life, a kingdom of holiness and grace, a kingdom of justice, love and peace.'[53]

Finally, Christ communicates his kingly power to all Christians in order that 'creation itself be delivered out of its slavery to corruption and into the freedom of the glory of the sons of God' (cf Rom 8:21).[54]

Living in the world 'the laity, by their very vocation, seek the kingdom of God by engaging in temporal affairs and by ordering them according to the plan of God'.[55] The proper and special, although not

[51] G. Schrenk, art. *hieros* in TWNT, III, p. 250.
[52] DCC, n. 36.
[53] *Ibid.*
[54] *Ibid.*
[55] *Ibid.*, n. 31.

exclusive, object of the layman's vocation is temporal affairs. This should correct any propensity to the idea of a mere 'Sunday Christianity'. If this was the impression created in the past its cause may be sought in the fact that professional theologians and spiritual writers were predominantly clerical and religious and these tended to conform the mission of the laity to their own. In this regard one can only bemoan the dearth of lay theologians. They would have offset the Church's past theological onesidedness. For the layman has a mission properly and exclusively his own. He fulfils his Christian and ecclesial vocation directly and above all in his weekday temporal occupation. He is to order it according to God's plan. In his case there can be no disjunction between religious and secular existence and activity.

The Council was on the way towards a new vision of the Church in the world which would have overcome this dichotomous view of reality. Nature and grace, temporal obligation and the life of faith, creation and redemption, should not be thought of dualistically. 'The division between the faith and the daily life of many should be considered as one of the most grave errors of our times.'[56] If more insistence were given to this point the oft-remarked contradiction or chasm between Sunday and weekday Christian life might be effaced. In the offering of the sacrifice of the Mass, and in his formal prayers, the layman renews the consecration of his whole life to God and obtains the strength to maintain the Godward direction of his life and of temporal affairs. But the immediate concretization of his Christian vocation takes place in his daily profession: he is a good Christian in so far as he is a good doctor, teacher, scientist, lawyer, politician, farmer, shop-owner or assistant, civil servant, factory worker, and so on. Certainly the offering of the Mass is an essential part of the layman's life. But it is not the unique fulfilment of his Christian vocation. Without the necessary correlative insistence on the fulfilment of his vocation above all in his everyday life there is the danger that worship and external religious practice will be used as a substitute or cover for social responsibility—in words heard before: there is the danger that 'religion' will be used as an 'opiate' (unconsciously to be sure) of the people.

Already in the Old Testament this type of thing was severely criticized by the prophets Amos, Isaiah (cf 1:16–17; 19–20) and Micah (cf 6:8). All these prophets emphasize the social iniquity of Judean society, and the iniquity or incongruity of rites of worship

[56] *Pastoral Constitution on the Church in the Modern World*, n. 43.

which are unrelated to common life. It is the great merit of secularization theology to have brought Christianity and the world together again, and for that reason it is capable of making a positive and valuable contribution precisely to the understanding of the mission and function of the Christian layman. The lay Christian's spirituality, mission and function is specifically incarnational, terrestrial, this-worldly, secular. His temporal and secular concerns and drives are one with his spiritual destiny. As a Christian he is the man for others, the pragmatic, functional, secular man, the builder of the technopolis and its inhabitant. It is to this that God's grace calls and drives him. This grace is of course from above. It is God's gift and justification, calling and sending him to involvement in the secular city. If the Christian cannot give himself unreservedly to man and his temporal existence it is hard to see how he will ever live in the present. As Teilhard de Chardin says: 'In the name of our faith, we have the right and duty to become passionate about the things of the earth.'[57] When one thinks of the work to be done in the fields of, for example, justice, peace, liberty, politics, the production and equable distribution of goods, the immensity and responsibility of the laity's task will be realized. Christ's reign over 'the principalities and powers, the world rulers of this present darkness' (Eph 6:12), is to be extended to the whole cosmos through human labour, technical skill and civic culture. 'Clearly then a great promise and a great mandate are committed to the disciples: "For all are yours, and you are Christ's, and Christ is God's" (I Cor 3:22–23).'[58]

Thirdly, all Christians are also in a true sense *prophets,* with a prophetical task. We can accept the term 'prophecy' here in the sense of a living witness to, and proclamation of, Jesus Christ. It corresponds to what Barth describes as the existence of the community for the world.[59] It must be pointed out immediately that the various aspects of the prophetic function of the whole community are not easily and clearly distinguished from one another. One need only think of the overlapping involved in terms such as mission, evangelization, preaching the Gospel, teaching the faith, proclamation, instruction, confession of the faith, apostolate, catechesis.

Just as the priestly and kingly functions of all Christians cannot be dissociated so both are closely linked with a prophetical function. According to I Pet 2:9 the very purpose of the royal priesthood of the

[57] Cited in *The Secular City Debate,* ed. by D. Callaghan, New York–London, 1966, p. 118.
[58] DCC, n. 36.
[59] Cf *CTKB*, pp. 315f.

people of God is *'that you may declare* the wonderful deeds of him who called you out of darkness into his marvellous light'. The 'wonderful deeds' are Christ's incarnation, life, death, resurrection, ascension and sending of the Spirit for the salvation of the world. According to Is 61:6 the priesthood of the community is not confined to the community but is meant to be a 'ministry of witness for humanity'.[60] St Paul brings out the necessary connection between priesthood and prophecy when he writes of 'the grace given me by God to be a minister of Christ Jesus to the Gentiles in the priestly service of the Gospel of God, so that the offering of the Gentiles may be acceptable, sanctified by the Holy Spirit' (Rom 15:15b–16). The whole people of God has a prophetical function in close relationship with its priestly and kingly. 'It spreads abroad a living witness to him, especially by means of a life of faith and charity and by offering to God a sacrifice of praise.'[61]

Jesus Christ is the one great prophet who proclaimed the kingdom of his father both by his example and his words. In this time between his ascension and final return he himself continues to fulfil his prophetic office. 'He does this not only through the hierarchy who teach in his name and with his authority, but also through the laity.'[62] The whole people of God has an active function in the transmission and interpretation of the unique revelation of Jesus Christ. Through the anointing of his Spirit Christ grants a participation to his people in his own messianic fulness of revelation so that it cannot err *in credendo*, in matters of belief. 'But you have been anointed by the Holy One, and you all know the truth.'[63] Through this sense of faith (*sensus fidei*), aroused and sustained by the Spirit, the people of God 'clings indefectibly to the faith once delivered to the saints (cf Jude 3), penetrates it more deeply by accurate insights, applies it more thoroughly to life', and cannot err 'when "from the bishops down to the last member of the laity" it shows universal agreement in matters of faith and morals'.[64]

Christian life is a participation in the love which motivated the Father's sending of his Son for the reconciliation of the whole world.[65] Because it is a participation in the life of *this* God it cannot be complacent or self-centred—nor even exclusively God-centred. It must

---

[60] G. Schrenk, *art. cit.*, p. 251.
[61] DCC, n. 12.
[62] *Ibid.*, n. 35.
[63] I Jn 2:20–1. Cf 2:27; I Cor 2:12, 16; Jn 14:17; 16:13.
[64] DCC, n. 12, quoting Augustine, *De Praed. Sanct.*, 14, 27 (*PL*, 44:980).
[65] Cf *CTKB*, pp. 315f.

also be man- and world-centred. Christians must bear witness to, and proclaim, God's 'wonderful deeds' (I Pet 2:9), his 'mighty works' (Acts 2:11), in an effort to lead all men to God. At Pentecost all were granted a special gift of speech, and recounted in various tongues the 'mighty works of God'.[66] St Peter saw in this the fulfilment of the prophecy of Joel: 'And in the last days it shall be, God declares, that I will pour out my Spirit upon all flesh, and your sons and your daughters shall prophesy.'[67] Here we are obviously dealing with special charisms of the Holy Spirit. Every Christian by virtue of his reception of the sacraments has a special prophetic ministry to perform in the Church. But the Holy Spirit does not act in the Church solely through the sacraments and sacramental ministries, as we have already seen.[68] Through special graces, distributed to whomsoever he wills, he inaugurates and sustains directly special ministries in the Church for its renewal and upbuilding (cf I Cor 12:7–11, 28). Both sacramentally and charismatically, and because the life they share in is the life of Christ for the world, all Christians share, and must actively share, in Christ's prophetic function. They have the right and the duty of 'bringing the Gospel to the world'.[69] In the last resort, it is not the Church which converts the world. 'Unless the Lord builds the house, those who build it labour in vain' (Ps 127). But God uses the Church as the channel of his grace, so that the Church can also be said to build the house. The Church is not the Holy Spirit. But the Holy Spirit indwells the Church. He ensures that there will be always true service, despite the sinfulness of men. He enables human beings to speak his Word, and to administer his baptism—not merely the baptism of water of the precursor of Jesus.[70]

Just as Jesus Christ exercised his prophetic function both through the 'testimony of his *life* and the power of his *words*', so must his followers also. For St Peter the 'declaration' takes place both through 'good conduct' (I Pet 2:12) and words (3:15). The Council includes both of these forms of implementing one's prophetic function under the one name of *evangelization*. This can be taken in the sense of Karl Barth as the proclamation of the Gospel to the Church's non-Christian immediate environment.[71] And in the case of the layman this proclamation has specific force. As the Council says: 'This evangelization,

---

[66] Acts 2:4, 11, *ta megaleia tou theou* corresponds to the *tas aretas* of I Peter 2:9. Cf Schelkle, *Die Petrusbriefe* . . ., p. 65.
[67] Acts 2:17. Cf 2:16–21; Jl 2:28–32.
[68] Cf DCC, n. 12 and above, chapter twelve.
[69] DCC, n. 35.
[70] Cf *CTKB*, p. 324.
[71] Cf *ibid*, p. 330.

that is, this announcing of Christ by a living testimony as well as by the spoken word, takes on a specific quality and a special force in that it is carried out in the ordinary surroundings of the world.'[72] The reason for this is that people are naturally more affected and provoked to reflection by the proclamation coming from one of themselves. And in addition, as those who live 'in the world', the laity understand the world. Their psychology and language is attuned to it. Hence they can diagnose better its ills, prescribe more relevant solutions, and administer better the remedies.

Christians must witness to him by the *example of their lives*. 'You are the light of the world. A city set on a hill cannot be hid. . . . Let your light shine before men, that they may see your good works and give glory to your Father who is in heaven' (Mt 5:14, 16). In this text our Lord is speaking to his disciples (*mathētai*, v. 2). Originally, the *mathētai* were a group of closer followers. But in the eyes of Matthew and of the early community they represent the whole Church, all believers. They are not merely the heads of the communities, or those with hierarchical ministry. This is clear from Matthew 28:19f where the eleven disciples are told to make disciples of all. Discipleship is not limited to the original disciples at the time of Jesus, nor to any group within the Church.[73] Matthew says that the whole Christian community is 'the light of the world' and 'the city set on a hill'. This ecclesiological application was natural for him. In the Old Testament and in Judaism these terms were applied to the eschatological Israel.[74] The Christian community is exhorted to be a light for the world, just like eschatological Israel. One should not push too far the 'indicative' character of *lampsatō* (Mt 5:16), or deduce from it that this giving of light outwards simply *is* the existence of the community.[75] The Church is essentially missionary. That is, it is essentially sent by Jesus Christ. It fulfils its mission in so far as it exists as a fellowship of the Holy Spirit and exercises its three ministries of priesthood, prophecy and kingship. It is not solely a function, nor is its function solely one of witness.[76]

According to Mt 5:14f one of the essential functions of the community is to give light. This is not its sole function, much less its whole

---

[72] DCC, n. 35.

[73] Cf R. Schnackenburg, in *Mélanges E. Tisserant*, vol. I, pp. 374–7: 'Der mathetes-Begriff bei Matthäus'.

[74] Cf Is 60:1–3; 2:2–4 Mic 4:1–2; Midrash on Cant. of Cant. 1–3; Gen rabba 59 in Str.–Bill., 1,237, under c and e (references in Schnackenburg, *art. cit.*, pp. 379f). Cf G. von Rad, 'Die Stadt auf den Berge' in *Evang. Theol.*, 8 (1948–49) 439–47, and A. Oepke art., *lampo* in *TWNT*, IV, 23f.

[75] Cf *CTKB*, 316.   [76] Cf above, pp. 147f.

existence. The Bible uses other images to describe the Church besides that of a shining lamp or city on a hill. Moreover, even if the lamp is put under a bushel it still lights. However, it would be a denial of God's gifts if one were to hide them. The whole Christian community is exhorted to be a light for the world. God's gifts are to be let shine before men so that they may give glory to God. 'The disciples of Jesus should let (*lassen sollen*) the light received through him from the heavenly Father shine forth in the world, in order to give glory to God.'[77] What is meant is not missionary work in particular, but the total life-conduct of the disciples. In their 'good works' (Mt 5:16) they have a responsibility before men. They must show themselves 'sons of light' (Lk 16:8) in the midst of a dark, godless world. The same idea recurs in I Peter 2:12 (cf 3:1–2). 'Maintain good conduct among the Gentiles, so that in case they speak against you as wrongdoers, they may see your good deeds and glorify God on the day of visitation.' It is not they, but God, who is to receive the honour, for their good works and light are ultimately his. There is nothing pharisaical about this 'giving of light'. It is but the acknowledgment of God's gift and the fulfilment of their mission and function. There is a difference between the open, fearless confession of faith in one's whole life conduct, and the hypocritical showing off before men mentioned in the very next chapter of Matthew's Gospel (6:1f).

Besides the witness of their lives Christians are also called to witness to Christ by their *words*. St Peter speaks of a certain *declaration* (*exaggellō*) of God's great redemptive acts, and indeed as the final aim of the royal priesthood of the whole body (I Pet 2:9). St Paul speaks of a certain *confession* (*homologia*) with the lips which is necessary for salvation. 'If you confess with your lips that Jesus is Lord and believe in your heart that God raised him from the dead, you will be saved.' Faith and confession are intimately linked (cf Rom 10:9, 14; II Cor 4:13). Both are necessary for salvation. This confession must be distinguished from preaching. Confession presupposes faith, faith hearing, hearing preaching, and preaching mission (Rom 14–15). *Preaching* has acquired the connotation of transmitting the Gospel message with authority and fidelity. In Catholic practice it is a hierarchical ministry. Normally, it takes place in the community gathered for worship, and thus forms part of the liturgical action. In the New Testament *kērussein* is connected with a special sending (*apostellein*).[78] During Jesus' lifetime only the

[77] A. Oepke, *art. cit.*, p. 26.
[78] Cf Lk 9:1–2; 4:18–19 (Is 61:1–2); Mk 3:14; Lk 4:43–4; I Tim 2:7; II Tim 1:11; Rom 10:14–15.

twelve, and the seventy or seventy-two (mentioned by Luke alone, 10:1), were sent to preach. The mission really confers the power of preaching God's Word. Their words are not simply a 'pure promise' of the Word of God.[79] But while preaching is connected with this special mission, St Paul mentions people who cooperated with him in the proclamation of the Gospel, and there are instances in the New Testament of a certain speaking of all in the Church.[80] Some of the laity will be permanently and professionally engaged in the task of catechesis and preaching and of closer cooperation with the hierarchy. They participate in some way in the ministry of the Word entrusted by Jesus to those specially sent.[81]

Furthermore, amongst the charisms mentioned by Paul we find 'the utterance of wisdom', 'the utterance of knowledge', 'prophecy', 'the ability to distinguish between spirits', 'tongues', 'the interpretation of tongues' (I Cor 12:8, 10). And amongst the charismatics there are 'apostles', 'prophets', 'teachers', 'speakers in various kinds of tongues' (I Cor 12:28). St Peter says that we should always be prepared to defend our faith to anyone who calls us to account for the hope that is in us (I Peter 3:15). St Luke recounts a splendid example of this. After being 'instructed in the way of the Lord' Apollos 'spoke and taught accurately the things concerning Jesus'. 'When Priscilla and Aquila heard him, they took him and expounded to him the way of God more accurately.' The result was that 'he gently helped those who through grace had believed, for he powerfully confuted the Jews in public, showing by the Scriptures that the Christ was Jesus' (Acts 18:24–28).

A prerequisite, however, for the fruitful exercise of all forms of the Church's prophetic witness is *instruction*. Instruction, both active and passive, is a right and a duty incumbent on all the members of the Church. If all Christians have the right and duty of witnessing to their faith then all have the right and duty of an adequate understanding of their faith and of being adequately instructed in their faith. As Barth says,[82] every Christian has the right and duty to inform himself and be informed. The duty falls primarily on professional biblical scholars, theologians and catechists, whether lay or clerical.[83] The duty falls also on the laity themselves. 'Therefore, the

[79] Cf *CTKB*, pp. 329, 323–4, 127f, 128.
[80] Cf Eph 4:3; Rom 16:3f; Acts 18:26; I Cor 14:23.
[81] Cf DCC, n. 33; Hamer, *The Church is a Communion*, pp. 146–7, note 1; L. Ryan, in *Vatican II: The Constitution on the Church*, ed. by K. McNamara, pp. 247–8.   [82] Cf *CTKB*, p. 330.
[83] Because of this right of all Christians to an adequate instruction and the duty of others to provide it one can understand the urgency and necessity of

laity should strive towards a more profound understanding of revealed truth, and insistently beg of God the gift of wisdom.'[84] Paul begins his discourse on spiritual gifts with the words: 'I do not want you to be uninformed' (I Cor 12:1).

All Christians must strive to understand their faith more and more in its implications for their concrete position in life. All must be, and are to some extent, *theologians*. Not in a scientific and professional sense but in the sense of a sufficient understanding of their Christian faith to be able to live a consciously Christian life and fulfil their prophetic mission. But professional lay theologians are also necessary, especially from the point of view of a concrete and existential understanding of the laity's mission and task in the world. Judging from history, and trusting in the Spirit's presence in the whole people of God, graces of wisdom and understanding and the distinguishing of spirits will never be lacking.[85] But the laity's understanding of their faith and their being informed is destined for their own active service of instruction. In ordinary ecclesiastical usage instruction refers to the preparation for the reception of the sacraments. But it can be extended to many other activities as well. One thinks immediately of parental instruction of children, of the various forms of catechesis, of the various levels of school-teaching, of literature, the press, the cinema, the radio, television, of public speaking and lecturing—either in exposition and defence of the faith, or in the adjustment of political and social ills. All these are legitimate exercises of the Christian's prophetical function.

There is an immense field of cooperation possible in this respect between the hierarchy and the laity. The laity must know what is going on in the Church. They must be adequately informed. On the other hand, the hierarchy must know what is going on in the world. Otherwise they cannot fruitfully exercise their prophetic mission. And they must be informed. They must not be allowed to live in a world of their own, distinct from the real one. They must be instructed as regards reality, and learn to read 'the signs of the times'. As I said, instruction, both active and passive, is a right and duty incumbent on all the members of the Church.

---

such things as the biblical and catechetical renewal and the introduction of theological facilities in all universities.

[84] DCC, n. 35.

[85] Justin, Tertullian, Clement of Alexandria, Origen (although he became a priest later), Catherine of Siena are among the lay theologians of history whose names immediately spring to mind. In our time there are many who could be mentioned.

Chapter Fifteen

The Mission and Ministry of the Hierarchy

THE basic difference between the Protestantism of Karl Barth and Catholicism does not lie in ecclesiology but in justification and christology—even if the difference is most apparent in ecclesiology. He interprets ecclesiology and christology in the light of his doctrine of justification. The ecclesiological formulation of Luther's concept of justification is the common priesthood of all believers. Barth radicalizes Luther's doctrine of justification according to an ultra-Calvinistic *soli Deo gloria*. As a result he also radicalizes Luther's concept of the priesthood of all. Barth's doctrine of justification expresses itself ecclesiologically in a denial of all true human participation in Christ's one ministry of priesthood, kingship and prophecy. No one participates in the sense that he is enabled to act salvifically in, with and under Christ. The basic fontal discussion with Barth lies in justification and christology. For this reason, a discussion concerning a hierarchical ministry in the Church is only of derivative importance. But in another sense it is not. For the discussion of each manifestation of the basic difference is a discussion of the basic difference itself. I am convinced (i) that Barth does not give due consideration to the important part of Scripture which points to a hierarchical ministry in the Church, and (ii) that his repeated accusation against the Catholic Church's understanding of Scripture on this point are not well-founded—and often not very kind. Since his understanding of Scripture on this point is determined by his pre-conception of the salvific activity of God *alone* in the history of salvation, the demonstration of the institution of a hierarchy by Christ will be again a refutation of his basic principle.

I. THE NEW TESTAMENT BASIS OF THE CHURCH'S TRIPLE HIERARCHICAL MINISTRY

According to the New Testament the whole new people of God is a prophetic, priestly and kingly body. It has been sent for a definite purpose, and accomplishes its mission in the exercise of definite ministries. There is only one ministry. It is a differentiated one. There is a differentiation of priestly, kingly and prophetical aspects. And there is a differentiation in participation in this one, threefold ministry. All participate in it initially in the same way, through the basic Christian virtues of faith, hope and charity, and the basic Christian sacraments of baptism, confirmation and the eucharist. This common initiation is concretized or actualized then in essentially different ways. In the last chapter we considered its actualization in the case of the lay Christian. Not all members of the Church, however, are lay. There is an *essentially different* concretization in the Church of the one basic ministry of the Church and of Jesus Christ. While the laity concretize it in one way others in the Church concretize it in another and essentially different way. And for this they receive a special participation in Christ's power. They represent Christ to the community in an altogether special way and so serve Christ and the community. This ministry is usually called 'monarchico-hierarchical' or 'hierarchical', and gives rise to what is also usually called the 'monarchico-hierarchical structure' of the Church.

The word 'hierarchical' comes from the Greek *hiera-archē*, and means priestly origin or holy power. The whole community is hierarchical in the sense that it participates in Christ's holy power. But the word 'hierarchy' has become a technical term denoting the holy power given to some only in the Church for the exercise of a particular ministry essentially different from all others, and therefore denoting the essential differentiation of holy power in the Church. The words 'hierarchico-monarchical' are unfortunate, because of possible historical connotations and associations with worldly sociological structures. It is to be noted that the Bible in speaking of ministry in the Church avoided all the words used in secular Greek for civil and religious authority—such as *archē, timē, telos*. The word it chooses is *diakonia*, ministry.[1] If I use the words 'hierarchical' and 'monarchical' it will be only because of their common usage and because I wish to indicate the scriptural basis for this usage, in so far as they refer to the participation in Christ's messianic and spiritual offices in the sense explained. But their use in reference to the Church must be freed of all undertones of absolutism, arbitrariness, power and domination, which may often accompany them in their historical and secular usage. The Church is not monarchical in the sense that the ministry of the college of bishops, for example, is a derivation from or participation in that of its head. Bishops are not simply civil servants or

[1] Cf below pp. 192f.

officials whom the Pope can abolish at will. They are a constituent element of the Church willed by Christ.[2] It would be better to adopt some other more biblical name for this special ministry. Hans Küng suggests 'pastoral ministry'.[3] He limits this, in distinction to purely charismatic ministry, to instituted or specially commissioned ministry. In what follows I will not be so much concerned with the actual way in which this special ministry is conferred (ultimately both are always charismatic and spiritual) even though of necessity I emphasize above all the aspect of instituted or pastoral ministry, since Barth's denial is aimed directly at it. The special minister and ministry I refer to is described thus by Küng:

> 'The pastor is from the first a special person in the community, since he is authorized as one with special powers to exercise a special ministry in the public life of the community. He has power to found and to govern communities, to call together, unite and build up the community; he has power to preach the word in the public assembly and to carry it out into the world as a missionary; he has power to lead public assemblies, to baptize and celebrate the Lord's Supper, to bind and to loose and to commision others like himself.'[4]

1. THE HIERARCHICAL MINISTRY ACCORDING TO THE GOSPELS[5]

Jesus Christ came to preach and to cast out demons. 'For that is why I came out' (Mk 1:38-39). He himself chose twelve disciples to participate in his messianic mission. 'And he went up into the hills, and called to him those whom he desired; and they came to him. And he appointed twelve, to be with him, and to be sent out to preach and to have authority to cast out demons' (Mk 3:13-15). The establishment of this group of twelve by Jesus during his pre-Easter historical life

[2] For the relationship between primacy and episcopacy cf Rahner-Ratzinger, *The Episcopate and the Primacy* (Quaest. Disp. 4), 1962.
[3] *The Church*, p. 428.
[4] *Ibid.*, p. 440.
[5] In an outline of the New Testament basis for this special pastoral ministry one might expect me to begin with the witness of Paul as the oldest historical testimony in our possession. One could begin like that of course. But the Gospels still remain, despite the realization that they have a 'history of redaction', and therefore reflect theological preoccupations of a later time, the Gospels of Jesus Christ and retain a certain historical validity in this regard. Therefore one can, and indeed ought, with the necessary criticism, of course, to begin with their account in an attempt to represent the basic historical exegesis of the Church's ministry.

is beyond doubt, even though the time and circumstances are not recorded.[6] The twelve represent symbolically eschatological Israel (cf Mt 19:28; Lk 22:30b). His formation of this special group reveals his claim on the whole of Israel.[7] His purpose in selecting them was that they be 'with him', that is, that they be his disciples par excellence,[8] the most intimate associates and witnesses of his life, teaching and mission. 'To you it has been given to know the secrets of the kingdom of heaven, but to them it has not been given.'[9] The second purpose for which he selected them was that they be 'sent out to preach and have authority to cast out demons'. According to the obvious meaning of the text they are going to be subjects in these actions. *They* are going to preach, and *they* are going to cast out demons and *have* the power to do so. The power is that of Jesus. But he will grant a participation in his power to the twelve (cf Mt 12:28).

Later, Jesus fulfils the purpose for which he called them. He sent them out to preach and gave them authority to cast out demons. 'And he called to him the twelve, and began to send them out two by two, and gave them authority over the unclean spirits. So they went out and preached that men should repent. And they cast out many demons, and anointed with oil many that were sick and healed them.'[10] Jesus gave them authority. The twelve have gone beyond the stage of promise. They are now those sent with power. Barth denies this historical development in the 'apostolate' because, for him, it is impossible, *a priori*, that men be enabled to act with the power of God. The apostolate is the 'status of the receiver of a

[6] Cf the articles of Rigaux, Cerfaux (in (*Mélanges E. Tisserant*), Giblet, Vögtle (in *Sentire Ecclesiam*, and art. 'Zwölf' in *LTK*) in the bibliography. W. Schmithals and G. Klein deny the existence and institution of this group by Jesus during his public life because it would contradict his expectation of an imminent *parousia*. Some ancient authorities (cf the critical edition of Merk) add 'whom also he named apostles' after the word 'twelve' in Mk 3:14. It is disputed whether Jesus used the word 'apostle'. Most probably he did not. Paul invented it, and it was only later that it was applied to the twelve (cf Dupont, *art. cit.*). Vatican II intentionally avoids this historical question (cf DCC, n. 19 and the commentary of K. Rahner in *Commentary on the Documents of Vatican II*, ed. by H. Vorgrimler, vol. I, p. 189).

[7] Cf R. Schnackenburg in *LTK*, 6, p. 168. It is a principle of Protestant exegesis to say that as representatives of eschatological Israel the twelve received what they receive as representatives of *all*. This is true, and expresses the profound union of office and community. But, on the other hand, it overlooks the position apart which the twelve had in the life of Jesus.

[8] 'His twelve disciples', as Mt 10:1 and 11:1, with the definite article in the Greek, put it.

[9] Mt 13:11: 'them' refers to the crowds he taught in parables; cf v 2f.

[10] Mk 6:7, 12–13. Cf the parallel texts in Lk 9:1f; Mt 10:5f.

promise', and was already instituted in the calling of the twelve in Mk 3:13f.[11]

Against this it must be pointed out that calling and sending are two different things. Jesus called the twelve, firstly, in order to be with him, and secondly, to be sent out. They are first disciples, then apostles. In the temporary mission to Israel the ultimate scope of their calling is fulfilled. They are sent to preach and to heal with power. Their sending is 'an authoritative sending in the sense of a full empowerment'.[12] They are made participants in Christ's messianic mission so that those who receive them receive him.[13]

St Luke speaks also of the mission of seventy or seventy-two others, with exactly the same directions and power as the twelve (10:1f). Barth deduces from this that the mission of the twelve is identical with the mission of the Church as a whole.[14] This, however, is not at all clear. Firstly, it must be noted that even with respect to the seventy or seventy-two a special appointment and mission by Jesus is necessary (Lk 10:1). What can be deduced from it is that the proclamation of the kingdom is not the sole responsibility of the twelve.[15] Secondly, at this stage Jesus did not think of the mission of his Church to all nations. What he was concerned with was the mission to Israel. 'Go nowhere among the Gentiles, and enter no town of the Samaritans, but go rather to the lost sheep of Israel.'[16] The refusal of the message of Jesus by the greater part of the people of Israel leads to a new stage in God's plan of salvation. Jesus realizes[17] the necessity of his death for all, including the Gentiles, which will be the foundation of a *new* covenant of God with his people. He retains the circle of the twelve, recognizes their election by God,[18] reveals to them the mystery of his passion and death,[19] as well as his intention of founding a universal Church.[20]

Before he ascended to heaven Jesus sent his eleven disciples definitively and permanently, with the power to bring the reconciliation accomplished in him to all nations, and all nations to the reconciliation

[11] Cf *CTKB*, pp. 125f, 128.
[12] Rengstorf, *TWNT*, I, p. 425. Cf *ibid.*, pp. 424–5.
[13] Cf Mt 10:40; Lk 10:16; Jn 13:20; Gal 4:14.
[14] *CTKB*, p. 128.
[15] Cf P. Grelot, in *Recherches Bibliques*, VII, p. 161.
[16] Mt 10:5–6.
[17] The possibility of a development in Jesus' consciousness of his mission is not excluded: cf K. Rahner, *Theological Investigations*, V, pp 193–215; Vögtle, in *Gott in Welt*, I, pp. 608–67; Schnackenburg, in *LTK*, 6, 168.
[18] Mk 4:11 (par.); Mt 11:25; Lk 12:32.
[19] Mk 8:31; Mt 16:21f; Lk 9:22f.
[20] Mt 16:18f; Lk 22:19; I Cor 11:24–25.

accomplished in him. For this purpose he grants them a share in his prophetical, priestly and kingly ministry.

> 'And Jesus came and said to them, "All authority in heaven and on earth has been given to me. Go therefore and make disciples of all nations, baptizing them in the name of the Father and of the Son and of the Holy Spirit, teaching them to observe all that I have commanded you; and lo, I am with you always, to the close of the age." '[21]

In his resurrection from the dead Jesus was designated or constituted Lord and Christ (Acts 2:36), Son of God in power (Rom 1:4). This supreme and universal authority of Jesus is the basis of his mission of his disciples. The passage from Matthew just quoted is addressed to the eleven alone. Their mission is one of power, and to the whole universe. Because I have all power go *therefore* (*oun*) and make disciples of all nations in my power, baptize them in my power, teach and direct them in my power. 'Make disciples' includes what follows in the other two injunctions. A disciple is one who receives the Word in faith and is baptized.[22] The missionary command includes baptism—'baptizing them'. The making of a disciple does not consist solely in preaching and the acceptance of the Word in faith. Jesus Christ creates disciples through the baptism administered by those he sent. Its administration and reception is necessary. Through baptism the disciple becomes God's possession, is placed in a special relationship to the Trinity (*eis to onoma*). But even faith and baptism are not sufficient. The disciple must also fulfil the moral directions of Jesus (cf Mt 7:21f). And for this reason the eleven are sent to teach, direct and guide. They are the ministers of Christ's prophetical, priestly and kingly office in the subjective realization of reconciliation.

The apostles do not become Jesus Christ. He remains the supreme Lord and head of his Church. None the less, they do really teach, sanctify and govern in his power. They do so in the power and according to the commission given to them by Christ, and therefore neither against his will nor in arrogant usurpation of his lordship. They are the instruments of the glorified Christ in his subjective realization of reconciliation in a way analogous to the instrumentality of his human visible nature in his objective reconciliation.

By the positive precept of Christ salvation is connected with the activity of those he sent. As Barth so well points out, their activity is to be a witness and reflection of Christ's activity. 'You shall be my

[21] Mt 28:18–20. Cf Mk 16:15–16; Lk 24:47–48; Acts 1:8.
[22] Cf Acts 2:38–41; 8:12f, 36; 19:30–33; Eph 4:5.

witnesses' (Acts 1:8). This aspect should not be forgotten. But their activity is also a *mediation* of Christ's activity. This cannot be understood unless we recall that the apostles received the gift of Christ's Holy Spirit. With this gift it is quite intelligible, for the Church is more than 'merely human'.[23] It is a divine-human reality in one. Barth denies this because he excludes *a priori* the possibility of an inherent presence of the Spirit in the Church, as well as the salvific activity of the human Church.

The mission given to his eleven disciples envisages all times and places, and all peoples. 'Make disciples of all nations.' 'All nations' means the whole of humanity, Jews and Gentiles. 'You shall be my witnesses . . . to the end of the earth' (Acts 1:8). 'I am with you all days (*pasas tas emeras*), to the close of the age.' Christ's vision is prophetic. He sees this activity of his apostles taking in the whole time between his ascension and final *parousia*. His command is that this activity continue for ever. There is only one mission. It is spoken directly to the eleven. But it is Christ's intention that the 'eleven' and their task exist always. 'And lo, I am with *you* always.' One mission and authorization which envisages the whole future Church. This is all that is meant by saying that Christ *instituted* a Church. To this Church he promises his assistance until his final coming.

The mission and holy power given by Jesus before his ascension to his eleven disciples is further clarified in Mt 18:18 and Jn 20:21-23. In chapter 18, Matthew groups together (as is his wont) a series of passages concerning the relationships of his disciples in community or with one another. Verse 18 is an independent passage. Its lack of connection with the three preceding verses is indicated by the transition from the singular to the plural 'you'.[24] Jesus confers on a particular group of his disciples[25] the power of binding and loosing. 'Truly, I say to you, whatever you bind on earth shall be bound in heaven; and whatever you loose on earth shall be loosed in heaven' (v 18).

To bind and loose[26] were technical terms in Judaism at the time of

---

[23] *CTKB*, p. 241.

[24] The RSV uses the word 'you' in both cases. Other versions (among them Knox and the Confraternity) bring out this distinction by the use of 'thee' and 'thou' in vv 15–17; and 'you' in v 18. The Greek has *sou* and *soi* in vv 15–17, and *humin* in v 18.

[25] Jesus confers this power on his twelve disciples and not on the whole community. Cf J. Jeremias, in *TWNT*, III, p. 751. In addition to the arguments of Jeremias, the disconnection of v 18 from the preceding v 17 should be noted. Cf J. Schmid, *Das Evang. nach Matth.*, pp. 272-3.

[26] Greek *deein–luein*; Aram. *asar–sharah*.

Jesus. They denoted the act of the Jewish rabbis in forbidding or allowing something; and, more rarely, in imposing or lifting a ban of excommunication, that is, in expelling or re-admitting a sinful member of the community.[27] In Mt 18:18 they do not mean exclusively the act and power of excommunicating and re-admitting, but a general forbidding and allowing, opening and closing, in the kingdom of God. This follows from (i) the usual meaning of these terms at the time; (ii) their use in conjunction with the 'keys of the kingdom of heaven' in Mt 16:19; (iii) their specification in Jn 20:23 as the forgiving and retaining of sins; (iv) the expression of their object by means of the word 'whatever' (the neutral Greek *hosa*). According to the words of Jesus, his disciples have authority to teach, sanctify and rule in his Church.[28] Their activity is one of service, the service of Christ and his Church. Their holy power is the power given to them by Jesus Christ. They are really given this power, so that what they do in the building up of his Church is acknowledged by God.

The mission of his disciples is a continuation of Jesus' own mission. This is emphasized by St John. ' "As the Father has sent me, even so I send you." And when he had said this, he breathed on them, and said to them "Receive the Holy Spirit. If you forgive the sins of any, they are forgiven; if you retain the sins of any, they are retained." '[29] Barth appeals to the two different Greek words used in Jn 20:21b (which describes Jesus' mission by the Father and the mission of the disciples by Jesus) to deny the idea of continuation.[30] Against this, however, it must be pointed out that Jesus uses *both* words to describe his own mission by the Father.[31] If there is any difference at all between his use of these verbs it is that he uses *apostellein* when he bases the authority of his word and work in the authority of God who sends him, and *pempein* when he speaks of the participation of God in his Word and work in the very act of his sending. One refers more to the authority behind the sending, the other more to the act of sending.[32]

It must be further pointed out that Jesus in Jn 17:18 uses the same verb (*apostellein*) to describe his mission by the Father and his own sending of his disciples. The apostles are sent with the power of Jesus in the service of his kingdom just as Jesus was sent with the power

---

[27] Cf the examples from rabbinic literature in Str.-Bill., I, p. 738f.
[28] Cf A. Vögtle, in *LTK*, 2, 480–2.
[29] Jn 20:21b–23; cf 17:18; 13:20.
[30] Cf *CTKB*, p. 124.
[31] Cf Jn 5:36–37; 6:29, 38, 39; 7:28–29.
[32] Cf Rengstorf, in *TWNT*, I, pp. 403–4.

of God in the service of his kingdom. This is the New Testament meaning of *apostellein*.[33] Barth wishes to point to a difference between the mission of Christ and that of the twelve. In this he is certainly correct, even if the attempt to deduce it from the two different verbs would not seem to be happy. The mission of the twelve is not identical with the mission of Jesus. Yet there is a comparison between their missions, as Barth also notes. Both are 'missions' or 'processions'.[34] Both involve investing with power. Both are sent to accomplish the one ministry in different ways. Barth denies a continuation. However, the analogy between them is precisely one of continuation. The apostles continue the mission of Jesus in the sense that Jesus continues his mission through them. There is no contradiction between these statements. The apostles themselves really act, really continue the mission of Jesus (which envelops both the objective and subjective aspects of reconciliation), but the power in which they act is the power of Jesus, so that it is really Jesus who acts through them. Just as John expresses his own specific christology, namely, the fullest possible unity between the Father and the Son, through the sending (*apostellein* and *pempein*) of Jesus by the Father,[35] so also he expresses the closest possible unity between Jesus Christ (his Holy Spirit) and the Church he instituted, through the sending (*apostellein* and *pempein*) of his disciples by Jesus. This union of the Spirit and the institution is one of the basic tenets of Catholic ecclesiology.

St John makes this quite clear when he adds that Jesus gave them his Holy Spirit (v 22). Again, it is the particular group of eleven disciples, and they alone, who receive and are promised the Holy Spirit, or power, of Christ.[36] They really share in his power. Barth says this also.[37] But we do not mean the same thing even though we say the same thing. For Barth the sending of the disciples is on a 'lower level' in the sense that it is solely human. Jesus' action continues in their action in the sense that he alone acts salvifically in the secondary form of their action. The 'continuation' of the work of Jesus Christ is always the event of his own direct act. He 'remains its free and independent presupposition'. This, however, seems very foreign to the mind of John, as is clear from what we have seen. Apostleship (whether of Jesus or of his disciples) is a sending with

[33] *Id., ibid.*, pp. 405, 25f.
[34] 'Quaedam processio': *Summa theol.*, I, q. 43, art. 1. Cf Card. Franzelin's exegesis of Jn 20:21 in his *Theses de Ecclesia Christi*, thesis IX.
[35] Rengstorf, *art. cit.*, 405, 7f.
[36] Cf Jn 20:22, 24. Cf Acts 1:2, 8.
[37] Cf *CTKB*, pp. 124, 126f.

power (or with the Spirit) in the service of the kingdom. The one sent acts in and with the power and authority of the one who sends.

John concludes by specifying the power of binding and loosing promised to the apostles in Mt 18:18; it is a power of forgiving and retaining sins. Here is quite clearly expressed again the continuation of the mission of Jesus by his disciples. The power which Jesus exercised during his life (Mk 2:5 and par; Lk 7:47f), he now confers on his disciples.

So far I have outlined the mission and power promised and given by Jesus to a special group of disciples. Within this group he promised and conferred the same power of teaching and governing on one, namely, Peter, who had been one of his most intimate disciples (cf Mk 5:37; 9:2; 14:33), indeed the spokesman of his disciples (Mk 8:29; 9:5; 10:28; 11:21), and whose name always headed the list (cf Mk 3:16; Mt 10:2; Lk 6:14; Acts 1:13). The promise is expressed in the following words of Mt 16:18–19:

> 'And I tell you, you are Peter, and on this rock I will build my church, and the powers of death shall not prevail against it. I will give you the keys of the kingdom of heaven, and whatever you bind on earth shall be bound in heaven, and whatever you loose on earth shall be loosed in heaven.'

Scarcely anywhere else in the whole New Testament is there such a concentration of Aramaic expressions. It must be interpreted accordingly.[38]

Jesus says he 'will build' his Church, and 'will give' the keys. The reference is therefore to the future—although J. Jeremias is of the opinion that the underlying Aramaic imperfect has more a voluntative character and refers to Jesus' present will.[39] Barth has his usual

---

[38] Cf J. Jeremias, in *TWNT*, III, 749, 10f; A. Oepke, *art. cit.*, p. 149; F. A. Sullivan, *De Ecclesia*, I, p. 105. This logion is found only in Matthew; it is probably not in its original context, but was introduced by Matthew from his own source between vv 29 and 30 of Mk 8; it was probably spoken shortly before Jesus' death or after his resurrection; its historicity is denied only by those who say that Jesus expected an imminent *parousia*, or that he considered himself sent only to the Jews (cf above, chapter ten); the idea of later interpolation is excluded by its semitic character, amongst other reasons.

[39] The Aramaic imperfect underlying the Greek *dōsō*, 'I will give' (v 19), is used only very occasionally, he says, with a future sense. It expresses more intention, desire, command. The case is different with Judaean Aramaic (the Targums) for there the imperfect has been influenced by Hebrew and more often has a future meaning. Cf Jeremias, *art. cit.*, 749, 16f; also his *The Eucharistic Words of Jesus*, London, 1966, p. 210. This would accord better with the opinion that the logion Mt 16:18–19 is a post-resurrection saying.

THE MISSION AND MINISTRY OF THE HIERARCHY 181

deduction from the future tense, namely, that the proclamation of the Word will always depend on the event of Christ's own direct act.[40] This is a bit far-fetched, but anything else is for him *a priori* inconceivable. Jesus expresses his will then to build his Church. He himself is the builder, and that which is to be built is, and will always remain, his Church—as Barth so often and admirably reminds us. '*I* will build *my* Church.'

Jesus wills to build his Church on Peter as on a rock. The disciple Simon is given the new name 'rock'.[41] In the Old Testament and in Judaism the giving or changing of a name expressed or signified a certain function.[42] The idea of 'building' a people was familiar in the old Testament,[43] and at the time of Jesus.[44] Nor was the metaphor of building on a man as upon a rock unknown.[45] Peter is willed to be the solid foundation which will give stability to his Church. This is clear from the sayings of Jesus about the wise man building his house upon the rock. 'And the rains fell, and the floods came, and the winds blew and beat upon that house, but it did not fall, *because* it had been founded on the rock.'[46] Jesus says that the powers of death shall not prevail against it (v 18c). The Church, founded as it is on the rock, victoriously resists the powers of death or the devil. It is indestructible. Implicitly, Christ announces the permanence of the rock (the person of Peter) on which it is founded.

Jesus gives the keys of the kingdom of heaven to Peter (v 19a). In the Old Testament,[47] and in rabbinical literature,[48] to 'have the keys' meant to have authority over something, and to 'give the keys' was to give this authority to another. The handing over of the keys meant installation to power (*Einsetzung zum Bevollmächtigung*),

[40] Cf *CTKB*, pp. 125f.
[41] The English word 'Peter' comes from the Latin Petrus, which comes from the Greek *Petros*, and which in turn merely adds a masculine termination to the Greek translation (*petra*) of the Aramaic word *Kepha* (meaning 'rock')— the word originally used by Christ. The original words were then: 'And I tell you (Simon), you are the rock (*Kepha*), and on this rock . . .'. Cf Sullivan, *op. cit.*, pp. 106f.
[42] Cf Gen 3:20; Is 7:14; Mt 1:23.
[43] Cf Jer 31:1–4, 27–28; 33:7. This use comes from the frequent designation of a people as a house, cf Jer 33:14, 17; Mt 10:6; 15:24.
[44] Cf the commentary on Ps 37, fragment A, col. 2, found among the Qumran documents.
[45] Cf Is 51:1–2, and the rabbinic commentary on Num 23:9, cited in Str.-Bill., I, p 733. This and the preceding reference cited in Sullivan, *op. cit.*, pp. 112–13.   [46] Mt 7:25. Cf 7:24–27; Lk 6:47–49.
[47] Cf Is 22:15–25.   [48] Cf the examples cited in Str.-Bill., I, p. 736f.

and the possession of the keys meant possession of full power (*Vollmacht*).⁴⁹ According to the explicit rabbinical explanation of Is 22:22 the power of the keys includes the power of teaching. The specialist in the knowledge of the Torah exercised the power of the keys. What he opens no one closes, that is, his teaching enjoys 'absolute validity'.⁵⁰

The power Jesus confers on Peter is not, however, that of the Jewish rabbis. Their power was based on their knowledge of the Torah. Peter's power is not based on his own knowledge, but on the fact that what he opens and closes is opened and closed in heaven, that is, 'with God'. This is explained in v 19b, where Jesus grants to Peter the same power which he grants to the eleven collectively: whatever he binds and looses on earth will be bound and loosed in heaven.⁵¹ Jesus, who has the key of David (Rev 3:7), grants his power to Peter. The power concerns Christ's rule on earth, in the Church. Jesus is speaking of building his Church (v 18b), and gives to Peter the power of binding and loosing 'on earth' (v 19b). The 'kingdom' is the kingdom of the future, the eschatological kingdom, which is the goal of the earthly Church.⁵² Peter is given the capacity and power to guide and direct men so that they can enter the kingdom of God. He leads men effectively into God's kingdom. 'Peter is to lead the people of God into the kingdom of the Resurrection.'⁵³

As will be seen from the above, there is no question of a 'Romanist exegesis or theory which asserts a Church independent of its Lord'.⁵⁴ Jesus grants authority in his Church, and the power of binding and loosing, to Peter. In the light of its Semitic background this can hardly be denied to be the meaning of the text. Peter, as the rock on which Christ builds his Church, is not independent of Jesus Christ. Jesus himself has installed him as such. He has given him a share in his own power and authority. Peter acts only as Christ's vicar, in his power. Acting with the power which Christ has given him he is not independent of Christ. Without Christ he is nothing. Without Christ Simon is not Peter. With him he is, and really is. Christ's authority is his authority—without ceasing thereby to be Christ's authority.

Mt 16:18-19 is confirmed by Lk 22:31-32 and Jn 21:15-17. In

⁴⁹ Cf J. Jeremias, *art. cit.*, 749, 21f.
⁵⁰ Cf *id., ibid.,* 747, n. 42; 750, 11f.
⁵¹ Cf above for the explanation of 'binding' and 'loosing'.
⁵² Cf Schnackenburg, *God's Rule and Kingdom*, Freiburg, 1963, pp 227f.
⁵³ O. Cullmann, cited (from German ed. of his book *Petrus*, Zürich, 1952, p. 229) in Schnackenburg, *God's Rule . . .* , p. 228.
⁵⁴ Cf *CTKB*, p. 126.

Lk 22:31 Jesus speaks to Simon of the temptation of all by Satan.[55] He prays for Simon alone, that his faith may not fail, and that he may strengthen his brethren. Jesus is thinking of his future community when he himself will be no longer visibly present. He obviously recognized the special position of Peter as the guardian and strengthener of the faith. The connection with the rock of Mt 16:18 is clear.

According to Jn 21:15-17, Jesus commits to Peter the function of 'feeding' and 'tending' his sheep. Shortly to ascend into heaven he made Peter the pastor on earth of his followers. The meaning of feeding and tending is clear from the Old Testament, from Jewish literature, and from St John himself.[56] It means to care for the flock, to go before them, to lead them, to know them, to call them by name, to defend them, to be willing to lay down one's life for them. Our Lord, therefore, installs Peter as the one who has to care for, lead and defend his whole Church.

2. THE HIERARCHICAL MINISTRY ACCORDING TO THE REST OF THE NEW TESTAMENT

Apart from these basic provisions for his Church the pre- and post-Easter historical Jesus left all else to his promised Spirit. 'But the Counsellor, the Holy Spirit, whom the Father will send in my name, he will teach you all things, and bring to your remembrance all that I have said to you.'[57]

After the ascension, the eleven apostles who remained after the defection of Judas were very anxious to fulfil Scripture's prophecy concerning his replacement, and to maintain the college of twelve established by Jesus (Acts 1:15-26). They do not make the replacement themselves. They chose 'one of the men who have accompanied us during all the time that the Lord Jesus went in and out among us' (v 21), and pray the glorified Lord to manifest *his* choice through lot. Matthias is the one selected to 'witness with us to his resurrection' (v 22), and thus to take the 'share which was allotted to Judas in this ministry' (vv 16-17).

This special ministry of the twelve includes that of *preaching and teaching with authority*. 'Every day in the temple and at home they did not cease teaching (*didaskein*) and preaching (*euaggelizein*) Jesus

---

[55] The 'you' is plural in v 31, and singular in v 32. The RSV, in a note, points explicitly this time to the distinction.
[56] Cf the references in J. Jeremias, art. *poimēn* in *TWNT*, VI, pp. 484-501.
[57] Jn 14:26; cf 14:16-17; 15:26; 16:12-14.

as the Christ.'[58] They consider this ministry as an obedience to God (Acts 5:29). They are aware of the assistance of the Holy Spirit, and that their word is the Word of God. 'And they were all filled with the Holy Spirit and spoke the word of God with boldness.'[59] Their witness is the witness of the Holy Spirit who has been given to them. 'And we are witnesses to these things, and so is the Holy Spirit whom God has given to those who obey him. . . . It has seemed good to the Holy Spirit and to us. . . .'[60] Taken in conjunction with the promise of the Holy Spirit this latter text is an indication of what we would now call collegial infallibility.[61]

Amongst the twelve Peter is especially marked out as the first witness to Christ's resurrection (cf I Cor 15:5; Lk 24:34). As such he may be regarded as the rock of the Church which exists because of the preaching and acceptance of the Gospel, the risen Christ. He was the leading figure in Jerusalem up to the time of the 'apostolic' council (cf Gal 2:7f). He was the driving force of the young missionary Church, being the only one of the twelve who definitely undertook missionary work outside Jerusalem.[62]

Paul, too, the charismatic par excellence,[63] 'called by the will of God to be an apostle of Christ Jesus' (I Cor 1:1), does not preach the Gospel (*euaggelizein*) with mere human wisdom but with power (cf I Cor 1:17). 'And my speech and my message were not in plausible words of wisdom, but in demonstration of the Spirit and power, that your faith might not rest in the wisdom of men but in the power of God. . . . For our Gospel came to you not only in word, but also in power and in the Holy Spirit and with full conviction.'[64] His word is the Word of God.[65] It is not a different word from that of the twelve. He preaches what he, too, 'received' (I Cor 15:1–11), and is anxious to have his Gospel approved by those in Jerusalem, 'lest somehow I should be running or had run in vain'.[66]

Besides the prophetic ministry of the twelve and Paul, other

[58] Acts 5:42. Cf 4:2 (*didaskein, kataggellein*); 2:42 (*didachē tōn apostolōn*); 4:33: 'And with great power. . . .'
[59] Acts 4:31.
[60] Acts 5:32; 15:28.
[61] Cf Jn 14:16–17; Mt 28:20; Jn 16:13.
[62] Cf Acts 2:14; 4:8f; 10:9f; 11:1f; 15:6–12; Gal 2:11f. Cf Küng, *The Church*, pp. 456–7.
[63] As I have already mentioned, I am not really concerned here with the distinction between charismatic and instituted ministry, but simply with the New Testament's witness to the existence of this special ministry.
[64] I Cor 2:4–5; I Thess 1:5.
[65] Cf I Thess 2:13, 8–9, 2.
[66] Gal 2:2; cf 2:1–10.

ministers and ministries of the Word are mentioned. 'Now in the Church at Antioch there were prophets and teachers, Barnabas, Symeon who was called Niger, Lucius of Cyrene, Manaen....'[67] 'And his gifts were that some should be apostles, some prophets, some evangelists, some pastors and teachers, for building up the body of Christ.'[68] There is no determined list of ecclesiastical ministries. They are as varied as the charisms on which they are based. They are treated only in passing. They are not all of the same order. 'And God has appointed in the Church first apostles, second prophets, third teachers, then....'[69] These ministries do not belong to everybody in the community nor do they belong to the community. They belong only to some in the community. They prolong the ministry of the apostles in a special way. Paul sends Timothy to the Churches at Corinth and Thessalonica 'to remind you of my ways in Christ, as I teach them everywhere in every Church'.[70] In the early epistles there is no reference to a form of appointment. They receive their ministry with their *charisma*, direct from the Holy Spirit. Their ministry and charism are identical. In the later epistles, however, there is mention of an appointment to this ministry by the apostles. 'And when they [Paul and Barnabas] had appointed elders (*presbuteroi*) for them in every Church, with prayer and fasting, they committed them to the Lord in whom they believed.'[71] The appointment takes place through the imposition of hands: 'Till I come, attend to the public reading of Scripture, to preaching, to teaching. Do not neglect the gift you have, which was given you by prophetic utterance when the elders laid their hands upon you.'[72] These in turn are to appoint others. 'And what you have heard from me before many witnesses entrust to faithful men who will be able to teach others also.'[73] All must remain faithful to tradition: 'O Timothy, guard what has been entrusted to you.'[74]

In addition to the special ministry of preaching and guarding the Gospel authoritatively, there was also in the New Testament community a special ministry of *sanctification* or of *priesthood*.[75] The

---

[67] Acts 13:1; cf 11:19–27. Luke may have had these in mind when he spoke in his Gospel (the only one to do so) of the seventy or seventy-two sent by Jesus (10:1).
[68] Eph 4:11–12; cf Rom 12:6–8.   [69] I Cor 12:28f.
[70] I Cor 4:17; I Thess 3:2–6; 5:12; Col 1:7; 4:7–17.
[71] Acts 14:23. Cf I Tim 4:11–16.
[72] I Tim 4:13–14.   [73] II Tim 2:2.
[74] I Tim 6:20. Cf II Tim 1:14; 2:2; 3:13–14.
[75] The New Testament writings do not tell us very much about this ministry in the community's practice. This is probably due to the character of these writings, whose scope was precisely the exercise of ruling and teaching power.

apostles reproduce the sanctifying gestures committed to them by the Lord. They administer baptism.[76] They preside at the eucharistic assembly, pronouncing the words spoken by the Lord, in fulfilment of his command.[77] The elders anoint the sick with oil, and if the sick man has committed sins they will be forgiven.[78] The Spirit is communicated through the imposition of hands: 'Then they laid their hands on them and they received the Holy Spirit. Now when Simeon saw that the Spirit was given through the laying on of the apostles' hands. . . .'[79]

Imposition of hands and sending by the prophets and teachers of Antioch is equivalent to sending by the Holy Spirit. 'Then after fasting and praying they laid their hands on them and sent them off. So, being sent out by the Holy Spirit they went . . . [and] proclaimed the word of God.'[80] Ministry is conferred through the imposition of hands. 'Do not neglect the gift you have, which was given you by prophetic utterance when the elders laid their hands upon you.'[81] Titus, whom Paul left at Crete, is directed to appoint elders.[82]

Very frequent in these writings is the mention of a *guiding*, leading, directing, ruling *ministry*. The twelve apostles give directions,[83] make decisions,[84] inspect,[85] and exclude the unworthy from the community.[86] Amongst the twelve Peter shows a particular responsibility.[87]

Paul is more stringent. 'Shall I come to you with a rod, or with love in a spirit of gentleness?' he writes to the Corinthians (I Cor 4:21). And in his second letter to them: 'I write this while I am away from you, in order that when I come I may not have to be severe in my use of the authority which the Lord has given me for building up and not for tearing down.'[88] He, too, gives directions,[89] judges the unworthy in the community and excludes them from it,[90] and sets a norm for the various *charismata*.[91]

---

[76] Cf Acts 2:38; Rom 6:3f; Acts 19:5–6.
[77] Cf I Cor 11:23–26; Acts 20:7–12; 2:42.
[78] Cf James 5:14–16.
[79] Acts 8:17–18. Cf 9:17; 19:1–6; II Tim 1:6.
[80] Acts 13:3–5.   [81] I Tim 4:14. Cf Acts 6:1–6.
[82] Tit 1:5. For Timothy cf I Tim 5:22.
[83] Acts 2:37–38.
[84] Acts 6:2f; 15:1–2, 6, 22–31; 16:4.
[85] Acts 8:14; 11:22.   [86] Acts 5:1–11; 8:20f.
[87] Cf Acts 1:15f; 2:37f; 9:32: 'Now as Peter went here and there among them all'; 15:7–12; Gal 1:18.
[88] II Cor 13:10.
[89] I Cor 11:17f, 27f; I Thess 7; 4:2.
[90] I Cor 5:3–5, 11.   [91] I Cor 14:37–40.

Besides the twelve and Paul others, too, exercise the ministry of shepherd or guardian. On his departure from them, Paul says to the elders (*presbuteroi*) of the Church of Ephesus: 'Take heed to yourselves and to all the flock, in which the Holy Spirit has made you guardians (*episkopoi*), to feed (*poimainein*) the Church of the Lord which he obtained with his own blood.'[92] Similarly, Peter, in his catholic epistle: 'So I exhort the elders (*presbuteroi*) amongst you, as a fellow elder and a witness (*sumpresbuteros kai martus*) of the sufferings of Christ. . . . Tend the flock of God that is in your charge (*poimanate to en humin poimnion tou theou episkopountes*). . . . Likewise you that are younger be subject to your elders.'[93]

The elders are appointed by the apostles (Acts 14:23). Paul appoints Timothy in Ephesus with the task of judging (even the elders), rebuking, commanding (I Tim 5:9, 20, 7; II Tim 4:2). He did similarly with Titus in Crete (Tit 1:5, 13).

Thus we have Jesus Christ sent by the Father (Lk 4:18, 43; Jn 3:17-34; Heb 3:1); Paul sent by Jesus Christ (I Cor 1:1; 15:8f); Timothy, Titus, elders sent by Paul (I Cor 4:17; I Thess 3:2-6; I Tim 1:3; Tit 1:5; Acts 14:23); others sent by Timothy (II Tim 2:2): is this not a clear indication already in the New Testament (when the Church was just beginning to realize the practical problem of continuation and universalization) of apostolic succession? Is it not an indication of the understanding granted by the Holy Spirit into Jesus' intention in relation to his Church (cf Jn 14:26; Mt 28:18-20)?[94]

From what we have seen of the intention of Jesus expressed in his words shortly before his ascension, and from what we have seen of the realization of his intention through his Holy Spirit in the New

---

[92] Acts 20:28.
[93] I Pet 5:1, 2, 5. Cf also Eph 4:11 (pastors, *poimenas*); I Tim 5:17 (presbyters); Acts 11:30 (presbyters); 15:2-4, 6 (presbyters).
[94] Cf above, pp. 183f. It is of the utmost importance to note the convergence of two eminent modern Lutherans (E. Schlink a theologian and J. Jeremias an exegete) with Catholic teaching on the transmission of ministry through the imposition of hands, that is, with this form of apostolic succession. 'The commission to the concrete ministry also bequeaths upon the believer, who is driven by God's spirit, the concrete charism for the concrete ministry to which God calls him. . . . According to the testimony of the New Testament, the request is granted through the laying on of hands, the charism is likewise bestowed for the concrete ministry to which a member of the community is sent forth through prayer and the imposition of hands. "Ordination was not regarded as a mere form or as a symbolic action but as an act of the imparting of the Spirit" (J. Jeremias)'. E. Schlink, 'Die apostolische Sukzession' in his *Der kommende Christus und die kirchlichen Traditionen*, Göttingen, 1961, p. 167, quoted in Küng, *Structures of the Church*, pp. 170-1.

Testament Church itself, it is very hard to understand how Karl Barth can say that 'an organ of mediation or institution is not an integral constituent of the essence of the Church'.[95] The Church has a divinely instituted structure. Certainly this structure will and must find different historical realizations. But these realizations must be faithful in transposing, transforming or reforming the original. There is no question of the Church determining its constitution and institution in the fulfilment of its task.[96]

The statement of Barth just quoted is, of course, in complete fidelity to his basic principle. But it is not a statement which is completely faithful to the whole of Scripture and consequently, as I have already indicated,[97] jeopardizes the fundamental principle on which his theology is based.

Recent New Testament exegesis, precisely amongst Protestants, is of course posing an ever greater problem to Protestants with regard to Church order and ministry. One time the problem was not thought to be so serious. The so-called typically Catholic concept of the Church (that is, the Church of doctrine, law and order, of institutional office) was thought to be a late corruption of primitive Christianity. However, Protestant historians are compelled by historical research to push the point in time at which 'Catholic decadence' began further and further back. For Luther it began with the Middle Ages and he felt he could identify himself with the Church of the first millennium. For A. von Harnack it began with the first century through the Church's struggle with gnosticism. For E. Käsemann of the Bultmann school it begins even earlier: in the New Testament itself.[98] H. Schlier, even before he became a Catholic, came to much the same conclusion as Käsemann. This is a terribly serious development for the Protestant theologian and exegete whose unswerving loyalty has always been first of all to holy Scripture. Leading Protestant exegetes themselves acknowledge that the Catholic concept of a special office and order in the Church is found already in the New Testament. Käsemann is quite explicit: 'The time when one could confront Catholicism with the full text of Scripture is past beyond recall. Protestantism today can no longer apply the so-called formal principle without adopting an untenable position in terms of historical analysis.'[99] 'The

---

[95] Cf *CTKB*, pp. 267, 273f, 281f, 283–7, 303, 207.
[96] Cf *ibid.*, p. 248, and references in preceding note.
[97] Cf above, p. 171.
[98] Cf H. Küng, *Structures of the Church*, pp. 135f, for references.
[99] E. Käsemann, *Exegetische Versuche und Besinnungen*, I, Göttingen, 1960, pp. 221f, cited in Küng, *op. cit.*, p. 139.

dilemma of the protestant theologian is obvious: either to accept early Catholicism as an element of the New Testament and thereby definitely embark on the road to "late Catholicism", or else to reject early Catholicism as an element of the New Testament and correct the canon accordingly.'[100] H. Schlier chose the first path and became a Catholic in 1955. Basing himself, as I have just tried to do above, not only on the pastoral epistles but on the Epistle to the Ephesians as well as on the great Pauline epistles, he found that the Catholic understanding of order, office and succession was a genuine aspect of the New Testament. 'Hence it was, if I may say so, an authentic Protestant path which took me to the Church. . . . What led me to the Church was the New Testament as it presented itself to unbiased historical interpretation.'[101] E. Käsemann chose the second path. He limits the canon on the basis of a 'Gospel' to be determined by believers convinced by the Spirit in the Word.

On the basis of a private principle Käsemann limits the Church's canon. Using the same method of procedure K. Barth glosses over certain texts of Scripture. I have already noted this.[102] His omission of all mention of bishops (*episkopoi*) or of elders (*presbuteroi*) in an enumeration of New Testament ministers or forms of ministry is an obvious confirmation of this procedure. Strictly speaking he does not limit the canon. He says that at first, at least, the Church's witness must be accepted.[103] None the less, the canon is not for him definitively closed. And there is no principle in his theology which would forbid him limiting it. On the contrary, his actual minimalization of certain parts is in practice a limitation of the canon. In any case both Barth and Käsemann are constrained to limit Scripture. This is the great danger and high price involved in approaching the exegesis of Scripture with a pre-conceived principle. As H. Küng notes,[104] the Protestant protest on the basis of Scripture against the catholicity of the Church becomes a protest against the catholicity of Scripture and so cancels itself out by undermining the very foundation on which it rests.

On the one hand, it undermines its own basis. On the other, it leads to ever greater divisions. 'The wrongly understood *sola Scriptura* leads to a *sola pars Scripturae* and this in turn to a *sola pars Ecclesiae*

[100] H. Küng, *op. cit.*, p. 139.
[101] H. Schlier, 'Kurze Rechenschaft' in *Bekenntnis zur katholischen Kirche*, ed. by K. Hardt, Würzburg,[4] 1956, pp. 176f, cited in Küng, *Structures of the Church*, p. 141.
[102] Cf *CTKB*, pp. 38f.
[103] Cf *ibid.*, pp. 204–5.
[104] *Op. cit.*, pp. 144–5.

(party); in short to a devastating chaos in the proclamation of the Gospel and to a progressive fragmentation of Protestantism.'[105] Needless to say, Catholic writers are not entirely blameless in this respect. As regards the point in question our one-sided emphasis on the pastoral epistles amounted in practice to a restriction of Scripture and to a consequent one-sided and restricted emphasis on Church law, tradition and institutional order to the detriment of the charismatic Church of the great Pauline epistles, for example. At the moment, however, in assimilating this aspect also of the New Testament witness we are showing ourselves more truly faithful to the whole of Scripture (Catholic) than our Protestant brethren, who have to have recourse to a limitation of the canon or refuse to face up to the whole of Scripture in order to safeguard a primary principle.

In conclusion it is very interesting to note the similarity between Käsemann's selective principle and Barth's: the justification of the sinner.

'The Bible is neither the Word of God in an objective sense, nor is it a doctrinal system. It is the record of the history of the proclamation of the message of primitive Christianity. The Church, which canonized it, asserts, however, that it is precisely in this way that she becomes the bearer of the Gospel. The Church maintains, and can maintain this position here only because she views history portrayed and manifesting itself in terms of the justification of the sinner. Since her claim, however, is an attestation and a confession, she thereby summons us to submit our own history to a scrutiny in terms of the justification of the sinner. Thus we would be forced to make a decision not only as to whether we wish to follow the above summons or not, but likewise as to whether the core of Scripture is correctly grasped by such a confession.'[106]

II. THE THEOLOGICAL UNDERSTANDING OF THE CHURCH'S TRIPLE HIERARCHICAL MINISTRY

Jesus Christ is the supreme prophet, priest and king. He accomplished his prophetical, priestly and kingly offices once and for all and perfectly in time and as man, the unique mediator between God and man. This perfect mediation had to be offered, presented, effected in all

---

[105] Küng, *op. cit.*, p. 146.

[106] E. Käsemann, in *Exegetische Versuche und Besinnungen*, vol. I, p. 232, cited in Küng, *Structures of the Church*, p. 142.

men of all times and places. For this purpose he called and sent his disciples. Through his Spirit he granted them a share in his three offices. They are to continue his work in applying it to men and the world. Rather, he continues his work through them. Ascended to heaven, he wished that his unique mediation be offered to all men and effected in them in the same connatural way in which it was objectively realized.

All his disciples are called and sent in his service, which is the service of all men. All exist for and in the one service. But all do not accomplish it in the same way. Some are called to serve by teaching in his name, with his authority, by presiding at and performing certain sacrificial and sacramental actions, by guarding and ruling and leading others as their shepherd.[107] Christ through his Spirit empowers them in a special way, grants them a special participation in his own messianic offices. In doing so, he gives a certain structure to his Church—a hierarchico-monarchical structure. Some have an essentially different service from others, and an essentially different power to accomplish it.

The post-apostolic Fathers of the first two centuries, who ought to be reliable interpreters of the intention of the apostles and of the original community, affirm quite explicitly both the hierarchical structure of the Church (not, of course, in such words, but in the sense explained), and apostolic succession, in the sense that the apostles constituted others to succeed them in their ministry, and commanded these others to do the same.[108] Ignatius of Antioch is the first to mention the triple hierarchical degree of bishop, priest and

[107] Through the definitive commission of Jesus (Mt 28:18f) 'a number of men become his representatives (*Stellvertretern*) in the sense that they take his place and therewith receive an authoritative position first of all within the small group of Christians': Rengstorf, in *TWNT*, I, p. 432.

[108] Cf Clement of Rome (towards the end of the first century), *Ep. ad Cor.* 44:2, 3; 57 (ed. Funk, *Patres Apostolici*, I, 154f, 171f); Ignatius of Antioch (beginning of second century), *Ep. ad Eph.* 3:2–4:1 (Funk I, p. 217); 5:3–6:1 (Funk p. 219); *Ep. ad Smyrn.* 8:1, 2 (Funk I, p. 283); Polycarp of Smyrna (beginning of second century), *Ep. ad Philipp.* 5:3 (Funk I, p. 303); Hegesippus (towards the end of the second century), quoted by Eusebius, *Hist. Eccl.* 4:22, 2–3 (*PG*, 20, 378f); Irenaeus (towards the end of the second century), *Adv. Haer.* III, 3, 1–3 (*PG*, 7, 848f); Tertullian (at the end of the second century), *De Praescript. Haeret.* 32 (*PL*, 2, 44–5). There is no need to enter into the historical problem of the actual successors to the apostles or the development of the monarchical episcopate. The basic ecclesiological difference between Barth and Catholicism is not that of apostolic succession, but of the participation by the Church in Christ's offices, or of the Church's salvific activity. If Barth admitted the possibility of such a participation the problem of succession would present no difficulty to him.

deacon.¹⁰⁹ The New Testament and St Clement mention only a twofold, namely, a college of 'presbyters' or 'bishops', and deacons.¹¹⁰ Deacons have been present from the beginning.

1. DIACONATE

The ministry of the whole people of God is a *diakonia*, a service. This applies especially to members of the hierarchy. 'If any one would be first, he must be last of all and servant of all,' our Lord said to the twelve (Mk 9:35). That which was characteristic of the Saviour's actions must be the characteristic of their actions. 'A disciple is not above his teacher, nor a servant above his master; it is enough for the disciple to be like his teacher, and the servant like his master.'¹¹¹ Service of God and of neighbour is the really distinctive mark of the apostle, as it was of Christ.

> 'You know that the rulers of the Gentiles lord it over them, and their great men exercise authority over them. It shall not be so among you; but whoever would be great among you must be your servant, and whoever would be first among you must be your slave; even as the Son of man came not to be served but to serve, and to give his life as a ransom for many.'¹¹²

It is not without significance therefore that the task of those whom the Lord specially commissioned is termed 'service' or 'ministry' (*diakonia*) in the New Testament.¹¹³ The sacred power they receive is not for domination or tyranny, not for their own aggrandizement or exploitation, but is solely a power of service—service of Jesus Christ, the world and the Church. Even philologically the New Testament excludes any identity between authority in the Church and authority in the world.

> 'The New Testament speaks of right and authority in office, in its task of *oikonomia* (I Cor 4: 1f; Col 1:25), in the *exousia* conferred on it by the Lord for the building up of the Church (II Cor 10:8; 13:10); it speaks of the task of judging (Mt 19:28), of punishing (I Cor 5:5), of superintending (Rom 12:8), of leading (Heb 13:17). But all this is ultimately service. *Diakonia* in the New Testament

---

¹⁰⁹ *Ep. ad Magn.* 6:1 (Funk I, p. 235); *ad Trall.* 2:13 (Funk I, pp. 243f).
¹¹⁰ Cf Phil 1:1; I Tim 3:8, 12; Acts 11:30; 14:23; Clement of Rome, *First Ep. to the Cor.*, 42 (Funk I, pp. 152f).
¹¹¹ Mt 10:24–5. Cf Jn 12:26.
¹¹² Mt 20:24–28.
¹¹³ Cf Acts 1:17–25; 21:19; Rom 11:13; I Tim 1:12; DCC, n. 24.

is the all-comprehensive, the most profound word for "office". The New Testament seems to be incapable of using words otherwise frequently met in Greek as designation of office (like *archē, timē, telos*) for an office in the church. The New Testament knows these words but does not use them in the realm of the church. *Archē* is restricted to the authority of synagogue and state or to the angelic powers; *timē* to the dignity of office of the Old Testament high priest. The result of such lexicographical investigation is impressive evidence that office in the Church is an institution essentially ordered to service. The result also makes manifest the self-understanding of the New Testament that order and law mean essentially different things in the Church and in the world. Therefore they cannot be named with the same words.'[114]

But while diaconate denotes the general ministry of the community it also denotes a specific ministry within the community, as Barth points out.[115] Paul addresses one of his letters 'to all the saints in Christ Jesus who are at Philippi, with the bishops and deacons'.[116] This is the oldest reference we possess to the existence of a special Christian ministry called diaconate. Its origin and exact function is not easy to determine. Material assistance to the poor in the community was a characteristic of apostolic activity from the beginning.[117] It is possible that this became the object of a specific ministry and of specific ministers.

The original sense of *diakonein* in the New Testament is to 'wait at table'.[118] The ministry of the diaconate in the New Testament community retained this original sense, and it is made the symbol of all charitable and administrative activity. The retention of the original sense explains also the later history of the diaconate, namely, its connection with the liturgy.[119] For its service at table was above all service at the common meal of all, the eucharist. Hence the diaconate is both an external service of the community as well as a liturgical service. From the Middle Ages onwards it has been reduced to a mere stepping-stone to the priesthood. Vatican II has restored its importance and breadth.

We can understand also how from the beginning it was regarded as sacramental and hierarchical. Acts 6:16 records that the Apostles

[114] K. H. Schelkle, *Discipleship and Priesthood*, p. 39, note 1.
[115] Cf CTKB, pp. 334f.
[116] Phil 1:1. Cf I Tim 3:8–12.
[117] Cf II Cor 8–9; Acts 4:34–37.
[118] Cf Lk 17:8; 22:27; Jn 12:2.
[119] Cf Jungmann, *art. cit.* in *LTK*, 3, 319–21.

prayed and laid their hands upon seven chosen men and appointed them to the duty of serving at table—which till then was part of the apostles' own task. Even if this passage cannot be regarded as narrating the origin of the diaconate[120] it does witness to the fact that the apostles considered it within their right and power to grant a participation to others in their apostolic task through the laying on of hands.[121] According to the New Testament, as we have seen, the latter action conferred the Spirit, that is, it was regarded as sacramental.[122] According to the early post-apostolic tradition the diaconate is attributed to the institution of the apostles, is always placed amongst the Church's hierarchical functions,[123] and is conferred through a rite of ordination.[124] There is no contradiction of Scripture when the Catholic Church speaks of diaconate as sacramental and hierarchical.[125]

2. UNIQUENESS OF THE ORIGINAL APOSTOLIC CHURCH

Just as the mission of the apostles by Jesus bears a certain similarity to that of Jesus by the Father, the mission of others by the apostles bears a certain similarity to that of the apostles. It is not identical. The apostles were sent above all to *found* the Church. Theirs was a unique historical situation. As O. Cullmann says, continuity must not be at the expense of uniqueness. 'An application to the future is conceivable which respects the historical uniqueness of the situation in which the Church was founded.'[126] The apostles received many gifts for the foundation of the Church which were intransmissible. Yet the mission of others is a continuation of their own mission. The others receive from them the ministry of guarding faithfully the deposit, imposing hands, and guiding others, so that Christ may be the truth, the life and the way for all. This is the meaning of 'apostolic succession', which is not a succession of 'apostles'.

'Go into all the world and preach the gospel to the whole creation. He who believes and is baptized will be saved; but he who

[120] Cf Meyer, in *TWNT*, II, pp. 84, 30f; 90, 35f; Gewiess, in *LTK*, 3, 319.
[121] K. Rahner, in *LTK*, 3, 322.
[122] Cf I Tim 4: 14; II Tim 1:6; Acts 8:17–18; 9:17;13:3–5; 19:1–6.
[123] In the New Testament itself it is always mentioned in close connection with bishops, and after them. Cf Phil 1:1; I Tim 3:1–13.
[124] Cf Rahner, *loc. cit.*
[125] In the Council of Trent, *Sess.* 23, cap. 4 and can. 6 (DS 1767, 1776); Vatican II, DCC, ch. 3, n. 29.
[126] O. Cullmann, *Peter* . . . , p. 162.

does not believe will be condemned. . . . And they went forth and preached everywhere, while the Lord worked with them and confirmed the message by the signs that attended it. Amen.'[127]

This passage presupposes the existence already of the 'Gospel', of the message to be proclaimed. Revelation ceased with the apostles. This does not necessarily mean that it ended 'on the day in the calendar when the last apostle died', but that it ceased when the foundation of the Church was complete.[128]

The revelation, destined for the faith of the world, is unique. It occurred once and for all. Catholic theology asserts this no less than Barth.[129] We do not say, therefore, that the post-apostolic Church is 'in the same immediate relationship to God, Christ and the Holy Spirit'.[130] As Barth points out, there are no new prophets and apostles who receive revelation in the same direct way.[131]

Barth's objection has, however, a deeper ring to it, if I understand him correctly. We assert the uniqueness of revelation in the sense that it took place in a definite period of time through a direct and immediate relationship between certain men and Jesus Christ, and his Holy Spirit. This revelation and this relationship occurred only once. But we also assert that this uniqueness does not exclude a continuation, in the sense that the unique revelation has to be transmitted by the Holy Spirit in and through, and therefore also by, human-historical means so that it can reach the end of the world. We do assert, therefore, a direct contact with revelation in the Church (as the whole complex of the tradition of revelation, including Scripture and the Church's institutions). This does not mean the identity of revelation and the Church, as Barth repeatedly affirms.[132] Nor does it mean a repetition of the original direct relationship between God and man. It means a direct relationship with the revelation *transmitted*. There is no new revelation in the Church. The Church is bound to the once and for all, unique revelation.

3. THE CHURCH'S HIERARCHICAL TEACHING MINISTRY

Here we come up against another very frequent Barthian objection to Roman Catholic doctrine. In affirming a continuation of revelation

[127] Mk 16:15–16, 20. Cf Gal 1:6–12; 2:2.
[128] Cf Rahner, *Inspiration in the Bible*, Quaest. Disp. I, 1961, p. 60, n. 34; pp. 68–9.
[129] Cf e.g., DS 3421, 548, 2905, 3020.
[130] Cf *CTKB*, p. 198.
[131] Cf *ibid*.   [132] *Ibid.*, pp. 198–200.

in the Church (in the sense of a human-historical tradition or transmission) the Catholic Church, he says, ceases to be obedient to revelation. It controls Jesus Christ and his revelation. It relativizes his majesty.[133] The fact that it renders present the Gospel which was once and for all revealed, and in this sense lives in direct contact with revelation, means that it rules itself, that it controls revelation, that it controls Jesus Christ. Many questions converge here. I will mention two points bearing on the Church's teaching authority, which should show that, at least in theory, his accusations are not justified.

Firstly, according to Catholic ecclesiology, the Church does not control revelation, but revelation controls the Church. The Church's teaching does not constitute a new revealed truth. Its function is to preserve, to guard, to proclaim the unique, once and for all revelation. There is progress in understanding, but it is a progress in the understanding of what has been once and for all revealed. It cannot go beyond what has been already revealed. Here we see the distinction between the original apostolic Church and the post-apostolic Church. The post-apostolic Church does not proclaim new truths, but guards and interprets what has been revealed. It is tied to revelation.

This is quite clear precisely in that which Barth calls the 'culmination of the identification of the Church with Jesus and his revelation',[134] namely, the infallibility of the pope. Infallibility is not revelation. In itself infallibility is something negative. It means immunity from error because of Jesus Christ's prayer that Peter's faith may not fail, or because of his promise of being with his Church always. It is the negative expression of a positive assistance. It does not of course preclude error on the part of individuals, including the individual who is the Church's head. But it does mean an immunity from error on the part of the Church as a whole, and on the part of the pope acting as the head of the Church in the interpretation of revelation. Positively it means a fundamental remaining in the truth. The Church, and the pope as its head, has the positive assistance of the Holy Spirit to guard and faithfully to interpret revelation according to Scripture and the apostolic tradition.

The head of the Church's infallible declaration is not revelation, for two reasons. Firstly, because it *is* not the Word of God. To use scholastic terminology, man is its secondary principal cause under the action of the sole first cause, God, or the Holy Spirit. Because man is a secondary principal cause, that is, because the pope's infallible declaration is due to the reflection of a faithful mind (expressing the faith of the Church and always under the influence of the

[133] Cf *ibid.*, pp. 198–202.   [134] Cf *CTKB*, pp. 199–200.

primary cause) it cannot be called, strictly speaking, the Word of God. It is the word of a human person infallibly interpreting revelation.

'Unlike God's revelation the charism of infallibility bestowed on the successors of Peter by the Spirit signifies a. not a new authoritative divine word, but only an explanation and a defence of the revelation that has already occurred; b. the main cause always remains the human subject (the pope); c. for it, the assistance of the Holy Spirit does not have the character of a special inner revelation, but only that of an external preservation from error; d. hence it is not a divine word but only a human utterance about the word of God.'[135]

It is precisely because it is a human word that it needs a special divine assistance to prevent error.[136]

The head of the Church's infallible declaration is not revelation, secondly, because it only interprets and guards revelation by means of a faithful interpretation of revelation as it comes down to us. It is tied to Scripture and tradition. The definition of papal infallibility given by Vatican I expressly forestalls Barth's misinterpretation. The assistance of the Spirit is promised not for a new revelation but for the faithful custody and exposition of the revelation once made to the apostles.

[135] H. Küng, *Structures of the Church*, p. 322, following S. Tromp, *De sacrae scripturae inspiratione*, Rome,⁴ 1945, p. 96: 'That which makes the Roman pontiff as teacher infallible, very clearly differs from revelation. a. There is no new authoritative speaking of God, but what he has spoken before is explained, unfolded, and defined. b. The principal cause speaking *ex cathedra* is and remains the Roman pontiff. c. The infallibility of the pronouncement does not come from internal influence but out of external assistance presupposing the ordinary gifts of the Holy Spirit and human effort; God is prepared to correct if the pontiff should deviate from the truth. d. The pontiff's speaking is not the word of God but about the word of God.'

[136] The case is different with regard to the hierarchical *priestly* ministry. In the proclamation of the Word of God, or the celebration of the mysteries of the liturgy, the human word is truly the Word of God and the sacramental actions (consecration of the species at Mass, absolution in the sacrament of confession, conferring of the Spirit by the imposition of hands) involve the divine agency. For then they are pure instruments, and not secondary principal causes. They no longer act by a power which truly resides in them. They act in complete dependence on God who uses them. For he alone can perform these acts. Cf Congar, *The Mystery of the Church*, pp. 45–6 (in the French original, *Esquisses* . . . , p. 49, n. 1, he refers to an article of his in *Irenikon*, 1933). This is very near Karl Barth's conception of the Church's ministry. For him it is an act of God alone through human instrumentality. The human instrument is not a cause. Still, as far as I know, all Catholic authors attribute some causality to the human instrument.

'The Holy Spirit is not promised to Peter's successors that they may reveal new doctrine through his revelation, but that, with his assistance, they may preserve holy and faithfully explain the revelation transmitted through the apostles or the deposit of faith.'[137]

This doctrine is repeated by Vatican II:

'This teaching office is not above the word of God, but serves it, teaching only what has been handed on, listening to it devoutly, guarding it scrupulously, and explaining it faithfully by divine commission and with the help of the Holy Spirit; it draws from this one deposit of faith everything which it presents for belief as divinely revealed.'[138]

Thus instead of controlling Christ, and denying the uniqueness of revelation, papal infallibility and the infallibility of the Church assert and safeguard both. Jesus Christ mediates his unique revelation through the Church's teaching office. The ministries and sacraments of the Church are nothing but the proclamation of the uniqueness of Christ's reconciliation and revelation. To say that Catholic doctrine identifies the Church (pope, bishops, teaching office) and revelation, or attributes to it a control over revelation, is certainly a misinterpretation, even if misleading terminology by Catholics themselves (such as 'the Church is the continuation of Christ', etc.) contributed to this misunderstanding.

'As difficult as it is for a Protestant Christian to understand the infallibility of the pope, it can be understood only in the perspective that has just been sketched: not as a self-glorifying appropriation of divine revelation but as a humble, obedient, non-partisan service of interpretation, directed and protected by the Holy Spirit, that remains a human interpretation. All understanding of papal infallibility which, in one way or another, would amount to an

---

[137] 'Neque enim Petri successoribus Spiritus Sanctus promissus est, ut eo revelante novam doctrinam patefacerent, sed ut, eo assistente, traditam per Apostolos revelationem seu fidei depositum sancte custodirent et fideliter exponerent': DS 3070.

[138] 'Quod quidem Magisterium non supra verbum Dei est, sed eidem ministrat, docens nonnisi quod traditum est, quatenus illud, ex divino mandato et Spiritu Sancto assistente, pie audit, sancte custodit et fideliter exponit, ac ea omnia ex hoc uno fidei deposito haurit quae tamquam divinitus revelata credenda proponit': *Dogmatic Constitution on Divine Revelation*, n. 10. Cf also DCC, n. 25.

identification of the Church with revelation, is a misunderstanding of papal infallibility.'[139]

▼ The second point I would like to emphasize is that the Church's teaching office does not control Jesus Christ or relativize God's majesty. We must understand Barth's difficulty with Catholic thought. For him the uniqueness of revelation excludes all human-historical tradition. It does not exclude all continuation. But its continuation must take place exactly as it took place originally, namely, as God's act alone. This is the sense in which it is unique. There can be no givenness of the Word of God in human, oral or written words. He thus rejects both the Catholic doctrine of Scripture as well as of tradition. The basis of his rejection is clear from his answer to the 'cleverer exponents of Catholic and neo-Protestant theology', and from his rejection of the theology of 'and': it denies the sole subjectivity of God.[140] There can be no such thing as a union of the divine with the human which enables the human to act as a divine-human principle. Barth asserts an indirect mediation of revelation now. It comes through Scripture. But as God's act alone. The human word does not mediate the Word of God. Whence he can only understand the Catholic teaching of a 'tradition' of revelation to mean an identification of the Church and revelation, and a control of Jesus Christ.

Now, my whole investigation of the doctrine of Scripture with regard to the Church's hierarchical ministry shows that human beings have been equipped and sent to speak, proclaim and teach the Word of God. Barth's exegesis is determined by a preconceived principle. I am always coming back to this point. But the fact that human beings are so empowered does not mean that they control Jesus Christ. On the contrary, Jesus Christ controls them precisely through this power. For the power is his. It is the power of his Spirit. St Paul puts this quite vividly:

> '. . . of which I became a minister according to the divine office which was given to me for you, to make the word of God fully known. . . . For this I toil, striving with all the energy which he mightily inspires within me. . . . For we cannot do anything against the truth, but only for the truth. . . . I write this while I am away from you, in order that when I come I may not have to be severe in my use of the authority which the Lord has given me for building up and not for tearing down.'[141]

[139] H. Küng, *Structures of the Church*, p. 324.
[140] Cf *CTKB*, pp. 200-1.   [141] Col 1: 25, 29; II Cor 13:8, 10.

The power which *he has* does not spring from himself but *from God*. Paul expresses this through his recurrent theme of divine power in human weakness. 'But we have this treasure in earthen vessels, to show that the transcendent power belongs to God and not to us.'[142]

Barth's veiled reference to the semi-Pelagianism of the Catholic doctrine of tradition and of the Church's authority[143] has no justification in the Church's own explanation of her teaching. The Church simply repeats what Scripture says: St Paul proclaims (and infallibly)[144] God's Word. And yet the power in which Paul does so belongs to God. The pope proclaims (and infallibly) God's Word. And yet the power in which the pope does so belongs to God. The pope, or bishops, are not successors of Christ. They are only his vicars. That is to say, they receive from him the power to be the visible representation of his action. Christ is not now visibly present. But he is present invisibly. He is the Lord of the Church through the spiritual power of his visible representatives.

We are grateful to Karl Barth for his persistent reminder to theology and Christian life that Jesus Christ is the unique mediator between God and man, that he is the unique source of grace and power. In this we are entirely in agreement with him. It is Christ himself through his apostles who teaches, sanctifies and rules. As Cullman says, since it is Christ himself who presides at the transmission of his Word there is no more *opposition* between apostolic tradition and direct revelation.[145] Unfortunately, Barth's christocentrism is coloured and mitigated (yes, mitigated) by his theory of Christ's sole subjectivity, which seems to spring originally from his conception of justification, and which has profound and negative effects in his christology and ecclesiology.

It is precisely because the risen Christ preaches the Word of God to all nations through the service or ministry of the Church[146] that we can really speak of an 'authoritative tradition of the Word of God'.[147] For this reason we can and must speak of a mediation of the Word of God by the Church. Karl Barth rejects this.[148] His former attempt at a theology of mediation was unsuccessful.[149] The authority

---

[142] II Cor 5:7.   [143] Cf *CTKB*, p. 199.   [144] Cf Gal 1:8–9.
[145] Cf O. Cullmann, *La Tradition* . . . , p. 28.
[146] This is excellently formulated in ch. 3, n. 21, of Vatican II's Constitution on the Church, with relation to bishops. Jesus Christ is the subject.
[147] Cf *CTKB*, p. 202.   [148] Cf *ibid.*, p. 197.
[149] Cf. *ibid.*, pp. 77f. Theology must be both *Vermittlungs-* and *Reflexions-Theologie*. The mediation takes place through the response of the human subject to the divine gift bestowed on him, or through the human response created by the divine action.

which he attributes to the Church under the Word is really no authority *of* the Church.

Again, it is precisely because the risen Christ acts through the ministry of the Church that the Church's teaching authority involves no *sacrificium intellectus*. Barth is quite right in saying that freedom is just as necessary for the mediation to us of God's Word in Holy Scripture, for the exercise of its sway in the Church, and therefore for the creation of the Church itself.[150] I cannot agree, however, that the Church's teaching authority according to Catholic doctrine excludes a true human response and liberty, and I cannot help but think that Barth's exposition of Church authority does not differ from what he castigates as liberal neo-Protestantism.

Since the Church's authority has been given it by Christ, and exists solely in his service, it does not exclude but creates the true and free human response. The fact that Christ's teaching authority comes through the service of a human medium does not destroy its divine creative power, just as its human mediation did not destroy it in the case of Jesus himself, or Paul. There is no contradiction between dogmatic intolerance and a true Christian response. As the Protestant author De Albornoz remarks: 'We sincerely consider it unjust to think that the Roman Catholic Church is intolerant because it is dogmatic. The illation, even in Protestant thinking, is most defective.'[151] The truth or Word of God is the true liberating force of the world. Through the indwelling presence and assistance of the Holy Spirit it comes to man through the Church, despite human weakness, error and sin. Truth and freedom is the effect of the Church's decisions precisely because they are infallible, that is, precisely because they infallibly witness to the truth and freedom of Christ.

Acceptance of the Word of God, through the same Holy Spirit acting in the mind and heart of man, is the required and liberating response of all Christians (cf Jn 8:31–32). But even from this point of view it is not right to say that Catholic teaching eliminates all freedom and responsibility of personal decision, no matter how fallible, in the face of an infallible authority. For Catholic doctrine, too, the individual conscience is always the direct norm of action. Even when it is invincibly erroneous the individual person must follow his conscience. It is a misinterpretation to say of Catholic as of Protestant doctrine that the fallible subjective conscience is effaced or overpowered by an infallible objective norm.

[150] Cf *ibid.*, pp. 209f.
[151] De Albornoz, *Roman Catholicism and Religious Liberty*, Geneva, 1959, p. 23, n. 4.

'For the Catholic, too, it is not ultimately the objective norm of the teaching voice but the subjective decision of *conscience* which has finally to decide on a believing acceptance of the revealed truth laid down by the authority of the Church. It is really not the case that the faith of a Catholic is entirely accounted for by slavish obedience to the rigid law of the Church. He, too, is making a personal act, an act of reflective thought and moral decision springing from the deep centre of his freedom, an act of choice. For him too it is an act that can only be performed in the conscience itself. Indeed, if his conscience, on subjectively cogent grounds, becomes involved in invincible error and he finds himself compelled to refuse his assent to the Church's teaching, he is, in the Catholic view, bound to leave the Church. The most eminent of Catholic theologians, St Thomas Aquinas, expressly declares that a man is bound in conscience to separate himself from the Christian body if he is unable to believe in the divinity of Christ (*Summa theol.*, I–II, q. 19, ad. 5). Thus the two confessions [that is, Lutheran and Catholic] meet each other in their recognition of an ecclesiastical teaching authority and in the decisive place they give to the judgment of the individual conscience.'[152]

Barth is quite right in saying that the basis of all true authority and freedom is christological. But he has no right to preclude *a priori* the possibility that Christ exercises his authority and freedom through human instruments. Is not Barth himself guilty of his own accusation, namely, of the limitation of God's freedom and lordship?

Barth once said in conversation that his decisive objection against the apostolic succession of the primacy of Peter in the bishop of Rome was that 'I cannot hear the voice of the Good Shepherd as coming from this "chair of Peter" '.[153] Even if he did, of course, this would not mean that he would accept the Catholic doctrine of the infallibility of the pope. None the less, this statement calls attention to the fact that the theoretical elaboration of the Church's ministry as a humble service of Jesus Christ is of little use unless it is put into practice.

'The teaching office of the Church is, at all levels, continually faced with the task of showing in all things that it is a selfless, humble, helpful service of human beings. An arrogant tone, a loveless attitude, frequent denunciations, authoritarian interventions without reason given and condemnations without a man's being

[152] K. Adam, *One and Holy*, London, 1954, p. 40.
[153] Related by H. Küng in *The Living Church*, London, 1963, p. 301.

heard in his own cause, totalitarian repression of free discussion—all this makes the Church's teaching authority something *incredible* to people both inside and outside the Catholic Church. All this is incredible because it is *unevangelical*, contrary to the Gospel.'[154]

Since the interpretation of the Bible is often pre-conditioned and coloured by existing reality must we not say that the failure of exegetes of different confessions to come to agreement as regards an office of unity in the Church is due in great part to the unbiblical historical realizations of that office? Does not the historical appearance of the Petrine ministry as a papal and Roman power- and dominion-structure not automatically preclude the attempt to find even its kernel in Jesus Christ's message of freedom and service? The office of unity can thus lead in fact to disunity, or to the prolongation of disunity, however paradoxical that may sound. It must embody the biblical Petrine ministry, and to the world of today. How much of the existing structure would disappear if only it became more open to the Gospel and to the technological and especially secularized world of today! But until this takes place the possibility of the reunion of all Christians is very slight. In this respect Pope John XXIII achieved a tremendous ecumenical breakthrough. As H. Küng so admirably puts it:

'It is not the claims, the "rights", the "chain of succession" as such which are decisive, but the exercise and carrying out of a ministry in practice, service in action. When John XXIII began his great ecumenical work for the Church, for Christendom and for the world, mankind was not very interested in his place in a chain and whether the legitimacy of his office was historically founded. What mankind saw with relief and joy was this: here was a man who for all his human weakness was a real rock in the modern age, able to give a new anchorage and a new sense of communion to Christianity (cf Mt 16:18). Here was a man who from his own deep sense of faith was able to strengthen and encourage the brethren (cf Lk 22:32). Here was a man, who was able to tend his sheep, as his Lord once did, with unselfish love (cf Jn 21:15–17). Not that the whole of mankind therefore became Catholic. But they felt spontaneously that these actions and this spirit had the Gospel of Christ

---

[154] *Id., ibid.*, pp. 299–300. We may recall the already cited words of H. de Lubac: 'If the Church is not the sacrament, the effective sign of Christ, then she is nothing': *The Splendour of the Church*, p. 161. Cf *CTKB*, pp. 302, 268, for Karl Barth's truly evangelical concept of authority and leadership in this respect.

behind them and were at all events justified by that Gospel. And this kind of legitimacy is more decisive for the Petrine ministry than any other.'[155]

4. THE CHURCH'S HIERARCHICAL SANCTIFYING MINISTRY

Turning now to a theological consideration of priesthood I hasten to stress that the Catholic conception of the hierarchical priesthood, of the Mass and the sacraments, in no way denies or impugns the unique high-priesthood of Jesus Christ, nor the uniqueness and perfection of his once and for all act of redemption.[156] Barth is quite justified in his assertion of the uniqueness and perfection of Christ's priestly sacrifice.[157] But this uniqueness and perfection does not exclude but includes the Catholic priesthood, Mass and sacraments.

Jesus Christ entered once and for all into the holy place offering himself as a sacrifice for sin. In this offering he accomplished once and for all, and perfectly, the reconciliation of the world. His sacrifice is a once and for all act in the sense that it is eternal. Seated at the right hand of God he is a priest for ever according to the order of Melchizedek. 'But he holds his priesthood permanently, because he continues for ever. Consequently, he is able for all time to save those who draw near to God through him, since he always lives to make intercession for them.' This is the teaching of the Epistle to the Hebrews.[158]

I agree with Karl Barth in interpreting the once and for allness of Christ's priesthood and sacrifice as an eternal actuality, and in seeing in this eternal actuality the basis and efficiency of its mediation here and now.[159] Christ's objective reconciliation was a divine–human, an eternal–temporal act. As a human, temporal, historical act, it is past. But as the personal act of God it is eternal. As such it is not past, but takes place eternally at the right hand of the Father. The mysteries of his life endure for ever in Christ's existence in glory.[160] The heavenly Christ is the real and true prolongation of the earthly Christ—and not

---

[155] *The Church*, pp. 463–4. Cf also pp. 471–2 where Küng styles this reincarnation of the Gospel ministry by John XXIII, in distinction from his immediate predecessors, 'a voluntary evangelical renunciation of spiritual power' and sees in this voluntary renunciation the only hope for Catholic renewal and the reunion of Christians.
[156] Cf, e.g., DS 1513, 1740.
[157] Cf *CTKB*, pp. 77f, 173.
[158] Heb 7:24–25; 6:20; 7:27; 8:1; 9:12; 9:26; 10:10, 12.
[159] Cf *CTKB*, pp. 176f.
[160] Cf Schillebeeckx, *Christ the Sacrament*, 64–75.

the Church or the sacraments. The problem of mediation, or of the subjective realization of reconciliation, is not so much (again in agreement with Barth) one of a spatio-temporal before and after, as of an above and below. The risen Christ remains the mediator in the subjective realization of reconciliation. He is so in the same personal act in which he accomplished the objective reconciliation. As Barth says, the objective and subjective are but 'moments' of the one redemptive occurrence coming to man in the *simul* of the one event. The act of salvation is one simultaneous event, whose subject is the one God by the one Christ, through the one Spirit.[161] This is the *ephapax* of his eternal priesthood and sacrifice.

His subjective realization of reconciliation is sacramental, just as his objective was. It is realized at a particular point in space and time, through visible *media*. It is always *his* reconciliation. Thus before he ascended to heaven he granted to certain men a participation in his own unique priesthood and sent them to bestow his Spirit through determined visible means. This is the visible form of his heavenly, invisible action. It is the visible sign, projection, offering, efficacy of the heavenly Christ's redemptive will. As such it prolongs the function of Christ's body in its earthly-historical state. Christ's objective redemption reaches us in the only form connatural to us, and which has meaning for us. As the personal act of God the mysteries of Christ's earthly historical life are eternally actual (or are eternally prolonged) and temporally actual in the Church's liturgy. The Church is the earthly-historical form of the glorified and invisible Christ. Her liturgy is the celebration in mystery or in sacrament of the once and for all redemption of Christ.[162]

The hierarchical priesthood in the Church is not a denial of Christ's unique high-priesthood. It is a participation in Christ's priesthood, given by Christ himself to his Church. Surely the freedom of God does not exclude this! His priests are not 'other Christs' in the sense that they remove or replace the heavenly Christ. Christ is always the supreme high-priest. Human priests are simply the selected visible

---

[161] Cf *CTKB*, p. 173.
[162] Thus St Thomas held that it is not only the *Christus passus* who effects salvation now, but the actual passion, death and resurrection of Christ. Cf *Summa theol.*, III, q. 48, art. 6; q. 50, art. 6; q. 56, art 1, ad 3. This insistence on the perennial aspect of Christ's earthly life is very frequent in the Church's liturgy. There is a transtemporal identification of past and present in one perennial 'today'. Cf, e.g., the antiphons to the *Benedictus* (Lauds) and *Magnificat* (Vespers) in the office of the Roman breviary for the feast of the Epiphany, 6 January. All this is but a commentary on Heb 13:8: 'Jesus is the same yesterday and today and for ever.'

forms through whom he acts. They take the place, not of the glorified Christ, but of his earthly, visible form. In this sense they are 'other Christs'.

Scholastic terminology (even if one rejects both it and medieval theology, one must at least acknowledge that it does not deny the above but in some way explains it) explains this by saying that they are merely the second instrumental agents of the ascending movement of sacrifice and the descending movement of the sacraments. The sole primary cause is always God, or Jesus Christ as God. A secondary cause acts under the influence of the primary cause. It can be principal or instrumental. It is principal when its own human qualities are active as a cause. It is instrumental when its own human qualities are not active as a cause. The instrument is a cause, too, but solely in the power of the primary cause. That is, it is a cause in its factual use by God.

In the exercise of his kingly and prophetical office the man Jesus is a secondary principal cause. Those who participate in these two offices of Christ in his Church are also secondary principal causes of their teaching and guiding. In the exercise of his priestly office Christ's human acts and words are solely an instrumental cause, but an instrumental cause joined in personal unity to the sole primary cause. Those who participate in his priestly office in the Church are secondary, instrumental causes, joined to the divine Spirit, but not in personal unity (only in this sense 'separate'). This means that they act solely in virtue of a power received from the sole primary cause. They have been designated and sealed for a certain office. While good moral and human qualities are intrinsically demanded, the fulfilment of the priestly office is independent of these qualities. It is God who performs the priestly acts, using man as his *ex officio* instrument.[163] This is the reason, and the sole reason, for the infallible effectiveness (*ex opere operato*) of the Church's priesthood. The priest is merely the visible form of the heavenly Christ's once and for all, supreme, eternal, high-priesthood.

There is an analogy between the hierarchical and common priesthoods in the Church—an analogy which stresses the dissimilarity more than the similarity.[164] Both are related as true and real

[163] 'Sed consecratio non est actus personalis ipsius sacerdotis, sed Dei cuius verbis consecrat. Ergo non impeditur propter propriam qualitatem': St Thomas, *IV Sent.*, dist. 13, q. 1, art. 1, quaestiuncula III. Cf St Augustine, *In Joann.*, tract. V, n. 18 (*PL*, 35, 1423), and tract. VI, n. 7 (*PL*, 35, 1428) (cited in Congar, *Chrétiens Désunis*, p. 97, n. 2).

[164] For this analogical conception of the types of priesthood in the Church cf Vatican II, DCC, ch. 2, n. 10, and the commentary of A. Grillmeier in

participations in the one priesthood of Christ. But the hierarchical priesthood is not simply a higher degree or intensification of the priesthood of all. It is an *essentially* different spiritual power. Christ, the eternal high-priest, consecrates his once and for all sacrifice through the hierarchical priest *alone*. They alone as his ministers, acting in his name and not as representatives of the community,[165] render Christ present on the altar. Of course, acting in his name they do actually represent the community, because they act as the visible form of him who in his person represents all. This last point is the christological basis of the practice in the Latin Catholic Church of the so-called 'private' Mass.

The sacrifice of the Mass does not deny or impugn the uniqueness and perfection of Christ's once and for all sacrifice on the cross. For *it is* Christ's once and for all perfect sacrifice. Christ's sacrifice has no need of perfection, repetition, representation or actualization. In this I am in agreement with Karl Barth, no matter what he thinks.[166] Christ's sacrifice on the cross is an eternally actual reality. His redemptive act takes place eternally at the right hand of the Father. It also takes place on earth in sacramental form for our subjective sanctification. There is no confusion here of 'ultimate and penultimate things'.[167] Christ himself is the subject in his one redemptive act sacramentally accomplished on earth. What his ministers do is the 'response' to *his* institution. In his pure mercy Jesus Christ has willed to present himself in his eternal redeeming act sacramentally in time, and in all times. Through his visible presentation of his mystery he achieves the subjective realization of reconciliation.

Christ's objective reconciliation was sacramental. The mode in which he achieves subjective reconciliation is also sacramental. He is the one sole mediator. But he exists now in a glorified form. To present his one sacrifice to us as he accomplished it once and for all in time, he uses a visible, human Church. He thus continues the economy of salvation he inaugurated while on earth in his visible form as man. He offers himself to us in his redeeming act in the only way connatural to us. This is the infinite mercy of his redeeming will. The purpose of this sacramental offering is man's subjective reconciliation. He created man, and saved him objectively, without him. He saves him

---

Commentary on the Documents of Vatican II, ed. by H. Vorgrimler, vol. I, pp. 156–9.

[165] Cf also Vatican II, *Decree on the Ministry and Life of Priests*, ch. I, n. 2.

[166] Cf *CTKB*, pp. 77f, 173, 289–90.

[167] Cf *ibid.*, pp. 77f.

also subjectively, but not without him. He does everything possible to accommodate himself to man, including his desire to leave man free to accept him or not. He places his once and for all redeeming act in visible proximity to man through his Church. He cannot do any more. It is up to man, under the interior invitation of God, to join himself to the ascending offering by Christ of Christ's eternal sacrifice, in order to participate in the communion of the one Spirit in God's descending action of sanctification in the sacrament. This is the theological reason underlying the Catholic's obligation of frequent offering of the Mass.

I will have to ask whether Barth really safeguards a subjective realization of man's reconciliation. If all is absorbed into Christ's act alone then obviously there is no reason for a sacramental economy. In any case, in the above explanation of the Catholic view, I can see no denial whatever of the perfection and uniqueness of Christ's sacrifice accomplished once and for all. There is the same high-priest and the same victim. The Mass is Christ's one, perfect, once and for all sacrifice, in sacramental form, for the subjective reconciliation of the world.[168]

My last point concerns the sacraments proper. Here too we not only can but must agree with Barth in saying that Christ's objective redeeming act is 'the one *mysterium*, the one sacrament, and the one existential fact before and beside and after which there is no room for any other of the same rank'.[169] But here again I do not agree that this excludes the reality and efficacy of the Church's seven sacraments. On the contrary, it is precisely that which guarantees their efficacy.

Christ's objective, once and for all, eternally actual redeeming act, is actual on earth in a visible form in and through the sacraments of the Church. The risen Christ is himself the sole principal cause. The sacraments are only secondary instrumental causes, in the sense already explained. What they do is done solely in the power of Christ. Thus the well-known expression of the efficacy of the sacraments by the phrase *ex opere operato*, instead of being a denial of Christ's

[168] It is not a new sacrifice—cf St J. Chrysostom, *Hom.* 17 *in Hebr.*, n. 3 (*PG*, 63, 131); Pius XII, Encycl. *Mediator Dei, AAS*, 39 (1947), 548f; Vatican II, *Constitution on the Sacred Liturgy*, nn. 2 (beginning), 7. For a bibliography on the recent discussion in Catholic theology (due to the writings of Odo Casel) on points I have raised above, cf R. Lachenschmidt, 'Heilswerk Christi und Liturgie. Verständnis der Fortdauer des Heilswerkes Christi in der Liturgie aus der Überzeitlichkeit des Christusgeheimnisses' in *Theol. und Phil.* (formerly *Scholastik*) 41 (1966), 211–27.

[169] Cf *CTKB*, p. 173.

unique lordship, redemption and merciful freedom, *expresses* that lordship, freedom and merciful redemption.[170]

The sacraments are efficacious by the very fact that the rite is performed. This does not mean that faith or the personal dispositions of the recipient have no role in the reception of the sacraments.[171] Very often in Catholic sacramental theology of post-Reformation times the teaching that the sacraments infallibly (*ex opere operato*) conferred grace on those who did not obstruct their efficacy (*non ponentibus obicem*) was given such prominence that the necessity of faith and personal dispositions for a fruitful reception was glossed over. Baptism, and especially infant baptism, should not be seen as a means of circumventing or as a denial of the personal decision of faith which is absolutely necessary for the constitution of a member of the Church and of the Church itself. On the contrary, baptism is a sign both of the grace of God and of the faith of man (*sacramentum fidei*): a sign of faith which must be personally ratified by man at the time, or, in the case of children, at a later stage. To say then that the efficacy of the sacrament does not depend on the faith or dispositions of the recipient, nor on the moral or religious disposition, simply reiterates God's fidelity to his new covenant. There is no particular type of magic or mechanics involved. All it says is that the efficacy of the rite is the work of Jesus Christ himself fulfilling his promised alliance. Grace is infallibly offered. As St Thomas explained: 'Baptism justifies *ex opere operato*: this is not man's work, but God's.'[172] The sacrament is only an instrumental cause, that is, 'an instrument which does not have its effect by the power of the minister, who is an instrument himself, but rather by the power of Christ and God'.[173] *Ex opere operato* means therefore 'by the power of Christ or of God'. The primary *opus operatum* is the objective, once and for all, personal, redeeming act of Christ. This *opus* actualizes itself sacramentally and infallibly through the earthly minister and rite. There can be no question of the sacraments 'forcing' the giving of grace, for Christ has instituted his sacramental Church. The sacrament brings about the unmerited application of the redemption to this person.

[170] Cf E. Schillebeeckx, *Christ the Sacrament of Encounter with God*, pp. 100–9; K. Rahner, *The Church and the Sacraments*, pp. 24f; L. Bouyer, *Du Protestantisme à l'Eglise*, pp. 211f.
[171] Cf above pp. 112f.
[172] St Thomas, *IV Sent.*, d. 15, q. 1, art. 3, sol. 3, ad. 2.
[173] *Id., ibid.*, d. 5, q. 2, art 2, quaestiuncula 3, ob. 1, and sol. Both this and the preceding reference cited in Schillebeeckx, *op. cit.*, pp. 103–4, from the critical ed. of St Thomas by E. Moos, Paris, 1947, vol. 4, pp. 656, 216, 218–19.

▼ 'In this sense *ex opere operato* is a reference to the universal causality of Christ's grace, to the unicity of Christ's mediation, to the pure gratuity of redemption; it says, in other words, *gratis estis salvati* by sacramental means; sacraments effect what they signify.'[174]

In concluding this consideration of the Church's hierarchical priesthood I would like to mention a point which I consider of great import in the dialogue with Karl Barth, and in the whole ecumenical dialogue between Catholicism and Protestantism. We have seen that the original, once and for all mission of the apostles was to last until the end of the world through a historical, horizontal appointment of successors. But this appointment is sacramental. This has been clarified by Vatican II:

'This sacred Synod teaches that by episcopal consecration is conferred the fulness of the sacrament of orders, that fulness which in the Church's liturgical practice and in the language of the holy Fathers of the Church is undoubtedly called the high priesthood, the apex of the sacred ministry. Episcopal consecration, however, together with the office of sanctifying, also confers the offices of teaching and of governing. . . . For from tradition, which is expressed especially in liturgical rites and in the practice of the Church both of the East and of the West, it is clear that, by means of the imposition of hands and the words of consecration, the grace of the Holy Spirit is so conferred, and the sacred character so impressed, that bishops in an eminent and visible way undertake Christ's own rule as teacher, shepherd, and high priest, and that they act in his person.'[175]

The priesthood is the apex of the Church's ministry, and the whole mission and ministry of the Church is sacramentally conferred. The Council states this explicitly in relation to bishops, but from them it radiates to the whole Church. The mission and ministry of the whole Church is sacramentally conferred. From what we have seen this

[174] Schillebeeckx, *op. cit.*, p. 107. The freedom and causality of God in the sacraments is brought out excellently in the liturgy of the Eastern Church by the eucharistic *epiclesis* and deprecative third-person formulas in the administration of the sacraments of baptism and penance. There the role of the Holy Spirit is emphasized—something deficient in Western theology (as we have already seen, cf above, pp. 128f), even if the Western *ex opere operato* expresses the same thing from a christological point of view. Cf R. A. Adams, 'The Holy Spirit and the Real Presence' in *TS*, 29 (1968), 51.

[175] Vatican II, DCC, ch. 3, n. 21. For the biblical, patristic and liturgical basis of this teaching, cf *ibid.*, n. 21, notes 19, 20, 22.

means simply that not only the original mission of the apostles, but the prolongation and continuation of this mission, and therefore also the mediation of objective reconciliation, is the personal act of Jesus Christ. For the ministry of the Church is based on 'the grace of the Holy Spirit' and the 'sacred character'. These are spiritual, internal effects of the sacrament of order. But, as St Thomas, and St Augustine before him, emphasized, the spiritual, internal effect of the sacrament is the work of God alone.[176] *The sacramentality of apostolic succession is fundamentally the expression of the universality and unicity of Christ's lordship and redemption in the Church.*

5. THE CHURCH'S HIERARCHICAL GUIDING MINISTRY

We can be brief with regard to the third hierarchical ministry in the Church, namely, its participation in Christ's kingly office. We have just seen that it is based on a spiritual sacramental gift of God. It is a spiritual power of service in the Church of Jesus Christ gifted by Jesus Christ. Its object and nature are thereby quite closely defined. It is not a power of dominion, tyranny or control over Jesus Christ or over his Church. It is exclusively a power of service of Jesus Christ and of those placed in its charge. Its exemplar must always be the good shepherd who came not to be ministered unto but to minister, and to lay down his life for his sheep.[177] It is not a gift for personal enjoyment and aggrandizement, but one 'solely for the edification of their flock in truth and holiness, remembering that he who is greater should become the lesser and he who is the more distinguished, as the servant' (cf Lk 22:26–7).[178]

The guiding authority of the Church has nothing to do with a denial of liberty, just as true Christian liberty has nothing to do with a denial of the Church's authority. This can be understood only on a Christological basis. That is to say, it is only when we realize that both the authority and freedom of the Church are the authority and freedom of Jesus Christ (or of his Word) that we understand how the authority of the Church is neither tyranny nor authoritarianism involving servitude and denying freedom, and how the freedom of the Church is neither libertinism nor subjectivism denying all true authority. Jesus Christ exercises his kingly rule through a human ministration. When one realizes the tender, loving care and direction Jesus desires for his followers, one realizes how easily his sinful human ministers

[176] *Summa theol.*, III, q. 64, art. 1, 2, 4; St Augustine, *In Joann. Evang.*, tract 6, 6–8 (*PL*, 35, 1427–9).   [177] Cf Mt 20:28; Mk 10:45; Jn 10:11.
[178] Vatican II, DCC, ch. 3, n. 27. Cf above, pp. 192f.

can deviate from the ideal. In this respect a continual reformation and renewal is necessary. But all things are possible to God. Since he has entrusted his flock to the care of human shepherds he will also see that their true spiritual guidance will not be lacking. He will not fail to draw all men to himself through their poor ministry.

Obedience to God's ministers is not a denial of liberty. It is always wrong to oppose authority or obedience and liberty. The principle of religious liberty is not defined with regard to God or his spiritual ministers, but with regard to human secular institutions, which have no right to intervene in a sphere outside their competence. Obedience to the authority of God is always liberating. Obedience to men whom God has established as the instruments of his will does not deny liberty, but attaches one to the source of all liberty, life, joy and spontaneity, which is Jesus Christ.[179] As Vatican II says:

> 'For the nurturing and constant growth of the people of God, Christ the Lord instituted in his Church a variety of ministries, which work for the good of the whole body. For those ministers who are endowed with sacred power are servants of their brethren so that all who are of the people of God, and therefore enjoy a true Christian dignity, can work toward a common goal freely and in an orderly way, and arrive at salvation.'[180]

The Church's hierarchical participation in Christ's kingly office is a real power exercised personally by certain men in the Church in the name of Christ, and therefore as his vicars and ambassadors. They 'have the sacred right and duty before the Lord to make laws for their subjects, to pass judgment on them, and to moderate everything pertaining to the ordering of worship and the apostolate'.[181] Karl Barth rightly draws attention to the fact that all ecclesiological law and order is christological. Jesus Christ is the 'primary subject'.[182] Through his once and for all mission of his apostles, and through his sacramental prolongation of this mission, it is Jesus Christ himself who teaches, sanctifies and rules in and through the Church. As Pius XII already stated in his encyclical *Mystici Corporis*:

> 'He it is who through the Church baptizes, teaches, rules, saves, binds, offers, sacrifices.'[183] Or as Vatican II puts it: 'In the bishops,

[179] Cf above, p. 201. The true notion of Church authority can only be understood from within, from the freedom and joy of actual life under its exercise.
[180] DCC, n. 18.   [181] *Ibid.*, n. 27.   [182] Cf *CTKB*, pp. 296f.
[183] 'Ipse est qui per Ecclesiam baptizat, docet, regit, salvat, ligat, offert, sacrificat': *AAS*, 35 (1943) p. 218.

therefore, for whom priests are assistants, our Lord Jesus Christ, the supreme high priest, is present in the midst of those who believe. For sitting at the right hand of God the Father, he is not absent from the gathering of his high priests, but above all through their excellent service he preaches the Word of God to all nations, constantly administers the sacraments of faith to those who believe, by their paternal role (cf I Cor 4:15) he incorporates new members into his body by a heavenly regeneration, and finally by their wisdom and prudence he directs and guides the people of the New Testament in its pilgrimage toward eternal happiness.'[184]

I am in agreement with Barth in his opposition to Rudolph Sohm and Emil Brunner.[185] But I deny that the christologico-ecclesiological basic law of the community excludes human beings as true secondary acting subjects of his law, or conversely, that the personal exercise of spiritual authority in the Church by certain men is a denial of the christological basis of the Church's law and order. It is a 'spiritual' law in the sense that it is exercised by the Spirit of Christ in and through his ambassadors. I have already amply demonstrated the biblical basis for this conception, as well as the fact that it in no way denies Christ's lordship and freedom. Apart from this fundamental disagreement I wholeheartedly concur in his list of basic presuppositions of all true Church law, and can only wholeheartedly desire that they be taken into account in the formulation of the laws of all Christian Churches.

---

[184] DCC, n. 21. Commenting on this passage Karl Rahner remarks: 'The subject really spoken of, even grammatically, is Christ': in *Commentary on the Documents of Vatican II*, ed. by H. Vorgrimler, vol. I, p. 192. Cf also Vatican II's Constitution on the Sacred Liturgy, n. 7; and St Augustine, *In Joh. Evang.*, tract VI, n. 7 (*PL*, 35, 1428). St. Thomas describes the role of the pope as that of a faithful minister who preserves the entire Church subject to the interior action of Christ who, by his Spirit, consecrates his Church to himself, impressing upon it his seal and image: cf Congar, *Esquisses* . . ., p. 88, and note 2 (Engl. transl., p. 72; the note is not given).

[185] Cf *CTKB*, p. 297, note 49.

Chapter Sixteen

Scripture and Tradition

In his whole presence and manifestation, words and deeds, signs and miracles (especially in his death and resurrection), and mission of the Holy Spirit, Jesus Christ is the fulness of revelation. He is the 'good news' (Gospel) of God's presence with us for our reconciliation. He called and sent his disciples to witness to him before all nations, so that those for whom he had lived and died and rose could participate, through faith and baptism, in his reconciliation.[1] His disciples accomplished this task in two ways: under the assistance of the Holy Spirit by their oral preaching, example and institutions (tradition); and under the inspiration of the same Holy Spirit by committing the message of salvation to writing (Scripture).

In this all Christians are in agreement. The same cannot be said as regards the nature and relationship of these two channels of revelation in the post-apostolic Church. The difference between Karl Barth and Catholic teaching on these points is even more pronounced than the usual difference between Protestant and Catholic thought.

I. SCRIPTURE

1. SCRIPTURE THE SIGN OF REVELATION

With Karl Barth[2] we may begin with the fact of the Church's faith. The Catholic Church, too, acknowledges the Bible as the indispen-

[1] Revelation is not simply a 'body of doctrine'. It is above all a person. Its transmission, likewise, is not simply the handing on of a series of intellectual truths, but a living witness to a living person. Thus Mk 16:15 ('Go into all the world and preach the Gospel to all creation') can be said to be equivalent to Acts 1:8 ('And you shall be my witnesses in Jerusalem and in all Judaea and . . .'). The faith which accepts this revelation is not solely an intellectual assent, but 'an obedience by which man entrusts his whole self freely to God' (Vatican II, *Constitution on Divine Revelation*, ch. I, n. 5). This christocentric and personal aspect of revelation and faith has been recently developed in Catholic theology. It is one of the *leit-motifs* of Vatican II (cf *loc. cit.*, ch. I). It is also one of the *leit-motifs* of Karl Barth's theology (cf *CTKB*, p. 68 and *passim*; *C.D.*, IV/1, pp. 740–79 = SS. 826–72).   [2] Cf *CTKB*, pp. 193f.

sable sign or form of divine revelation. But I do not agree with him—and in this I think I can claim the tradition of both the Catholic and Protestant Churches in support—in his understanding of the nature of this sign. His actualist doctrine of Scripture is the logical consequence of his doctrine on justification and christology. This is its strength and weakness.

The essence of his position is this: the written word of the Bible never is *in itself* the Word of God. That would entail the possibility of a human control of God's Word, and therewith the denial of God's lordship and freedom. He makes the comparison, *mutatis mutandis*, with the union of God and man in Jesus Christ. It is an indirect unity, he says. That is, the unity of God's Word and the written word exists solely by an ever new act of God, solely as it is 'brought about by the decision and act of God'. We have seen already that this is not Scripture's conception of the hypostatic union, nor of the union of Christ's Word as God and his human word as man. As regards the Bible, is not Barth saying, in effect, that the union is brought about, and, at the same time, that it is not *brought about*? Is he not denying an earthly human effect of the divine action which expresses or is that union *in concreto*?

We must not misunderstand Barth—at least in view of his later thought. The human witness expressed in Scripture is an answer (*Antwort*) to the Holy Spirit speaking the Word (*Wort*) of God. The divine act has an effect, therefore, on human history. But it has not an effect which expresses a union of the divine and human words—of the *Wort* and *Antwort*. It seems to touch history only to set off a movement on a completely different plane. It then utilizes this movement or answer to touch off a similar reflection in others. It utilizes it, however, in the sense that the answer never aids the Word in the furtherance of its cause. The speaking of the Word of God always remains a divine act *alone*. Looking at it from the point of view of the human word, God seems to use it 'as if he used it not'. There is no cooperation on the part of the human writer in and under God's inspiration, just as there is no cooperation on the part of the human act of faith in and under God's justifying grace. The same functional (or economic) monophysitism (or mono-actualism) which is apparent in Barth's doctrine of justification, christology, and the Church's ministry, is also apparent in his doctrine of Scripture.

Barth asserts a factual limitation of God's Word to the word of the Bible, and a factual identification of God's Word and the written word. At the time in which he wrote his doctrine of Scripture his two great adversaries were Roman Catholicism and liberal Protestantism.

The factual limitation of God's Word to the word of the Bible can be seen as an attempt to exclude the Catholic doctrine of tradition and the liberal Protestant doctrine of history.³ Its factual identification with the written word, through God's ever-new act, can be seen as an attempt at a mean between Catholic objectivism and liberal Protestant subjectivism. Barth liked to regard himself as a mean between these two. Asserting the identification of the Word with the word he tried to safeguard the authority of the Word over against subjective inspiration of the Spirit. Asserting the identification to be solely the event of an ever-repeated divine act he tried to safeguard the freedom of the Spirit over human control.

But the factual identification is more probably an attempt at mediation within Protestant theology itself. Ever since the Reformation there has been a literal and a spiritual current: the former (which was the position of both Luther and Calvin) identifies the Word of God with the written and proclaimed word *in itself*; the latter (which was the position of the Anabaptists or *Illuminati*, and still is that of the Quakers and numerous sects) asserts the freedom and independence of the Spirit over the text.⁴ In identifying the Word with the word Barth wishes to ward off total spiritualism and subjectivism. In predicating the identity solely of the divine act he wishes to safeguard the freedom of the Spirit. He obviously considers the doctrine of the Reformers inconsistent with his own more consistent interpretation of their doctrine of justification. For my part, I cannot see how he safeguards either the factual limitation or the factual identification.

In Catholic theology, the written word of Scripture is the sign of the Word of God in the sense that it is in itself the human expression of the Word of God. The comparison with Jesus Christ is illustrative —Catholic theology is also 'consequent' christology. In listening to the words of the man Jesus the apostles heard the Word of God in human form or sign. 'For he whom God has sent utters the words of God.'⁵ In a similar way the reader of the Bible reads the Word of God expressed in human form. Scripture is not immediately the Word of God. That is the prerogative of the *Logos* alone. It is not the Word of God in the same way that the words of Jesus are the Word of God. It is the witness to and expression of the revelation given by the man Jesus. None the less, Scripture is formally the Word of God. It is

---

³ Cf *CTKB*, pp. 198f.
⁴ Cf J. Hamer, *Karl Barth* . . ., ch. 2: 'The Word of God in Protestant Tradition'.
⁵ Jn 3:24. Cf the words of the Lord to Jeremiah: 'Behold, I have put my words in your mouth': Jer 1:9.

God's Word through the word of the human writer. We do not say that the Church makes the Bible the Word of God. It is the Holy Spirit who does that. There can be no denial of the 'one single fundamental and indestructible priority of God'.[6] But by a special charism God elevates the faculties of the human writer so that what he writes is in itself the Word of God in human form.

2. THE INSPIRATION OF SCRIPTURE

Obviously, both Barth's and Catholicism's different conceptions of Scripture as the Word of God depend on their different conceptions of inspiration. The fact of inspiration is based originally on the Bible's own witness as regards itself.[7] Writing to Timothy Paul says that 'all Scripture is inspired by God'.[8] Peter provides an indication of what *theopneustos* means: 'First of all you must understand this, that no prophecy of Scripture is a matter of one's own interpretation, because no prophecy ever came by the impulse of man, but men moved by the Holy Spirit spoke from God.'[9] Scripture is, therefore, the work of man written under an impulse or movement by the Holy Spirit. I agree with Barth in saying that the decisive centre in both passages is that the Holy Spirit is the real author of Scripture. The human authors are also real authors, but *secundarii*. The biblical concept of *theopneustia* is a description of what God does in the humanity of his witnesses.[10]

I cannot see any basis, however, either in Scripture or in the whole history of the Church which lives from Scripture, for Barth's further assertion that the word of the Bible is not in itself the Word of God in human form, that the Church cannot of itself read God's Word in the Bible, that the identification of God's and man's word in the Bible (inspiration) is an ever new act of God.[11] This is an obvious and quite consequent interpretation of Scripture in the light of his 'primary principle'.

[6] Cf *CTKB*, p. 193.
[7] There is no need to go into the question as to the possibility of proving from Scripture itself its consciousness of its own universal inspiration. The texts to be quoted are quite explicit as regards the Old Testament. II Pet 3:15–16 and I Tim 5:18 refer to at least some writings of the New Testament. Karl Rahner, in his work on inspiration (cf bibliography), gives food for new thought on the question.
[8] II Tim 3:14–16.
[9] II Pet 1:20–21.
[10] Cf *CTKB*, p. 195.
[11] *Ibid.*, pp. 194f.

For St Paul, it is the 'sacred writings' themselves 'which are able to instruct you for salvation', are 'profitable for teaching, for reproof, for correction, and for training in righteousness' (II Tim 3:15–16). In their references to the Old Testament, the New Testament writers obviously understand the written word which can be read with human eyes to be identical in itself with the Word of God. 'And as for the resurrection of the dead, have *you* not *read* what was said to you by God, "I am the God of Abraham, and the God of Isaac, and the God of Jacob"?'[12] How often do they refer to the *written word* as the Word of God spoken by the mouth of the prophet! 'This was to fulfil what the Lord had spoken by the prophet, "Out of Egypt have I called my son." . . . Brethren the Scriptures had to be fulfilled, which the Holy Spirit spoke beforehand by the mouth of David. . . .'[13] This obvious realism of the New Testament should not be modified in order to make it fit in with any preconceived idea of *solo Deo*.

The written word of Scripture is both a human and a divine word in one. In itself it is the Word of God because it is spoken by the Holy Spirit through a human writer. The Holy Spirit is the primary (or principal) mover (or author). The human prophet is the secondary mover (or author). Both together produce one effect (the written word) which is attributed completely to both. It is the Word of God in the word of man.

Through the charism of inspiration, the word of man is itself the spoken Word of God, and for this reason enjoys full authority and inerrancy. This is quite clear in Scripture. 'How is it then that David, inspired by the Spirit, calls him Lord, saying. . . . Jesus answered them, "Is it not written in your law." . . . If he called them gods to whom the word of God came (and scripture cannot be broken). . . .'[14] It is quite clear in the whole of patristic tradition.[15] Amongst the Reformers, it is clear in the theology of Calvin—who, for Barth, is the great authority.

'Truth is exempt from all doubt because without any aid it can hold its own. How properly this power belongs to Scripture is seen

---

[12] Mt 22:31–32, quoting in v 32 the written words of Ex 3:6.

[13] Mt 2:15, quoting Hos 11:1; Ex 4:22; Peter in Acts 1:16, who goes on to cite Ps 69:25 and 109:8. Innumerable other texts could be adduced. Cf, e.g., Mt 1:22–23; 22:43–44; Lk 24:25–27, 44; Mt 4:4–10; Jn 5:39 ('You search the *Scriptures* . . . and it is *they* that bear witness to me'); 10:34–35; Rom 1:2; Heb 4:3–7; Gal 3:8 and Gen 18:17–18.

[14] Mt 22:43; Jn 10:34–35. Cf texts in preceding note.

[15] Cf the multitude of references in Tromp, *De Sacrae Scripturae Inspir.*, pp. 8–21.

from the fact that among human writings there is none, however polished and adorned, that has such a power to move us . . . they will touch us so vividly, they will pierce our hearts so deeply, they will implant themselves so firmly in the very marrow of our bones, that the power of rhetoricians or philosophers compared to the force of such feeling is but a wisp of smoke. Thus it is easy to perceive that the Holy Scriptures have a peculiarly divine quality of inspiring men.'[16]

In trying to explain further the nature of inspiration, theology has invoked the aid of the Aristotelian-Thomistic category of instrumental causality. By this means it safeguards and explains in some way the mystery involved. The whole impulse comes from the Holy Spirit. He is the sole principal cause. He uses the human writer as his secondary instrumental cause. This means that the human writer really acts, really exercises his faculties to the full, but solely in virtue of the impulse received from the Spirit. He is not, therefore, an instrument in the same sense in which a pen is an instrument of the hand. He is a spiritual, free, self-moving instrument, acting under the divine impulse according to his own form, that is, freely and intelligently.[17]

Since God is the sole principal author of the whole of Scripture his inspiration extends to the whole of Scripture. It extends to everything the human author wills to express, and to the words and literary form in which he expressed it. It is 'verbal inspiration'. It is not dictation. Barth rightly points out that such would imply a docetic dissolving of its real human authorship.[18] It would be a scriptural monophysitism. In the explanation I have given the human author remains a true author. He wills, conceives, chooses the words and literary form of

[16] *Inst. Christ.*, I, 8, 1 (C.R., III, c. 99), cited in Hamer, *Karl Barth*, pp. 97–8. Calvin is treating of the criterion of inspiration. For him the human word of Scripture in itself has a 'peculiarly divine quality'. Barth himself is obviously aware of a difference between himself and the Reformers when he has to have recourse to a certain 'intention' behind their statements (cf *CTKB*, p. 196). If Barth is more consistent than Calvin to Calvin's own principles (as he claims he is) there is something obviously wrong with the principles.

[17] All Catholic authors agree on this. Their attempt at further explanation differs. The Thomist school speak of a 'physical pre-motion' which moves the will of the human author efficaciously but in a way consonant with its nature, that is, freely (cf Synave-Benoit, *La Prophétie* . . ., p. 305; Vosté, *De Divina Inspiratione* . . ., p. 56). The broad outlines of the doctrine of inspiration as presented in Pope Leo XIII's Encyclical *Providentissimus Deus* (cf DS 3291–4) are agreed upon by Catholic authors. Within this consensus many points remain disputed.

[18] Cf *CTKB*, p. 196.

the work, but always under the influence of the Spirit.[19] Neither is it a mantically-mechanical materializing of the concept of inspiration. Inspiration is a spiritual elevating influence on man's spiritual faculties of will and intellect, and through them on his executive faculties. Neither does it deny the grace, mystery and freedom of the Word of God. This can only be thought if one begins with the idea that God is not free to do such and such. God has in fact expressed his Word in a permanent human word—according to the testimony of Scripture itself. Consequently, we must say that he is free to do so.

According to Barth, inspiration concerns the knowing and understanding of Scripture as well as its writing. For him revelation and inspiration are identical. Just as he distinguishes an objective and subjective aspect of revelation he also distinguishes an objective and subjective aspect of inspiration.[20] The Catholic Church has always recognized the necessity of the intervention of the Holy Spirit for the *understanding as well as for the writing* of Scripture. Written under the impulse of the Spirit Scripture can only be really understood under the impulse of the same Spirit. The verbal inspiredness of the text by no means excludes 'the work of the Holy Spirit in the knowledge of Scripture'. In so far as the Catholic Church has not sufficiently emphasized this activity of the Spirit Barth has something to say to it. The objective written word of Scripture does not by itself meet us as the Word of God. The sense of that objective word must be perceived today by a living spirit through a new act of God communicating the meaning of his objectively inspired word to his people.

One could institute a comparison between the written word of Scripture and its perception as the Word of God and the fruitful reception of the sacraments. Just as the sacraments infallibly offer grace (*ex opere operato*) but require of necessity subjective dispositions of faith and penance, and therefore a new act of God through his Spirit, for their fruitful reception, so God's Word infallibly meets us in Scripture but requires a new act of God to the individual for its fruitful perception. And just as post counter-Reformation Catholic theology needs to insist more on the subjective action of the Spirit in the receiver of the sacraments so also it must insist more on the subjective action of the Spirit in the reader and hearer of Scripture.

---

[19] Cf Vosté, *op. cit.*, pp. 80f; Synave-Benoit, *op. cit.*, p. 302: The human writer is neither a purely instrumental cause, nor a principal cause, but a 'dependent principal cause or an instrumental cause in a large and improper sense'.

[20] Cf *CTKB*, pp. 195f. I have read identical statements in J. Baillie, *The Idea of Revelation in Recent Thought*, New York–London, 1960, pp. 64–6.

'Scripture is not, by itself, the word and message by which God purposes to give life to men. It is, to be sure, the word of God inasmuch as God has assumed responsibility for it, but of itself it is not God's word in the sense that God could be called the subject of the act of speaking to me. His Word is, in a sense, laid down or deposited; it has become an object, a "thing", in the scriptural text, and by this means what was said once can span the centuries and reach me in the present. But in order that its content may be rendered actual in a living mind, its meaning must be perceived in the present moment by such a mind, as a result of a new act by God: this is no longer the original act by which the sacred writer was inspired, but an act by which God communicates the meaning of his Word to his people, in the fellowship of the prophets and apostles.'[21]

The word 'inspiration' was used by the Fathers in a very broad sense and included the whole of the Spirit's action in the Church.[22] Consequently, it can be applied to the subjective illumination of God in the understanding of Scripture, as Barth does. Still, in a scriptural context, the word 'inspiration' has become technical, and denotes the impulse of the Spirit in the *writing* of Scripture. The words illumination, understanding, *gnosis*, are usually reserved for the reader's perception, under the influence of the Spirit, of the sense of the written word, that is, for his encounter with God in the word of Scripture. This corresponds to the usage of Scripture too. When it refers to the existing written word it uses the word 'inspiration', whereas when it speaks of the understanding of Scripture it speaks of interpretation, of the opening of the mind.[23] The preservation of this distinction would be less conducive to ambiguity.

For the second point of the circle of inspiration Barth has recourse to II Cor 3:4–18 and I Cor 2:6–16. The first text refers to the understanding of the old dispensation through conversion to the Lord (who is as such the Spirit). In the second text Paul affirms the necessity of the true wisdom granted by the Spirit for the understanding of 'the gifts bestowed on us by God' (v 12). For Barth this spiritual understanding is an ever new act of the Spirit alone, whereas for St Paul man himself receives and possesses this spiritual wisdom and is able to impart it to others. 'We do impart wisdom. . . . But we impart a secret and hidden wisdom of God. . . . Now we have received the

[21] Y. M.-J. Congar, *Tradition and Traditions*, p. 400.
[22] Cf Congar, *op. cit.*, pp. 125f, 387f.
[23] Cf II Tim 3:14–16; Mt 22:43; Lk 24:27, 45.

Spirit . . . that we might understand. . . . And we impart this. . . .
But we have the mind of Christ.'[24] Barth's 'circle of inspiration' is
confined to the Holy Spirit.

In Barth's concept of inspiration where lies the necessity of
exegesis? Is not the whole science of textual and literary criticism
based on the presupposition that the word of the inspired author, as
expressive of his formal judgment, is the Word of God, and can be
humanly ascertained as the Word of God? It by no means eliminates
the necessity of prayer and the interior action of the Spirit for the
understanding of this Word. But the subject who understands is the
human person who reads the Scriptures, and the word understood is
the human word of the inspired author.

3. THE AUTHORITY OF SCRIPTURE: *Sola Scriptura*

It is solely the fact of inspiration which explains and safeguards the
authority of Scripture. That is, it is solely because the written word
is in itself the Word of God by virtue of a special divine charism that
Scripture is authoritative for the Church. In denying this, I cannot
see how Karl Barth can attribute any authority at all to Scripture.
This is a very hard statement to make as regards one who has
studied and loved the Scriptures all his life. It concerns, therefore,
his theoretical explanation of Scripture's authority. But as such it
must stand. When Barth speaks of the 'authority of the Word of God'
he does not mean the authority of the written word of Holy Scripture.
The written word has no authority. It does not mediate the Word of
God. The unique subject of the mediation of God's Word is the Holy
Spirit.[25] The authority of the Word is solely the authority of the divine
act.

We have already seen that the Catholic Church does not deny the
uniqueness of the original revelation. We have also seen that it does
not claim to identify itself with revelation. Barth's objections to the
Catholic concept of tradition in this regard do not really touch it.[26]
Moreover, recent Catholic ecclesiology, in the light of patristic and
historical studies, also speaks of a *sola scriptura*. Scripture contains
in itself, in some way, the fulness of the apostolic Church's witness
to revelation. All post-scriptural reception of and witness to revelation
is dependent on and bound to Scripture. As Barth says, the Church
can no longer appeal past Scripture directly to God or Christ or the

[24] I Cor 2:6, 7, 12, 13, 16.
[25] Cf *CTKB*, pp. 197, 194.
[26] Cf above, chapter fifteen, art. 2, 2-3, and *CTKB*, pp. 198f.

Holy Spirit. Or again, the Church exists according as it obeys Scripture. It does not control Scripture, but is controlled by it.

What, then, of the fixing of the canon? Or who, and by what authority, determines which books are inspired? The question is important, for if they cannot be authoritatively determined how can we speak of an authority of a written word?

Despite his *sola scriptura* Barth acknowledges a certain form of Church authority in this regard.[27] He rightly points out that the Church does not give authority to the Bible, does not stand at the origin of its inspiration, or even of its canonicity. In Catholic theology, the inclusion of a book amongst the authentic collection of inspired books (canonization) is an act of the Church. But by the very fact that a book is inspired it tends towards this recognition. It is canonical *in actu primo*.[28] The Church merely acknowledges and confirms publicly this intrinsic canonicity. It does not establish Scripture as a source of revelation. In this I agree with Barth.

But I cannot agree when he none the less goes on to state that the canon is not definitively closed. Absolutely speaking, the canon of the Church's Scriptures does not exclude the possibility of extension. But Barth means more than this. For him the list already decided upon by the Church can be changed. The Church's word is fallible like everything else. For Catholics, on the contrary, what the Church has once solemnly proclaimed as Holy Scripture is irrevocably Holy Scripture. This does not mean that the Church makes Scripture the Word of God. The Church is only the guardian and interpreter of God's Word. But as such it is infallible. Barth's invocation of the decrees of the Councils of Florence and Trent as an indication of the Church's awareness in the past of the fallibility and perfectibility of its decision as regards the Canon of the Bible is hardly a strong argument.

Protestants have usually said that the Bible's inspiration is determined by the Bible itself to each individual.[29] Barth is more radical. The inspiration or canon of Scripture cannot be humanly determined. He does progress beyond the former Protestant individualism in that he speaks of an act of the Church, of the necessity of subjection to the judgment of the Church. But his attempt at mediation is not successful. In his explanation, the Church has no real authority. The ever new act of the Holy Spirit is the sole criterion. But then how can one possibly speak of an authority of *Scripture*?

[27] Cf *CTKB*, I, pp. 204f.
[28] Cf H. Höpfl, art. 'Canonicité' in *DBS*, I, 1030.
[29] Cf the quotation from Calvin above, pp. 218–19.

With Catholic theology obviously in mind, Barth says that the establishment of Scripture as the source of revelation means the possession and control of revelation, and the denial of *sola scriptura*.[30] I have already pointed out that Catholic theology does not claim to establish Scripture as the source of revelation. In its ministry of promoting and guarding the Word of God, it receives and acknowledges it as such. In its accomplishment of this task it neither possesses nor controls revelation. Here we touch on the Catholic Church's criterion for the recognition of an inspired book, and therefore of its reception into the canon. Usually it is explained as a divine revelation given to the apostolic Church and transmitted in an oral witness through apostolic succession. It owes its origin to God alone. In this explanation there is no question of the Church possessing or controlling revelation. It affirms the inspiration of Scripture solely on the basis of an act of obedience to a second channel in which revelation comes to it, namely, tradition.

But how can we say that Scripture is the sole Word of God (*sola scriptura*), in the sense that it transmits the fulness of the apostolic Church's witness to revelation? This is the greatest obstacle in the way of the recent attempt on the part of Catholic theologians to draw as near as possible, through a new look at the decree of Trent and a return to pre-Tridentine theology, to some of the legitimate demands of Protestant theologians on this matter. From a consideration of the nature of inspiration Karl Rahner has presented a solution which plausibly reconciles the necessity and relationship of the twofold authority of Scripture and the Church, while retaining the sufficiency of Scripture.[31]

The apostolic Church, he says, in its ministries, sacraments, revelation and also Scripture, is the canon or norm for the Church of all succeeding time. 'The Bible, too, belongs to the constitutive elements of this Apostolic Church as the qualitatively unique work of God and the permanent "canonical" origin for the later Church.'[32] Forming the Scriptures in itself the Church addresses itself to the future as the norm-giving apostolic Church; conversely, addressing itself to the future as the norm-giving apostolic Church, it forms the Scriptures. In willing the Church, God wills the Bible. Inspiration is simply 'the causality of God in regard to the Church, inasmuch as it refers to that constitutive element of the apostolic Church which is the Bible.[33]

[30] Cf *CTKB*, p. 198.
[31] K. Rahner, *Inspiration in the Bible* (Quaestiones Disputatae I), New York–Edinburgh–London, 1961.
[32] *Id., ibid.*, pp. 47–8.   [33] *Ibid.*, p. 51.

The criterion of inspiration is still revelation. But the revelation takes place through the inspired Scripture revealing itself to the Church (the reflex recognition may happen much later) as an intrinsic homogeneous piece of its apostolic or normative self-constitution. Filled with the Holy Spirit, the Church infallibly recognizes and judges a writing as connatural and apostolic.[34]

From the nature of inspiration as explained, it follows also that the Scriptures and the later infallible teaching of the Church are intimately connected. They are but 'two instances of the same process', for the Scriptures are 'the act of the early Church teaching infallibly'.

'The infallibility of the teaching authority of the later Church is, by definition, the inerrant interpretation of Scripture, because it includes by definition the link with the teaching of the early Church, which necessarily teaches the later Church and has expressed her teaching in Scripture.'[35]

Fr Congar has presented us with a mine of historical information as regards the relationship between Scripture and tradition.[36] The position up until the time of the Reformers was that Scripture contained all truth necessary for faith and salvation. It was a materially sufficient norm of revelation, and in this sense *sola*. But the Fathers and scholastics by no means professed the *sola scriptura* of the Reformers. Intending to 'restore' the sovereignty of *God alone* the Reformers affirmed not only the material, but also the formal, sufficiency of Scripture. For them Scripture was not only the objective norm of all truth: it became also its own norm for the discernment of all truth. For the Fathers and scholastics, on the contrary, Scripture *as read in the Church* was the material source of revelation. Scripture was not sufficient to yield its own sense.[37]

The sufficiency of Scripture cannot mean therefore the elimination of 'oral tradition'.

'Precisely because the Scriptures are an objectivization of the "beginnings" of the faith in the early Church and carry within

---

[34] Cf *ibid.*, pp. 66–7.   [35] *Ibid.*, p. 72.

[36] Y. M.-J. Congar, *Tradition and Traditions*, London, 1966.

[37] Cf Congar, *op. cit.*, pp. 107–18: Excursus A: 'The Sufficiency of Scripture according to the Fathers and the Mediaeval Theologians'; pp. 409–22: '*Scriptura Sola?*' Card. Franzelin, despite his anti-Protestant polemic, did not completely reject the idea of the material sufficiency of Scripture, and recognized it to have been taught by the Fathers; cf his *De Divina Traditione et Scriptura*, Thes. XIX, 227–8, 231.

themselves the essential characteristics of historical development, the sufficiency of the Bible is, as it were, a living protest against its mummification and reduction to the level of a dead letter. The Church derives her life from her own beginning, thus from her Scriptures, and has no other beginning beside or beyond it. It is, however, of the essence of this beginning that it is not also the end. It is not only not the end of theology, but also it is not the end (of the unfolding) of the faith and of the authoritative teaching of the Church.'[38]

In line with the whole of patristic and medieval thought, and in opposition to the disjunction introduced by the Reformers in the sixteenth century, the Council of Trent merely re-asserted the necessity of both Scripture and tradition for the knowledge of the Gospel. It asserted the existence of two qualitatively distinct channels of revelation. It did not resolve the question of whether Scripture and tradition are two partial or total channels of the one source. It did not determine their relationship.[39] The post-tridentine affirmation by most Catholic authors (not all) of the material insufficiency of Scripture is an accessory to Catholic doctrine and not the basic point in the dialogue with Protestantism.[40] Scripture, tradition and the Church cannot be separated.

'The whole foregoing discussion shows how the whole activity of the early Fathers tends to unite these terms which the disjunctions of the sixteenth century were to set up in opposition: Scripture, Tradition, Church. . . . Tradition is that interpretation of Scripture which is the interpretation of the *Church*. Its criterion is the apostolicity of that Church, guaranteed by the succession of hierarchical ministers.'[41]

The 'and' of Scripture and tradition means that these two ways in which the apostolic witness to revelation is transmitted to us are inseparable. It does not mean that they are two ways which can be used independently. They are two distinct ways. But they are two ways indissolubly bound together. Both together yield the knowledge of revelation in all its true significance. Due to the rediscovery of the Church, and also due to the ecumenical movement, many modern Protestant theologians are beginning to understand and develop more the sense of tradition. They recognize that Catholics are correct in

[38] K. Rahner, *op. cit.*, p. 74. Cf Congar, *op. cit.*, pp. 130–1 on the presence of the Spirit in his Church for the interpretation of all truth.
[39] Cf J. Dupont, in *NRT*, 85 (1963), 348; Congar, *op. cit.*, pp. 167f.
[40] Cf Dupont, *art. cit.*, 453.   [41] Congar, *op. cit.*, pp. 37–8.

saying that the opposition between Protestantism and Catholicism cannot be classed as one between 'Scripture' and 'Scripture and tradition'. Scripture, tradition and Church are being seen more and more as inseparable. For first of all Scripture itself is tradition. The very existence of 'form criticism' in modern biblical research is a proof that the Bible and the Church are inseparable—even in origin, for it presupposes that the present Gospels are accounts by the evangelists reproducing the kerygma of the apostles handed on and shaped by and in the Church. The modern approach to the Gospel formation has therefore brought the Church and tradition into greater focus in Protestant theology. The Protestant insistence on the Bible and the Catholic insistence on the Church were originally the same thing. Similarly, the renewed study of the Church by Protestant theologians, of its nature and necessity, in continuing dialogue with Catholicism, has re-awakened the sense of authority and community, and destroyed the old individualism. Finally, modern Protestant theologians realize also that they, and the Reformers before them, live in fact from unwritten traditions.[42]

[42] The influence of form criticism can be seen from the following words of R. Bultmann: 'There is no faith in Christ which is not at the same time faith in the Church in as much as she was the bearer of the kerygma': *Das Verhältnis der urchristlichen Christusbotschaft zum historischen Jesus*, Heidelberg, 1962, p. 26 (cited in R. E. Brown, *New Testament Essays*, London–Dublin, 1965, p. 24, n. 21). The realization of the necessity of the Church in all times can be judged from the following words of the Methodist theologian Albert C. Outler: 'The ruptures which quickly opened between the various Protestant traditions are sad enough proof that their common profession of *sola Scriptura* could not prevent the emergence of discrepant confessions of faith and rival systems of doctrine': in *TS*, 27 (1966) 712. In a very important passage H. Rückert sums up this whole change amongst his Protestant colleagues: 'Der Katholizismus hat einfach recht, wenn er uns darauf hinweist, das in dem dilemma "Schrift" oder "Schrift und Tradition" eine falsche Alternative steckt. Denn erstens ist auch die Schrift Tradition, und zweitens leben auch wir von nicht-geschriebener Tradition. Auch Luther hat von ihr gelebt. Er wäre von seinen Voraussetzungen aus niemals zum trinitarischen und christologischen Dogma gekommen, sondern hat es aus der Überlieferung der Kirche. . . . Luther versteht unter dem Wort Gottes immer die *viva vox evangelii*, das lebendig in der Kirche verkündigte Wort, so dass damit die Geschichte deiser Kirche mit umgriffen ist als das Element, in dem Verkündigung und Weitergabe erfolgen. Trüge die Prinzipienlehre der evangelischen Dogmatik dieser *viva vox evangelii* Rechnung und liesse sie sich von daher durchformen, so wäre in ihr die echte Zusammengehörigkeit und Einheit von Schrift, Tradition und Kirche geborgen, auf die uns die katholische Arbeit an diesem Problem aufmerksam machen will': *Schrift, Tradition, Kirche*, Lüneburg, 1951, pp. 22–3 (cited by R. Geiselmann, in Schmaus, *Die mündliche Überlieferung*, p. 126). For trends in modern Protestantism on this question cf Congar, *op. cit.*, pp. 469–93.

Karl Barth was in the mainstream of the modern ecclesiological development in Protestantism. He has much to say on tradition, and quite obviously lives from it. At the same time he does not see any contradiction in berating Catholicism for doing the same. However, his criticism on this point has mellowed. The attitude of the Western separated brethren to article nine of Vatican II's Dogmatic Constitution on Revelation, especially its statement that 'it is not from sacred Scripture alone that the Church draws her certainty about everything which has been revealed', cannot be, he says, a simple *non placet*. For did not the newly created Churches of the sixteenth century, he asks, appeal to the early Councils? And have *we* not also necessarily and legitimately established certain unwritten traditions in the form of confessions? As regards a teaching office or *magisterium*, does not one of the evangelical Churches still go under the name of 'Lutheran-Evangelical' and not simply Evangelical? And did not Calvin exercise a role in the sixteenth century over the whole of French Protestantism and indeed far beyond it, which is not very unlike the office of Peter? We have always had, and always should have, authentic charismatic interpreters of the *Verbi scripti et traditi*. Consequently, we must be careful in our protest to the Roman Catholic Church. 'We, too, do not live, think or teach on the basis of a Bible in solitary elevation, and thus not *sola*, in the sense of *solitaria, Scriptura*.'[43]

The basic difference between Barth and ourselves in the question of tradition is one of ecclesiology—indeed, before that it is a question of pneumatology, of our doctrine of the Holy Spirit. He is a systematic theologian, so that the basic reason for his non-recognition of the Catholic position is systematic. It would be a denial of his primary principle. I cannot see, however, how with the same primary principle he can speak of an authority of Scripture itself.

Barth is not correct in saying that it is essential to Catholicism to reject 'the narrowing down of revelation to its biblical attestation'.[44] What is essential to Catholicism is that the Bible be read in the Church. The Bible enjoys supreme authority. It does not receive its authority from the Church, as was falsely stated by some fourteenth- and fifteenth-century theologians, and against whom the reaction of

---

[43] 'So sollte man auf unserer Seite vorsichtig sein im Protest gegen den im Artikel 9 (im Zusammenhang allerdings reichlich ungeschützt und verwirrend) auftauchenden Satz: *Ecclesia certitudinem suam . . . non per solam Sacram Scripturam haurit*. Wir leben, denken und lehren auch nicht aufgrund einer in einsamer Höhe schwebenden Schrift, insofern nicht *sola* (=*solitaria*) *Scriptura*': K. Barth, *Ad Limina Apostolorum*, Zürich, 1967, pp. 53–4; cf ibid., pp. 52–4.   [44] Cf *CTKB*, p. 198.

the Reformers was in some sense justified. But the written word of God exercises its authority in the living, preaching and teaching word of the Church. Christ created his Church first of all, and committed his Word to his human ministers. Their witness is codified once for all in Scripture. But the Church did not then cease. The Church is sent to the ends of the world and time. The Holy Spirit is in her midst. It must remain absolutely faithful and obedient to its beginnings, that is, to Scripture. But it has always its original mission to accomplish. It has the care of Christ's flock. This mission of the Church is alone that which ensures and guarantees the authority of *Scripture*. The theology of 'and', instead of being a relativization of Scripture and God's majesty, is precisely that which guarantees both. The majesty of God and the authority of Scripture are exercised through the Church. The theology of 'and' merely asserts the union of God and man in Jesus Christ, of the Word of God and the word of man in Scripture, of God's grace and human action in justification, of God's revelation and human reason in theology, of the Holy Spirit and certain men in the Church's ministry. It is simply the assertion of the truth and reality of the Son of God incarnate, of the written Word of God, of the justified man, of man's knowledge of God's mysteries, of the indwelling of the Holy Spirit. All of these owe their existence solely to God's initiative and action. But they do exist and live. There is no Pelagianism or semi-Pelagianism involved. Nor is there a preconceived *analogia entis* involved, determining the interpretation of Scripture. This may be invoked as an explanation. But the existence and reality of these phenomena are facts attested in Scripture. Barth's separation of Scripture and the Church does, as he says,[45] point like a sign to the barrier between the Church and its Lord. But who wants to erect a barrier between the Lord and his Church? Surely not its founding Lord? Again, as he says, the factual authority of Scripture safeguards the authority of Jesus Christ. That is quite true. Unfortunately again, it goes too far. It takes authority away from Scripture. And who wants to do that? Surely not the Lord who inspired it?

II. TRADITION

1. ORIGIN

Together with the Church's Scriptures, and intimately connected with them there is also the Church's tradition. Karl Barth acknowledges this.[46] The latter owes its origin, he rightly says, to the

[45] Cf *ibid.*, pp. 201–2.   [46] Cf *ibid.*, pp. 202f.

communitarian character of the Church, that is, to the desire of the Word to be present to all times and individuals in and through the Church. In founding his Church Jesus sent his apostles to 'hand on' his Gospel by witnessing to him. Others believe and are saved because the Word is preached to them on the basis of mission. The apostolic mission, or the mission of the Church, stands at the basis of all transmission of the good news.[47]

The Epistles of St Paul which, with the exception of the pastorals, are the oldest of the New Testament writings, witness especially to the fact of oral tradition in the original apostolic Church. Paul hands on a message received from the first apostles:

> 'For I delivered to you as of first importance what I also received, that Christ died for our sins in accordance with the scriptures, that he was buried, that he was raised on the third day in accordance with the scriptures, and that he appeared to Cephas, then to the twelve. . . . Whether then it was I or they, so we preach and so you believed.'[48]

He hands on a message received directly from the risen Lord: 'As we have said before, so now I say again, if any one is preaching to you a gospel contrary to that which you received, let him be accursed. . . . For I did not receive it from man, nor was I taught it, but it came through a revelation of Jesus Christ.'[49]

He guards what he hands on, commending others to 'maintain the *traditions* even as I have delivered them to you' (I Cor 11:2). He demands obedience to them, warning others to avoid everything 'not in accord with the *tradition* that you received from us' (II Thess 3:6). He warns against 'those who create dissensions and difficulties, in opposition to the doctrine you have been taught'.[50] Echoing the words of Jesus himself he says: 'I know that after my departure fierce wolves will come in among you, not sparing the flock. . . . Therefore be alert.'[51] There is no reason to suppose that this danger ceased, and this remedy was no longer needed, once the apostolic witness was written down—most of the New Testament writings were already in existence when the Acts of the Apostles was written.

It is hard to know where exactly Barth stands on this question.[52]

[47] Cf Rom 10:14–18; Mk 16:15–16, 20; Lk 24:44–49; Acts 1:8.
[48] I Cor 15:3–5, 11; cf 11:23f; Gal 2:2.
[49] Gal 1:9, 11–12.
[50] Rom 16:17. Cf I Tim 1:3–4; I Jn 2:18f.
[51] Acts 20:28, 31. Cf Mt 24:11, 23f.
[52] Cf *CTKB*, pp. 199f.

He says tradition ceased with Scripture, but that the Church continues as the bearer and proclaimer of Scripture's witness. This bearing and proclaiming of the Church he also terms tradition.[53] Seemingly he denies the continuation of tradition in the sense of a continuation of the original apostolic Church, and therefore of direct contact with revelation, Jesus Christ and the Holy Spirit.[54] Catholic theology also asserts the uniqueness of the original apostolic Church, as well as the fact that tradition is now but the continual expression and proclamation of Scripture's witness.

The fact of the continuance of this way is clear enough from Scripture itself. Others will have to build on the foundation laid by Paul (I Cor 3:10), 'for building up the body of Christ, until we all attain to the unity of the faith' (Eph 4:12–13). Conscious of his approaching end, he leaves his companion Timothy (cf I Thess 3:2) at Ephesus (I Tim 1:3), instructing him to preserve and guard what he has received, to attend to the public reading of Scripture, to preaching and teaching (I Tim 4:11–13). 'O Timothy, guard what has been entrusted to you. . . . Follow the pattern of the sound words which you have heard from me . . . guard the truth that has been entrusted to you by the Holy Spirit who dwells within us.'[55] And Timothy is to entrust to others what Paul has entrusted to him. 'What you have heard from me before many witnesses entrust to faithful men who will be able to teach others also' (II Tim 2:2). The original unique witness to revelation is to be handed on and guarded by successive ministers of the Gospel.

2. AUTHORITY

The Council of Trent decreed that the Scriptures and traditions preserved by apostolic succession in the Catholic Church must be received with equal respect (*pari pietatis affectu*).[56] By traditions it means divine traditions, that is, truths regarding faith and morals received from Christ or the Holy Spirit and transmitted, as it were, from hand to hand (*quasi per manus*).

In this decree, therefore, there is no question of traditions which owe their origin to the Church itself and which have grown up over the centuries. Again, the traditions mentioned do not necessarily contain truths which are not contained in the Scriptures, nor are they

[53] *Ibid.*, pp. 202f.
[54] *Ibid.*, pp. 198f.
[55] I Tim 6:20; II Tim 1:13–14.
[56] Cf DS 1501.

a source independent of Scripture. In answer to the Reformers, the Council wished to affirm the 'living Church as the possessor, custodian and authentic interpreter of the Scriptures'.[57] Its traditions are completely bound up with the Scriptures, as their commentary, interpretation, clarification. Finally, it can be pointed out that the traditions are not the Word of God in the same sense in which Scripture is. They are not inspired. They are not formally God's Word. They contain the Word of God. With these reservations, Scripture and tradition must be said to be equally authoritative and must be received *pari pietatis affectu*. Together (for they cannot be separated) they constitute the authoritative transmission of the Word of God.[58]

The difference between Barth[59] and Catholic doctrine with regard to tradition is pneumatological and, as a result, ecclesiological. The Catholic doctrine of tradition and its authority cannot be understood unless we believe in the indwelling presence and action of the Holy Spirit in his Church. We say, with Barth,[60] that tradition is not a mere historical mediation bound up with human truthfulness and credibility. The primary acting subject, as in every other aspect of the Church, is the Holy Spirit. But we say that the Holy Spirit is sent by Christ to be present in his Church until the end of the world. He is sent by Christ and received by the Church.[61]

We believe that the Holy Spirit really teaches the Church, and will always be present in it, creating its faith in infallible progressive conformity with the original message of salvation. The Church will always be as it was at Pentecost: filled with the Holy Spirit, and believing and speaking as the Spirit gives it utterance. We believe that the Spirit acts in a special way through the twelve, and through their successors in their role of proclaiming and guarding what the twelve once and for all proclaimed. 'You shall receive power when the Holy Spirit has come upon you; and you shall be my witnesses' (Acts 1:8).

On the other hand, Karl Barth's doctrine on tradition can only be understood on the premise that the presence and action of the Holy Spirit always remain transcendent to his Church. The Pauline saying: Shall I come to you in power? as well as all the other New Testament assertions of human possession and exercise of the power of the Spirit,

[57] K. Rahner, *Inspiration* . . . , pp. 35–6.
[58] The attitude of Anglicanism with regard to this interdependence of Scripture and tradition is the same; cf *The Lambeth Conference*, London, 1958, pp. 2, 3–5, cited in Congar, *op. cit.*, p. 465, n. 2.
[59] Cf *CTKB*, pp. 202–3.
[60] Cf *ibid.*, p. 173.
[61] Cf Jn 14:17, 26. Cf above, chapter twelve.

have no meaning in his system. The exercise of power in the Church is always a divine act alone. He acknowledges that the hearing and preaching of God's Word is primarily an action of the community. This is an important point over against all subjectivism. But he does not safeguard any real authoritative tradition of the Word by the Church. He cannot speak of a real authority *of the Church*, just as he cannot speak of a real authority of *Scripture*.

3. FORMS

It is obvious that there can be no possibility in Barth's ecclesiology of enumerating forms of Church authority,[62] just as there can be no possibility of determining the canon of Scriptures. The authority of the forms he enumerates is always and solely the authority of the ever-new act of the Holy Spirit. He accuses the Catholic Church of an 'immanentism in which Church and revelation are equated, violating the divine authority of Holy Scripture and therefore returning the Church to that solitariness in which ultimately there can be no Church life at all and therefore no genuine Church authority'.[63] This cannot go without a comment, even though I have harped on it several times already.

This whole exposition so far of the Catholic concept of the Church should go to show that it cannot be, in all fairness, accused of immanentism (if I understand correctly Barth's use of the word). The Church is not a purely human reality. It does not proudly usurp the authority of God or of his written word. It does not identify itself with revelation. If it believes in the immanent presence of the Spirit it does so solely on the basis of faith in, and obedience to, God's own will and work. I would like to ask Barth to reflect on his own accusation. Is the authority of *Scripture* solely 'divine'? Can he really claim for his *Church* a 'life' and an 'authority'? Is the Church, too, a solely divine reality? Does he not opt for such a transcendentalism that (to repeat his own accusation to Catholicism) 'there can be no Church life at all and therefore no genuine Church authority'? Justice is done to the witness of Scripture neither by a pure immanentism nor by a pure transcendentalism, but by a transcendentalism with and in immanentism.

This can be seen in that form of tradition which Barth terms 'Ecclesiastical teachers'. Amongst these the 'Fathers of the Church' occupy a particular place. What is the basis of the authority of the Fathers? Amongst Catholic writers it is usually connected with the orthodoxy

[62] Cf *CTKB*, p. 204.   [63] Cf *ibid.*, p. 209.

of their doctrine, their antiquity, sanctity, and approval by the Church.⁶⁴ The ultimate basis is the special presence and action in them of the Holy Spirit. The Fathers lived at the very beginning of the Church's self-consciousness. Both as an answer to their own *fides quaerens intellectum*, and as a result of confrontation with the surrounding religious and cultural world, they had to give their faith precise expression in human language and discipline for the first time. For the accomplishment of this task they received the special assistance of the Holy Spirit. 'But the Counsellor, the Holy Spirit, whom the Father will send in my name, he will teach you all things, and bring to your remembrance . . .' (Jn 14:26). The transcendent Spirit is immanent to his Church in a special way in its earliest Fathers.

Holy Scripture was their standard and norm. But they did not merely repeat Scripture. They interpreted and made it more explicit. They gave a definite existence, norm and form to the whole Church's future life and history. They are its 'fathers'. They are not Fathers as individuals. Catholic theology speaks of a 'unanimous consent' as a necessary condition for their normativeness. They lived and died in the communion of the Church. The Spirit was promised to the Church. Nor is it up to us, as individuals, to determine their authority. This is the task of those whom 'the Holy Spirit has made guardians, to feed the Church of the Lord' (Acts 20:28). This does not mean that the Church today confers authority on the Fathers, just as its 'canonization' of Scripture does not confer its authority on Scripture. Prior to the Church's recognition the Fathers are in themselves authoritative, for they had the special assistance and enlightenment of the Holy Spirit. But, no less than the written word of Scripture, their words remain dead to us unless they are preached by the mouth of the Church. It is to human ministers that Christ gave the charge of his flock. To these the Spirit has been given 'to be with you for ever' (Jn 14:11) and to bring to remembrance all that Christ himself had said (Jn 14:26). This Spirit makes these ministers live in this time between the times in ever progressive fidelity and obedience to Scripture and tradition—or, better, to Scripture in tradition—as their living proclaimer and interpreter.

There is no reason why less ancient ecclesiastical writers (Luther and Calvin, for instance) could not become also Fathers of the Church. The Church is apostolic and patristic in the whole of its historical life.⁶⁵ The Holy Spirit is present at all times and places, and always

---

⁶⁴ Cf E. Amann, art. 'Pères (de l'Eglise)' in *DTC*, XII, 1192–1215.

⁶⁵ Fr George Florovsky, the Orthodox patristic scholar, reacts against the fairly widespread designation of the Orthodox Church as 'the Church of the

creates new 'Fathers'. These will be normative as the instruments of the Spirit. But, once more, their normativeness *for us* is determined by the Church, and especially by its living *magisterium*. Christ's command and mission envisage in a special way his apostles and their successors, and to them he promised the special assistance of his Spirit. As Barth says,[66] the standard of judgment will be Scripture and the Church's confession. But in stipulating the conformity of their teaching with that of Luther and Calvin, is he not, in fact, if not in theory, admitting a human and infallible interpretation and tradition of Scripture? In theory, of course, for him, the true authority of the Church is the authority of the Spirit alone.

The immanence of the transcendent Spirit is that which explains also the normativeness of the two forms the Church's confession can take. The unanimous consent of the whole people of God in their profession of faith is an infallible form of the tradition of Scripture's witness to revelation.[67] This consensus is not the same as the testimony of the Church's teaching office. They are, however, intimately connected, for the recognition of this form, too, depends upon those to whom Christ committed his flock in a special way.[68]

The solemn confession of faith of the whole college of those whom Christ constituted guardians of his Church is an infallible form of the tradition of God's Word in Scripture. Before his ascension Jesus prayed for his eleven disciples:

'And now I am no more in the world, . . . I have given them thy word. . . . Sanctify them in the truth. . . . As thou didst send me into the world, so I have sent them into the world. . . . I do not pray for these only, but also for those who believe in me through their word, that all may be one.'[69]

I agree with many points of Barth's definition of the Church's confession.[70] The unanimous confession of faith of the whole episcopal body, the successors of the apostles, is not a new revelation, nor based

---

Fathers', or 'the Church of the seven Ecumenical Councils', as if it had known no creative visitation of the Spirit since the eighth century. Cf the citation in Congar, *op. cit.*, pp. 441–2, from *Istina*, 8 (1961–2), 116–19.

[66] Cf *CTKB*, p. 206.
[67] Cf Vatican II, DCC, n. 2.
[68] Cf Card. Newman, *On Consulting the Faithful in Matters of Doctrine*; H. Fries, 'J. H. Newmans Beitrag . . .' in Schmaus, *Die Mündliche Überlieferung* . . ., p. 115.
[69] Jn 17:11, 14, 17, 18, 20, 21. Cf 14:16–17, 26; Mk 16:15f; Mt 28:18–20; 18:18.
[70] Cf *CTKB*, p. 206.

on a direct revelation. It safeguards the authority of Scripture. The whole of its power derives from its mission as *witness* to the original revelation. Its voice can only be that of the *una, sancta, catholica* to the *una, sancta, catholica*. But I disagree with him when he denies the competency of some, in virtue of their mission by Jesus Christ and assistance by his Spirit, to interpret and proclaim Holy Scripture infallibly for the whole Church and the whole world. They are not the commissioned voice of the community, but the commissioned voice of Jesus Christ and the instrument of his Spirit. Their authority is not originally their own. It is the authority of Jesus Christ. He has empowered and sent *them* to act in his name. 'All authority in heaven and on earth has been given to me. Go therefore and make disciples of all nations . . . teaching them to observe all that I have commanded you. . . .'[71]

Once it is realized that the ministry the Catholic Church attributes to its hierarchical members is not a purely human one, but a participation in the ministry of Jesus Christ through his Spirit, it will also be realized that in it there can be no question of a denial of the freedom of the Word of God, or of freedom under the Word of God. The Word of God is powerfully free. It has created the Church, and continues to create the Church through the Church's ministry. It creates a response in the Church. This response is an authoritative mediation of the Word of God. It is an infallible witness to the Word, in the power of the Word. The acceptance of the original revelation in faith through this infallible mediation by men does not mean any *sacrificium intellectus*. As Barth so rightly says, subordination to the Word of God can only mean the greatest freedom.[72]

Unless one excludes *a priori* the possibility of a participation by human beings in the liberating power of God's Word, one should have no difficulty in taking the further step and saying that subordination to the Word of God in its infallible proclamation by the Church can only mean the greatest freedom. Barth makes this *a priori* exclusion. Whence, for him, and rightly so (for a merely human word cannot create a truly free response, nor demand entire submission), authority exercised by a human subject would connote a *sacrificium*

[71] Mt 28:18, 19, 20. Cf Jn 14:26.
[72] 'Where the Lord's spirit is, there is freedom. She [the Church] is the "where" of spiritual freedom. In so far as she is different from the *pneuma* living and ruling within her, the Church is the historical quasi-sacramental sign of this *pneuma*, and hence also of freedom, by which the "pneumatic" freedom is signified and made present': K. Rahner, *Theological Investigations*, II, p. 97. Cf the second essay or 'investigation' *ibid.*, pp. 89–107: 'Freedom in the Church', and cf above, pp. 201, 211f.

intellectus. For Barth, authority and freedom in the Church are 'only predicates of the Word'. This is the manifestation of his basic principle: the limitation of salvific activity to God alone. Until he allows some salvific reality and activity to the human Church there can be no real confrontation of ecclesiologies.

Chapter Seventeen

The Justification of Sinful Man

IN this second volume of my study I am trying to outline some of the basic points of agreement and disagreement in Karl Barth's and the Catholic conception of the Church, as well as the basic reasons underlying these. I think that Barth's difference from us in the question of justification is the factual source of all our other differences. I say 'factual' because in both our (professedly) Christocentric theologies the ultimate basis should be christological. This does not seem to be the case, even though it is not easy to pin things down exactly. From the very beginning Barth's primary concern was the relationship *solo Deo* between God and individual man.[1] Even when the individual man became Christ justification still remained the 'red thread' which runs through all the Dogmatics.[2] The *solo Deo* became a *solo Christo*. Finally, and this is the decisive point, Barth himself acknowledges that his 'consequent' christocentrism is interpreted in the light of his justification *sola fide*.[3]

The question of the agreement or disagreement of Karl Barth's and the Catholic Church's (the Council of Trent's) doctrine on justification has been the subject of much recent Catholic thought and writing. This was sparked off by Hans Küng's provocative book.[4] In it the author claims to establish 'a fundamental agreement between Karl Barth's position and that of the Catholic Church in regard to the theology of justification seen in its totality'.[5] Here I can consider only those points which I believe to be really critical in any comparison between Barthian and Catholic theology. This is rather unfortunate, as it may give a false impression about the large area of agreement which does in fact exist, as well as a false impression about the value of Barth's exposition.

[1] Cf *CTKB*, pp. 34f, 38f, 43, 49f.   [2] Cf *ibid.*, pp. 215f.
[3] Cf above, pp. 19–20, and below, pp. 337f.
[4] *Rechtfertigung. Die Lehre Karl Barths und eine katholische Besinnung.* Einsiedeln, 1957. Engl. transl., New York, 1964 (references will be to this latter).   [5] H. Küng, *op. cit.*, pp. 277–8.

My ecclesiological dialogue with Karl Barth is not based on the discussion here. I treat of this problem of justification (apart from the fact that it would be very difficult to treat of the Church without touching at some point on justification and the life of the justified) because it happens to be the factual source—or, better, the primary appearance—of the basic difference between us. My ecclesiological answer to Barth is valid in itself. In fact, since Barth interprets christology, ecclesiology, Scripture, etc., in the light of justification I answer his doctrine on justification in the doctrines of the Church's ministry, the Mystical Body, etc. It is well, however, to see our basic difference in its primary appearance.

My conclusions will differ from those of Küng. This was already to be expected. For if Barth is consequent with regard to justification, and if his justification is fundamentally in agreement with Catholic doctrine, he should be also in agreement with us in ecclesiology, Scripture, christology. He is not. Certainly, there are fundamental agreements between Barth's doctrine of justification and Catholic doctrine. One need only read Hans Küng's profoundly theological work to realize this. But there is also a fundamental disagreement.

For Barth, the relationship between God and man in the subjective realization of reconciliation does not take place through a cooperation or sub-operation of man under God, but depends always and exclusively on God's action. 'It does not depend at all on what man had or has or will have to contribute from below.'[6] This is the particular point which renders it difficult to assert a 'fundamental agreement' between Barth's and the Catholic doctrine of justification. Barth's doctrine on this point is uniform in the three moments which he distinguishes in God's one grace, namely justification, sanctification and vocation, as can be seen from my outline in *The Church in the Theology of Karl Barth*. He does not say that man is passive in this whole process of his subjective reconciliation. His human acts of faith, love and hope are required and created as a response (*Antwort*), correspondence (*Entsprechung*) and reflection of the solely divine reconciling act. But these human acts play no role, effective or conditional, in man's own reconciliation. All human action is the acknowledgment ('realization' in the sense of knowledge) reckoned by the good pleasure of God to 'correspond' to his action.[7]

Barth does speak of a certain 'cooperation' of man, in the sense that man provides the sphere of God's action. But, for him, man does not cooperate in the sense that he is a subject, under God's action,

[6] Cf *CTKB*, p. 234.
[7] For human faith and God's righteousness, cf *ibid.*, pp. 227-32.

of his own subjective reconciliation. The actions of which man is the subject are sinful. What he seems to say is that God's action really touches man and causes a human corresponding action to take place. This is his gift and gracious creation.[8] But it is a gift which is not given. The resulting human action is always sinful. Man is not elevated to be himself a subject of good works. His works may be new within the human sphere, but they are not good in the sense that they participate in God's goodness. If they are good in this sense man is not as such their subject. They are good because God accepts the necessarily sinful human result as good, or himself directly creates it good. We must now consider more closely the *reasons underlying* Barth's position. These become clear in his opposition to Roman Catholicism.

Barth understands the Roman Catholic doctrine of man's cooperation with God to mean that man is in some way a subject of his subjective reconciliation. From the restricted outline of Barth's doctrine which I have given in *The Church in the Theology of Karl Barth* it will be clear that it is precisely this doctrine he opposes all along. *He objects to it for two reasons, which in turn are but manifestations or consequences of a third and fundamental reason.*

His *first objection* to the Roman Catholic doctrine of cooperation is that it presupposes a false doctrine of the man of sin, of man's *status corruptionis*. Barth acknowledges that Catholic doctrine teaches the necessity of a prevenient grace and of the grace of baptism in man's justification. But it also teaches, he says, the necessity of man's free assent to, and cooperation with, these graces. This presupposes that man's *liberum arbitrium* is not completely perverted by original sin. 'All this can and must take place in the Romanist view because even in a state of original sin the *liberum arbitrium* of man is *minime extinctum, viribus licet attenuatum et inclinatum.*'[9] In other words, it is not so weakened or perverted that on the presupposition of *gratia praeveniens* man is not *incapable* of that *assentire et cooperari*, of that *se disponere et praeparare*.[10] A fortiori he can cooperate on the basis of the grace received in baptism,[11] and its renewal in penance.[12] On the basis of grace, therefore, man can perform good works.[13]

---

[8] One can speak of a *gratia creata* in Barth in the sense that God's action really takes place in time and history, really touches man, but not in the sense that it becomes man's.

[9] *Conc. Trid.*, Sess. VI, *Decr. de Iustif.*, cap. I; can. 5.

[10] *Conc. Trid., ibid.*, can. 4. Barth, *C.D.* IV/2, p. 497 (=S. 563).

[11] *Conc. Trid., ibid.*, cap. 7.   [12] *Conc. Trid., ibid.*, cap. 14.

[13] *Conc. Trid., ibid.*, cap. 10. Cf Barth, *C.D.* IV/2, pp. 497-8 (=SS. 562-563); IV/1, p. 625 (=S. 698).

There are many things of real value in Karl Barth's own doctrine of sin and the man of sin.[14] Amongst these may be mentioned his emphasis on God's grace, mercy and love in his Son as the source of our knowledge of sin; on the christological, socio-ecclesiological, as well as the individual character of sin; on the inter-connection which exists between man's sinful act and his sinful being; his description of the nature of man's sin as pride, sloth and falsehood; his doctrine on the radicality of sin; on the misery of the man of sin; on the non-existence of indifferent acts; on the distinction between freedom of decision and true Christian freedom; his insistence on sin as man's own responsible *act*. Indeed, his whole doctrine is a powerful, sustained, and laudable argument against all forms of Pelagianism, semi-Pelagianism or 'synergism'. ∅

None the less, he differs from Catholic teaching. According to him, man's *liberum arbitrium* is totally perverted. This means for Barth that man is so perverted that not even with grace can he perform good actions. Man's actions are always, and can only be, totally sinful. Therefore, not even with the grace of God can he be the subject of good works.

'We speak of men who are always sinners like others; who at every moment and in every respect need forgiveness, the justification before God which is sheer mercy. Their sanctification takes place here below where there is no action that does not have the marks of sloth or can be anything but displeasing to God. This is true even of their lifting up of themselves, even of their looking to the Lord, which is their action as saints. . . . Is it really more than the eddy which may arise and be seen in a powerfully flowing stream but which cannot alter the course of the stream as a whole?'[15]

Barth's *second objection* to the Roman Catholic doctrine of co-operation is that it presupposes a false doctrine of grace.[16] It divides grace, he says, and in so doing denies it as God's or Christ's one, ever-new, sovereign and free act.

'The heart or guiding principle of the Romanist doctrine of grace is the negation of the unity of grace as always God's grace to man, as His sovereign act which is everywhere new and strange and free. It is the negation of the unity of grace as His grace in Jesus Christ.

[14] Cf *CTKB*, pp. 217–22, and the references to Barth's exposition; cf, *ibid.*, p. 217, notes 9, 10, 11.
[15] *C.D.* IV/2, pp. 527–8 (=S. 597). Cf *CTKB*, pp. 218–22.
[16] Cf *C.D.* IV/1, pp. 84–8 (=SS. 89–94).

It is the division of grace by which it is first of all His, but then—and this is where the emphasis falls—effected and empowered by His grace, it is also our grace.'[17]

Grace, says Barth, is not first God's and then man's. It is always God's, and never man's. Man's state in relation to it can never be that of one who has something. It can only be one of absolute need, the state of a beggar. Grace is not first *increata* and then *creata*, *actualis* and *habitualis*. *Gratia praeveniens* is *gratia concomitans*, *operans co-operans*, *sufficiens efficax*, *actualis habitualis*, *increata creata*. It is *creata* only because it is *increata*, *co-operans* only because it is *pure operari*, etc. There is no such thing as *gratia inhaerens*. Grace is always *God's* sovereign and free *act*. 'Is there in Paul anything like a sacramentally infused and therefore inherent righteousness?'[18]

Both these objections of Barth's are, however, but manifestations or consequences of his *one fundamental accusation* against the Roman Catholic doctrine of cooperation: it denies, he claims, the justification of man as God's sovereign and free act of grace. That this is his basic difficulty will be already clear. It need only be briefly illustrated here.

For even though the Council of Trent, he says, sincerely forbids all self-confidence and self-glory on the part of the Christian,[19] it is hard to see what meaning or force this statement can have in conjunction with a doctrine 'the whole point of which is to maintain man in an unshaken self-consciousness balancing not only the grace of God but also and primarily his own sins'.[20] And even though Roman Catholic doctrine speaks also of the unity of grace, it does not make any use of it. It merely commemorates the fact. It is definitely much *more* interested in 'man's state and life and activity of grace than in Christ as the One who accomplishes the divine act of sovereignty and what man is in and by Him'.[21] The Catholic ascription of grace to man, and therefore its division of grace, is a denial of the atonement as God's free act of grace. For then man is no longer needy and cannot be the recipient of the one complete grace of Christ. It is the denial of God as the sole subject of reconciliation.[22]

With its Tridentine doctrine of justification the Roman Church, Barth continues, closed the door to self-reformation, and deprived

[17] *C.D.* IV/1, p. 84 (=S. 89).
[18] *C.D.* IV/1, p. 625 (=S. 698), referring to Trent, *Sess.* VI, cap. 16.
[19] Trent, *Sess.* VI, cap. 16.
[20] *C.D.* IV/2, p. 498 (=S. 563).
[21] *K.D.* IV/1, S. 92 (=p. 87).
[22] Cf *C.D.* IV/1, pp. 84–8 (=SS. 89–94); IV/3, 2, pp. 514–20 (=SS. 591–8).

itself of all possibility of seizing the initiative in uniting the divided Church. For its decree completely ignored what was to the Reformers and Paul the very climax of justification, namely, its character as a *divine* work *for* man.[23]

Barth cannot subscribe, therefore, to the Roman Catholic doctrine of justification because he thinks its assertion (i) of a subjectivity of man in his own justification, (ii) of only a partial perversion of man's will, and (iii) of a grace which inheres in man, is a denial of justification as God's sovereign and free act of grace, or an assertion of at least a partial justification of man by himself, independently of God.

The inestimable ecumenical service rendered by Hans Küng's work on justification in Barth's and in Catholic doctrine is its demonstration that this supposedly fundamental objection by Barth is in fact no objection. He has convincingly demonstrated that it is in the best tradition of Catholic doctrine: i. negatively, that man of himself, without God's grace, is absolutely incapable of justifying himself in any way or to any extent; and ii. positively, that justification is God's sovereign and free act of grace. 'Hence, Barth's fundamental objection to Catholic teaching can be rejected as unjust and untenable, that is, the charge that Catholic theology relativizes the sublimity and sovereignty of God and diminishes Jesus Christ and His grace.'[24]

Father Küng's work is a good example of the many recent efforts at restoring the Church to its true 'balance'. In the Council of Trent's decree on justification, emphasis was polemically, and justifiably, laid on certain 'subjective' aspects, such as *gratia creata*, man's *liberum arbitrium*, man's cooperation. Post-Tridentine Catholic theology continued this emphasis, but in too exclusive a manner. There was a danger of distorting the true order of values. And this order always gives primacy to God, his grace and his Word.

This was the positive and truly evangelical insight of the Reformers. Modern Catholic theologians, through a renewed study of the sources, equally stress this. Küng has expressed this agreement admirably as

---

[23] 'dass ihnen das, was wirklick nicht erst den Reformatoren, sondern schon dem Apostel als die Hoheit der Rechtfertigung in ihrem Charakter als einem *göttlichen* Werkes *für* den Menschen vor Augen stand, eine unbekannte Grösse war': *K.D.* IV/1, S. 698 (=p. 625).

[24] H. Küng, *op. cit.*, p. 193. Cf *id., ibid.*, pp. 276f. The value of this service of Küng's will be understood when it is realized how widespread the Protestant misunderstanding of Catholic doctrine on this point is. Cf J. L. Witte, in *Münch. Theol. Zeit.*, 1959, pp. 38–9, and references; Küng, *op. cit.*, pp. 190f. This can be seen in the fact that Barth, even after Küng's work, still expressed misgivings about the genuineness of Küng's 'Catholic' doctrine. Cf his letter to the author, in Küng, *op. cit.*, pp. xxf.

regards the problem of justification. In Catholic theology also, primary emphasis must be given to *gratia increata*, to man's sinfulness, to God's subjectivity.[25] This primacy of emphasis is not something merely relative. It is not merely intended as a corrective to post-Tridentine theology. It is an absolute primacy, which always and everywhere must be acknowledged.

There are, however, secondary elements in the Catholic doctrine of justification, which are not less 'fundamental' to it than the primary. Both must be stressed in a truly 'Catholic' presentation. The primary must remain primary, but not to the detriment, glossing over, or exclusion of the secondary. It is precisely as regards these secondary elements that Barth will be found to be not so 'Catholic'.

The doctrine of the Catholic Church and the doctrine of Karl Barth agree on the fundamental point: justification is originally and primarily God's gracious act alone. They also agree in many other points. But Barth disagrees with us on this equally fundamental point: while God is the sole ultimate subject, he is not the sole subject of justification. The Christian is also its subject. Not just a subject *in* justification, but, in complete dependence on God, a subject *of* justification. This difference is based on two other differences, namely, our varying doctrines as regards grace and the man of sin. It is quite to be expected that Barth rejects our doctrine of cooperation. Our presuppositions are different. *We* may say that man cooperates with God and, at the same time, that God remains always the sole ultimate subject. On Barth's presuppositions those two statements are mutually exclusive. For if one accepts his doctrine of the total perversion of man's *liberum arbitrium*, and his doctrine of grace as God's *coup d'état* which never becomes man's, then one could not possibly accept the Catholic doctrine of cooperation, because one could not possibly understand how such a doctrine safeguards the sovereignty and freedom of God's grace.

The sovereignty, freedom and primacy of God's grace is as much a concern of Catholic doctrine as it is of Barth's. Admittedly, Catholic theology since Trent has devoted too much attention to grace as a private reality inherent in each individual. Grace is not primarily a created reality. It is primarily a description of God himself, of his gracious and benevolent disposition towards man, of his merciful love for man.[26] Recent Catholic studies, especially of Scripture and of the Greek Fathers, have brought this primary aspect of grace more into

[25] Cf Küng, *op. cit.*, chs. 23–5, 27, 30–2.
[26] Cf, e.g., Eph 1:2–8; II Tim 1:9.

focus, together with its christocentric, personal, ecclesiological and trinitarian aspects.[27]

This does not mean that the traditionally Western way of considering grace is false. God's grace to man is not in vain (I Cor 15:10). His benevolence or favour posits something in man. He effects in man the favours he wishes him. His gracious love achieves its end. God gifts something to man, creating him as his love wishes him to be. He makes him good, a sharer in his own eternal goodness.[28]

That grace is something given to man, God's gift to man, is recognized by modern-day Protestant exegetes and theologians as well.

'In Paul, *dikaiosune* is simultaneously an imparted and a received *dōrea*: Rom 5:17 (*tēs dōreas tēs dikaiosunēs*: genitive of apposition). It also means a gift bestowed, in Rom 8:10; 9:30; 10:6. Thus we can speak of a state of justification because in this giving the whole of the life of faith is founded. Thus what is stressed in Phil 3:9 is the always valid position that faith based on *dikaiosunē* is something given.'[29]

God's grace effects in man a new reality, a new being. This new being does not abolish or replace his original, created being. Nor is it something merely superimposed. It is his greater insertion into the origin and foundation of all being, Jesus Christ.[30] For he receives this free gift from God through Jesus Christ.[31] It is his justified being, the perfection of his created being in Christ. And as such it is man's new relationship to the Trinity of divine persons, who come to him and make their home with him.[32]

Grace, therefore, is a created reality, inherent in man.[33] It is his real participation in divine life. This does not mean that it ceases to be divine, or that it ceases to be God's. According to Catholic theology, man does not possess grace in the sense that he controls it, that it is some kind of an intermediate reality between Christ and the

---

[27] Besides the articles in the various dictionaries, and besides the various text-books, cf, e.g., J. Loosen, 'Ekklesiologische, christologische und trinitätstheologische Elemente im Gnadenbegriff' in *Theologie in Geschichte und Gegenwart* (Festschrift Schmaus), München, 1957, pp. 89–102; H. Volk, 'Gnade und Person', ibid., pp. 219–36.

[28] Cf St Thomas, *Summa theol.*, Ia IIae, q. 110, art. 1; q. 113, art. 2.

[29] G. Schrenk, art. *dikaiosunē* in *TWNT*, II, p. 208 (cited in Küng, *op. cit.*, p. 204). Cf also G. Stählin, *RGG*3, II, pp. 1634f, and other Pauline texts such as Rom 1:5; 5:5; I Cor 12:11.

[30] For creation as a christological and redemptive event cf Küng, *op. cit.*, chapter 22.   [31] Rom 5:15–17.

[32] Cf Jn 14:23; Rev 3:20; Rom 8:9–17; Gal 4:5–6; I Cor 3:16–17; I Cor 6:19; II Cor 6:16; Acts 2:38.   [33] Trent, *Sess.* VI, cap. 7; can. 11.

Christian, which the Christian is free to use or not as he wills. Barth's accusation is unjust.[34] Grace is not a *habitus* in the sense that possessing it we have no further need of God. We always have need of God's repeated intervention. The point is, however, that with and under God's intervention man himself really performs holy actions. Grace is God communicating himself to man, creating in him a new life-principle, enabling him to live a life which is a participation in his own divine life.

'God becomes, so to speak, a new soul for man, a new life-principle, in virtue of which man's personal decisions and actions obtain a value which immeasurably transcends all purely human significance, a value which is truly divine. Man is, as an ancient tradition put it, "made divine".[35] Grace is therefore not so much a gift God has given away and established in man to be administered by man alone, a gift which would thus experience a fate God has no control over: grace is God himself who communicates himself to man, sinks into his innermost being, and in this way sanctifies him. This sanctification makes of man a new reality not unlike the new existence effected by the soul when it animates the human body. The life of this man is now a participation in the very own life of the triune God himself.'[36]

The human life of the Christian is holy because it is a participation in God's own life. It is only because man's actions are preceded, accompanied and followed by the power of Christ that they are pleasing to God and meritorious.[37] Hence Barth's accusation against the Catholic doctrine of *liberum arbitrium* is also unjust.[38] This doctrine does not mean for us that man of himself is in any way the cause of his own justification. In saying that man's will is not totally perverted we do not mean that he contributes something independently of grace.[39] What we do mean is that he retains the possibility of appropriating, of living out, of transforming his own life—provided God gives him the grace.[40] This does not detract in any way from justification

---

[34] Cf above, p. 241.

[35] Cf K. Rahner, 'Some implications of the Scholastic concept of uncreated grace' in *Theol. Investigations*, I, pp. 319–46; *id.*, in *LTK*, IV, p. 994f.

[36] O. Semmelroth, *The Preaching Word. On the theology of Proclamation*, New York, 1965, p. 155. Cf also H. Küng, *op. cit.*, pp. 205f for other references.

[37] Trent, *Sess.* VI, cap. 16. [38] Cf above, p. 240.

[39] This was, after all, the very first doctrine explicitly rejected by the Council of Trent, cf *Sess* VI, cap. 1, 5f; can. 1–3.

[40] Trent, *Sess.* VI, cap. 5; can. 4–5.

as God's pure gift. On the contrary, the greatness of God's gift becomes really apparent in man's cooperation or sub-operation.[41]

Man does not do anything as regards his salvation which he has not been empowered to do by God. God therefore crowning man's works merely crowns his own gifts.[42] God does *everything*, and yet he wishes that man should do it as well.

'Human action is subordinated to the divine action. It is not only God and man, grace and freedom, but God through man, grace through freedom, that does the good act. . . . There are many things God does without me; there are others he does only through me. "God", says St Augustine, "who created thee without thee will not justify thee without thee".'[43]

The divine life is truly a human life as well. Man lives out the divine life gifted to him by God. Justification is a horizontal as well as a vertical process. It is not only God's action to and in man. It is God's action to and in and through man's action. With God's grace man really cooperates or sub-operates salvifically. He is not just a passive object of God's action, but he is made its true, active instrument. Consequently, his subjective reconciliation is not the work of God *alone*. Man is permeated by divine life. He receives in himself the principle of divine life, and is consequently the 'subject' of divine life. He is sanctified, and is able to perform good or holy works. His actions are not always and completely sinful. God is the sovereign and free subject of salvation. Yet under and with God, and only so, man is also its free subject. It is totally from God and yet totally from man. This is the problem of the cooperation or sub-operation of human liberty with divine grace, which Catholic theology has always recognized as a profound mystery. The explanation given is the only one which does justice to revelation and Catholic dogma.[44]

The principle of salvation is God's grace through the faith which

---

[41] Cf St Augustine, *Ep.* 194, 19 (*PL*, 33, 880).
[42] Cf K. Rahner, *art. cit.* in *Tüb. Theol. Quart.*, pp. 63–4 and note 9.
[43] C. Journet, *The Meaning of Grace*, p. 21. Cf St. Augustine, *Enarr. in Ps.* 70:2 (*PL*, 36, 877); *Sermo* 169, 13 (*PL*, 38, 922–3). Cf also St Bernard, *De gratia et libero arbitrio* (*PL*, 182, 1002, 1026f) reproduced in Küng, *op. cit.*, p. 266.
[44] 'Catholic theology has always recognized a profound mystery in this subordination-cooperation (total mutual compenetration of the two categories) of human liberty and divine grace. At bottom it is the mystery of the analogy of being considered in the sphere of action. . . . In this there is question solely of a philosophical doctrine which Catholic theologians judge necessary for the explanation of divine revelation and Catholic dogma': J. Alfaro, 'Justificacion Barthiana y Just. Cat.' in *Greg.* 39 (1958) 768.

issues in charity, and not the mere observance of the Mosaic Law. This is what Paul means in Rom 3:28.[45] He does not mean that all observance of the divine law has no intrinsic, contributory value to justification. A Catholic can also say that justification takes place *sola fide*. But faith is a divine-human action or work—the divine through the human, and the human by and under the divine. Paul insists on the human act of faith as the necessary condition of justification, or salvation.[46] He also insists on the works of faith. God alone saves, but through human works of faith. Justification is from God but through man whom he has enabled to cooperate with him.[47] Man's works are good as man's works.[48] This is the cooperation explicitly mentioned by Paul himself: 'For we are God's fellow-workers.'[49] What I have just given is the clear teaching of the Council of Trent.[50]

According to Barth, God's grace is his simultaneously condemning and freeing action. Man's condemnation as a sinner is also his liberation for new acts. In the event of God's grace man is always the sinner he was and is. But in this same event he is set in movement towards the new man he already is and will be. God's grace is effective. It really condemns and liberates man. But it is an event. It does not become man's. Man always remains the sinner he was and is. Yet when it occurs he is set in movement from his past to his future which is also his present. He is *simul peccator et iustus*.

It is very difficult to understand how Barth can assert a real alteration or sanctification of man. As he himself points out: if there are no good human works is not our attestation of a real alteration of the human situation pointless and empty?[51] What he says about creating an eddy in the stream of sin would seem to be an expression of his embarrassment. For if grace is not something which is given to man, does not really become man's, how can it possibly be said that he is sanctified? Barth admits a real change. But if man's acts in so far as they are man's are not good, what more can this mean than merely a change from one bad act to another? How can Barth assert a real

---

[45] For a detailed exposition of Pauline texts cf H. Bouillard, *Karl Barth*, vol. II, pp. 73–101.
[46] Cf Rom 1:16–17; 3:22; 10:9–10; 11:20.
[47] Cf Rom 2:6; 2:13; 10:9–10; 13:8–10; I. Cor 7:19; Gal 5:6, 13–14; 6:7, 15; Eph 2:1–10; Phil 2:12; Rom 8:3–9; 7:6. And cf James 2:14–26.
[48] Cf Rom 6:12–18; Eph 2:1–10; II Pet 1:10; James 2:8; Phil 2:12–13.
[49] I Cor 3:9. Cf II Cor 6:1.
[50] *Sess* VI, cap. 5–6, 10–11; can. 4–9, 24–5, 32.
[51] *C.D.* IV/2, p. 585 (=S. 662). One cannot simply say that 'Barth's stand on intrinsic justification fulfils the requirements of Catholic dogma': H Küng, *op. cit.*, p. 262.

alteration of man's life, or his real participation in divine life, or his real justification or sanctification, when he also asserts that the life of which man is the subject always remains totally sinful?[52]

Because of his doctrine on grace as the event of God's action to and in man, but which never becomes man's, and on the total perversion of man's *liberum arbitrium*, Barth is unable to perceive a third possibility between an action of God alone and an action of man alone in man's subjective salvation. For him there can be no *via media* between the doctrine of Luther and that of Pelagius in this respect. Either God justifies man, and the human act of faith is but a necessary consequence but not an intrinsically necessary condition, or man simply justifies himself by means of his human acts. The Catholic solution is for him no solution at all. It is merely the assertion of man's self-justification, of synergism. He fails to see the possibility of an act which would proceed from God and man in union, which would as such be the cause of man's subjective justification and which would be completely God's and yet also completely man's.

For him, the subjective accomplishment of reconciliation is an act of God *alone*. Man's actions, under the divine action, do not contribute to it or condition it. They are a purely human reflection of God's action. This is an exact parallel to his doctrine on the person and work of Christ. Just as he denies the inherent sanctification of Christ's human nature, and consequently its true cooperative instrumentality in the objective work of reconciliation, so also he denies the inherent reality of created grace in the individual Christian, and consequently his cooperative instrumentality in his subjective reconciliation. We can see here, too, the basis of his ecclesiological and mariological differences with us.

[52] The formula *simul iustus et peccator* is susceptible of a Catholic interpretation. Compare on this R. Grosche, 'Simul peccator et justus' in *Catholica*, 4 (1938), 132–9; von Balthasar, *op. cit.*, pp. 378–86; Küng, *op. cit.*, chapter 30. With the latter's exposition Barth can and does express his agreement— cf his letter to the author in Küng, *op. cit.*, p. xx. However, have we not here a question of the whole absorbing a part, or the more radical agreeing with the less radical? Where does Barth say that grace becomes 'man's possession as an intrinsic reality'? (H. U. v. Balthasar, *op. cit.*, p. 379, and cited in Küng (!), p. 248; cf *Conc. Trid., Sess.* VI, cap. 7; can. 11.) Or where does he say that man's actions with God's grace are not totally sinful? (Cf, for the contrary, *Conc. Trid., Sess.* VI, cap. 11; can. 25.)

The correction of Luther by modern Lutheran theologians is significant in this respect: 'The NT knows nothing of the *simul iustus et peccator*. The Christian is "holy" and not a "sinner" '; *Theol. Abteilung Bericht* 1957-63, *Dokument No. 7, Vierte Vollversammlung des Lutherischen Weltbundes*, 30 July to 11 August 1963, Helsinki, p. 16.

Barth says that the basis of our differences lies in our different conception of Jesus Christ. 'We are not at one with the Catholics and humanists—even those in our own ranks—in the knowledge of Christ, and therefore we cannot be at one with them in this as in so many other matters.'[53] He also points out that his doctrine of *sola fides* is the necessary consequence of his doctrine of *solus Christus*.[54] On the other hand, he acknowledges that his *solus Christus* is the necessary consequence of his *sola fides*.[55] Both the *solus Christus* and the *sola fides*, in his theology, are other ways of saying *solus Deus*. The original concretion of this *solus* took place, for him, in the question of justification. All his theology safeguards this primary conclusion.

[53] *C.D.* IV/1, p. 500 (=S. 557).
[54] Cf *CTKB*, pp. 231f.
[55] Cf above, pp. 19-20, 238, and below, pp. 337f.

Chapter Eighteen

The Church is Event and Institution

As Karl Barth says, the community is an assembly which comes into existence in response to a call.[1] The New Testament Greek word for Church, namely, *ekklēsia*, was taken over from the Septuagint's translation of the Hebrew word *qahal*.[2] The best English equivalent would be 'assembly',[3] although the words 'community', 'Church', 'congregation' should also be used to bring out the richness and many-sided meaning of the original reality. In the New Testament *ekklēsia* has various meanings. It can mean the one universal Church,[4] the local Church at Jerusalem, Antioch, Corinth,[5] and the Church actually assembled for worship.[6] It is now generally agreed that the universal was the original meaning.[7] This intermingling is also understandable, since the word was and could be used in all its senses of the original Jerusalem community.

There is no appreciable difference between St Paul's and the other New Testament writers' use of the word *ekklēsia*. What is important, and what distinguishes the New Testament assembly from every other type of assembly, is its description as the assembly *of God* (*ekklēsia tou theou*). The concept of the community is not therefore one of quantity but of quality. It is not numbers which count, but the call of God and answer of man: God assembling and man allowing himself be assembled. It is an assembly based on the response of *faith*

---

[1] Cf *CTKB*, pp. 250f.
[2] Cf K. L. Schmidt, art. *ekklēsia* in *TWNT*, III, pp. 502–39; M. Schmaus, *Katholische Dogmatik*, III/1, pp. 26–37; J. Hamer, *The Church is a Communion*, pp. 35–44; H. Küng, *The Church*, pp. 81–7.
[3] Cf Schmidt, *art. cit.*, p. 507.
[4] Cf, e.g., Acts 20:28; Gal 1:13; I Cor 15:9; 12:28.
[5] Cf, e.g., Acts 8:1, 3; 11:26; I Cor 1:2.
[6] Cf, e.g., I Cor 11:18; 14:19, 28, 34–35.
[7] Formerly, the Catholic authors Battifol, Leclerq and Kösters, basing their views on the etymological sense of the word *ekklēsia*, and not on its relation to the *qahal Yahweh* of the Old Testament, thought the original use was of the particular local community.

to a *divine* summons—not just another free association of and by individuals. This corresponds to the use of *qahal Yahweh* in the Old Testament, and shows the continuity of the new people of God as the remnant of Israel with the people of God of the Old Testament. St Paul adds *en Christō*. This brings out the newness of the New Testament community as the people founded in the death, resurrection and ascension of Jesus Christ, and in the mission of his Holy Spirit.[8]

From this brief examination it is clear that the *ekklēsia* of the New Testament has both an ontological and an actual meaning.[9] In this it follows the Septuagint use of the word. I do not think Barth does justice to both these meanings. He brings out strikingly the qualitative idea of the Church as a dynamic event or act of assembling and being assembled. The Church *is* an event, a coming together, a congregating in response to a call, particularly for worship. This event nature of the *ekklēsia* is brought out in the word 'congregation', although it also finds expression in the word 'Church', as for instance when we say that 'it is time for Church'. But can one say that the being of the Church is solely act? Or can one say that the human Church, in the image of John the Baptist in Grünewald's painting, is merely a figure pointing to a salvific reality which always remains 'outside' it? And is the Church never continuously the Church? Even the use of the word in the New and Old Testaments indicates that this view cannot be exclusive. The Church is also a constant reality, and the source of the constantly repeated event of its gathering. The community exists also *ausser Akt*, that is, apart from its actual assembling by God and by itself. The author of Acts brings this out when he says: 'Take heed to yourselves and to all the flock, in which the Holy Spirit has made you guardians, to feed the Church of the Lord [or 'of God'] which he obtained with his own blood.'[10] As well as signifying the act of its assembling and being assembled the word *ekklēsia* also denotes the assembled community, or the people of God as such.[11]

It is also clear, from what we have seen, that the word *ekklēsia* in the New Testament signifies the universal, the local and the cultic 'Church'. It signifies the Church as a whole, its manifestation in a particular locality, and its most intensive actualization in community worship. All these aspects should be theologically evaluated and find

[8] Cf Schmidt, *art. cit.*, 507, 511.
[9] The terminology is that of Schmaus, *op. cit.*, p. 29.
[10] Acts 20:28.
[11] Cf, e.g., Dt 23:1–8; II Chron 1:3, 5; 6:3; 30:2–4; Neh 8:17; Ps 22; Phil 3:6; I Cor 12:28; Col 1:18, 24; Eph 1:22; 3:21.

a place in the ecclesiologies of all Christian Churches today. The Church's universality means the fulness of its differentiation in unity, or the fulness of its unity in differentiation. Universality and unity should not lead to uniformity or the suppression of local and individual differentiation. On the contrary, as the dynamic life of the Church, it should create this differentiation.[12]

Catholic ecclesiology has been one-sided in this respect in its insistence on the primacy of the pope, on centralization, on universal law. Recently this one-sidedness has been balanced by a corresponding insistence on the episcopacy, with its correlative evaluation of the local Church, and by the liturgical renewal, especially in its insistence on the eucharist as the greatest manifestation and actualization of the whole Church. The universal and institutional Church is directed towards the local Church, that is, towards the Church as *event*. This does not mean that it exists solely when it celebrates the eucharistic mystery. It exists continually as an institution and in invisible love and worship of God. But of its very nature the Church is sacramental. Its invisible unity and worship must be repeatedly enacted visibly.

'It is a visible society; as really visible it must continually realize its historical, spatio-temporal tangibility through the actions of men. It must become "event" over and over again. It is not as if these "events" in their separated individuality in space and time founded the Church anew. An actualism of this sort, which would basically deny the social constitution of the Church, tradition, apostolic succession and any real Church law of divine right, is foreign to Catholic ecclesiology.'[13]

The Church as an institution has a more intense degree of actuality in the actual exercise of its functions. As an institution it must repeatedly become event. This appears also from the consideration that it is an institution for service, an institution for the service of Christ and therefore of the world. No one shares in Christ's three offices for his own benefit. He is called and sent in the service of Christ, his Church and his world. The apex of this service, and the greatest intensive actualization of the Church, takes place in the celebration of the eucharist.

The Church is the continuing presence of Christ with men through his Spirit in ministry, word and sacrament, and the continuing presence of men with Christ through his Spirit in faith, hope, and love for God and one another. In the eucharist the Lord and source

[12] Cf Vatican II, DCC, ch. 2, n. 13.
[13] K. Rahner, in *The Episcopate and the Primacy*, p. 24.

of the Church is made present, and the union of the faithful with Christ and one another is most tangibly visible and interiorly realized. Hence the eucharist is the most intense actualization of the Church. The eucharist exists because the Church exists, but also the Church exists because the eucharist exists. The personal body of Christ, sacramentally present through the Church's ministry, effects his mystical body. 'The Head makes the unity of the Body, and that is how it is that the *"mysterium fidei"* is also the *"mysterium Ecclesiae* par excellence".'¹⁴ Or as William of Thierry put it: 'Eating the body of Christ is nothing else but becoming the body of Christ.'¹⁵ The eucharistic celebration, in which the people of God gather round its invisible Pastor and its visible pastor, is of necessity a local event. But in it the *whole* Church is re-presented and actualized. The local Church is not a 'section', 'province' or 'sub-division' of the real or whole Church. The local Church *is* the whole Church.

'This Church of Christ is truly present in all legitimate local congregations of the faithful which, united with their pastors, are themselves called Churches in the New Testament. For in their own locality these are the new people called by God, in the Holy Spirit and in much fulness (cf I Thess 1:5). In them the faithful are gathered together by the preaching of the Gospel of Christ, and the mystery of the Lord's Supper is celebrated, "that by the flesh and blood of the Lord's body the whole brotherhood may be joined together". In any community existing around an altar, under the sacred ministry of the bishop, there is manifested a symbol of that charity and "unity of the Mystical Body, without which there can be no salvation". In these communities, though frequently small and poor, or living far from any other, Christ is present. By virtue of him the one, holy, catholic and apostolic Church gathers together. For "the partaking of the body and blood of Christ does nothing other than transform us into that which we consume".'¹⁶

---

¹⁴ H. de Lubac, *The Splendour of the Church*, p. 107. On the relationship between the eucharist and the Church cf J.-M. R. Tillard, *The Eucharistic Pasch of God's People*, New York, 1967, and W. Elert, *Eucharist and Church Fellowship in the First Four Centuries*, St Louis, 1966.
¹⁵ William of Thierry, *PL*, 184, 403. Cf St Thomas, *Summa theol.*, III, q. 73, art. 3c. Copious texts in de Lubac, *Corpus Mysticum*, Paris, 1949.
¹⁶ DCC, n. 26. The council document refers to Acts 8:1; 14:22–23; 20:17; Mozarabic Prayer, *PL*, 96:759B; St Ignatius of Antioch, *Ad Smyrn.*, 8:1 (ed. Funk, I, p. 282); St Augustine, *C. Faustum*, 12, 20 (*PL*, 42:265); *Sermo* 57, 7 (*PL*, 38:389); Leo the Great, *Sermo* 63, 7 (*PL*, 54:357C).

The Church as the local and liturgical event is the whole Church in its local manifestation and realization: the Church *at* Corinth, *at* Rome, *at* Antioch.[17]

The Catholic concept of the Church as universal and institutional does not exclude, therefore, but demands, the realization of the Church as event. I do not think that Karl Barth does justice to the universal and institutional Church. Basically, his position is that of Congregationalism. The community is an assembly which comes into existence in a definite place in response to a call. The Scripture text he loves to quote is Mt 18:20: 'For where two or three are gathered together in my name, there am I in the midst of them.' This idea of a local community has and should have a definite place in ecclesiology, as we saw. But for Barth the local assembly takes place solely in the event of its gathering, and in response to a call which is always God's action alone. There is no salvific human mediation between Christ and the Christian. There is no permanent ministry or order instituted by Christ. Even the form or order witnessed to in Scripture is the *norma normans* only in so far as the community now hears in it again the 'immediate direction' of Jesus Christ through his Spirit. In this sense its law will be a living and liturgical law of service.[18] 'No office, no clerical group may intervene between the Lord, Christ in Heaven, and the Christian community of the land, sovereign on earth. Its formal aristocracy is only representative Christian democracy, the corollary of the autocracy of Christ.'[19] Certainly, since the Church is a priestly people in its totality all Christians have direct access to God in Christ through the Spirit. No clerical group claims to intervene between it and its risen Lord. Yet a clerical group does exist, and by divine will, in the service of this direct encounter of the Christian and of the Christian community with God. As the sacramental and visible means of God's presence to man, and as the service of man's response to God, the Church's hierarchical ministry and sacraments do not 'intervene' between God and man but aid their encounter. Barth denies the existence of such a ministry in the Church. He penned the above words in 1925. He has not changed. Already then, too, he rejected the possibility of a universal reformed creed.[20] In his

---

[17] Cf I Cor 1:2; II Cor 1:1; DCC, n. 28. As St Peter Damian says: 'Sancta ecclesia in omnibus una et in singulis tota. . . . In universitate una, et in suis partibus tota': *Dominus Vobiscum*, cap. V–VI (*PL*, 145:235). Cf the reflections of K. Rahner (*loc. cit.*, pp. 28f) on the relationship between the episcopate and the primacy as based on this relationship between the local and the universal Church.

[18] Cf *CTKB*, pp. 296–7, 302–4.

[19] *Ibid.*, p. 207.   [20] Cf *ibid.*, p. 208.

conception there can be no such thing as a visible universal Church, just as there can be no such thing as a permanent Church. This is explained ultimately by his refusal to allow any real human participation in the grace and ministry of Jesus Christ. Barth would even seem to be a radical Congregationalist. For even the act of human response to the direct call of Christ is not a holy action in the sense that it participates in Christ's holiness. It is on a totally different plane.

The Church is not solely event in the sense that its being is solely act. It is not solely in a process of becoming. It is also an ontological permanent reality of grace, due to the indwelling of the Holy Spirit. While all human action is more or less sinful there is a real ontological sanctification. Faith in the Holy Spirit demands this. The Church is not solely event in the further sense that it is not solely the local community. It is a universal, and universally visible one Church of Christ. There is a third sense in which the Church is not solely event. It is not solely the event of the direct action of the Holy Spirit. It is this, just as it is an act and a local community. But it is also an institution. The Church is an institution *and* an event.

Ever since the first assembly of the World Council of Churches in Amsterdam in 1948, where theological thought was strongly under the influence of Karl Barth, it has become customary to oppose Catholic and Protestant ecclesiology as 'institutional' or 'horizontal' and 'eventful' or 'vertical'. Shortly afterwards, on the occasion of a highly interesting book by a Protestant theologian, the consideration and relationship of these two aspects was even considered the 'capital problem of contemporary ecclesiology'.[21]

As Barth says, the Church is primarily a divine action. Catholic ecclesiology neither denies nor forgets this. The difference between us lies in our explanation of the mode or way in which this divine action creates the Church. In further agreement with him we also say that this divine action takes place in a direct immediate intervention of the risen Lord in his earthly-historical body. In modern terminology this is known as the charismatic aspect of the Church, and is receiving increased attention by Catholic authors. The Church is not solely an institution. The action of the risen Lord through his Spirit does not take place solely through the means (Word and sacrament, triple participation in his messianic ministry) which he instituted once and for all. The Holy Spirit, who indwells his Church, intervenes directly, suddenly and unexpectedly when and where he wills, for the good of the Church. The Spirit blows where he wills.

[21] R. Aubert, in *ETL*, 28 (1952), 688. He was reviewing the book of J.-L. Leuba, *L'Institution et L'Evénement*.

This is manifest as regards many of the graces or *charismata* mentioned by St Paul. Their object is the 'common good'. Their source is direct 'inspiration' by the Holy Spirit.

'To each is given the manifestation of the Spirit for the common good. To one is given through the Spirit the utterance of wisdom, and to another the utterance of knowledge according to the same Spirit, to another faith by the same spirit, to another gifts of healing by the one Spirit, to another the working of miracles, to another prophecy, to another the ability to distinguish between spirits, to another various kinds of tongues, to another the interpretation of tongues. All these are inspired by one and the same Spirit, who apportions to each one individually as he wills.'[22]

It is manifest in the whole history of the Church. One need only cast a glance at the Church's saints, social and charitable workers, founders of religious orders, missionaries, to be convinced of this. This direct action of the Spirit is not necessarily an extraordinary and therefore rare phenomenon. It is a necessary, constant and widely diffused aspect of the Church's life.

'It is not only through the sacraments and Church ministries that the same Holy Spirit sanctifies and leads the people of God and enriches it with virtues. Allotting his gifts "to everyone according as he will" (I Cor 12:11), he distributes special graces among the faithful of every rank. By these gifts he makes them fit and ready to undertake the various tasks or offices advantageous for the renewal and upbuilding of the Church, according to the words of the Apostle: "The manifestation of the Spirit is given to everyone for the common good" (I Cor 12:7). These charismatic gifts, whether they be the most outstanding or the more simple and widely diffused, are to be received with thanksgiving and consolation, for they are exceedingly suitable and useful for the needs of the Church.'[23]

The direct action of the Spirit does not take place in independence of, much less in opposition to, his indirect action through his human ministers and earthly sacraments. This is understandable when we remember the identity of their source (the Holy Spirit) and object (the building up of the body of Christ). It is clear also from the fact that the charisms are given to all members of the Church (whether they

[22] I Cor 12:7–11. Cf Rom 12:4–8; Acts 8:26–40.
[23] Vatican II, DCC, ch. 2, n. 12.

share in the institutional ministry or not), and that the charismatics are often candidates for the ministry (cf Gal 2:2, 9–10). Both are constituent elements of the Church, and should work in harmony, in mutual recognition, safeguarding and encouragement.[24]

The Spirit's action is not absolutely conditioned by the exercise of the instituted ministry. The Holy Spirit acts directly without the mediation of the Church, and the action of the Church is solely a response. Here there is a justification for Karl Barth's theology of *act and response*. There is no mediation on the Church's part, but solely an action of response to the direct internal action of the Spirit. This action of the Spirit is personal and transitory. But it is not transitory in the sense that it does not confer a grace and power, or that it remains an ever new act of the Spirit alone. A charism, too, is a real gift which enables the Church member to act in the power and grace of God. Barth's theology of act and response would seem to be tarnished by his theology of reflection.

In general agreement with Barth as regards the Church as event, I must however question him on his denial of a mediated action of the Holy Spirit in the creation of his Church. The Church is neither exclusively an event nor exclusively an institution. It is both an institution and an event. The question is basically pneumatological, and only as such ecclesiological. It concerns the mode of the Spirit's presence and action in the Church. From all we have seen of the doctrine of Holy Scripture it should be beyond dispute that there are certain *media* in the Church to which the conferring of salvation is infallibly and perennially connected.

> 'As the Father has sent me, even so I send you. . . . Receive the Holy Spirit. If you forgive the sins of any, they are forgiven; if you retain the sins of any, they are retained. . . . Whatever you bind on earth shall be bound in heaven, and whatever you loose on earth shall be loosed in heaven. . . . All authority in heaven and on earth has been given to me. Go therefore and make disciples of all nations, baptizing them . . . teaching them to observe all that I have commanded you; and lo, I am with you always, to the close of the age, . . . he who receives any one whom I send receives me; and he who receives me receives him who sent me. . . . They laid their hands on them and they received the Holy Spirit. . . . Take heed to yourselves and all the flock, in which the Holy Spirit has made you guardians, to feed the Church of the Lord. . . . I know

---

[24] Fr Semmelroth terms the relationship between the two a *Füreinander im Gegeneinander*, in *Geist und Leben*, 36 (1963), 450.

that after my departure fierce wolves will come in among you, not sparing the flock. . . .'[25]

I must try to be clear in what I mean and do not mean here by institution in its distinction from event. The Church is an institution as the permanent reality through apostolic succession of the ministries and means of salvation. This institution took place through Christ's mission of his apostles and mission of his Holy Spirit. It was, of course, originally an event—the event of Christ's direct intervention in human history. But this event took place only once—in the sense that it was limited to the time of the apostles. The Church of succeeding time takes place through the mediation of this apostolic Church. The aim and result of the original event was an institution. The ministries and means of salvation instituted once and for all continue for all time through historical, horizontal, apostolic succession. The action of the risen Christ in his Church of today takes place (not exclusively, as we have seen) through the mediation of the means created in the Church once and for all.

The greatest obstacle to the understanding of this would be to consider this permanent structure of the Church as a merely human and historical reality. The Church in its structure is a divine-human reality, in analogy to the divine-human reality of the historical Christ. The source and principle of its permanence and continuity is the Holy Spirit in and through the visible, sacramental, human and historical actions. This is particularly apparent when we remember that apostolic succession is a sacrament, the sacrament of episcopal consecration. Jesus Christ alone is the principal cause of the sacraments and of sacerdotal action. He alone grants a participation in his own power and mission to continue his mission in the same sacramental way. But he does really grant a participation so that their action is action in his power.

Another cause of misunderstanding (and here I think there is room for further development in Catholic ecclesiology) might be a too great association of the Church's mediatory action with a Christ of the *past*. Certainly, Christ instituted the visible sacramental means of salvation in a time which is now past. But the power in which these means act is the power of the risen Christ, and therefore something supra-temporal. Thus the action of the institutional Church, as a divine and human action in one, is also a temporal and supra-temporal action in one. Christ can be said to institute his Church here

[25] Jn 20:21–23; Mt 18:18; 28:18–20; Jn 13:20 (Lk 10:16; Mt 10:40); Acts 8:17; 20:28–9.

and now as he did there and then. This would seem to have been the conception of the Fathers.

'According to the modern mind, for example, Christ *founded* the Church, and *instituted* the sacraments. For the Ancients—and in this category we include the Middle Ages—, Christ *is* the *auctor* of the sacraments and all that makes up the Church; which is to say that he is always *actually*, and therefore immediately, responsible. Certainly the early Christians were not unaware that these realities had an historical origin, but that origin interested them less than the authority permanently present and then operating in what was believed and lived.'[26]

This consideration is reinforced when we recall what I have already mentioned: that the Church-institution is destined to actualize itself as the Church-event, especially in the sacrament of the eucharist. 'The liturgy is the summit toward which the activity of the Church is directed; at the same time it is the fountain from which all her power flows.'[27] Just as the scope of the original event of the foundation of the Church was the Church as institution, so the scope of the Church as institution is the Church as event. In the eucharist the Church is continually created and renewed. It is continually re-created because it is precisely and solely here that Christ re-presents himself in sacrament in the *ephapax* of his sacrifice on the cross. 'If the eucharistic hour is the hour of Christ *in sacramento*, it is equally the hour of the foundation of the Church *in sacramento*.'[28]

I have mentioned many ways in which Catholic ecclesiology can and must speak of the Church as event. Yet it has a fundamental dissatisfaction with Barthian ecclesiology. For it maintains that the Church mediates salvation, in and under the power of the risen Lord. Formerly, at least, Barth too asserted a certain 'mediation' of the Church. But it was mediation in the sense that the subject remained Christ alone. In the later volumes of his Church Dogmatics he 'demythologized' his former use of the term 'sacrament' and 'mediation', and resorted to a pure theology of response and reflection.[29] This is quite consistent, of course, with his position in pneumatology, christology and justification. The event of the Church is for him solely an invisible, spiritual action of the Holy Spirit. The exclusiveness of this statement is certainly not biblical.

[26] Congar, *Tradition and Traditions*, London, 1966, p. 12.
[27] Vatican II, *Constitution on the Liturgy*, n. 10.
[28] A. de Bovis, in *NRT*, 85 (1963), 137.
[29] Cf *CTKB*, pp. 77f.

Catholic ecclesiology, on the contrary, maintains that the Spirit, or the risen Christ in power, acts through the means of salvation which he instituted once and for all, in a way similar to his action in and through his visible historical humanity during his life on earth.[30] The *pure docere* and *recte administrare*, while primarily a divine action, are not solely a divine action. The risen Christ acts infallibly in the means he himself instituted. While we can never know who is saved or not, we can say that the Church is *there where* the Church exercises the means of salvation instituted by Christ. The Church is not solely dependent on a purely spiritual and unpredictable act of God.

Karl Barth's 'mono-actualism' leads necessarily to a 'demythologization' of the terms 'institution', 'mediation', 'sacrament', 'written word of Scripture', 'tradition', 'Church authority'. Other trends in Protestantism are fortunately not wholly in agreement with him in this. This is evidenced by the following passage from the already mentioned and highly interesting work of Pastor Leuba:

> 'In giving his Spirit once and for all to his apostles and those who were with them he renders the Church capable of continuing the task he had commenced on earth. In his name, in his place, the Church will accomplish the work of God. The apostles, having received the Spirit, will be the witnesses of Jesus in Jerusalem and in all Judea and Samaria and to the end of the earth.'[31]

The Church is both institution and event, event and institution. The future union of the diverging Christian traditions is largely dependent on the recognition of both of these aspects. This is particularly apparent with regard to the basic strictly ecclesiological point of divergence, namely, the nature of Church ministry and of apostolic succession. For long, Catholics have insisted more or less exclusively on instituted hierarchical ministry and on institutional apostolic succession, i.e. through the imposition of hands. In modern Protestantism there is a renewed interest and awareness of instituted episcopacy and episcopal succession, and of the recognition of the presence of this episcopacy in the Catholic Church. I have already

---

[30] Fr Congar terms it extremely noteworthy that the theological development of the theory of apostolic succession was effected by St Irenaeus in the second half of the second century over against a heresy (Gnosticism) which sought to destroy the meaning itself of the incarnation. Cf Congar's *Le Christ, Marie et l'Eglise*, pp. 42–3.

[31] *L'Institution et l'Evénement*, p. 25. And in note 8 he adds: 'This is a unique and definitive authorization.'

quoted Schlink and Jeremias on this point.[32] On the other hand, Protestants have always insisted, more or less exclusively, on the Church's charismatic ministry and on charismatic succession in this ministry. In modern Catholicism there is a renewed interest in and awareness of charismatic ministry and charismatic succession, and the acknowledgment of the presence of this charismatic ministry and charismatic apostolic succession in Protestant Churches. Schlink had of course already posed the problem to Catholic theologians.

'In the primitive Church we must from the outset reckon rather with the coexistence and overlapping of these different foundations and forms of ministry. The ministry of founding and guiding the Church was exercised partly on the basis of a special commission by the apostles or by others called to be the founders and leaders of the communities, partly on the ground of a commission by the community or by outstanding members assigned to office, but not on the basis of a special commission, and finally the ministry of founding and guiding the Church was also charismatically exercised without a special commission.'[33]

Hans Küng, amongst others, leaves himself open to the question, saying it requires a whole new exegetical, historical and dogmatic enquiry.[34] From the Catholic side the future of the ecumenical movement and its likelihood of leading to the reunification of Christians depends to a great extent on its answer to this question. Of course all this goes beyond the position of Karl Barth in the sense that the recognition of a charismatic as well as an institutional ministry attributes to the Church or recognizes it as possessing a true share in Christ's own salvific ministry. And because it goes beyond Barth on this point it will also go beyond him, and indeed has already done so, on the questions of Christ's human existence and of justification.

---

[32] Cf above, p. 187, note 94.
[33] E. Schlink, 'Die apostolische Sukzession' in *Der kommende Christus und die kirchichen Traditionen*, Göttingen, 1961, p. 173 (cited in H. Küng, *Structures of the Church*, p. 175).
[34] Cf H. Küng, *op cit.*, p. 172f; *The Church*, pp. 442–4; 'What is the Essence of Apostolic Succession?' in *Concilium*, 4/4 (1968), 16–19. Cf also esp. M. Villain, 'Can there be Apostolic Succession outside the Continuity of the Laying on of Hands?' *ibid.*, 45–53.

Chapter Nineteen

The Church is Visible and Invisible

KARL BARTH's sincere concern for the visibility of the Church is obvious.[1] And what he actually says can, for the most part, be interpreted *in meliorem partem*. However, what he means by these words is not exactly the same, if I interpret him correctly, as what we mean by them. I hope I am not being too querulous, but I believe that his treatment of this point, too, shows signs of the general weakness in his ecclesiology and theology.

The basis of Barth's position is this: the Church is essentially visible in its organization, *cultus*, members, etc., as the human reflection of the direct spiritual act of its invisible essence, namely, the power of the Word made flesh. Its invisible essence presses from within outwards, from invisibility to visibility. In Catholic ecclesiology the Church's visibility is usually considered in connection with a theology of mediation, that is, in connection with the Church as the instituted means of grace. Both these viewpoints are valid, and should complement one another. When isolated, they represent a unilateral consideration of the Church as event or institution, whereas the Church is both an event and an institution, as we saw.

One of the constituent factors of the Church's visibility is undoubtedly the action (worship, prayer, charity, etc.) which wells out from the invisible, internal, direct action of the Spirit. With its increasing acknowledgment of the Church as a charismatic event Catholic ecclesiology should incorporate Barth's explanation of the Church's visibility. The Church in its visibility should be an epiphany of Jesus Christ, a christophany. The grace of Christ, as the grace of the Word made flesh, of its very nature seeks 'incarnation'. It seeks visible expression, and in a social form. On the other hand, Barth should incorporate the truly evangelical explanation of the Church's visibility as an instituted means of grace. The Church is universally visible as the society which has one visible head to whom all render

[1] Cf *CTKB*, pp. 254f.

obedience; in which salvation is obtained through visible social relations to persons and things.

Barth, however, cannot accept this, for it would be a denial of his basic principle: the mediation of salvation by God *alone* in his direct act. But because he denies it he is unable to explain the permanency, universality and uniqueness of the Church's visibility. In his view, there is nothing to prevent the Church being visible now in one way, now in another. Its visibility is solely an ever-new response to the invisible and internal action of the Spirit. Certainly, the Holy Spirit is constant and one in his action. But how is any one to recognize where and when he acts? Or is it possible, humanly speaking, to recognize the Church of which the New Testament speaks? Karl Barth says it is possible on the basis of the internal action of the Spirit. But his only appeal against my holding a contrary opinion is again the personal, internal action of the Holy Spirit.

I am not even completely satisfied with Barth's explanation of the Church's visibility on the basis of event-response ecclesiology. He seems to save visibility at the expense of unity. That is, he safeguards the *inconfuse* of the Church's two 'natures', but is not so clear as regards the *indivise* and *inseparabiliter*. His explanation of the Church's visibility seems to reveal a type of ecclesiological Nestorianism based on an ecclesiological monophysitism. Lest these words seem over-peremptory and unfraternal I must explain exactly what I mean.

The kernel of the problem is this: If what the Church 'really is'[2] is not visible, how can the Church really be said to be visible? If there is no 'direct unequivocal identity' (I would prefer to say 'unity') between its real being and its historical manifestations, how can the Church be said to be visible? If the visible Church can be the mere semblance of the real Church, and if it can be termed the body of Christ only 'poetically or mythologically', how can one say that the real Church is really visible?

As far as I can see, the only way in which visibility is really safeguarded in an event-response ecclesiology is when the charisma of the Spirit is recognized to be a gift to the human Church, empowering its action. Only then is there unity between the invisible and visible Church, and only then can it be said that what the Church really is, is visible. This does not exclude by any means the necessity of faith in the Holy Spirit. I shall come back to this. But Barth's explanation of the visibility of the Church is not entirely satisfying. He says the unity of the invisible and visible Church is the work of an ever-new direct

[2] Cf *CTKB*, pp. 256f.

act of God alone. According to his explanation we can never say that the real Church is visible, or that the visible Church *is* the real Church. The charism of the Spirit for him is not a gift to men in the sense that what the Spirit does he does through men, and what men do they do in the power of the Spirit. The visible resulting Church is a purely human reflection of its invisible essence (the power of Christ through his Spirit). For him, the terms 'body of Christ', 'communion of saints', etc, refer solely to the 'divine operation which takes place in the Church'. On the other hand, the human visible Church is an empirical magnitude like the 'kingdom of France or the republic of Venice, as they used to put it in the sixteenth century'.[3] There seems to be a separation between the visible and invisible Churches. The real Church is solely a divine action. This is what I mean when I say that Barth effects an illegitimate Nestorian separation of the visible and invisible Church on the basis of a functional monophysitism.

When we say that the invisible and visible Church is the one Church we do not say that the whole reality of the Church is perceptible to the human senses. The Church is in the world but not of the world. It is an other-worldly and this-worldly reality in one, a divine and human reality in one, an eternal and temporal reality in one. It is a *complexio oppositorum*: of divine power and human weakness, of divine holiness and human sinfulness, of eternity and time. Its eternity, divine power and holiness cannot be seen by human eyes. This aspect of the Church can be understood only in a 'lively spirit of faith', as the encyclical *Mystici Corporis* says.[4] Faith is absolutely necessary if we are to understand the Church for what it really is.

But that which is believed is not distinct from what is seen. The invisible and visible Church form one reality.

'But the society furnished with hierarchical agencies and the Mystical Body of Christ are not to be considered as two realities, nor are the visible assembly and the spiritual community, nor the

---

[3] Cf *ibid.*, p. 259. This was a phrase used by Card. Bellarmine (cf Hamer, *The Church is a Communion*, pp. 83f.). In his reaction to the invisible Church of the Reformers Bellarmine overstressed, and to a certain extent isolated, the Church's visible aspect. He did not deny either the invisible aspect or the unity of the two. The opening words of his famous definition of the Church run: 'There is only one Church, not two.' Barth seems to come to a similar isolation of the visible Church but from nearly an opposite principle, namely, that the real Church is solely divine.

[4] *Vivido fidei spiritu*, in *AAS*, 35 (1943), 238 (=Engl. transl., CTS, London, p. 56). Cf p. 197 (=Engl. transl., p. 10). Cf Barth in *CTKB*, pp. 257f.

earthly Church and the Church enriched with heavenly things. Rather they form one interlocked reality which is comprised of a divine and human element.'[5]

That which is seen is not as such believed. That which is believed is not as such seen. Yet that which is seen and believed is the one reality. The object of faith is not something *other* than the visible Church. It is the visible Church seen in the light of faith in God's revelation. This cannot be understood if one excludes the gift and indwelling of the Spirit in the Church, and his action through the human instrumentality of the Church. What is believed is not a solely 'divine operation' in and under a human operation, but the divine reality and power *of* the human operation. The visible Church is the sacrament and instrument of the invisible. The comparison which Barth institutes between the Church and Jesus Christ is very illuminating.[6]

For him the *caro Christi*, Jesus Christ in his appearance as man, is not the object of faith. For us the man Jesus *is* the object of faith. Thomas did not see the man Jesus and confess another who was God. The man he saw he confessed to be God. Similarly, we see the visible Church and confess its divine sanctity and power.[7] What we really confess is the presence and action of the Holy Spirit. The Church is not united to the Spirit in personal or hypostatic union. It is united to him through his created gifts. Because of the Spirit's gift to it the Church is one divine-human reality. While we see the human we confess the divine. That is, we confess the presence and operation of the Holy Spirit *in* and *through* the Church.

---

[5] Vatican II, DCC, ch. 2, n. 8. Cf Schnackenburg, *The Church in the New Testament*, pp. 142–9.

[6] Cf *CTKB*, p. 257.

[7] 'Ipsa Ecclesia visibilis est objectum fidei, quamvis sub alia ratione ac consideratione sit visibilis et naturaliter intelligibilis, et sub alia ratione per fidem supernaturalem credenda. Ita etiam in capite Ecclesiae Christo Domino Apostoli non *alium* videbant et *alium* credebant; sed eum ipsum quem videbant sub ratione sensibilis humanitatis, credebant sub ratione divinitatis, non *alium et alium*, quae haeresis deinde erat Nestorii, sed *aliud et aliud*': Franzelin, *Theses de Ecclesia*, p. 365.

Chapter Twenty

The Church is the Body of Christ

THE theme we now enter, in dialogue with Karl Barth, has been amongst the most discussed exegetical and theological questions of the past thirty years, and indeed still is. It is highly complex. It has unmistakable kinship with other New Testament images of the Church, such as the vine and the branches (Jn 15:1-8), the spiritual house (I Pet 2:4f), the bride of the Lamb (Rev 12:2, 9; 22:17). While the Pauline image of the Church as the 'body of Christ' should not be made the expression of the whole ecclesiology of the New Testament, it should never be omitted. It brings out more graphically than most of the other images used in the New Testament in description of the Church the essential characteristic of the Church of the New Testament, namely, its dependence on and union with Christ. It expresses admirably the christological dimensions of the Church. It prohibits any disjunction or separation of christology and ecclesiology.

For this reason it would be very strange if it did not occupy a prominent place in Barth's synthesis. And in fact it does play a dominant role in his ecclesiology. Indeed, if one wished to gain a quick insight into Barthian ecclesiology I could recommend no better starting point than this. He does not grant it a special section, nor devote much explicit attention to it. None the less it stands always behind the scenes, and is the usual phrase he employs for a quick reference to the Church: the Church is the earthly-historical form, or body, of Christ. In it are apparent the dominant themes of his ecclesiology, namely, its christocentric, functional, missionary or teleological, 'eventful' and purely 'reflective' aspects.

It is not easy to enter into exegetical dialogue with him on this point. This is certainly due to the complexity of the problem itself, and to my own limitations. It is due also to Barth's inconsistency in expression, and to a possible indecision in his own mind. Three times he explicitly returned to it in his definitive ecclesiological doctrine. But the difficulty is due above all to his method of theological exegis.[1]

[1] Cf *CTKB*, p. 38f, and above, chapter one.

Rather than institute an exhaustive exegesis of the text of St Paul he seems to apply to him his own fundamental christological and ecclesiological principles and then finds their confirmation in Paul. For the greater part Paul does confirm his insight. But there are aspects in Paul's doctrine of the body of Christ which Barth does not mention, and which would modify his 'christocentrism'. Once more, the analysis of a particular theme of Barth's synthesis will show that the part on which the whole is built is deficient.

The discussion, as always, takes place more on the level of christology and justification, and only then on the level of ecclesiology. Is the reality of salvation and salvific activity to be attributed to Jesus Christ *alone* (to the exclusion of the Church)? Or does the Church possess a mystery of its own, in a certain sense autonomous and distinct from Christ? It is on this (by now quite familiar) level that we can understand what exactly Barth means, and that we ought to enter into dialogue with him.

The basis and starting point of Karl Barth's doctrine on the Church as the body of Christ is this: the body of Christ is the universally-*representative* dead and risen personal body of Christ which creates on earth its likeness and reflection. From this follow the dynamic and missionary concept of the community.[2] On the generality of Paul's doctrine most exegetes, I think, would have nothing against this conception (apart, of course, from Barth's understanding of 'reflection'). On the contrary, many would endorse its christological, dynamic and teleological aspects. I say 'on the generality of Paul's doctrine' because all admit progress in Paul himself from his earlier great epistles to his later captivity ones. What Barth says would seem to be a legitimate interpretation of Paul, even if not necessarily of his doctrine in the earlier epistles. His exposition might seem to imply that Paul already in the great epistles spoke of the body of Christ as the head of the community, for example, whereas this theme is only introduced later.[3] However, Barth's aim is not the genesis but the substance of Paul's whole doctrine.

While the origin of the Pauline image of the Church as the body of Christ is disputed, we can say, with Barth, that it is not called 'body' because it can be likened to an organism. Its source is not extra-biblical, except possibly for its literary form. Its basis lies in Paul's own specifically Christian thought.[4] In substantial agreement with

---

[2] Cf *CTKB*, pp. 260–3.
[3] Cf Cerfaux, *La Théologie de l'Eglise* . . ., pp. 281–2.
[4] Cf Benoit, 'Tête et Plérôme . . .' (present opinion), p. 110; Schnackenburg, *The Church in the N.T.*, pp. 167–8.

Barth we say that the 'body' of which Paul speaks is not a moral and therefore metaphorical union of a collectivity of Christians, but the real, physical, personal body of the risen Christ. Mgr Cerfaux has long championed this view amongst Catholic exegetes,[5] and today there is large agreement with him.[6] The 'Christ', or risen body of Christ, of I Cor 12:12 is the cause and unificatory principle of the life of the community. Barth says that the community is one in many and many in one because the principle which constitutes its unity and plurality is itself one in many and many in one creating an earthly reflection.

The personal body of the glorified Christ, of which Paul speaks, is the body which died and rose again as the *representative* of all mankind. In his body all are one dead and living body. It may be disputed whether this formed a specific part of Paul's conception of the 'body of Christ' in the great epistles, but it can hardly be disputed with regard to the captivity epistles.[7] In the one body of Christ Jews and Gentiles are included or represented in ontological unity. 'For he is our peace, who has made us both one . . . by abolishing in his flesh the law of commandments and ordinances, that he might create in himself one new man in the place of two . . . and might reconcile us both to God in one body through the cross.'[8]

In the light of this fact, and in continuing agreement with Karl Barth, we must go on to say that the mystery of the community is in the first place christological and therefore teleological (missionary and eschatological). As the earthly-historical creation and reflection of their heavenly body (or head) the community cannot regard itself as its own end. The fulness of the divine life which dwells in Christ (Col 1:19), that is, in his pneumatic body which is the life-giving spirit (I Cor 15:44, 45), is a dynamic power which fills the Church (Col 1:9), and through it unites all things in heaven and on earth in Christ (Eph 1:10).[9] 'And he has put all things under his feet and has made him the head over all things for the Church, which is his body, the fulness of him who fills all in all.'[10] Sharing in the fulness of its heavenly head

---

[5] Cf Cerfaux, *op. cit.*, pp. 225–6, 228f, 286f.

[6] J. Havet, 'La doctrine Paulinienne du "Corps du Christ" . . .' in *Recherches Bibliques*, V, p 187, presents an imposing list of exegetes who agree with Cerfaux on this point.

[7] Cf Benoit, *art. cit.*, pp. 123f.   [8] Eph 2:14, 15, 16. Cf Col 3:15; 1:19–22.

[9] The Greek text of Eph 1:10 has *anakephalaisōsasthai ta panta en tō Christō*; the Vulgate has *instaurare omnia in Christo*. I have followed, as usual, the RSV rendering. As Barth points out (cf *CTKB*, p. 263) Eph 1:10 means 'to give to all things their head in Christ'.

[10] Eph 1:22–23: *hētis estin to sōma autou, to plērōma tou ta panta en pasin pleroumenou*. Cf Cerfaux, *op. cit.*, pp. 272–5.

the Church cannot be 'a house with closed doors and windows', but is driven and must strive to realize the fulness which is already an ontological reality in its Head. As R. Schnackenburg so succinctly puts it:

> 'The body of the crucified and risen Lord expands into the ecclesiological Body of Christ by means of the Spirit; through the latter the Lord (the head) builds up his Church (the body) for himself and becomes with it a full unity. In this way the Church becomes a reality which is already present in Christ's body on the cross and which then is built up by inner and outer growth deriving from its head, Christ, and takes possession of the cosmos in order to achieve its perfect form. That may be alluded to in the pregnant statement of Eph 4:13 that we are all to attain "to the perfect man, to the full measure of the plenitude of Christ", whether *hēlikia* is to be understood in a spatial or a temporal sense. At all events the Church is regarded as a cosmic and eschatological reality which in its temporal and earthly existence only unfolds and strives after what in its head, Christ, is already a reality. Viewed from Christ, the Church as his body is his instrument for bringing the cosmos more and more under the blessing of his rule, in order to make the universe (cf 1:10) subjected to him share as far as possible in the grace of redemption.'[11]

Thus far I have been in joyful agreement with Karl Barth. It is to be noted that our considerations have concerned mostly the christological, functional, missionary, and eschatological aspects of the Church. But when we continue further our investigation of Pauline doctrine we come to the disheartening insight that we do not even agree in that in which we seem to agree. Karl Barth has been speaking all along of christology alone. We have been speaking of the christological dimensions of *ecclesiology*.

Barth continues[12] what we have just been considering with the observation that there are, therefore, not three but one body of Christ. In a certain sense this is true. The 'body of Christ' for St Paul is primarily and always (at least implicitly) the personal body of the risen Christ. When he says that the Church is the body of Christ he means that it is this personal body of Christ. What is this relationship of identity between the Church and the personal risen body of Christ? I shall recall briefly Barth's solution, and then go on to see if it accords with Pauline doctrine.

For Barth there is 'real identity' between the head in heaven and

---
[11] R. Schnackenburg, *The Church . . .,*' pp. 175–6.
[12] Cf *CTKB*, p. 263.

the body on earth.¹³ This does not mean that there is a real identity between Christ the head and the human Church.¹⁴ What it means is that 'Jesus Christ is the community', that 'his being is its being'.¹⁵ This is a concise formulation of Barthian ecclesiology. The phrase must be taken literally. It cannot be reversed. The human community is not Jesus Christ, but his 'merely human reflection'.¹⁶ It does not *become* identical with the body of Christ, but through the direct action of the Spirit it *learns* that it is already the body of Christ, and must create a purely human reflection.¹⁷ We are on familiar ground. Justification is not an event in the history of the community between the times. What is event is its knowledge.

Again, 'Jesus Christ is the Church' because he alone is the primary and proper subject. He is the invisible being of the community. Not in his form as its head, but in his secondary, earthly-historical form in the midst of the community.¹⁸ In this form he is the body which is the Church. That is how Barth would interpret Col 1:18. Here, too, we are on familiar ground: mono-actualism. We can recall what we have already come across on the question of the Church's visibility: the terms 'body of Christ', 'communion of saints', refer solely to the 'divine operation which takes place in the Church'.¹⁹ 'Jesus is the Church' means that he alone possesses divine life, and he alone acts with the power of divine life. This is Barth's 'christological constriction' at its clearest in relation to ecclesiology.

Can this be said to be St Paul's doctrine of the 'body of Christ'? We must examine some of the principal texts in which the phrase occurs.

I shall begin with I Cor 10:16–17: 'The bread which we break, is it not a participation [or communion] in the body of Christ? Because there is one bread, we who are many are one body, for we all partake of the one bread.' Reacting against the idolatrous tendencies at Corinth, Paul shows that they are incompatible with the true notion of the eucharistic supper which unites to Christ as the pagan sacrifices to the demons, and one must choose between one or other of these

---

¹³ Cf *ibid.*, p. 260.

¹⁴ There is no question therefore of the error repudiated in the encyclical *Mystici Corporis* (cf *AAS*, 35 (1943), 197, 234 = Engl. transl. 9, 51), namely, that which asserts such a union between Christ and his Church that 'the invisible frontiers between things created and their Creator are obliterated', and 'divine properties are attributed to human beings'. This error is very far from the thought of Karl Barth!

¹⁵ Cf *CTKB*, pp. 259–60.

¹⁶ Cf *ibid.*, p. 259.   ¹⁷ Cf *ibid.*, pp. 263f.

¹⁸ Read carefully *ibid.*, pp. 259–60.

¹⁹ Cf *ibid.*, p. 256.

'communions'.[20] The body spoken of is the individual dead and risen body of Jesus Christ (v 16). This one body, present in the eucharist ('one bread'), makes Christians identical with itself through the act of partaking of the one bread. The body of which Paul primarily speaks is the risen body of Christ which is the bread.[21] This individual and eucharistic reference stands at the origin of everything Paul says of the body of Christ. Christ's one eucharistic body creates the Church one with him, makes it this body of his.

Already we notice some improbabilities in Barth's exegesis.[22] I am in agreement with him in his general imposition of the question. Thus he observes quite rightly that the primary form of Christ's presence after his ascension is his heavenly presence at the right hand of the Father. All other forms of his presence are secondary. He does insist that Christ has a secondary form of presence, namely, an earthly-historical form as the body which is the real essence of the Church. To be faithful to Paul we must insist, in addition, on the *sacramental realism* of this presence of Christ. There are many secondary forms of Christ's presence in his community.[23] In one of these, that of which Paul is speaking in our text, Christ is so present that his body is bread, and bread is his body.

Christians are in communion (*koinōnia*) with one another because they participate in the one body of Christ. What is this communion? It is a union amongst themselves based on their real participation in the one life-giving body of Christ. Because Christians are in Christ, or because Christ is in Christians, they are one amongst themselves. Here we see Paul's basic thought, which he so often expresses by the formulas 'we in Christ' and 'Christ in us'. Christians, while remaining on earth, already live the life of heaven, the life of their celestial head.[24] They are already 'spiritual',[25] living the life of Christ through his Spirit who 'really dwells in you',[26] while remaining pilgrims away from the Lord, groaning for what is to come.[27] Hence Paul can say: 'It is no longer I who live, but Christ who lives in me' (Gal 2:20). In

[20] Cf Cerfaux, *op. cit.*, pp. 224f; Benoit, *art. cit.*, pp. 117f.
[21] Cf I Cor 11:27–29, where Paul explicitly equates the bread and body.
[22] Cf *CTKB*, pp. 260f, 262f.
[23] Cf Vatican II, *Constitution on the Liturgy*, n. 7; Instruction on the Worship of the Eucharistic Mystery, 25 May 1967, nn. 9, 55.
[24] For a full exegesis of the Pauline formula 'in Christ' cf Cerfaux, *op. cit.*, ch. 10, pp. 179–94; Malevez, 'L'Eglise, Corps du Christ . . .' in *Rech. Sc. Rel.*, 32 (1944), 52f.
[25] Cf Gal 6:1; I Cor 14:37; 2:15; 3:1.
[26] Cf Rom 8:9–11, 23; II Cor 5:17, 4–5; Eph 2:19; 3:17.
[27] Cf Rom 8:23; II Cor 5:6; Phil 3:3, 12f.

our text (I Cor 10:16–17), Paul says that the sacramental body of Christ creates the communion of Christians by identifying them with him, that is, by granting them a participation in his own life. 'There is neither Jew nor Greek, there is neither slave nor free, there is neither male or female; for you are all one in Christ Jesus' (Gal 3:28).

The human Church is not, therefore, a 'purely human' reflection or documentation of its heavenly head. Christ 'identifies' the Church with his body through his sacramental presence, granting it a share in his life. The Church does not merely 'learn' of its identity with his personal body. It is made 'identical'. The partaking by Christians of the one bread is not a mere documentation, or public acknowledgment, of their already existing unity. Certainly, the eucharistic celebration has also the aspect of witness. This is a valid element in Barth's theology of response. But above all, the eucharistic celebration creates their unity or their 'identity' with the body of Christ. 'We who are many are one body, for [*gar*] we all partake of the one bread.'

The second text I will consider is I Cor 12:12–13. Paul wishes to show that the diversity of charisms should not lead to anarchy.[28] Just as the human body, he says (using a classical metaphor to illustrate his originally Christian thought), acts as the unifying principle of its members, 'so it is with Christ' (v 12). He is the body in that he has many members (Christians) and acts as their unifying principle by 'identifying' them with himself through Spirit and sacrament. 'For by one Spirit we were all baptized into one body—Jews or Greeks, slaves or free—and all were made to drink of one Spirit' (v 13).

Here again we find Paul's sacramental realism. The risen Christ creates and unifies his Church through sacramental contact. In v 13a of our text Paul mentions baptism explicitly.[29] The individual Christ is body because he unites Christians to himself through baptism. Baptism is not therefore simply a documentation of an already existing identity with Christ, but a *means* by which Christ *makes* Christians his members. Salvation is had solely by union with Christ's pneumatic, vivifying body (I Cor 15:14f). This union is had by faith and the baptism of faith.

'Do you not know that all of us who have been baptized into Christ Jesus were baptized into his death? We were buried therefore with him by baptism into death, so that as Christ was raised from the dead by the glory of the Father, we too might walk in

[28] Cf Cerfaux, *op. cit.*, pp. 227f; Benoit, *art. cit.*, pp. 118f.
[29] Benoit, Cerfaux and Käsemann think v 13c refers to the eucharist, as in I Cor 10:16–17; Percy and Schnackenburg think it refers to baptism. Cf Benoit, *art. cit.*, p. 119, and nn. 3, 4.

newness of life. For if we have been *united* with him in a death like his, we shall certainly be *united* with him in a resurrection like his.'³⁰

'At the root of this key passage is a conception of salvation whose physical realism our modern way of thinking is too prone to tone down.'³¹ In the sacrament of baptism there is physical and sacramental union of the body of the Christian with the body of Christ in death and resurrection. In another place Paul emphasizes again this realism by comparing it with sexual union. He also emphasizes that the result of this union is that Christians are made members of Christ, and have his Spirit.

'Do you not know that he who joins himself to a prostitute becomes one body with her? For, as it is written, "The two shall become one". But he who is united to the Lord *becomes* one spirit with him. . . . Do you not know that your body is a temple of the Holy Spirit within you, which you have from God?'³²

In all this we come across the great paradox of Christian life—a paradox, however, on whose basis alone this 'time between the times' can be called a history of salvation. With his doctrine of justification Barth diminishes radically the meaning of the Church's history as a history of salvation. The paradox is this: while we are *already* dead and risen and therefore justified in Christ,³³ we must also believe, die and rise in baptism and conduct and *be* justified.³⁴ Fr Benoit terms it the 'dialectical tension' of indicative and imperative.³⁵ In a similar vein, Mgr Cerfaux describes the Church's reality distinct from Christ (as the fulness and upbuilding of his body, Col 2:10 and Eph 4:16) as one of the many ways of expressing 'the paradox of the Christian life, which depends totally on grace and demands at the same time the acquiescence of the human will'.³⁶ The same thought often recurs in the writings of Fr Congar.

'The mystery of the Mystical Body, like that of the kingdom, brings us in contact with a twofold and paradoxical truth. Everything is already fulfilled in Christ; the Church is simply the manifestation of what is in him, the visible reality animated by his Spirit.

---

³⁰ Rom 6:3–5.
³¹ Benoit, *art. cit.*, pp. 110–11.
³² I Cor 6:15–17, 19. Cf Rom 8:11, 23.
³³ Cf Eph 2:14–16; Col 1:22; 2:20.
³⁴ Cf Col 1:23; 3:5; Phil 3:8–14; Rom 6:3f.
³⁵ *Art cit.*, p. 112.
³⁶ *Op. cit.*, p. 288.

Yet, we have still to bring Christ to fulfilment and build up his body. This twofold truth we would call a "dialectic of gift and task" (*dialectique du "donné" et de "l'agi"*); it is closely bound up with the mystery of the theandric reality of the Church, and we meet it also in connection with the sacraments.'[37]

We return now to our text in I Cor 12:12-13. Christians are one amongst themselves because they are united by Christ to his personal body. They are one 'in Christ' because they are 'from Christ' as their unifying principle (that is, body). This is the same thought which we have encountered in I Cor 10:17 and Gal 3:28. It is the same as in Rom 12:5: 'So we, though many, are one body in Christ.' And in the text under consideration Paul concludes: 'Now you are body of Christ (*humeis de este sōma Christou*) and individually members of it' (v 27). He does not say *to sōma tou Christou* (with the articles, that is), as he usually does.[38] He does not mean that they are comparable to a human body; nor that they are directly the physical body of Christ (with the articles). What he says is that Christians are Christ's body, that is, that they are in some way identified with it because they share in his life and unity in dependence on him.

Turning now to the captivity epistles we find that Paul introduces some new dimensions to his doctrine of the body of Christ. This body still remains (at least implicitly) Christ's own personal risen body. 'Body' denotes the Church only by reference to the personal body of Christ, which is the source of its life, activity and unity. There is, however, a tendency to separate the effect from the cause, and to attribute the name 'body of Christ' to the Church in its own proper life. There is a tendency, therefore, to present the Church as a reality *distinct* from the physical body of Christ.[39]

This *distinction* appears, *firstly*, in Paul's introduction of the theme of Christ *head* of the body, the Church. He did not introduce this theme as a deduction from that of 'body of Christ' (in the sense that he deduced Christ's headship from the fact that he is Saviour or vital principle of life), but adapted its biblical usage, in reaction to the speculations of the Colossians, to express Christ's authority and supremacy over the angelical powers.[40] In relation to the Church, Paul speaks of Christ the head first in this sense of superiority and supremacy.[41] The origin of the physiological or vital principle sense,

[37] *The Mystery of the Church*, p. 27 (French original: *Esquisses* . . ., p. 26).
[38] Cf Rom 7:4; I Cor 10:16; Eph 4:12; I Cor 11:27.
[39] Cf Cerfaux, *op. cit.*, pp. 275f; Benoit, *art. cit.*, pp. 123f.
[40] Cf Benoit, *art. cit.*, p. 132; cf Col 2:10, 18-19; Eph 1:20-21.
[41] Col 1:18; Eph 1:22-23.

Fr Benoit maintains, is Hellenistic. Paul also speaks of Christ head of the Church in this sense.[42] The theme of head, understood solely in the sense of superiority, could have resulted in a separation of Christ and his body. Understood solely in the physiological sense of vital union it could have resulted in absolute identity. In blending the two Paul safeguards both the superiority of the head over the body and the intimate union between them. The synthesis is achieved in Eph 5:23–32, which can be regarded as the 'ultimate development of Paul's thought as regards the Church the body of Christ'.[43]

The *distinction* appears, *secondly*, in Paul's explicit designation of the Church itself (the universal Church, which is the usual sense of *ekklēsia* in the captivity epistles) as the 'body of Christ': 'His body, that is, the Church'.[44] As L. Cerfaux points out: 'The Church which was first called *sōma* because of its identity with the body of Christ ends up by being called itself "the body of Christ", and even *sōma*.'[45] The Church is this body because it is the realization and expansion of its activity and life. The nature of this union is not easy to express. Cerfaux says that similarity errs by defect and identity errs by excess. It is, none the less, he says, a veritable mystical identification.[46]

It is for *this* reason that Christ can say to the persecutor of the *community*: 'Saul, Saul, why do you persecute me?' (Acts 9:4), and of that which is done, or not done, to the least of his brethren: 'You did it (or did it not) to me' (Mt 25:40, 45). Jesus does not say this because he is the community, or because he is alone its invisible being, or because he is alone the primary and proper acting subject. He says it because the community is in some way identified with him. The object of the action of persecution or of charity is the *community* or its *members*, and not *directly Jesus Christ*, as Barth would have it.

As the 'Church' the 'body' is more personified, and considered in its own proper life as a reality distinct from the physical body of Christ.

'In designating the body of Christ "the Church" Paul underlines the collective existence of this group of the saved as an organized and unified society, as a *living person which distinguishes itself*

---

[42] Eph 4:15–16; Col 2:19: '. . . . the Head, from whom the whole body, nourished and knit together through its joints and ligaments, grows with a growth that is from God'.
[43] Benoit, *art. cit.*, p. 135.
[44] Col 1:24. Cf Eph 1:22f; 5:23; Col 1:18.
[45] Cerfaux, *op. cit.*, p. 280.
[46] *Id., ibid.*, p. 287, and note 4.

from the personal Christ, while living by him alone. It would be too strong to term it autonomous, because its whole being comes from Christ and it subsists only *en Christō*. None the less, it is not identical with him. It is more the object of his redemptive work, of his love, of his vivifying influence. This is seen in the fine passage of Eph 5:23–32 where it appears before Christ as his spouse, *intimately united to him, yes, but still distinct from him* as that which he loves, for which he delivers himself, which he purifies and sanctifies.'[47]

In conclusion: While I agree with Barth as regards certain christological aspects of the Church expressed by the Pauline concept 'body of Christ' I do not agree with him in saying that it is solely a christological concept. His view represents an ecclesiological christocentrism which is certainly not Pauline. For at bottom it is a denial of ecclesiology, or, in other words, it is a christological constriction. That is, it is a christology which swallows up ecclesiology, a doctrine of Jesus Christ which denies the reality of salvation and of salvific activity to the Church. This is a constriction which continually recurs throughout Barth's theology. It is based ultimately on his doctrine of justification and on a certain christological economic mono-actualism, that is, that Christ as God is alone salvifically active in the history of salvation. This christocentric 'ecclesiology' accords ill with the Pauline doctrine of the 'body of Christ'. For if this Pauline image teaches us anything it teaches us that Christ does not possess *alone* divine life but that the Church exists over against him as the sharer of his divine life through his vivifying and loving influence. Barth's deficient interpretation of this image of the Church, since it is simply the consistent and consequent application of his basic principles in justification and christology (which, we must recall once more, he claims to be the correct interpretation of Luther and especially Calvin), reveals the deficiency of the basic principles themselves.

Certainly, when Paul speaks of the 'body of Christ' he means above all the personal and universally representative dead and risen body of Christ. And for this reason, as Barth justly points out, an ecclesiology based on this concept will have to be christological, dynamic, missionary and teleological. But I cannot agree with Barth when he says that St Paul by the expression 'the Church is the body of Christ' means 'Jesus Christ is the Church'. This is to absorb the mystery of the Church into the mystery of Jesus Christ. I disagree

[47] Benoit, *art cit.*, p. 127 (translation and emphasis mine). Cf also J. L. Witte, 'Die Katholizität der Kirche' in *Gregorianum*, 42 (1961), 220–1.

with Barth's understanding of this Pauline image above all, therefore, because of his denial of the *realism or actuality of the Church's union with Christ* or of its *participation in his mysterious life,* and consequently of the Church's existence as a mysterious reality in its own right—from Christ, yes, *but also distinct from him and over against him* as is quite clearly expressed by that other Pauline image which depicts the Church as the spouse of Christ (Eph 5:23–32), and which constitutes the ultimate development of Paul's thought as regards the Church the 'body of Christ'. My other disagreements with Barth's understanding of this basic Pauline image follow necessarily from the basic one outlined. I disagree with his denial that the union of the Church and Christ, the union by which it 'is' his body, *takes place* in this time between the times. This is basically a disagreement as regards the doctrine of justification. Barth radically minimizes the meaning of the Church's history as a history of salvation. By means of the image 'body of Christ' Paul says this union takes place or occurs here and now. In other words, he says that the Church *becomes* the body of Christ. Once more, we see that Barth's understanding of this Pauline image in the light of more basic principles in justification and christology reveals the deficiency of these principles. Finally, I must disagree with Barth not only as regards the Church's holy existence distinct from Christ through a union which takes place in this time between the times but also when we assert that this union takes place not only through a direct action of the holy Spirit but also through his sacramental action. Paul's sacramental realism cannot be gainsaid.

The Christian community is not simply a purely human reflection of what it is in Jesus Christ and is not in itself. It is the fulness and expansion of Christ's own glorious life. It is a holy and sanctifying reality *(sancta et sanctificans),* in total dependence on Christ, yet distinct from him. As the encyclical *Mystici Corporis* says (a statement which Barth rejects):[48] *est ipsa quasi altera Christi persona.* As is usual with Protestant authors, one looks to Karl Barth in vain for the concept of the Church as the spouse of Christ, that is, for an exegesis of Eph 5:22–32.

---

[48] Cf *CTKB,* p. 263.

Chapter Twenty-One

I Believe the Church

IN this and the following chapters I intend to confront Karl Barth's and the Catholic's understanding of the phrase taken from the so-called Nicene-Constantinopolitan Creed: 'I believe the one, holy, catholic and apostolic Church'.[1] I agree with him in many things, but not in all. I agree with him in his christological and dynamic conception of these predicates of the Church. But I insist that they are predicates *of the Church*. I can be brief, for the scriptural basis of the Catholic position has already been outlined. The Holy Spirit indwells his Church and uses it as his instrument so that the human Church lives the life of the Spirit and cooperates with him in the achievement of its unity, sanctity, catholicity and apostolicity.

The more one tries to understand the Church the more one realizes how ultimately unintelligible it is. It is a human, earthly and temporal society like all other human societies, whose members, practices and institutions can be seen and understood. And yet it is completely unlike all other human societies, for it is also the sign and instrument of the divine, heavenly and eternal life and power of the Holy Spirit. It is the mysterious unity of a human and a divine, a temporal and an eternal, an earthly and a heavenly reality. It is this because the divine Spirit of its heavenly eternal head indwells and vivifies its human, earthly, temporal manifestations. It is permeated by this Spirit. It is for ever thwarting the Spirit, but never completely successfully. While sinful and evil, it shares already the life of its risen Lord. Its words and actions are weak human words and actions, yet they are bearers of divine power and life and holiness. It is a sacramental reality. It points to the presence and action of the Holy Spirit, and effects what it points to. As St Paul says of the profound relationship of husband and wife in the unity of Christian marriage: 'This is a great mystery, and I take it to mean Christ and the Church' (Eph 5:32).

[1] Cf DS 150. Cf also DS, 10–13, 1862 and 1868; DCC, n. 8.

The presence and action of the Holy Spirit in and through his Church can only be known on the basis of the Spirit's own revelation. The Word of God tells us that the Spirit was given to the Church to be its principle of life and action.[2] On the authority of the revealing God we believe the Church *to be* this mysterious reality, as the seventh-century Bangor antiphonal puts it.[3] The Church is a mystery of faith.

As Barth points out,[4] we do not believe *in* the Church, but we believe the Church. Faith is above all the acknowledgment of, and total dedication to, a person. It cannot be reduced to a mere acceptance of a body of doctrine or mere adherence to objects and rules— a view which Barth in the footsteps of William Herrmann rightly criticizes.[5] Faith is something which occurs between persons, a personal activity.[6] And 'faith in', according to the traditional distinctive meaning of the phrase introduced by St Augustine,[7] includes a total and irrevocable self-giving of one person to another. In this sense we believe only *in* God. To believe in another human person or object in this sense of complete and unconditional self-surrender would be to idolize a creature and blaspheme against God who alone is worthy of such faith. We cannot give ourselves totally to another human person or object—not even to the Church. We do not believe *in* the Church. And we do not do so for the simple reason that the Church is not God, as Barth so often points out. While God works in and through the Church he cannot be identified with it or it with him.[8] We believe *in* God alone, Father, Son and Holy Spirit, because he is the sole personal and absolute self-revealing being. We believe the other articles of the Trinitarian Creed as the work of the three divine persons. Immediately after the mention of the Spirit comes the Church, as his primary work. We believe the Church as the work of the Holy Spirit, as the reality in and through which the Holy Spirit accomplishes the subjective reconciliation of the world. Thus the repetition of the so-called Nicene-Constantinopolitan Creed, while it gratefully acknowledges the spiritual and mysterious reality of the Church itself, that is, while it acknowledges the divine immanence, also and above all acknowledges the divine transcendence. We do not believe *in* the Church, but in God alone.

---

[2] Cf Jn 20:22; Acts 2:1–4. Cf above, chapter twelve.
[3] 'Credo et in Spiritum Sanctum . . . sanctam esse Ecclesiam catholicam': DS 29.   [4] Cf *CTKB*, pp. 241, 271f.   [5] Cf *ibid.*, p. 68, and *passim*.
[6] Cf J. Mouroux, *I Believe*, London–New York, 1959.
[7] Cf Augustine, *In Joann.*, 29, 6; 48, 3(*PL*, 36:287, 413).
[8] Cf above, pp. 125f.

This is why the earliest Creeds speak of believing *in* God and in the Holy Spirit but of believing the Church.[9] This is why the oldest Church order we possess, namely, the *Traditio apostolica* of Hippolytus of Rome dating from around the year 215, asks very precisely in its third baptismal question: 'Do you also believe in the Holy Spirit in the holy Church for the resurrection of the body?'[10] We believe in the Holy Spirit who is at work in the Church and the term of whose operation is the resurrection of the body. This is traditional Catholic teaching.

'This is why the great scholastics explained the article *credo ... unam, sanctam, catholicam et apostolicam Ecclesiam* as identical with the one that precedes it, *credo in Spiritum Sanctum,* and as really meaning: I believe in the Holy Spirit not only in himself in his eternal procession, but also in the Church, in his temporal procession; I believe in the Holy Spirit unifying the Church, sanctifying her, making her Catholic and apostolic.'[11]

---

[9] Cf DS 2, 11, etc.

[10] Cf P. Nautin, *Je crois à l'Esprit saint dans la sainte Eglise pour la résurrection de la chair* (Unam Sanctam 17), Paris, 1947.

[11] Y. M.-J. Congar, *The Mystery of the Temple*, London, 1962, Appendix III, pp. 288–9. Thus St Thomas says, for instance: 'Si dicatur "in sanctam Ecclesiam catholicam", hoc est intelligendum secundum quod fides nostra refertur ad Spiritum sanctum, qui sanctificat Ecclesiam, ut sit sensus: "Credo in Spiritum sanctum sanctificantem Ecclesiam". Sed melius est, et secundum communiorem usum, ut non ponatur ibi "in" sed simpliciter dicatur: "sanctam Ecclesiam catholicam", sicut etiam Leo papa dicit': II–II, q. 1, art. 9, ad 5um. And Albert the Great: 'Credo in Spiritum sanctum sanctificantem Ecclesiam catholicam, id est universalem Ecclesiam': *In 3 sent.,* d. 24, a.6. And very succinctly Faustus of Riez: 'Credimus Ecclesiam, quasi regenerationis matrem; non in Ecclesiam credimus, quasi in salutis auctorem': *De Spiritu sancto,* Lib. I, cap. I (*PL,* 62; 11A—under the name of Paschasius Diaconus). Copious other texts from the Church's tradition can be found in de Lubac, *The Splendour of the Church,* chapter one.

Chapter Twenty-Two

I Believe the Church is One

FROM what we have seen as regards the Church as the body of Christ it follows that we believe the Church to be one and unique. For St Paul the basis of the Church's unity lies in the existence and action of the one God, Father, Son and Holy Spirit; in the 'one bread' of the eucharist in which 'all partake'; in the one confession of the one Gospel; in the work of the ministry guaranteeing the faithful transmission of the one deposit, guarding the faith of the community, and directing and instructing with regard to liturgical and other practices; in the mutual service of charity; in the one 'work of faith and labour of love and steadfastness of hope'.[1]

The Church's unity is above all its participation in the unity of God's triune life. Its principle is the risen Christ through his Holy Spirit who dwells in the Church. 'God's love has been poured into our hearts through the Holy Spirit who has been given to us.'[2] Sharing in this one love or Spirit of God Christians, though many, form one body. 'For by one Spirit we were all baptized into the one body—Jews or Greeks, slaves or free—and all were made to drink of one Spirit.'[3] The Church's unity is primarily this internal, invisible and divine life which permeates all.

But even a cursory reading of some of the texts referred to from St Paul in note 1 reveals that the Church's unity must be visible as well as invisible. There must be the one profession of faith, the one baptism, the one eucharist, the one Gospel, the one ministry in the service of the Gospel, the one external communion. The necessity of visible unity follows from two considerations—which more or less correspond to what we have already often termed the theologies of institution and event, or mediation and response. The life of the

[1] Cf I Cor 12:3–13; 10:16–17; 4:17–21; 14:36–37; 8:6; 1:10–13; Rom 12:4–5; 15:5f; Col 3:14f; Gal 3:27–28; Rom 10:13; I Cor 1:2; I Thess 1:3–5; I Cor 11:2, 17f, 34c; Gal 1:6–9; 2:2; Acts 20:28–31; II Tim 4:1f; 1:13–14; 2:2; I Tim 6:20.
[2] Rom 5:5. Cf II Cor 1:22.
[3] I Cor 12:13.

glorified and incarnate (or pneumatic) Christ is transmitted to incarnate men incarnately, that is, by earthly-historical means. Secondly, the life of the incarnate Christ expresses itself in incarnate men incarnately, that is, in external and social forms. In its whole reality the Church must be the earthly-historical form of the risen Christ. In this sense it can be called a 'prolongation of the incarnation', or the 'incarnation' of the risen Christ. Both phrases are open to misunderstanding. It is better, as we have already seen, to say that the Church 'bodies forth' the risen Christ.

I have already expressed my regrets over Barth's neglect of the aspect of mediation. On the question of unity he does allow the possibility of 'a particular organ of mediation'[4] on the basis of love and prudence. But he denies that such an organ is an essential constituent of the Church's essence. The essential constituent of the Church's essence is for him the ever-new direct and invisible act of the risen Christ through his Spirit alone.

In Catholic theology the Church is visibly one primarily because the Holy Spirit uses human and earthly historical instituted instruments in his creation of its internal unity.[5] Christ founded one Church, his Church, on the rock who is Peter (Mt 16:18). For him he prayed that his faith might not fail, and he commissioned him to strengthen his brethren (Lk 22:32). The foundations are his apostles, who were the original witnesses, proclaimers and guardians of his revelation. These he empowered in a special way and sent them to make disciples of all nations 'to the close of the age' (Mt 28:18-20). The unity of all, which is an objective reality in Jesus Christ (I Tim 2:6; Eph 2:14f), becomes a subjective reality in all its *plenitude* only through visible contact with the teaching, sanctifying and guiding action of these men and their successors until the close of the age.

Strictly speaking, they neither 'supply' nor 'create' the unity of the Church,[6] but are the instruments of Christ's own salvific action through his Spirit. The power in which they act does not originate in themselves, but is the pure gift of its Lord. Their authority is the authority of the servant. The higher the responsibility the greater must be the service.[7] They exercise it, as Barth beautifully puts it, simply in the fact that they make the authority of Jesus Christ visible

---

[4] Cf *CTKB*, p. 267.
[5] I have given an indication above of the Scriptural basis of the Catholic assertion of the Church's mediatory function. Cf above, chapter fifteen, art. I.
[6] Cf *CTKB*, p. 267.
[7] This is recognized by the popes in their traditional self-description as *servi servorum Dei* (servants of the servants of God).

and audible in the Churches.[8] There should be no 'lording over' (II Cor 1:24). The unity of the visible institutional Church is not an end in itself. It exists solely in the service of its Lord and for the creation of invisible and visible unity.

I have already pointed out that the Church's visible unity is also due to the human action welling out from the invisible direct act of the Holy Spirit.[9] This visible unity should not be isolated or dissociated, however, from the instituted unity, as Paul himself recognized (Gal 2:1f). Least of all should it claim to be the exclusive representation of the Church's visible unity. Furthermore, I have already expressed doubts with regard to Barth's possibility of safeguarding the *unity* of the Church's visibility and invisibility on this explanation. Certainly, the Holy Spirit acts both indirectly and directly in the mediation of the unity accomplished in Jesus Christ. But if we are really speaking of the unity of the *Church*, and not of the unity of Jesus Christ alone all the time, then the Spirit's action must have a created effect in its human recipients. The invisible Church is not simply a divine action and the visible Church a purely human reflection. The Church is human and temporal, but elevated and enabled to live the divine eternal life. In faith and love these human beings, without ceasing in any way to be human, share in the knowledge and love of God's triune life. 'He who believes has eternal life.'[10] I do not think Barth does justice to the Pauline doctrine of our life 'in Christ' and Christ's life 'in us', as I have already pointed out in the chapter on the Church as Christ's body. According to him, our life in Christ is not actually *our* life but Christ's. Christ's life in us is not *our* life but always Christ's own life. Christ alone and always is the subject of the Church's invisible life. This leads to a separation of an invisible and visible, divine and human, eternal and temporal 'Churches'.[11]

That said, I agree with Barth in so far as he explicitly states that the *invisible* and *visible* Church is *one* Church. The Holy Spirit indwells and permeates the Church's human structure through his grace and power. The attempt to explain or justify the Church's divisions by appealing past the visible divisions to an invisible unity should be abandoned. What the Church is it is invisibly and visibly. If the Church is one invisibly it will be one also visibly for it is not the Church at all if it does not find concrete external expression. Similarly, I agree with Barth as regards the *unity* of the Church *triumphant* in heaven and the Church *militant* on earth. For 'we all,

[8] Cf *CTKB*, p. 268. [9] Cf above, pp. 263f.
[10] Jn 6:47; 5:24. [11] Cf above, pp. 264f.

although in a different way and to a different degree, partake (*communicamus*) in the same love of God and of the neighbour, and we sing the same hymn of glory to our God. For all who belong to Christ, having his Spirit, grow up into one Church and cleave together in him (cf Eph 4:16).'[12] This union is expressed through the intercession of the heavenly Church for the earthly Church, and the imploring of this intercession by the earthly Church.[13]

Eternal life, for Barth, is essentially 'historical', for it is the life of God. God lives his eternal life as the active ruler of his kingdom. Participation in this life means cooperation of service with God in the cause of God. In this life there is only the promise and pledge of this participation. The future life, however, will consist 'in the participation of man in the being and life of God, a willing of what He wills and a doing of what He does. It will be a being not only as object, but as an active subject....'[14] This, he says, is what synergism of every age and type has tried to ascribe to man at a place where it does not belong to him. Man's eternal life will not be one of rest, enjoyment or contemplation. It will be a life and being in active service of God in his fellowship with the created world and man.

I agree with Karl Barth in his active conception of eternal life. At the same time, I must ask where, in his conception, the unity of the heavenly and earthly Churches lies.[15] For us, the life of the earthly Church is already a participation, however imperfect and insecure, in the same life of the Spirit which is that of the Church of heaven.

Thirdly, and finally, we must say, and for the very same reason as the one just given, that the Church *before and after Christ* is *one* Church. I have already expressed a doubt whether Barth does not diminish the difference between the two Testaments in this respect.[16] His consideration of election solely *ab aeterno*, that is, his failure to view it in historical development and conditioned by human response

---

[12] DCC, n. 49. [13] Cf *Ibid.*, n. 49f.
[14] Karl Barth, *C.D.* IV/1, pp 113–14 (= S. 123).
[15] Cf Barth, *ibid.*, pp. 111–14 (= SS. 120–4). Compare the similar active view of eternal life expressed by St Thérèse of Lisieux in her *novissima verba*: 'I wish to spend my time in heaven doing good on earth.' For her, however, the charity of the Christian on earth is a present participation in that eternal life so that he can render already, in some way, that service. Cf J. Mouroux, *The Mystery of Time*, Desclée, 1964, pp. 23–30. This activist conception of life in the heavenly Church was an ancient patristic conception and to some extent was shared by the Middle Ages. According to it the saints in heaven are in a transitory state until the last judgment, and never cease to watch over the Church on earth with care. Cf H. U. von Balthasar, *Thérèse of Lisieux*, London, 1953, pp. 31f.
[16] Cf above, pp. 35f.

and human history, would seem to have its embarrassing repercussions in his doctrine of the Church's unity. The existence of an unbelieving Judaism, he says, is an 'ontological impossibility', and therefore the 'deepest obscurity' which faces the *credo unam Ecclesiam*.[17]

Apart from these reservations concerning his doctrine on the unity of the Church I wholeheartedly endorse Barth's sincere and moving words concerning the impossibility of a plurality of Churches, the scandal of actual division, its detrimental effect on missions, the penitence and effort demanded of each for its removal, and the solution he proposes to overcome it.[18] The New Testament does use the word 'Church' in the plural.[19] This plurality does not undermine the Church's simple unity, as Barth points out.[20] All live the same life of the Spirit, profess the same faith, celebrate the same sacrifice and cult, and are in union with each other. They are not simply parts of the whole Church, nor is the whole Church the sum of the local Churches. The one whole Church is present and actualized in the local and cultic Churches.

However, the New Testament also speaks of a universal Church. Indeed, the primary use of the word *ekklēsia* in the New Testament would seem to have been universal.[21] In Barth's ecclesiology there is no place for universality, nor consequently for the unity of a universal Church. Unity for him is always the unity of the local Church in response to the event of Christ's action. Universality is the plurality of forms in which its unity takes place. This is the price he has to pay for an exclusively 'response'—or 'reflex'—theology. It is the price of the denial of the pope as the successor of him to whom Christ said: 'I have prayed for you that your faith may not fail; . . . strengthen your brethren. . . . Feed my lambs. . . . Tend my sheep.'[22]

The confession *credo unam Ecclesiam* means that we believe the unifying presence and action of the Holy Spirit in his Church. We cannot doubt the effectiveness of this presence and action. We cannot doubt that the unity of the Church has always existed, despite human sin and rebellion. The Church's unity is a 'given unity'— not only in the sense that it exists ontologically and objectively in Christ, who has reconciled all in himself, but also that it exists ontologically and subjectively in the Church. It is a given unity because

---

[17] Cf *CTKB*, p. 267.   [18] Cf *ibid.*, pp. 268–71.
[19] Cf Acts 15:41; 16:5; I Cor 7:17; 11:16; 14:33–34.
[20] Cf *CTKB*, p. 267.
[21] Cf I Cor 12:28; 15:9; Eph 1:22; Acts 20:28; Eph 3:11, 21; Col 1:18, 24. Cf above, p. 251.   [22] Lk 22:32; Jn 21:15, 16, 17.

the ultimate principles of unity, namely, the Holy Spirit, the Gospel, Christian believers, ministers and sacraments, have always existed in the Church. This 'Church' 'subsists in the Roman Catholic Church', as Vatican II reminds us and as we have seen already.[23] It is not exclusively identical with the Roman Catholic Church. That is, it does not exclude other Churches. The reason for this statement was, the theological commission informs us, that 'it accords better with our recognition of ecclesial elements in other Churches'. The Church's 'given unity' includes therefore all these ecclesial elements. These are described in the Decree on Ecumenism thus:

> 'All those justified by faith through baptism are incorporated into Christ. They therefore have a right to be honoured by the title of Christian, and are properly regarded as brothers in the Lord by the sons of the Catholic Church. Moreover some, even very many, of the most significant elements or endowments which together go to build up and give life to the Church herself can exist outside the visible boundaries of the Catholic Church: the written word of God; the life of grace; faith, hope and charity, along with other interior gifts of the Holy Spirit and visible elements. All of these, which come from Christ and lead back to him, belong by right to the one Church of Christ. The brethren divided from us also carry out many of the sacred actions of the Christian religion. Undoubtedly, in ways that vary according to the condition of each Church or Community, these actions can truly engender a life of grace, and can be rightly described as capable of providing access to the community of salvation. It follows that these separated Churches and Communities, though we believe they suffer from defects already mentioned, have by no means been deprived of significance and importance in the mystery of salvation. For the Spirit of Christ has not refrained from using them as means of salvation which derive their efficacy from the very fulness of grace and truth entrusted to the Catholic Church.'[24]

The Church's given unity does 'subsist' in the Roman Catholic Church. It is the 'all-embracing means of salvation', possessing 'the fulness of the means of salvation'.[25] The Roman Catholic Church is, therefore, *par excellence,* the sign to the world of the unity of the Father and the Son in the Holy Spirit. 'That they may be one even as we are one. I in them and thou in me, that they may become perfectly one, so that the world may know that thou hast sent me.'[26]

[23] Cf DCC, n. 8, and above, p. 102.   [24] *Decree on Ecumenism,* n. 3.
[25] *Ibid.*   [26] Jn 17:22b–23.

While the Church's unity is a given reality it is also a growing and future reality. Like the unity of the God-man Jesus Christ it will not have achieved the culmination of its unifying mission and ministry except at the end of its historical earthly existence. It is the instrument of unity as well as its sign. In fact it is the instrument because it is the sign. Its *gift* of unity is its *task* of uniting. 'The Church exists in Christ as the sacrament or sign and instrument of intimate union with God and of the unity of the whole human race.'[27] This means that the given unity of the Church is not a static something which has simply to be treasured and preserved. It is the dynamic life of the risen Christ who wills to unify all things in himself.

'For he has made known to us in all wisdom and insight the mystery of his will, according to his purpose which he set forth in Christ as a plan for the fulness of time, to unite all things in him [that is, to recapitulate or bring to a head all things in Christ], things in heaven and things on earth.'[28]

The Church must participate in this unifying dynamism of its head, for it is 'his body, *the fulness of him who fills all in all*'.[29] Christ recapitulates or unifies all things through his apostles and his Holy Spirit. The Church's unity is its *task* of making 'disciples of all nations', of preaching the word 'to all the earth (*tēs oikumenēs*)' so that 'they may all be one', and Christ may be all in all.[30]

All that I have been saying has been but a commentary on the following passages of Paul's epistle to the Ephesians:

'There is one body and one Spirit, just as you were called to the one hope that belongs to your call, one Lord, one faith, one baptism, one God and Father of us all, who is above all and through all and in all. But grace was given to each of us according to the measure of Christ's gift . . . and his gifts were that some should be apostles, some prophets, some evangelists, some pastors and teachers, for the equipment of the saints, for the work of ministry, for building up the body of Christ, until we all attain to the unity of the faith and of the knowledge of the Son of God, to mature manhood, to the measure of the stature of the fulness of Christ; so that we may no longer be children, tossed to and fro and carried about with every wind of doctrine, by the cunning of men, by their craftiness in deceitful wiles.'[31]

[27] DCC, n. 1.   [28] Eph 1:9–10.   [29] Eph 1:23.
[30] Mt 28:19; Rom 10:18; Jn 17:21.
[31] Eph 4:4–7, 11–14.

Chapter Twenty-Three

I Believe the Church is Holy

THE same faith which compels us to confess the unity of the Church compels us to confess also its sanctity. 'The Church is believed to be indefectibly holy.'[1] And no less than its unity the basis of the Church's holiness is the life and action of the one God, Father, Son and Spirit. God alone is holy. 'For you alone are holy. . . . Holy, holy, holy Lord God of Hosts.'[2] Despite the uniqueness and transcendence of his holiness Scripture insists on the reality and obligation of man's participation in his holy life. The communication and participation takes place in Jesus Christ through the Holy Spirit. As our Saviour and Redeemer Christ possesses in himself the fulness of divine holy life (cf Col 1: 19-20; 2:9-10a). All of us share in this fulness of the Son (cf Eph 1:23; 4:7, 10). We do so through the Holy Spirit. 'God is love', says St John (I John 4:16). This love 'has been poured into our hearts through the Holy Spirit who has been given to us' (Rom 5:5; cf I Cor 12:3-13). The same Spirit who is the bond and expression of the love of the Father for the Son and the Son for the Father in the eternal unity of the one divine being is also the principle of the communication of this divine life to man. Thus the holiness of the Church is first of all the holiness of God himself, Father, Son and Holy Spirit. It is theological, christological and pneumatological.

But it is also ecclesiological. It is a true and real note or predicate of the Church itself. I agree with Barth[3] that Christ alone has the plenitude of sanctity, and that the Church is sanctified only as he enters into contact with it through his Holy Spirit. But given this 'contact' I maintain that the Church is in itself really and ontologically sanctified. It lives 'in Christ'. It lives the eternal life of God himself, however inchoatively and imperfectly. To say that the Church's sanctity is an ontological reality in Christ alone, and that

[1] 'Ecclesia . . . indefectibiliter sancta creditur': DCC, n. 39.
[2] Cf the *Gloria* and *Sanctus* prayers of the Roman Mass. Cf Lk 1:35; Mk 1:24; Lk 4:34; Jn 6:69; Acts 3:14; 4:27, 30.   [3] Cf *CTKB*, p. 272.

the subjective action of the Spirit does not intrinsically sanctify Christians; or to say that the holy activities of the Christian are not holy activities of the *Christian* but always Christ's own direct act: I cannot see how these assertions agree with Holy Scripture.

Catholic theology distinguishes in the Church an internal holiness of life and a structural holiness of means or mediation of that life. Both are objective and ontological. This distinction, or the reality and objectivity of the Church's holiness in these two senses, is clearly founded in Holy Scripture and witnessed to in the Church's entire tradition, as we have already seen when treating of the doctrine of justification and of the Church's ministry.

On the one hand, the people of God of the New Testament is called 'a holy priesthood', a 'holy nation', or simply the 'saints'.[4] This designation manifests its continuity with the people of God of the Old Testament, for the latter too is called 'a kingdom of priests and a holy nation' (Ex 19:6). Its holiness and priesthood consisted in its being chosen by God, set apart, and enabled to approach and serve him.[5] But it manifests also its discontinuity with the people of Israel, for it is called the 'saints in Christ Jesus', 'those sanctified in Christ Jesus, called to be saints together with all those who in every place call on the name of our Lord Jesus Christ'.[6] It has received of the fulness of Christ through the Holy Spirit who has been 'poured into our hearts'.

Those who believe and are baptized really share in the holy life of Christ through this Spirit and are enabled to act holily. They have eternal life. 'He who believes has eternal life' (Jn 6:47; cf 5:24). They share in the 'first fruits of the Spirit' (Rom 8:23), who 'has been poured into their hearts' (Rom 5:5). They share in God's divine nature. 'Partaking of the divine nature [and] participating in the Holy Spirit [they live] in fellowship (*koinonia*) [with one another and] with the Father and his Son Jesus Christ.'[7] They are holy. 'Do you not know that you are God's temple and that God's Spirit dwells in you? . . . For God's temple is holy, and that temple you are.'[8] They are called to act accordingly, in 'good conduct', and 'good deeds'.[9] How can they who have died to sin and been born to a new life still live in sin?

> 'How can we who died to sin still live in it? Do you not know that all of us who have been baptized into Christ Jesus were

---

[4] Cf I Pet 2:5, 9; Acts 9:13; 9:32; 26:10; Rom 1:7.
[5] Cf Num 16:3–5; Lev 27:16, 33.   [6] I Cor 1:2; II Thess 2:13–14.
[7] II Pet 1:4. Cf I Jn 1:3, 6; II Cor 13:14; Phil 2:1; I Cor 1:9.
[8] I Cor 3: 16–17. Cf 6:9.   [9] I Pet 2:12; I Thess 4:7–8.

baptized into his death? We were buried therefore with him by baptism into death, so that as Christ was raised from the dead by the glory of the Father, we too might walk in newness of life. . . . Let not sin therefore reign in your mortal bodies'.[10]

Possessing the Spirit they are to live by the Spirit.

'But you are not in the flesh, you are in the Spirit, if the Spirit of God really dwells in you. Any one who does not have the Spirit of Christ does not belong to him. But if Christ is in you, although your bodies are dead because of sin, your spirits are alive because of righteousness. If the Spirit of him who raised Jesus from the dead dwells in you, he who raised Christ Jesus from the dead will give life to your mortal bodies also through his Spirit which dwells in you. So then brethren, we are debtors, not to the flesh, to live according to the flesh—for if you live according to the flesh you will die, but if by the Spirit you put to death the deeds of the body you will live. For all who are led by the Spirit of God are sons of God. For you did not receive the spirit of slavery to fall back into fear, but you have received the spirit of sonship. When we cry, "Abba, Father!" it is the Spirit himself bearing witness with our spirit that we are children of God, and if children, then heirs, heirs of God and fellow heirs with Christ, provided we suffer with him in order that we may also be glorified with him.'[11]

Or as Vatican II says:

'The followers of Christ who, not according to their works, but according to his own purpose and grace are called by God and justified in the Lord Jesus, through baptism sought in faith (*in fidei baptismate*) truly become the sons of God and sharers in the divine nature, and in this way are really made holy (*ideoque reapse sancti effecti sunt*). Then, by God's gifts they must retain and perfect by living it (*vivendo tenere atque perficere*) the holiness they have received. They are warned by the Apostle to live "as becomes saints" (Eph 5:3), and to put on "as God's chosen ones, holy and beloved, a heart of mercy, kindness, humility, meekness, patience" (Col 3:12), and to possess the fruits of the Spirit unto holiness (cf Gal 5:22; Rom 6:22).'[12]

Barth does not do justice to this intrinsic holiness of the Church's life and action. Does he not in fact identify the *credo sanctam*

---

[10] Rom 6:2–4, 12. Cf I Thess 4:3, 7–8.
[11] Rom 8:9–17.   [12] DCC, n. 40.

ecclesiam with the *credo in Jesum Christum* or the *credo in Spiritum Sanctum*? That is, by denying the Church's real participation in the life and holiness of Christ, or by attributing holiness exclusively to Christ and his Spirit, is he not denying the very basis of the Church as a mystery of faith and reducing its mystery to the mystery of Christ? We believe the mystery which the Church *is*—through the Holy Spirit, yes, but *in itself*.

For the same reason Barth also denies the Church's structural holiness, that is, its holiness as a means of salvation. The Church not only is holy: as God's instrument it makes holy. It is the *communio sanctorum* or *sancta et sanctificans*, that is, the holy and salvific community. In both cases the sole ultimate principle of its holiness is the risen Christ through his Spirit. Not only does he grant a participation in his holy life. He also grants a participation in his holy action and ministry. Through his apostles and sacraments he sanctifies the Church. As his instruments the Church's apostles and sacraments sanctify the Church. The Holy Spirit is conferred through the laying on of the apostles' hands. 'They laid their hands on them and they received the Holy Spirit. Now when Simon saw that the Spirit was given through the laying on of the apostles' hands . . .' (Acts 8:17–19). Through their words sins are forgiven. 'Receive the Holy Spirit. If you forgive the sins of any, they are forgiven' (Jn 20:22–23). Through their witness all men are led to Christ.[13] Through the sacraments the faithful share in Christ's death and resurrection, body and blood, life and Spirit.[14] For this reason Scripture speaks of the Church as our 'mother', and us as her 'children' and 'offspring'.[15] This sanctifying power of the Church will never be lacking for it is but the bodying forth of Christ's own infallible sanctifying offer and action in his subjective accomplishment of reconciliation through his Holy Spirit. It will never be totally 'corrupt'.

In his Epistle to the Ephesians Paul had already clearly outlined this twofold aspect of the Church's mystery as *sancta et sanctificans*: 'Christ loved the Church and gave himself up for her, that he might sanctify her, having cleansed her by the washing of water with the word, that he might present the Church to himself in splendour, without spot or wrinkle or any such thing, that she might be holy and without blemish' (5:25b–27). In this text of Paul the divine origin of the Church's sanctification, the mediation of this sanctification through water and word, and the ontological sanctification of the

[13] Cf Acts 1:8; Rom 10:17; 16:15.
[14] Cf Rom 6:3f; I Cor 10:16–17; 12: 13; Acts 2:38–42.
[15] Cf Gal 4:26f; Rev 12:17.

Church in itself (distinct from Christ) are all apparent. The whole of
the Church's tradition witnesses to this same twofold mystery.[16]
H. de Lubac sums it up: The Church is a 'two-fold mystery of
communication and of communion: through the communication of
sacraments, of holy things (*sancta*), it is a communion of saints
(*sancti*)'.[17]

But the Church which confesses the presence and action of the Holy
Spirit in and through her, and therefore her own holiness, is conscious
also of her own sinfulness. The same ancient symbols of the faith
which proclaim the Church to be holy speak also of 'the remission of
sins'. Admittedly, Catholic ecclesiology has laid less emphasis on this
aspect of the Church as a sinful reality. And in this respect Barth's
and Protestantism's accusations of triumphalism, as well as reminders
of the Church's sinfulness, serve a useful purpose. Since the Church
is not God nor a divine reality but the human, earthly and historical
people of God, it cannot be free from the sin, error and change which
are part and parcel of all human, earthly and historical existence.
The Church is both holy and sinful.

The Catholic Church has not forgotten this aspect of sinfulness in
its liturgy. There it witnesses to the tension in its existence between
sin and holiness, death and life. On the one hand, it confesses itself
as the Father's 'holy catholic Church' and 'holy people'.[18] On the
other hand, and much more frequently, it confesses its sins, begs
'pardon', 'absolution', 'remission', 'mercy', 'purification', says the
Lord alone is holy, and in general proclaims its own sinful unworthi-
ness to 'go to the altar of God'.[19] After having pronounced the awe-
inspiring words of the consecration in obedience to Christ's command
(cf I Cor 11:23f), and through which Christ renders himself sacramentally present on the altar, the Church immediately prays:

'To us sinners also, your servants, trusting in the greatness of
your mercy, deign to grant some part and fellowship with your

---

[16] Commenting on Ephesians St Jerome writes: 'Et quomodo de Adam
et uxore eius omne hominum nascitur genus; sic de Christo et Ecclesia omnis
credentium multitudo generata est': *in Ephes.*, lib. III, cap. V, ad vers. 31
(*PL*, 33: 631). And Rabanus Maurus: 'Populo credentium, quem mater
Ecclesia per fidem et baptismum generavit': *In Genesim*, lib. II, cap. 19 (*PL*,
107:548B). Finally, St Bede leaves us this pithy summary in his commentary
on Rev 12: 'Nam et Ecclesia, quotidie gignit Ecclesiam': *Explan. Apocalypsis*,
lib. II, cap. 12 (*PL*, 93:1660). Other texts may be found in H. de Lubac, *The
Splendour of the Church*, pp. 71f.   [17] *Op. cit.*, p. 72.

[18] In the prayer of the canon and in the first prayer immediately after the
consecration and elevation in the Mass.

[19] These prayers are repeated throughout the whole rite.

holy apostles and martyrs . . . and all your saints. Into their company we implore you to admit us, not weighing our merits, but freely granting us pardon. Through Christ our Lord.'[20]

And immediately afterwards it repeats the prayer enjoined on it by the Lord himself: 'When you pray, say: "Father, hallowed be thy name.... Forgive us our sins." '[21]

The same tension can be seen in the Church's doctrine on the members of the Church. It is precisely the Catholic Church which has always maintained that the Church is not a pure communion of the just or of the saints, or of the predestined, but comprises sinners too —and who is not one?—within its ranks. If the Fathers sometimes seemed to speak differently they were speaking either of an ideal Church, or of the triumphant Church to come, for they explicitly say that the body of Christ also contains sinners.[22] All the Fathers see in the Gospel narrations about sin and sinners (e.g. Lk 11, Mary Magdalen, publicans and sinners) symbols of the sin and damnation in the Church. Often, too, they apply the warnings of the prophets to the people of Israel, and the lamentations of Isaiah and Jeremiah, to the Church. The doctrine of the Church concerning sin in her midst, that sinners can also belong to her, is traditional. Besides the liturgy and the Fathers it has often explicitly taught this.[23] It is clear also from her teaching as regards the sacrament of penance. While incorporation in the Church demands some form of supernatural life it does not demand the absence of all sin. The Church in its members is both holy and sinful.

And the Church does not confess the remission of sins, or pronounce its liturgical prayers, or teach its doctrine about penance and about its members as both holy and sinful, simply out of humility, or for others, or for some of its members, but in all reality and truth for itself. This was already explicitly stated in the fifth-century Council of Carthage, which also provides the biblical basis for this doctrine.

[20] The Prayer *Nobis quoque* . . . of the Canon.

[21] Luke 11:2, 4. Cf I Jn 1:8; Mt 13:24f, 41f, 47; 18:15f; James 5:15–16.

[22] Thus Augustine, e.g.: 'Benedictus est ex parte bene viventium, claudicat ex parte male viventium. Sed adhuc in uno homine est utrumque': *Sermo* V, 8 (*PL*, 38, 59). The same author also says that the Church *sine macula et ruga* is the future eschatological Church. Here on earth it can never cease to pray 'forgive us our sins': *Retract.*, II, 18 (*PL*, 32, 637–8). Cf St Thomas, *Summa theol.*, III, q. 8, art. 3, ad 2. Cf S. Tromp, *Corpus Christi quod est Ecclesia*, I, pp. 131f, for many other patristic references.

[23] Cf DS 1578, 1201f, 2472f; encycl. *Mystici Corporis*, in *AAS*, 35 (1943), 203–4 (English *CTS* transl., pp. 16–17); DCC, n. 14.

'Whoever thinks St John the apostle's statement: "If we say that we have no sin, we deceive ourselves, and truth is not in us" (I Jn 1:8), is to be taken in the sense that he is saying we have sin because humility demands us to say so, not because we actually do have sin: let him be anathema. For the apostle continues: "If we acknowledge our sins, he is faithful and just to forgive us our sins and to cleanse us from all iniquity" (I Jn 1:9). Hence it is quite clear that this is said not only from humility but truthfully. . . . Whoever says that the reason why the saints say, "Forgive us our debts" (Mt 6:12) in the Our Father is not that they are requesting this for themselves—for such a request is not necessary for them —but that they are requesting it for others of their people who are debtors; and whoever says that the reason why each of the saints does not say, "Forgive me my debts", but "Forgive us our debts," is that the just man is understood to make this request for others rather than for himself: let him be anathema. The apostle James was a holy and a just man when he said, "For in many things we all offend" (James 3:2; cf Ps 142:2; I Kings 8:46, etc.).'[24]

But if the Church is really and intrinsically holy, how can it be said to be sinful, or vice versa? The Catholic interpretation of the Church *simul iusta et peccatrix* is not the same as the Barthian. First of all, there can be no disjunction of an invisible, holy, divine Church and a sinful, visible, purely human Church. When we speak of the Church as *simul iusta et peccatrix* we speak of the visible, human Church, just as when we speak of the Christian *simul iustus et peccator* we speak of the visible human Christian. Secondly, when we say that this Church 'acquires a part in the holiness of its head' we do not mean that it none the less remains 'in itself not holy', 'standing absolutely in need of its justification'.[25] These are two points on which I would have liked clarification from Barth's side.

There are many points on which, on the other hand, I agree with Barth. The sole author of all holiness is God. Of himself man has only lying and sin. If he has anything of truth and justice it is from God.[26] Moreover, the holiness he does possess is not at all the same as the divine holiness. Man does not cease to be man when he lives the life

[24] Council of Carthage, DS 228–30.
[25] Cf *CTKB*, p. 272.
[26] 'De his quae hominum propria sunt. Nemo habet de suo nisi mendacium et peccatum. Si quid autem habet homo veritatis atque iustitiae, ab illo fonte est, quem debemus sitire in hac eremo, ut ex eo quasi guttis quibusdam irrorati non deficiamus in via'; Council of Orange, DS 392. Cf also Council of Trent, DS 1546.

of God. He lives God's own life in a human and imperfect way. If Barth had only developed his theology of reflection in this sense! Under the creative action of the Holy Spirit the community of men who believe, love and hope 'have eternal life' (Jn 6:47), do live God's life, in a human way.

What is the Catholic interpretation of the 'Church simultaneously holy and sinful'? The recent Council did not provide any solution, nor did it even pose the problem. Traditionally, a distinction was made between the Church as the instituted and infallible instrument of the Spirit's sanctifying action and as the communion of those who receive and respond to and live Christ's holy life (and this naturally includes those who exercise an instituted sanctifying ministry and thus form part also of the Church considered as a means of grace). Of the Church considered from the first point of view it was said that it was holy and not sinful. Certainly sin concerns the personal attitude and response of the individual to his God and therefore concerns the Church as a communion of life. One could scarcely speak of the rite of baptism sinning! Still, there is a certain sense in which we must also speak of the instituted means as 'sinful', as for example when a liturgical rite is so slovenly carried out that it is barely discernible as the rite of the Church, or when structures are allowed to become so outmoded that they no longer fulfil the service of truth and free human persons for which they solely exist. In so far as the Church possesses the means of grace and correctly, that is, objectively, uses them then it is as such holy and not sinful. Or it is *simul sancta* as the means of grace and *peccatrix* in her members as a communion of life.

But as the communion of those who respond to the invitation of Christ to live his life the Church is both simultaneously holy and sinful. Firstly, in so far as some of its members live in mortal sin and others live in venial sin which does not destroy the life of grace it is simultaneously sinful and just. Secondly, justification, while it frees from sin, does not free from the marks of past sin nor from the threat of sin. The members of the Church bear in themselves the marks and stains of past sin from which they must be purified before they become fit to enter into perfect communion with God. And they are continually assailed by the threat of sin. They are besieged, threatened and harassed from all sides. In this time between the times Christians are continually threatened by the world, the flesh and the devil— who, according to St Peter, goes about like a roaring lion seeking whom he may devour. They need the continual grace of God if they are to resist.[27] In the present they are not confirmed in holiness. They

[27] Cf the Council of Trent, DS 1541.

are threatened by sin, can yield to sin, continually struggle against sin, and often sin. The Church in these her members is sinful and just. Thirdly, the present holy life of Christians is imperfect. They must be purified before they can face God 'as he is'. They are not reborn to glory but to the hope of glory (I Pet 1:3). They must continually strive forward towards his perfect holiness. 'Not that I have already obtained this or am already perfect, but . . . I press on toward the goal for the prize of the upward call of God in Christ Jesus.'[28] The present life is a continual history and transition from sin to holiness. Because of this too the Church must be said to be holy and sinful in its members.

But the phrase *ecclesia simul sancta et peccatrix* can scarcely be reduced to *christiani simul peccatores et iusti*. For example, the Church itself, properly speaking, as the communion of the justified, must be said to be sinful.[29] *Ecclesia peccatrix* is not entirely equivalent to *Ecclesia peccatorum*, nor is it very realistic to make a distinction between a 'holy' Church and 'sinful' members. According to Vatican II the Church itself would seem to be the subject of sin. For it says that sins wound the Church itself and that the sacrament of penance effects reconciliation with the Church.[30] Again it says that the Church needs purification, penance and renovation, and thus implies that since it is the subject of penance it must also be in some way the subject of sin.[31] Finally, when it says that the Church exists in the Blessed Virgin Mary without spot or wrinkle it implies that apart from her it does not exist without spot or wrinkle.[32] Thus Augustine, for instance, could interpret Eph 5:25-27 eschatologically:

> 'Whenever in my books I have described the Church as being without spot or wrinkle, I have not meant to imply that it was already so, but that it should prepare itself to be so, at the time when it too will appear in its glory in the present time, because of the inexperience and weakness of its members it must pray every day anew: Forgive us our trespasses.'[33]

And St Thomas:

> 'That the Church will be glorious, without spot or wrinkle, is the final goal to which we are led through the sufferings of Christ. This

[28] Phil 3:12, 14. Cf H. Küng, Justification . . . , pp. 236-48, for a fuller exposition.
[29] Cf K. Rahner, *Die Kirche der Sünder*, pp. 14f.; *id*., 'Il peccato nella Chiesa' in *La Chiesa del Vaticano II*, ed. by G. Barauna, pp. 418-35.
[30] DCC, n. 11.   [31] *Ibid*., n. 8.   [32] *Ibid*., n. 65.
[33] *Retract*., II, 18 (*PL*, 32:637-8).

will only be true in our eternal home, not on the way thither, for now we would deceive ourselves if we were to say we have no sin, as I Jn 1:8 points out.'[34]

The Church's indefectible holiness and inevitable sinfulness is simply the expression of the union of the divine and the human, the Spirit and the flesh, in the one complex reality which is the Church. Both aspects must receive equal emphasis in order to preserve the mystery in proper perspective and balance.

Because of the reality of sin the Church must continually renew, reform and purify itself. It must be the *ecclesia semper reformanda*. Because of its sin and inclination to sin, because of proneness to error and failure, it must always question its relationship to its Lord and the fidelity of its witness to him. One recalls the phrase of Cardinal Newman: 'In a higher world it is otherwise, but here below to live is to change, and to be perfect is to have changed often.' The Church is 'always in need of being purified, and incessantly pursues the path of penance and renewal'.[35] Renewal is not simply change of course, but that which the Council in speaking of religious termed *accommodata renovatio*, that is, adaptation to the contemporary world through a return to the sources.

But the continual reformation and renewal of the Church is a consequence not only of its sinfulness but above all of its holiness. The Church's sanctity, like its unity, is not a gift for its own enjoyment but, as the participation in the life or love of the Trinity, it is a dynamic force which presses the Church ever forwards towards the 'measure of the stature of the fulness of Christ' (Eph 4:13, 15), towards the fulfilment of its mission to the world, towards its eschatological consummation in sanctity. In this sense especially the Church must be a continually reforming Church. Its sanctity must spring forth in ever new visible forms. This reformation does not originate in itself but is the result of the Holy Spirit's indwelling presence and action through his dynamic created gift of sanctity. As the Council said: 'The Holy Spirit [who] was sent on the day of Pentecost in order that he might for ever [*iugiter*] sanctify the Church . . . by the power of the Gospel he makes the Church grow, perpetually renews her, and leads her to perfect union with her spouse.'[36]

It is only through this continual renewal and reformation that the Church will be able to witness to the world of the holiness of Jesus

---

[34] *Summa theol.*, III, q. 8, art. 3, ad 2.
[35] DCC, n. 8. Cf also Decree on Ecumenism, n. 6.
[36] DCC, n. 4.

Christ. It is only through continual reformation that this quality of holiness will become a visible note of the Church. Reformation will not mean de-formation or denial of what have been true forms of holiness in the past. But it will mean the expression and concretization of the Church's holiness in ever new forms. This continual need for re-formation is due to the reforming action of the Spirit indwelling the Church and to the Church's existence in human history and as part of that history. The Church must bear witness to the contemporary world it lives in. Sanctity is a history. Living and sharing in the development and change of history it must continually reform to be 'the light of the world' (Mt 5:14-16), the 'ensign to the nations' (Is 11:12), the universal sacrament of salvation. The Church 'exhorts her sons to purify and renew themselves so that the sign of Christ may shine more brightly over the face of the Church'.[37]

The total splendour of its witness to the mystery of Christ will only take place in the future, in the *eschaton*. Here on earth the Church is on the way. It is a pilgrim Church. It already shares really and ontologically in the holiness of God but its perfect and consummated sharing belongs to the future. For the time being it strives towards that future, groans within itself (cf Rom 8:23) and desires to be with Christ (cf Phil 1:23).[38] Its cult and canonization of saints, and especially its cult of the Blessed Virgin Mother of God, concretely witnesses to this eschatological tension. In canonizing saints it witnesses to the reality of its present earthly anticipated participation in the future consummation, and at the same time proclaims the futurity of that consummation.[39]

Vatican II sums up this whole question:

> 'While Christ, "holy, innocent, undefiled" (Heb 7:26) knew nothing of sin (II Cor 5:21), but came to expiate only the sins of the people (cf Heb 2:17), the Church embracing sinners in her bosom, is at the same time holy and always in need of being purified, and incessantly pursues the path of penance and renewal. The Church, "like a pilgrim in a foreign land, presses forward amid the persecutions of the world and the consolations of God", announcing the cross and death of the Lord until he comes (cf I Cor 11:26). By the power of the risen Lord, she is given strength to overcome patiently and lovingly the afflictions and hardships which assail her from within and without, and to show forth in the world the

---

[37] DCC, n. 15.
[38] Cf *ibid.*, n. 48.
[39] Cf *ibid.*, n. 49, and below, chapter twenty-six, pp. 331f.

mystery of the Lord in a faithful though shadowed way, until at the last it will be revealed in total splendour.'[40]

I agree with Barth as regards the christological source of the Church's sanctity. I agree with him in his two positive deductions from this fact.[41] The Church's holiness is one, that of its head through his spirit. Participation in it means participation in the community. Its holiness is indestructible, for Christ dwells in and acts through his Church through his Spirit. I disagree with him in his third (critical) deduction. Christ is always the subject of the Church's holy actions. But he bodies forth his holiness infallibly through certain instituted (by himself) means of grace. The Church's holiness, in and under him, is also *activa sanctitas*. In certain holy actions (e.g. preaching, baptism, the Lord's Supper) it is indefectibly holy.

I agree with Barth in the basic assertion of his fourth, and again critical, deduction, namely, that purely visible membership of the Church is not necessarily membership of the Church.[42] The Church is both a visible and invisible reality, a sacramental structure and an invisible sacramental life. Full active membership connotes the possession of sanctifying grace through baptism, the profession of the Catholic faith, and union with its guiding authority. It means participation in Christ, the life, the truth and the way, through the triple means of salvation he instituted, and which are nothing else but the means of prolonging visible, human, connatural contact with himself. Full membership in the Church means therefore both participation in its visible structure and invisible life.

Barth, too, says in his fifth deduction[43] that the Church's sanctity must become visible in a human reflection. With this I am in wholehearted agreement. But as Catholics we mean more than this when we say that participation in the visible Church is necessary for membership of the *sancta ecclesia*. We mean that participation must be had in its visible instituted structure. We do not agree with his explanation of the *ex opere operato* of baptism. Baptism does not evade the lordship of God, or the real spiritual mystery of the community. On the contrary, it is the precise expression of his lordship, since he is its sole principal cause. In this lies its infallibility.[44] From its viewpoint members of the Church are those who are baptized. But its effect (the *res sacramenti*) can be hindered by the recipient. It does

[40] DCC, n. 8.
[41] Cf *CTKB*, pp. 272-3.
[42] Cf *ibid.*, pp. 274f.
[43] Cf *ibid.*, pp. 275f.
[44] Cf above, chapter fifteen, art. II, 4.

not confer, but presupposes, like all the sacraments, faith, for it is a sacrament of faith. Since this depends on the internal action of the Spirit we must say that mere visible participation in the Church does not necessarily constitute membership of the Church, or, in other words, we cannot say for certain who are members of the Church.

From the nature of the Church we must say on the one hand, and against Barth, that visible membership (in the sense explained) is necessary. On the other hand, and this time with Barth, we must say that since the Church is also, and indeed primarily, a communion with God in his holy life, some spiritual union with him is necessary for membership. We have already seen that sinners, or those who have forfeited sanctifying grace, are members of the Church. This means that they retain some union with God. The minimum is latent belief in him. Vatican II gives priority to the 'possession of the Spirit of Christ'.[45]

---

[45] DCC, n. 14. Cf the Council of Trent, DS 1531: the implication is that without faith one cannot be a Christian or incorporated in the Church. Cf also encycl. *Myst. Corp.*, *AAS*, 35 (1943), 203-4 (Engl. transl., pp. 16-17); Thomas Aquinas, *Summa theol.*, III, q. 8, art. 3. J. Hamer, *The Church is a Communion*, pp. 88-90; C. Journet, *L'Eglise du Verbe incarné*, vol. II, p. 175. The theological notion of Church membership demands the retention of some participation in the divine life. If one considers the Church solely as a juridical visible society then Church membership will depend solely on juridical visible ties. But if one considers the Church as both a visible juridical structure and an invisible communion of life in intimate union (and one must do so, I believe, for a theological understanding of the Church) then one cannot say that 'all and only those belong to the Church as members who are visibly, i.e. in the external forum, subject to these two powers (sacramental and juridical authority—the latter including the teaching and ruling authority) of the Church' (K. Rahner, *Theological Investigations*, II, p. 17), or that 'pure internal unbelief would not destroy Church membership' (id., in *LTK*, 6, p. 224). Fr Rahner claims to be interpreting the ecclesiastical usage of the term 'member of the Church'. If his interpretation is correct then ecclesiastical usage would seem to have been based solely on a counter-Reformation insistence on the visible and juridical nature of the Church, and certainly pre-Vatican II.

Chapter Twenty-Four

I Believe the Church is Catholic

THE basis of the third predicate of the Church mentioned in the Nicene-Constantinopolitan Creed (as of its other three predicates) is the triune life of God himself *ad intra* and *ad extra*. God's inner trinitarian life is the fulness of communion in union, of plurality in unity. His eternal salvific will, revealed in its objective realization in Christ,[1] envisages the subjective participation by all men, through his Holy Spirit, in this same communion in union (cf Eph 2:18–22). As the term of this external operation of the Trinity the Church will reflect in its own life and existence the diversity in unity and unity in diversity of the Trinity. It will be universal and one. 'Thus the *universal* Church shines forth as a people made *one* with the unity of the Father, the Son, and the Holy Spirit.'[2]

The mystery of the Father's will, set forth in Christ, is the unification or recapitulation of all things in him (Eph 1:9–10). Jesus Christ accomplishes this unification. This was precisely the scope of his mission and incarnation: the salvation of all men. He accomplishes it in two distinct phases.

Objectively, he accomplished it through human and visible actions which were divinely salvific because their subject was the Son of God become man.

> 'That which we have seen and heard we proclaim also to you, so that you may have fellowship with us; and our fellowship is with the Father and with his Son Jesus Christ. . . . For there is one God, and there is one mediator between God and man, the man Christ Jesus, who gave himself as a ransom for all.'[3]

This means that he possessed in himself the fulness in unity of the triune life of God, and the fulness in unity of the redeemed life of

---

[1] Eph 1:9–10. Cf I Tim 2:3–6.
[2] Vatican II, DCC, ch. I, n. 4 (emphasis mine).
[3] I Jn 1:3; I Tim 2:5–6a.

mankind. He was 'full of grace and truth. . . . For in him the whole fulness of deity dwells bodily, and you have come to fulness (*plērōma*) of life in him'.[4]

But Jesus Christ accomplishes this unification of all things also subjectively. This means that his life is a dynamic force which spreads out from his risen glorified body, permeating and unifying his community on earth, and through it the whole of creation. Thus St John adds: 'And from his fulness (*plērōma*) have we all received, grace upon grace.' And St Paul: 'He who descended is he who also ascended far above all the heavens, that that he might fill all things. And his gifts were. . . .'[5]

Jesus Christ accomplishes the subjective realization of his fulness of unity in the power of his Holy Spirit. But just as he accomplished the objective recapitulation through human and visible actions and words, so also he accomplishes the subjective recapitulation through human and visible actions and words. He accomplishes it through his Spirit, apostles and sacraments.

In analogy to what has been said of the incarnation of the Son of God in the man Jesus, this means that in the human visible Church the fulness of the Spirit dwells bodily. This is not just a nice comparison thought out by ourselves. St Luke describes the reality, fulness and universal capacity of the gift of the Spirit at Pentecost. The Holy Spirit was given in the form of tongues of fire, 'distributed and *resting on each one* of them. And they were *all filled* (*eplēsthēsan*) with the Holy Spirit and . . . devout men from *every nation under heaven* . . . were bewildered, because *each one* heard them speaking in his own language'.[6] The gift of the Spirit fills each one, is able to fill each one, fills all, and is able to fill all. This is what we mean by the universality (or catholicity) in unity of the Church's life, or Christ's life in and through his Church through his Spirit. It is able to satisfy the aspirations, no matter how different, of all and each to life and truth. The Church bears within it the fulness of revelation and truth (which is Christ) and the fulness of life (which again is Christ). Christ's life in his Church has the capacity to make all things one (while not only retaining but guaranteeing differentiation) because it is itself fulness in unity.

Christ's accomplishment of the subjective recapitulation through his Church means, again by analogy with what we have already seen concerning him, that the Church's life is a dynamic force which spreads outwards, seeking to recapitulate all things in its unity. Thus

[4] Jn 1:14; Col 2:9.
[5] Jn 1:16; Eph 4:10–11a. [6] Acts 2:3, 4, 5, 6.

Paul describes the Church as the 'fulness (*plērōma*) of him who fills all in all'.[7] This text brings out the fact that Christ himself is the ultimate subject, in and through his Church to which he has given fulness, of this dynamic movement towards universalization.[8] *In* him and *under* him, because *from* him, the Church participates in his fulness in unity, and in the dynamic force of its movement outwards. Thus Paul, further on in the same epistle, speaks of the 'gift given' to himself and others in the community 'for the work of ministry, for building up the body of Christ . . . from whom the whole body . . . makes bodily growth and upbuilds itself in love'.[9] And St John, in a parallel statement: 'The glory which thou hast given me I have given to them that they may be one even as we are one . . . so that the world may know that thou hast sent me. . . . I do not pray for these only, but also for those who believe in me through their word.'[10]

This, then, is what we mean by the catholicity of the Church: its possession of the *dynamic fulness in unity* of the divine life, and the means to that life, which it has received from the Father, in the Son, through the Holy Spirit.[11] Of its very essence the Church is one, catholic and catholicizing, or one, universal and universalizing. In this light we understand the absolute necessity and universality of its mission. 'The Church does not become universal (or "Catholic") because it engages in missionary activity but engages in missionary activity because by nature the Church is universal.'[12] 'Go therefore and make disciples of all nations . . . be my witnesses to the end of the earth. . . . Their voice has gone out to all the earth, and their words to the ends of the world (*tēs oikumenēs*).'[13]

After these primary considerations, which are meant to bring out, in conformity with the *basic legitimate demands of Karl Barth's theology*, the trinitarian and dynamic aspects of the Church's catholicity, we must now take a more detailed look at Barth's conception of this third predicate.[14]

[7] Eph 1:23. Cf Col 2:10.
[8] The Church is 'die Fülle des Christus, *der* durch sie das All und den Kosmos in seine Fülle hineinnimmt' (emphasis mine): H. Schlier, *Der Brief an die Epheser*, p. 99.
[9] Eph 3:7, 11–12, 16.   [10] Jn 17:22, 23, 20.
[11] It is the universal capacity of assimilation of its constitutive principles . . . the dynamic universality of its unity (Congar, *Chrétiens désunis*, p. 117), the participation in the dynamic expanding power of Christ in order to recapitulate the whole world in him (Witte, 'Die Katholizität . . .' in *Gregorianum*, 42 (1961) 223).
[12] Schnackenburg, *The Church in the N.T.*, p. 139.
[13] Mt 28:19; Rom 10:18. Cf Acts 1:8; Lk 24:47; Jn 20:21.
[14] Cf *CTKB*, pp. 276–9.

The *first point* we notice is that the Church's catholicity for Barth does not mean the universality of its unity but its sameness in all its forms. There is not a great difference between these two expressions, and yet I think there is a small nuance which reveals two different outlooks. When we speak of the 'Catholic' Church we speak of the universality, totality and universal dynamism of the one Church. The sameness of the Church in all its local actualizations does not constitute its catholicity but is rather the result of its catholicity. For the universal Church is not simply identical with its concrete local manifestation or realization. Nor is it merely the sum of these concrete local manifestations.

Barth speaks of catholicity as the Church's truth and self-identity in a plurality of forms. This he has to do, of course, because the Church and its catholicity is always the event of the living Word and work of Jesus Christ its head through his Holy Spirit.[15] Thus its simple unity in the plurality of forms is due, as we saw, to the simple unity of God himself acting directly in each time and place. The plurality of forms of its simple unity is due to the same direct action. For Barth there is no universal power of extension of the one Church, nor actual universal extension of one Church. There is a universal plurality of forms of the one Church in self-sameness. While we can adopt, and recently have begun to do so more, what Barth calls 'catholicity', in the sense that we have begun to evaluate more the local Church as the concrete actualization of the whole Church, he cannot adopt what we call 'catholicity'. As we have already seen there is no place in his ecclesiology for a universal Church, nor consequently for the unity of a universal Church.[16]

A *second point* in which I think Barth's explanation deficient concerns the inherence and permanence of the Church's catholicity.[17] We can agree, to a certain extent, with his explanation of the *ecclesia semper reformanda*. The Church must ask in every age whether its form, doctrine, order and ministry agree with its 'unalterable essence'. Many alterable inessentials will certainly have crept in. But what is this 'unalterable essence'? Is it an inherent reality of the human Church, or is it an extrinsic divine act of Christ alone through his Spirit?

For Barth it is not an inherent reality. Temporal catholicity does not mean for him that the Church possesses the life and means whereby it is able to fill all time and last for all time, endure permanently, historically and horizontally to the end of the age. 'And lo,

[15] Cf *ibid.*, pp. 278–9.   [16] Cf above, pp. 255f., 286.
[17] Cf *CTKB*, pp. 277f.

I am with you always, to the close of the age.'[18] It means that the Church is created the same in the historical sequence of its forms. No historical form of the Church represents as such the unalterable essence of the Church. None can be in itself the norm of catholicity for succeeding forms. This statement can and must be accepted in the sense that the Church, as a historical reality, will concretize itself in ever new historical forms. But it cannot be accepted in the sense that these forms are inessential to the Church, that they do not in their own time and culture really embody the Church, or that they need not be taken into account in the Church's present and future reformation. The Church's reformation must take into account at least its primary and original form, as witnessed to in Scripture. Indeed it must take into account the Church's own believing implementation of Scripture in the past, as more and more Protestant theologians are themselves coming to realize.[19]

The Church's catholicity is an ontologically inherent constituent of the human historical Church. In the next chapter we shall see that the Church's catholicity cannot be separated from its apostolicity in the sense of apostolic succession. The Church has one permanently enduring essential structure. Continual historical reformation can never deform this constituent of the Church's unalterable essence. But abstracting from the permanence of the Church's catholicity in its essential structure, there is also an essential ontological permanence of catholicity in its life. The Church is the fulness of Christ's dynamic recapitulating life, as well as the fulness of the means thereto. This fulness is an inherent permanent reality.

In dialogue with Barth one must continually ask the question: in speaking of the (in this case) catholicity of the Church, are we speaking of the catholicity of Jesus Christ alone, or are we speaking of the catholicity of Jesus Christ in and through his Church, and therefore of the Church as well under Jesus Christ? Barth seems to speak of the catholicity of Jesus Christ alone. We thus meet again his 'christological constriction', namely, that catholicity is not an inherent reality and salvific activity of the Church.

There is a *third point*. Barth rightly says that the catholicity of the Church is a matter of faith.[20] It is a matter of faith in the presence and action of the Christ who recapitulates all things through his Spirit in and through his Church. But he then goes on to state that this faith excludes the Church's visibility as the Catholic Church. Catholic

---

[18] Mt 28:20. Cf Eph 1:10.
[19] Cf above, pp. 225f.
[20] Cf *CTKB*, p. 278.

theology, on the contrary, maintains that this essential predicate is also a visible note of the true Church of Christ, which can be known by human reason. Certainly, catholicity is above all a spiritual invisible predicate of the Church. It is its participation in the fulness in unity of Christ's life. But there can be no disjunction between the invisible and visible. The dynamic fulness of the incarnate life of Christ must produce an incarnate effect. It presses from within outwards, to use a phrase of Barth's.

Again, the basic question is christological. St John, after saying that 'the Word became flesh and dwelt among us, full of grace and truth', immediately adds: 'we have beheld his glory, glory as of the only Son from the Father'.[21] He manifested his glory in signs (Jn 2:11). He who sees him sees the Father (14:9). 'That which was *from the beginning*, which we have *heard*, which we have *seen* with our eyes, which we have *looked upon* and *touched* with our hands, concerning the word of life. . . .'[22] This Johannine realism should not be attenuated, just as the Pauline sacramental realism with regard to Christ's present action in the Church should in no way be attenuated.[23] St John also says that Christ confers the 'glory', which the Father gave him, on his apostles, 'that they may be one even as we are one . . . so that the *world may know* that thou hast sent me'.[24]

Barth's exposition of the Church's catholicity seems to me to be a particularly weak point in his ecclesiology. The reason, too, is clear, for it is the hardest of the four predicates to explain on the basis of an exclusive event-ecclesiology. None the less, he has many points which merit the attention of both Catholic and Protestant ecclesiologists.

First of all, I have found his christological and dynamic thought extremely helpful in the brief introductory exposition which I have given of modern Catholic theology's concept of catholicity. Secondly, we can learn much from him in his spiritual conception of this predicate of the Church. Catholic theology has usually insisted on the apologetic aspect of catholicity as a note of the true Church. Recently more attention has been given to its dogmatic aspect. For it is, above all, part of the Christian confession of faith. Without prior consideration of the internal spiritual catholicity the external note is unintelligible. Catholicity can never be considered as primarily something geographical, numerical, sociological, cultural, temporal or historical. It is primarily an internal and spiritual reality. And it

[21] Jn 1:14.
[22] I Jn 1:1. Cf 1:1–3.
[23] Cf above, pp. 273f.
[24] Jn 17:22–23. Cf Acts ch. 2.

is only when we are sure that the Church has not denied or contradicted her internal spiritual catholicity that we can adduce all these external signs as really signs of her catholicity.

Thirdly, whatever his explanation, he brings out the necessity of treating of the Church under this aspect. It is an essential predicate of the Church, an essential part of its confession of faith. He rightly bemoans the abandonment by Protestantism of this word 'catholic'. For a 'Church is catholic or it is not the Church'.[25]

Fourthly, he reminds all that the plurality of Churches cannot mean that there are national, racial Churches. The Church's catholicity consists precisely in being able to absorb all nations, cultures, classes and races without destroying or being absorbed by them. It must be able to transcend all differences.[26] While there is a Church *in* England, there can be no such thing as a Church *of* England. This is in conformity with St Paul, who as we saw, when he speaks of the local Church, speaks of the Church *at* Corinth, *at* Rome, *at* Antioch.[27]

Fifthly, he points to the difference between 'catholic' and 'ecumenical'. 'Ecumenical' originally expressed the geographical dimension of the Church. In the course of history it came to mean the union of all Christians by faith and baptism, and the effort to unite them still further. 'Catholicity' denotes the dynamic movement of the Church to recapitulate *all things* in Christ. 'Ecumenicity' can be taken to mean that part of the Church's catholic dynamic movement which recapitulates in full unity all those partly separated.[28]

Catholicity is above all a task, a dynamic gift which seeks fulfilment. The Catholic Church cannot just sit back with assured consciousness of possessing the fulness of truth, life and holiness and expect the separated Churches to 'return' to it. The latter are also the 'catholic' Church, even though their catholicity is partial through a *denial* of certain truths. But the Roman Catholic Church is also only partially catholic, not through a denial of certain evangelical truths, but through a 'hiding' of them, or failure to develop them. The Church must demonstrate its catholicity, its fulness, and its capacity of really being able to take to itself all goodness and truth no matter where they are found. It must *existentially actualize* ever more and more the fulness of revealed truth, the catholicity of the divine life it shares in. In relation to the separated Churches it must

[25] Cf *CTKB*, p. 276.
[26] Cf DCC, n. 13.
[27] Cf above, pp. 251, 255.
[28] Cf H. van der Linde and J. L. Witte, in *Ecumenism and the Roman Catholic Church*, ed. by A. von Geusau, London, 1966, pp. 74–85.

demonstrate in itself, by learning from them, *their* catholicity. It must overcome onesidedness, which is a partial negation of its essence and mission—although onesidedness is hard to avoid because of the limitation of the human mind and will. All parts conspire towards that fulness in unity which is the goal and purpose of God for mankind (cf Jn 11:52; Eph 4:11ff).

'In virtue of this catholicity each individual part of the Church contributes through its special gifts to the good of the other parts and of the whole Church. Thus through the common sharing of gifts and through the common effort to attain fulness in unity, the whole and each of the parts receive increase.'[29]

In dialogue with other Christians and non-Christians it must strive to realize its one universality in unity, that universality which consists in its power to absorb all that is good in others. Its strictly Christian ecumenical movement consists in its attempt through dialogue to strive towards that fulness in unity of all the good which is present in all Christians and Christian Churches according to the Scriptures, and which may be and often is more perfectly actualized 'outside' itself. It must become concretely and existentially 'the universal sacrament of salvation'.

---

[29] 'Vi huius catholicitatis, singulae partes propria dona ceteris partibus et toti Ecclesiae afferunt, ita ut totum et singulae partes augeantur ex omnibus invicem communicantibus et ad plenitudinem in unitate conspirantibus': DCC, n. 13.

Chapter Twenty-Five

I Believe the Church is Apostolic

As Karl Barth notes,[1] the four predicates of the Church mentioned in the Creed describe the one being of the community. The being of the community consists in its service of the Father, Son and Holy Spirit, in the subjective accomplishment of reconciliation. Reconciliation is the *fulness* of *communion* in the divine *holy* life which descends from the Trinity in the person of the incarnate Christ, and from him in the person of his Holy Spirit 'incarnate'[2] in his *apostles* to the Church of today, and through it to the whole world, so that all may one day perfectly and definitively participate in God's eternal life.

The Church which participates in this descending and ascending movement is of its nature one, holy, catholic and apostolic. It cannot be one if it is not apostolic, nor can it be holy if it is not catholic. These are predicates of the man Christ's own indivisible life first of all, and since it is his life which constitutes the Church, the latter simply does not exist if it does not participate in all four aspects. Yet, again as Barth points out, they mount to a climax.[3] Apostolicity, or mission in the service of Christ to the world in agreement with the mission of the original apostles, is the 'concrete spiritual criterion' of the unity, sanctity and catholicity of the Church, just as Christ's apostolicity

[1] Cf *CTKB*, pp. 279f.
[2] As already pointed out above in chapter twelve, pp. 125f., and esp. pp. 136f., there is an absolute distinction to be made between the hypostatic union of two natures in Christ and the union of the Holy Spirit with human people and earthly realities to form the Church. There is no question of a 'continuation of the incarnation' in the sense that the members of the Church are united hypostatically with the Holy Spirit. The Church is united with the Spirit through his created gifts. It is a vital but non-personal union. It is a union of many human persons in the one divine life. As H. Mühlen puts it in the title of his work: 'One Person in many persons': *Una Persona mystica. Die Kirche als das Mysterium der Identität des Heiligen Geistes in Christus und den Christen: Eine Person in vielen Personen*, Munich–Paderborn–Vienna, 1964.
[3] Cf *CTKB*, p. 411.

or mission from the Father is the concrete spiritual criterion of the unity, sanctity and catholicity of his human life.

Catholic theology usually distinguishes three ways in which the Church is apostolic: It is apostolic in *origin*, in that it was founded in and through the apostles; it is apostolic in the *means of salvation*, in that its doctrine and sacraments agree essentially with those of the apostles, as documented in Scripture; it is apostolic in the uninterrupted *succession* of its bishops to the college of apostles. In dialogue with Barth I would like to treat briefly of the Church's apostolicity under the overall aspect of its *mission*. The scriptural and theological basis has already been outlined fairly extensively.[4] I wish to show once more how much I agree with Barth, and how much I still disagree.

An 'apostle' means, basically, 'one who is sent'. The Church's apostolicity consists in its mission and the fulfilment of its mission. This predicate of the Church, like the other three, is a predicate of the Church which exists today. It is a predicate of the whole Church, for each and everyone is sent, each and everyone is an apostle. It does not merely express a connection with the past. While the connection with the apostles *par excellence* is an aspect of the Church's apostolicity, it would be one-sided to regard it as the sole aspect. The Church's apostolicity is above all a description of the present-day Church. It expresses the *essence* of its *actual existence*.

Furthermore, apostolicity is not an 'essential' feature of the present-day Church in the sense that it is a perfect gift given to the Church, to be preserved and 'stored up' for the *parousia*. The Church's apostolicity is a perfect reality only in the risen Christ and in the *eschaton*. In this time between, on its way from the *Christus solus* to the *Christus totus*, the Church must continually strive to realize ever more perfectly its apostolicity or mission, and so build itself up to the measure of the stature of the fulness of Christ.[5] Its apostolicity is a participation in the apostolicity of Christ himself sent to do the will of His Father, and who now seeks to unite all things under one head through his Church (Eph 1:9-10). The essence which this note describes is the essence of its existence. The Church's apostolicity is its dynamic participation in Christ's own dynamic mission. It describes 'the living community of the living Lord Jesus Christ in the fulfilment of its existence'. It describes the Church sent in the actualization of its sending. It describes the Church's Christ-given mission in its existential fulfilment.

[4] Cf above, chapters thirteen to fifteen.
[5] Cf Eph 4:12-13, 15-16.

L

I agree, therefore, with Barth when he says that the Church's apostolicity is a history which continually takes place.[6] I agree with him when he says that the apostolic Church must not be centred in itself, but in Christ and the world.[7] It exists solely in the service of Christ to the world. 'Its mission is not additional to its being. It is, as it is sent and active in its mission.'

However, I do not agree with the exclusively actualist way in which Barth understands these statements. He excludes all human ontological participation in Christ's apostolicity, all historical ontological permanence of the apostolic Church. The reason behind this is not far to seek. Apostolicity is and always remains in fact a predicate of Jesus Christ alone. It occurs and is known solely in and by the direct act of Jesus Christ and his Spirit.

Moreover, I agree with him in his identification of apostolicity and mission only on the condition that this mission is not confined to the mission of preaching and witnessing to the world.[8] This is one aspect of its mission and ministry, and it is an aspect which should pervade its whole existence, as Barth so admirably illustrates. But it is only one aspect. Christ was sent to preach, sanctify and rule. Participating in his mission, the Church is sent to make Christ the truth, the life and the way for all by preaching, sanctifying and ruling. It is easy to understand why Barth speaks predominantly (although not exclusively) of the Church's witness. For him, the unicity and perfection of Christ's objective sacrifice and priesthood excludes the possibility of any participation in his priesthood or re-presentation of his sacrifice. Subjective reconciliation does not take place in this time between the times, but only its knowledge. Christ's apostolicity in this time between the times exists solely in its prophetic aspect. And in his explanation even this remains always Christ's own direct act.

I have said that the Church's apostolicity consists in its mission by Christ and in its fulfilment of this mission. How does it receive its mission from Christ? Barth says it receives it by the direct act of the Spirit in the word of Scripture, that is, in the word of the original apostles. This is certainly one of the ways in which the Church is 'apostolically' constituted. With its re-evaluation of the charismatic element in the Church Catholic ecclesiology is recognizing it more and more. In fact many see in it a possible way of solving the crux of the validity or invalidity of Protestant ministry and orders.[9] This should

[6] Cf *CTKB*, p. 282.
[7] *Ibid.*, pp. 283-4.
[8] Cf above, chapter thirteen, pp. 147f.
[9] Cf above, pp. 261f.

not however (in a way just as one-sided as the former Catholic insistence on succession and tradition) lead to a denial of apostolicity through apostolic succession of persons. I maintain that succession in the apostolate is also achieved through what is commonly called 'apostolic succession', that is, through an uninterrupted, historical, horizontal line of persons who have succeeded the original apostles in the fulfilment of the Church's mission.

Karl Barth protests strongly against this latter conception.[10] It is a denial, he says, of the freedom of the Holy Spirit in his creation of the community. It denies the spirituality of the Church's apostolicity, reducing it to a mere sociological and juridical criterion, and thus eliminating the necessity of the Holy Spirit and of faith. We can understand the vehemence of his protest, and if we thought for a moment that the Catholic view did in fact constitute such a denial our reaction would be no less vehement. However, I do not think that his accusation is just.

The basis of our difference with regard to apostolic succession lies basically in our differing conceptions of the role of Christ's human nature in the objective redemption, and of the Church's apostolicity of origin. I have already presented the clear biblical basis for both of these.[11] I believe that the Son of God accomplished the objective reconciliation as the incarnate Christ, and therefore that his human nature was salvifically active. As man he was full of grace and truth, filled with the Holy Spirit, and transmitted to others the power and spirit and life of God. For the accomplishment of subjective reconciliation he empowered his apostles through the gift of his Spirit to continue his mission to the ends of the earth and for all time. 'All authority in heaven and on earth has been given to me. Go therefore and make disciples of all nations, baptizing them . . . teaching them to observe all that I have commanded you; and lo, I am with you always, to the close of the age' (Mt 28:18–20).

Henceforth the Church is the Church of these apostles. Christ sent them forth once and for all. He founded and founds his Church in and through them. The Church of succeeding ages must come into contact with its *definitive apostolic origin*. St Luke sums up this concisely in his description of the New Testament community itself: 'And they devoted themselves to the apostles' teaching (*tē didachē*) and fellowship (*kai tē koinōnia*), to the breaking of bread (*kai klasei tou artou*) and the prayers (*kai tais proseuchais*).'[12] Since both the

[10] Cf *CTKB*, pp. 280f.
[11] Cf above, Section Two, chapter six, and Section Three, chapters thirteen to fifteen.   [12] Acts 2:42. Cf Rev. 21:41.

time and sphere of activity of those to whom Christ actually spoke was limited, he must have seen in the 'you' all those who would carry on their mission to the end. The apostles must see to it that their mission continues. Henceforth they are responsible. The execution of their mission in the power of Christ is not a control of Christ or of his Spirit but a humble obedience to his free command.

In fact, it is the Holy Spirit, who has been given to the apostles, who transmits himself. He is the sole ultimate principle of apostolic succession. He does not always act alone and directly. He acts in and through the apostles. He has been gifted to the apostles. What he does he does through them, and what they do is actually done by him. The Holy Spirit and the apostles form but one divine-human salvific principle. Multiple instances are witnessed to by Scripture. Christ sends his apostles to continue his own mission, grants them his Spirit, and tells them that what they do is done by the Spirit. 'As the Father has sent me, even so I send you. . . . Receive the Holy Spirit. If you forgive the sins of any, they are forgiven. . . .'[13] The execution of their mission is an act of the apostles themselves, but it is an act in the power of the Spirit. Again, Jesus took bread and wine, gave it to his disciples, and said: This is my body and blood. Do this in remembrance of me.[14] The apostles fulfil his command in the communities and the bread eaten and the wine drunk is the body and blood of the Lord. 'Whoever, therefore, eats the bread or drinks the cup of the Lord in an unworthy manner will be guilty of profaning the *body and blood* of the Lord.'[15]

The apostles lay on their hands and the Spirit is given. Barth interprets this[16] to mean that the Holy Spirit is free to execute and transmit the apostolic mission, or to give himself, also through the laying on of hands. But he is also free not to. What is important is that it is always his *direct act alone*. He has not been given to the apostles with the promise that certain actions and words of theirs are infallibly his actions and words. The power of the Spirit never belongs to the apostles. This is a mono-actualism which, I must say once more, cannot be reconciled with scripture. 'Then they laid their hands on them and they received the Holy Spirit. Now when Simon saw that the Spirit was given through the laying on of the apostles' hands, he offered them money, saying "Give me also this power, that any one on whom I lay my hands may receive the Holy Spirit".'[17]

[13] Jn 20:21–23. [14] Lk 22:19–20.
[15] I Cor 11:27.
[16] Cf *CTKB*, pp. 280f.
[17] Acts 8:17–19. Cf 9:17f; 5:32; 15:28; Jn 15:26–27.

Through Christ's gift of his Spirit to them the apostles confer the gift of the Spirit. This is quite clear in the text just quoted. If one refuses *a priori* to admit this, there can be no talk of an instituted apostolic succession through persons. For apostolic succession is simply the transmission of Christ's power and mission through the laying on of hands, that is, in the actual exercise of the power and mission given by Christ. Paul writes to Timothy: 'Command and teach these things. . . . Till I come, attend to the public reading of Scripture, to preaching, to teaching. Do not neglect the gift you have, which was given you by prophetic utterance when the elders laid their hands upon you.'[18]

This is an obvious illustration of how the original apostles sought to fulfil the Lord's command to make disciples 'of all nations to the close of the age'. As a Calvinist exegete remarks: 'If Timothy and Titus are not apostles like Paul, nor could they possibly be so, none the less they are his successors in the building up of the Church, and they themselves will have successors. . . .'[19]

The power with which these men act is not their own in the sense that it originated in them. It is a pure gift and task of the Holy Spirit. 'Receive the Holy Spirit. . . . You shall receive power when the Holy Spirit has come upon you. For we are weak in him, but in dealing with you we shall live with him by the power of God.'[20] The Holy Spirit is therefore absolutely necessary. Without him they can do nothing. Barth is not correct in accusing Catholic doctrine of denying this necessity of the Spirit. The unjustness of his accusation is emphasized by Catholic teaching with regard to sacramental causality. Christ alone is the principal cause of the Church's priestly and sacramental acts—and apostolic succession is sacramental.[21]

Certainly there has been too much insistence from the Catholic side on the visibility and historical demonstrability of apostolic succession as an apologetic note of the Church's apostolicity. Furthermore, since the First Vatican Council, this note, and therefore the other three, has been subjected to the word *Romana*, that is, to the primacy of the pope. As Barth correctly points out,[22] the word *Romana* does not stand in the Creed of 381. The whole of apostolicity does not reside in Peter and his successors, nor does it come from

[18] I Tim 4:11, 13–14. Cf II Tim 1:6; Tit 1:5; Heb 6:2.
[19] P. Menoud, *L'Eglise et les ministères selon le Nouveau Testament* (Cahiers théologiques de l'actualité protestante, 22), Neuchâtel–Paris, 1948, pp. 51f.
[20] Jn 20:22; Acts 1:8;; II Cor 13:4.
[21] Cf above, chapter fifteen, art. II, 4.
[22] Cf *CTKB*, p. 279.

them. Vatican I from this point of view has been corrected or complemented by Vatican II. Apostolic succession is primarily collegial under and with one head, that is, it is the succession of the college of bishops with the pope as head to the college of apostles with Peter as head. Vatican II has complemented many other aspects of the Catholic Church's doctrine of apostolicity as well, chief among them being its reminder that apostolicity is above all a spiritual reality and service, that its transmission is sacramental, and that it is a description and predicate of the *whole* Church, and not exclusively of the Church's hierarchical ministry.

The Church's apostolicity is primarily a spiritual predicate which can only be believed. It consists in the present Church's participation, through the Holy Spirit, the original apostles and their successors, in Christ's own mission from the Father. Since the mode of its participation in Christ's mission, and its actual exercise of the mission entrusted to it by the incarnate Christ, is sacramental, its invisible apostolicity has also a visible character which can be historically determined. But this historical determination does not prove the Church's *predicate* of apostolicity. As a dogmatic predicate the Church's apostolicity can only be believed. The determination of the Church's apostolicity as an apologetic note only shows the reasonableness of faith in its apostolicity as a dogmatic predicate. It shows that faith in the Word of God announcing and conferring on the Church a participation in Christ's own mission does not contradict the rational nature of the man who believes.

Apostolicity as a predicate of the Church denotes *its existence as that which is sent in the fulfilment of its sending*. It denotes, above all, its spiritual participation in Christ's spiritual mission. The means by which it participates in Christ's mission, namely, its connection with the past through apostolic succession, is only secondary. A person who is sent does not keep for ever looking backwards, but goes about his task with an eye to the way ahead. Otherwise, like Lot's wife, he is in danger of complete immobilization, and of disservice to his sender.

Apostolic succession must not be regarded as the handing on from person to person of an immobile and immutable gift, which has to be guarded and defended at all costs. It is much more a task which has to be accomplished at all costs—the dynamic participation in Christ's triple messianic prophetic, priestly and kingly task. This becomes clear when we remember that apostolic succession is not something which takes place outside or above the Church, and from there keeps the Church in conformity with its origins. Nor is it something which is additional to its being or mission. *Apostolic succession takes place in the fulfilment of the Church's apostolicity.* It is taking place here and now, and all over the world, because the Church, the whole Church, is engaged in the threefold task of its mission. Apostolic succession takes place in the fulfilment of the Church's mission from the ascension to the *parousia*.

Apostolic means 'in the discipleship, in the school . . . of the apostles . . . because listening to them and accepting their message'[23] only in so far as there are living human successors who safeguard and proclaim this word. Christ did not commit his mission to a word, but to his human apostles. Barth, possibly more consistently, certainly more drastically, goes further than the usual Protestant conception of apostolicity. For him, it is not simply the authoritative continuity of the apostles' written word. It is always the apostolicity of Jesus Christ himself alone. Thus the community has not to subject itself to the witness of the apostles, but to Jesus Christ himself who speaks through their witness.[24] This is a christological constriction which leaves very little room for any true ecclesiology.

No, apostolic succession is the succession of living person to living person. These persons are not in any way lords of the community. They are the servants, the emissaries, of Jesus Christ. As Barth so beautifully puts it, apostolic succession cannot consist in any other authority than that of service.[25] In the accomplishment of its mission, in the fulfilment of its task, Christ himself is present and continually sends his Church anew. It is in and through this *sending* (apostolicity) of the Church that Christ the head *unifies* (unity) all things in the *fulness* (catholicity) of his *holy* life (sanctity).

The Church is one, holy and catholic only because it is apostolic. In so far as it fulfils, and ever more perfectly fulfils, its apostolicity (mission, triple ministry) it is, and becomes ever more perfectly, one, holy and catholic. Apostolicity is the predicate of the Church which denotes its existence as that which is sent in the fulfilment of its existence, in identity with the original apostolic Church, through the mediation of its mission by apostolic succession. In the exercise of its apostolicity from the present Christ, in identity with the apostolicity of the original Church and of the intervening Church, the present-day Church is, and is ever more fully, one, holy and catholic.

---

[23] Cf *CTKB*, p. 279.
[24] Cf *ibid.*, pp. 282f.
[25] Cf *ibid.*, p. 282.

Chapter Twenty-Six

The Church is Eschatological

THE consideration of apostolicity as the Church's continual movement *from* leads us naturally to a consideration of its movement towards. In my exposition of Karl Barth's doctrine on the eschatological Church I have grouped together two problems which he considered separately, namely, the Church's eschatological tension, and the meaning of the Church's time.[1] The two are, of course, intimately connected. They present us with an overall view of the Church's history from Christ, in Christ, and to Christ. Once again we must admire the clarity, simplicity and breadth of vision of Barth's presentation of this general panorama of the Church.

In my dialogue with Karl Barth I shall begin with an investigation of the Old and New Testament concept of the 'kingdom of God'. It is a theme of primary importance in the whole of Scripture. In the Gospels alone we find it, or its equivalent 'kingdom of heaven', mentioned eighty-two times. The preaching of the 'Gospel of the kingdom of God' formed the object both of Jesus' own mission,[2] and of the mission of his disciples.[3]

In the Old Testament God was experienced and acknowledged as king in his actual kingly leadership and reign over Israel and over the whole world.

'Who is like thee, O Lord, among the gods? Who is like thee, majestic in holiness, terrible in glorious deeds, doing wonders? Thou hast led in thy steadfast love the people whom thou hast redeemed, thou hast guided them by thy strength to thy holy abode. The Lord will reign for ever and ever. . . . The voice of the Lord is upon the waters; the God of glory thunders. The voice of the Lord is powerful . . . is full of majesty . . . breaks the

---

[1] Cf *CTKB*, ch. 18. He treated the first aspect especially in his *C.D.* III/2 and the second in vol. IV, as the references given indicate.
[2] Cf Lk 4:43; 8, 1; Mt 4:23; 9:35.
[3] Cf Lk 9:2, 60.

cedars . . . shakes the wilderness. . . . The Lord sits enthroned as king for ever.'[4]

God is king in his active rule and leadership. The sphere of his kingship is occasionally termed kingdom.[5]

Already ruling over Israel and the world, God promises a new salvific and judicial intervention in the future through his Messiah.

'Behold my servant, whom I uphold, my chosen, in whom my soul delights; I have put my Spirit upon him, he will bring forth justice to the nations. . . . In those days Judah will be saved . . . the eyes of the blind shall be opened, and the ears of the deaf unstopped. . . . He will execute judgment among the nations. . . . He will feed his flock like a shepherd. . . . Your eyes will see the king in his beauty.'[6]

Corresponding to this new intervention there will be a new people of God. This people will be characterized by universality, by interiorness, by the knowledge of God, by the forgiveness of sins, by peace, plenitude and joy.[7]

Then 'Jesus came into Galilee, preaching the Gospel of God, and saying, "The time is fulfilled, and the kingdom of God is at hand (*ēggiken*), repent and believe in the Gospel." '[8] He gathered disciples around him and sent them out to preach 'the kingdom of heaven is at hand'.[9]

The kingdom is 'at hand' in the person of Jesus himself. As Barth says,[10] the kingdom of God is his lordship established in the world in Jesus Christ, the rule of God as it takes place in him. As Origen said, Christ is the *autobasileia*, that is, the kingdom in person.[11] 'Jesus' preaching of the reign of God and his salvific activity are not independent realities, but grow to form one unity and together attest

[4] Ex 15:11, 13, 18; Ps 29:3, 4, 5, 8, 10. Cf Ps 105; 23:7f; 104; 96; 97; 93. In the Old Testament the Word of God is the expression of God's sovereignty and notification of his reigning will. Cf Eichrodt, *Theol. des A.T.*, II/III, Stuttgart, 1961, pp. 41–2.

[5] G. von Rad (in *TWNT*, I, p. 569) refers to Ps 103:19; 145:11, 13; Dan 3:33. In the Old Testament, the term 'kingdom of God' is rarely used. God's kingdom is conceived as his actual kingly rule. It was only in Jewish postbiblical literature that the verbal propositions of the Old Testament (e.g. 'God rules') were replaced by abstract concepts (e.g. 'The reign of God'). Cf Kuhn, in *TWNT*, I, p. 570.

[6] Is 42: 1; Jer 33:16; Is 35:5; Ps 110:6; Is 40:11; 33:17.

[7] Cf Jer 31:31–34; Is 11:1; 2:2f; 19: 18–25; 41:18–20; 52:7; 35; 51:3, 11; Ps 97.   [8] Mk 1:14–15. Cf Mt 4:17.

[9] Mt 10:7; Lk 10:9, 11.   [10] Cf *CTKB*, p. 346.

[11] Origen, *Comment. in Matth.*, 14, 7 (*PG*, 13, 1197).

the eschatological happening which was event in him.'[12] Jesus is himself fully aware that the fulness of divine power has been given to him, and that God's reign, in both its salvific and judicial aspects, is breaking through in his actions. 'But if it is by the finger of God that I cast out demons, then the kingdom of God has come upon you.'[13] The miracles of Jesus are the 'kingdom of God in acts'.[14] Hence Jesus can say: 'The kingdom of God is in the midst of you.'[15]

God's kingdom is his absolutely free, powerful and personal intervention in the course of human history. It denotes above all his kingly action, calling men to penance and forcing them from the power of Satan. It results in the creation of a people who hear and obey his call and are liberated by him.[16] In Jesus it is already present, and those who come within the sphere of his action already participate in its blessings. But, as Barth again points out,[17] Jesus, and with him his disciples, continued to look forward to a future manifestation of the kingdom. The kingdom is present, yet not in its full manifestation. It is future, yet already breaking into the present.[18] Jesus predicted a future coming of the kingdom in two senses: (i) as coming within the present generation; and (ii) as coming at the end of the world. We must now examine these predictions more closely.

'Truly, I say to you, there are some standing here who will not taste death before they see the kingdom of God come in power.'[19] This obviously refers to an imminent coming of the kingdom. So do other texts of the Gospels. 'When they persecute you in one town, flee to the next; for truly, I say to you, you will not have gone through all the towns of Israel, before the Son of man comes.'[20] To

[12] R. Schnackenburg, *God's Rule and Kingdom*, pp. 123–4. Cf Schmidt, in *TWNT*, I, pp. 590–1.

[13] Lk 11:20; Mt 12:28. The aorist *ephthasen* can only mean 'has actually come'. Cf Schnackenburg, *op. cit.*, p. 124. Cf Jn 3:16–21; 12:31; Mt 3:10, 12; 23:13.

[14] L. de Grandmaison, *Jésus-Christ. Sa personne, son message, ses preuves*, vol. II, Paris, 1928, p. 366.

[15] Lk 17:21. Cf Mt 11:12–13 and Lk 16:16. Cf A. Feuillet, in *Introd. à la Bible* (ed. by Robert and Feuillet), vol. II, pp. 777f.

[16] Cf Feuillet *op. cit.*, pp. 774–5, 801; Cullmann, *Peter—Disciple . . .*, pp. 201f.   [17] Cf *CTKB*, pp. 343f.

[18] With the school of 'realized eschatology', against that of 'consequent eschatology', we must assert a present realization of the kingdom in Jesus. But with the latter, against the former, we must assert a future and fuller realization of the kingdom. For the various trends of Schnackenburg, *op. cit.*, pp. 114f.

[19] Mk 9:1 (Mt 16:28; Lk 22:69).

[20] Mt 10:23. Cf also Mt 26:64 (Mk 14:62; Lk 22:69); Mt 26:29 and Lk 24:35.

what do these texts refer? For long they have been disputed amongst exegetes. I believe that the solution adopted by Barth is the best, namely, that the synoptists, and Jesus himself, view the coming of the kingdom as one event, but one which takes place in different forms and moments. This conforms with the active conception of the kingdom which we have seen to be that of the Old Testament. Thus the texts I have just cited refer to the transfiguration, resurrection, sending of the Holy Spirit, and to the final *parousia*, for it is imminent in an anticipatory way in these other events and even imminent in a final consummatory way in a certain sense.

That they refer directly to the scene on the mount of transfiguration seems to be the mind of Mark, for he goes on immediately to narrate it.[21] On that occasion Jesus' face 'shone like the sun, and his garments became white as light', and Peter, James and John 'were eyewitnesses of his majesty', and 'made known the power and coming of our Lord Jesus Christ'.[22] However, the above texts do not refer solely to the transfiguration. Immediately afterwards, on the way down from the mountain, Jesus himself points forward to his resurrection. 'Tell no one the vision, until the Son of man is raised from the dead' (Mt 17:9). By his resurrection Jesus was designated 'Son of God in power' (Rom 1:4). In it the future coming has already begun, is already a reality. It involves both a judgment on unfaithful Israel, and the extension of salvation to all nations.[23]

But even the risen Christ, and in obedience to him his disciples, still look forward to another manifestation of his power, namely, the coming of the Holy Spirit. Paul speaks of the kingdom in terms of the Holy Spirit and of power: 'For the kingdom of God does not mean food and drink but righteousness and peace and joy in the Holy Spirit.'[24] Jesus had promised his Spirit of power: 'And behold, I send the promise of my Father upon you; but stay in the city, until you are clothed with power from on high. . . . But you shall receive power when the Holy Spirit has come upon you; and you shall be my witnesses. . . .'[25] This, again, is an imminent coming. From the right hand of God Christ pours out his Holy Spirit on his apostles, and in and through them 'many wonders and signs are done'.[26]

[21] Mk 9:2-8 (Mt 17:1-8; Lk 9:28-36; II Peter 1:16-18).
[22] Mt 17:1-2; II Peter 1:16.
[23] The rending of the temple veil (Mt 21:51f), the giving of the kingdom to a nation producing its fruits (Mt 21:43; 22:1f), the destruction of the temple (Mt 23:36-24:2 and par.), for example.
[24] Rom 14:17. Cf I Cor 4:20.
[25] Lk 24:49; Acts 1:4-5; 1:8.
[26] Acts 2:43. Cf 2:3, 6f; 11:19-26; Rom 15:19.

In all these senses Jesus proclaimed that his kingdom was 'at hand', imminent, to come within his own generation. But he also proclaimed it as coming at the end of the world, and imminent in the sense that the time of this final coming is known only to the Father, and therefore can take place at any moment. Unlike contemporary Jewish apocalyptic Jesus was not concerned so much with the exact day or hour of this final coming but with the necessity on man's part to repent and believe, to make his concrete decision for God and his reign (cf Mk 1:15).

'Men of Galilee, why do you stand looking into heaven? This Jesus, who was taken up from you into heaven, will come in the same way as you saw him go into heaven. . . . But of that day or that hour no one knows, not even the angels in heaven, nor the Son, but only the Father. . . . Watch therefore, for you do not know on what day your Lord is coming. . . . At the close of the age the Son of man will send his angels, and they will gather out of his kingdom all causes of sin and all evildoers, and throw them into the furnace of fire. . . . Then the righteous will shine like the sun in the kingdom of their Father.'[27]

Again, therefore, while the kingdom is a present reality through the Spirit in the time of the Church, we keep on praying 'Thy kingdom come', and yearn for its definitive and final coming at the consummation of the world in Christ's *parousia*.

I agree, therefore, with the general lines of Karl Barth's understanding of the kingdom of God sayings in Scripture. The future manifestation of the kingdom was viewed as one event but as taking place in different forms or moments. Hence I agree with him also in his rejection of all absolute and 'consequent' eschatology.[28] The futurity of the kingdom of God, and its imminence, cannot be limited solely to its definitive and final manifestation, when the consummation of all things will take place. We must say this if we are to do justice to the totality of Scripture texts regarding the kingdom, and regarding Christ's mission of his apostles to make disciples of all nations to the close of the age.[29]

The time of the community is the time of Christ's coming in the

[27] Acts 1:11; Mk 13:32 (Acts 1:7); Mt 24:42; 13:40–43.
[28] Cf *CTKB*, pp. 343–4, 348–9.
[29] Cf above, chapter ten. I have mentioned there some current upholders of 'consequent' eschatology. For the modern position, discussion and literature on the subject cf B. Rigaux, 'La seconde venue de Jésus' in *Recherches Bibliques*, VI, 173–216.

form of his Spirit, this is in an intermediary form between his resurrection and *parousia*.[30] The time of the community is, as Barth often says, the 'time between the times' of Christ's ascension and final coming.[31] It is the last time, the eschatological time *par excellence*, because it has its end before it, within it, and after it. It is an otherworldly and this-worldly reality in one because of the presence in it of Jesus Christ who sits at the right hand of the Father and is the beginning and end of all things (Rev 21:6).

What is the meaning of this last time? It is the time of the subjective realization of reconciliation. It is the time in which Christ continues to fulfil his mission from the Father, that is, the time in which he continues to execute God's 'plan for the fulness of time, to recapitulate all things in him, things in heaven and things on earth' (Eph 1:10). From the point of view of the Church it is the time of its *mission* in his service and of its execution of its mission. The whole meaning of its time is mission. It has time because it is sent by Christ to minister to him. It is sustained in time because it is sent. The Holy Spirit is the vital force behind and within it. He is the eschatological gift sent into it from the depths of transcendence and the Church's own future. Because of him it exists as the eschatological Church. It is transported into the *eschaton*. It exists 'in Christ Jesus'. It is an other-worldly and this-worldly reality in one. The indwelling Spirit drives it continually upwards and therefore forwards to the final consummation. Christ the *alpha*, the one, must become the *omega*, the many. He does so through his Spirit who is the vital force hurtling the Church through space and time from the resurrection to the *parousia* in the accomplishment of its mission. The time of the Church is, therefore, the incarnation or 'temporalization' of Christ's continuing execution of his mission from the right hand of the Father.[32]

Karl Barth considers this time more from the point of view of the individual Christian. I agree with him in general but none the less think there are points which reflect the general weaknesses of his theology. What is the meaning of the individual's time? It is the means of his subjective reconciliation. It is the space given him for the free acceptance of faith and salvation and for continual growth in love for God and man (Eph 4:15). As Barth says, the existence of this time 'is due solely to the free grace of God'.[33] Its basis lies in the

---

[30] For Barth Christ's 'coming', *parousia* and 'kingdom' describe the same event. [31] Cf *CTKB*, p. 340.

[32] It involves, from the point of view of the Church, all that I have already said concerning its ministry and apostolicity.

[33] Cf *CTKB*, p. 339.

fact that 'He does not will to be man's reconciler over his head'.³⁴ But it is still 'over man's head' if all that is required is a mere 'human realization (in the sense of knowledge) and correspondence'.³⁵ Does subjective reconciliation really take place in this time between the times, or merely its knowledge and acknowledgment? Paul is unambiguous: 'We were buried therefore with him by baptism into death, so that as Christ was raised from the dead by the glory of the Father, we too might walk in newness of life' (Rom 6:4). We cannot avoid Paul's realism. We, here and now, actually die and rise again through the sacraments of faith. The function of baptism is not simply the granting of knowledge of our objective death and resurrection in Christ, or the mere human reflection of our objective death and resurrection in Christ.³⁶

Again, this time is one of pure grace. But presupposing God's will of saving all men objectively and subjectively it is not an 'extra' manifestation of the grace of God once the objective reconciliation is accomplished. The objective reconciliation is not yet the subjective. As he came to save all men objectively and subjectively, his work through his Holy Spirit is not simply an 'extra' and, as it were, superfluous demonstration of his glory. History after Christ is not simply 'surplus history'.³⁷ It is necessary for man's salvation. If salvation is not to take place over his head, man must have a say and responsibility in the matter. *This* is the greatness of God's grace. Salvation does not originate in man in any sense, but he must pronounce his yes to it and live it if it is to be *his* salvation. This is a *conditio sine qua non*. Hence time is given to him. He has time for continual conversion, for death and resurrection in Christ (Rom 6:2f), for fidelity to the life that is in him (Rom 6:11f), for growth in faith and love towards the head, Jesus Christ (Eph 4:15).

I do not think this actual subjective realization (not in the sense of knowledge alone) of reconciliation is clear in Barth's theology. I thus find it hard to understand how, in his view, our time and history is really a time of salvation. All this shows the weakness of his justification *sola fide*.

We can come at the problem from another angle, which will remind us of Barth's nearness to the doctrine of *apokatastasis*. He says the *parousia* is one and the same event in three different forms. This can be correctly understood, as we have already seen, and will see again

³⁴ *CTKB*, p. 342.
³⁵ *Ibid.*
³⁶ Cf *ibid.*, pp. 232f.
³⁷ *Ibid.*, p. 341.

in a moment. But I find it hard to say that 'the final judgment has already been pronounced'.[38] Certainly, a judgment on all mankind is pronounced in Christ's death and resurrection. But this judgment can scarcely be identified with the final judgment. The final judgment concerns man's correspondence to the grace that has been given to him in this time between. If one says, of course, that the existence of this time is an additional manifestation of God's glory, and its scope merely man's knowledge of what has taken place solely in Christ, then one must also say that the final judgment has already taken place. If, on the contrary, one says that Christ must realize or actualize subjectively in each free human individual his objectively perfect reconciliation then one must say that the existence of this time is a necessity—a necessity included in the grace of total reconciliation —and that the object of the final judgment will be man's free correspondence to Christ's subjective action. In this explanation neither history nor the final judgment is superfluous. Man's cooperation under, in and with grace, is the necessary condition of salvation. If this is not acknowledged then obviously the final coming of Christ can only be the definitive revelation of universal salvation. Everything is in danger of being decided beforehand. There is no distinction between Christ as the *alpha* and Christ as the *omega*. The Church moves from fulness to fulness, from *plērōma* to *plērōma*, as a ship on the ocean with Christ on either shore but invisible to it. We maintain that the *omega* is also the *alpha* in the sense that everything in the *omega* comes from the *alpha* as from its principle. But we also maintain that Christ as the *omega* is the *Christus totus*, that is, as including the totality of Christ and those who have actually lived his life. Christ as *alpha* is the *Christus totus* only in the sense that he represents all, and is the principle of the life of all. But the living of his life by all obviously adds some distinction. Human time and history has decisive conditional value for the fulfilment of God's plan. This is its meaning and value.

After this all too brief exposition of the nature and meaning of the Church's time and history we go on now to examine the relationship between the kingdom of God and the Church. In this question everything depends on our understanding of the presence of the Holy Spirit in this time between. Barth says it is always Christ's own 'direct and personal coming', no less than the resurrection and the *parousia*.[39] An indirect and historical connection is necessary, he says, but only in the service or as a garment of the 'true and direct connection'.

[38] *Ibid.*, p. 339.
[39] Cf *ibid.*, pp. 338-9.

The Holy Spirit is not given once and for all time to the Church. He does not intrinsically indwell his Church. The Church never has the Spirit. He always acts in ever new events. But he is really present in an earthly-historical form. Christ, who is the kingdom, is the being of the community in the form of his Spirit. Hence Barth says that the kingdom is the Church, but that the statement cannot be reversed.[40]

Here we are back on familiar 'Barthian' ground. We have already encountered the same idea explicitly in his doctrine on Christ the head and body.[41] I have also often outlined my basic difficulties with this position. I shall briefly touch on them again in this new perspective.

The question of the relationship of kingdom and Church is complex and very much discussed. There is a relationship between them, but it is not a relationship of identity. The kingdom is the origin, scope and goal of the Church's mission. It is present in some way in the Church as its creative power and life. To this extent we can say that the kingdom is the Church, and the Church is the kingdom. But it is better to say the Church is the Church and the kingdom is the kingdom.[42] The kingdom, as such, is a future reality. It is at the consummation of the world that the Church and the kingdom will be identical.

While the Church is still the pilgrim Church on earth, journeying towards its consummation, we can neither identify the kingdom with it, nor it with the kingdom. The first of these positions is that of Karl Barth. For him the kingdom is the Church, but the Church is in no way the kingdom. This position is based on his christological constriction or mono-actualism. The second position is attributed by Barth to the Catholic Church.[43] This would constitute a denial of Christ's future coming, and of the Church's eschatological tension. While Barth may have some grounds for his accusation in past expositions of Catholic ecclesiology he can hardly say that the ecclesiology of Vatican II constitutes such a denial.

We maintain that the Church shares already in the good things of God's kingdom. Jesus 'called to him his twelve disciples and gave them authority over unclean spirits, to cast them out, and to heal every disease and every infirmity'—which were exactly the things adduced by himself as signs of the presence of the kingdom.[44] In this

[40] Cf *CTKB*, p. 346.
[41] Cf above, chapter twenty.
[42] 'God's kingdom means God's powerful eschatological action. Basically it indicates the God who acts, who effects and gifts salvation. God's people, on the other hand, indicates the receiver of salvation': A. Vögtle, in *Sentire Ecclesiam* (Fest. H. Rahner), p. 63.
[43] Cf *CTKB*, pp. 349f.
[44] Cf Mt 10:1, 7–8; 12:28.

respect his words to Peter are significant: 'You are Peter, and on this rock I will build my Church, and the *powers of death* shall not prevail against it.' The overthrow of Satan and victory over death are precisely those signs invoked by our Lord for the demonstration of the presence of the kingdom.[45]

Again, Christ prays the Father 'to give another Counsellor, to be with you for ever . . . to dwell with you . . . to be in you'.[46] He himself gives to his disciples a share in his own Spirit and power, and promises another and more perfect participation in the near future.[47] At Pentecost 'they were all filled with the Holy Spirit', and performed 'wonders' and 'signs' in testimony.[48] The Holy Spirit guides the Church into the fulness of truth (Jn 16:13), furnishes it with hierarchical and charismatic gifts, and adorns it with the fruits of his grace.[49] The apostles go forth and preach the Gospel, baptize and guard their flock in the power of the Spirit.[50]

The Church is 'the fulness of him who fills all in all'.[51] God 'has delivered us from the dominion of darkness and transferred us to the kingdom of his beloved Son, in whom we have redemption, the forgiveness of sins'.[52] We are already 'sealed with the promised Holy Spirit, the guarantee of our inheritance', and so 'are God's children now'.[53] We are 'dead to sin and alive to God in Christ Jesus' by dying with him in baptism and partaking in his body and blood in the eucharist.[54] We are the temples of the Holy Spirit. 'Do you not know that you are God's temple and that God's Spirit dwells in you? . . . For God's temple is holy, and that temple you are.'[55]

Because of this permanent presence and activity of the Holy Spirit in and through it the Church can be termed 'the initial budding forth of the kingdom'.[56] Because 'the Holy Spirit was sent on the day of Pentecost in order that he might for ever sanctify it, the Church, or

---

[45] Cf Mt 12:28; 10:1, 7–8; Mk 3:22–27; Lk 10:17f.
[46] Jn 14:16–17.
[47] Cf Jn 20:22; Lk 24:29; Acts 1:8; Mt 16:18f; 28:18f; 18:18.
[48] Acts 2:19, 43; 3:6, 12; 4:7, 16.
[49] Eph 4:11–12; I Cor 12:4; Gal 5:22. Cf Vatican II, DCC, ch. I, n. 4.
[50] Acts 4:8, 31, 33; 8:17–19; 20:28.
[51] Eph 1:23.
[52] Col 1:13–14; cf Rom 8:10–11.
[53] Eph 1:13–14; I Jn 3:1–2; Rom 8:14–17.
[54] Rom 6; I Cor 12:13; 10:16–17.
[55] I Cor 3:16, 17; 6:19.
[56] DCC, n. 5. Or, the Church is the 'avant-garde of God', 'the outrider of the secular city of man', to put it in more secularized language. Cf H. Cox, *The Secular City*, pp. 144–8; J. C. Hoekendijk, *The Church Inside Out*, London, 1967.

in other words the kingdom of Christ now present in mystery, grows visibly in the world through the power of God'.[57] It is not only the Holy Spirit or Jesus Christ who grows on earth. It is the Church which grows, the human communion of saints sanctified by the Holy Spirit. The Church is really and intrinsically sanctified and performs holy actions, however ambiguously. Barth will not admit this because of his constriction of all divine holiness and holy activity to Jesus Christ. Hence he says that the kingdom is the Church, but the Church is in no way the kingdom.[58]

The Church of course must credibly re-present or existentially actualize this sign of the kingdom. Its representation cannot be completely ambiguous. The appeal to the promise and guarantee of the Spirit must be demonstrated existentially: by his fruits you shall know him and his dwelling place. Much of today's failure to accept the Church's witness stems precisely from itself: it does not credibly 'bud forth' the kingdom. The peace, holiness, justice, racial equality, mutual respect, truth, freedom and love which are the characteristics of the kingdom are simply difficult to find in a Church closed in upon itself.[59]

But the Church is not identical with the kingdom. Catholic theology in the past has over-identified the present reality of the Church with the kingdom, and this resulted in a theology of glory and triumph.[60] Barth's objections were not without foundation. Vatican II has returned the relationship to its true perspective, reaffirming that the Church exists in the service of the kingdom and that the kingdom is essentially an eschatological reality towards which the Church in this present aeon strives. 'The Church receives the mission to

[57] DCC, nn. 4 and 3. Cf Schnackenburg, *God's Rule and Kingdom*, p. 188.

[58] Because of the scriptural and conciliar texts given above I would not be prepared to go quite so far as Hans Küng on this matter when he says: 'The transcendental and eschatological character of the reign of *God*, as the reign of God, makes *any* identity or even continuity [between the Church and the kingdom] out of the question': *The Church*, p. 92 (I have italicized the word 'any').

[59] Hans Küng has some profound observations to make regarding the Church which really and credibly exists in the service of the kingdom, and not in its own service: cf *The Church*, pp. 96–104.

[60] 'It is better not to speak of the Church as a "manifestation of the kingdom of God" (B. Bartmann and others), or the "present form of God's kingdom" (E. Walter). . . . The Church is the community of those who wait for the kingdom of God, the "threshold of the kingdom" [Die Ekklesia ist die Gemeinde der Reich-Gottes Anwärter, die "Vorstufe der Basileia"] (J. Jeremias, *TWNT*, III, p. 750, n. 70)': R. Schnackenburg, *God's Rule and Kingdom*, pp. 224, 230–1 (original German, pp. 155, 160). Barth's main source of knowledge of Catholic theology was B. Bartmann.

proclaim and to establish among all peoples the kingdom of Christ and of God. . . . While she slowly grows, she strains towards the consummation of the kingdom and, with all her strength, hopes and desires to be united in glory with her king.'[61]

The Church is essentially eschatological. We can say, with Barth,[62] that it is a provisional representation of its eschatological reality. It is a representation because already it shares in the first fruits of the Spirit. But precisely for this reason, as Barth also points out,[63] it is only provisional.

'Having the first fruits of the Spirit we groan within ourselves (cf Rom 8:23) and desire to be with Christ (cf Phil 1:23). . . . By the power of the Gospel he [the Holy Spirit] makes the Church grow, perpetually renews her, and leads her to perfect (*consummatam*) union with her spouse. For the Spirit and the bride say to the Lord Jesus, "Come!" (cf Rev 22:17).'[64]

The final consummation of the kingdom is a future reality. The Catholic Church does not maintain that it has already taken place in itself.[65] On the contrary, it acknowledges its own existence as one of tension between an 'already' and a 'not yet'. And the realization of this tension is repeatedly finding acknowledgment in all aspects of its theological self-awareness.

'Christian existence is lived between an indicative and an imperative, between present and future; the Christian community also lives in this tension, as the body of Christ and the people of God, as consecrated and yet sinful; the Holy Spirit has been given to it, but only as a guarantee (II Cor 1:22; 5:5), as the first fruits (Rom 8:23); baptism and the Lord's Supper are at once remembrance of things past and anticipation of things to come. All this is unthinkable without the idea of a real future. . . .'[66]

The Catholic Church does not claim to invest itself with the authority of Christ, but seeks to execute as faithfully as possible the mission it has received from the one to whom all authority belongs. Its representatives may behave differently, and often have, but the Spirit has always been present, leading it into 'all the truth' (Jn 16:13). It does

[61] DCC, n. 5. Cf A. Feuillet, *op. cit.*, p. 801.
[62] Cf *CTKB*, pp. 340f.
[63] Cf *ibid.*, pp. 345f.
[64] DCC, nn. 48 and 4.
[65] Cf Karl Barth in *CTKB*, p. 349, and Vatican II, DCC, n. 48.
[66] H. Küng, *The Church*, p. 65.

not claim equal dignity for its tradition with the original apostolic witness. It is the 'sacrament of salvation', the 'sacrament of union with God',[67] *the sacrament of the kingdom.* The other world already breaks into this world in the sign of this worldly reality.

But precisely because it is a sacrament it is only a preliminary reality. In this time and world the reconciliation of Christ envisages the whole man, body and soul, and uses sacramental, visible, earthly-historical means, in correspondence with his own incarnate reality and the nature of man. But this world is transitory. It, and the whole human race, will be perfectly re-established in Christ in the *eschaton.*[68] There will then be no more need of sacramental mediation, since we will be like God, for we will see him as he is.[69] Thus the Church *as such,* in her sacraments and institutions, is a passing reality. 'It is herself she confesses as preliminary and destined for dissolution *(Aufhebung).'*[70]

'The final age of the world has already come upon us (cf I Cor 10:11). The renovation of the world has been irrevocably decreed and in this age is already anticipated in some real way. For even now on this earth the Church is marked with a genuine though imperfect holiness. However, until there is a new heaven and a new earth where justice dwells (cf II Pet 3:13), the pilgrim Church in her sacraments and institutions, which pertain to this present time, takes on the appearance of this passing world. She herself dwells among creatures who groan and travail in pain until now and await the revelation of the sons of God (cf Rom 8:19–22).'[71]

The Church will not go unscathed in the final consummation. None the less, it will not lose its identity. While the future reality of the Church will be again wholly and utterly the work of Jesus, I cannot agree with Barth in saying that it will be in no way identical or continuous with its earthly reality.[72] As he points out, the holy city, the bride adorned for her husband, the new Jerusalem, does not grow up from the earth but comes down from God out of heaven.[73] But this new Jerusalem is already a present reality in Jesus himself and, in some sense, in his Church on earth through his Holy Spirit. The

[67] Vatican II, DCC, ch. 7, n. 48; ch. I, n. 1.
[68] *Ibid.,* ch. 7, n. 48.
[69] *Ibid.,* n. 48; I Jn 3:2.
[70] O. Semmelroth, *Commentary on the Documents of Vatican II,* ed. by H. Vorgrimler, vol. I, p. 281.
[71] Vatican II, DCC, ch. 7, n. 48.
[72] Cf *CTKB,* pp. 347–8.
[73] Cf Rev 21:2; II Pet 3:13; Is 65:17.

coming down from God out of heaven is not limited to the future Church of the *eschaton*. God has already come down from heaven in his Son and Spirit. The *eschaton* has already broken into the present. The word used in the texts which describe the future heavenly Jerusalem is not *neos*, 'which signifies the newness of that which has recently arisen in time and was not there before', but *kainos*, 'which signifies the newness and peculiarity of something in comparison with another, that is, new in its mode of being (*der Art nach*), different from the usual, better than the old form'.[74] The final consummation is an absolutely gratuitous creation from above, but this new *aiōn*, the *eschaton*, has already broken into the present in Christ and through him in the Church.

This is clear from St Paul.

'Therefore, if anyone is in Christ, he is a new creation; the old has passed away, behold, the new has come. All this is from God, who through Christ reconciled us to himself and gave us the ministry of reconciliation. We beseech you on behalf of Christ, be reconciled to God.'[75]

Here we find expressed the whole meaning of the Church's existence and history. Reconciliation comes completely from God in Christ through the Spirit. But it becomes a subjective reality in man only when man 'lets himself' be reconciled. God does not wish to do anything for man without man's own acquiscence and cooperation. He does not wish to create the new heaven and the new earth without man himself already living in some imperfect way his reconciliation. This present subjective realization of reconciliation is above all the life of charity. And Paul says that charity remains (I Cor 15:8f).

It is precisely in her canonization and cult of the saints, especially in her cult of the Virgin-Mother of God, that the Church at the same time acknowledges her relationship and yet difference with the Church

---

[74] J. Behm, art. *kainos* in *TWNT*, III, pp. 450, 8f. Just as there is identity of subject between the man created by God and re-created by the grace of his Spirit, so also there is identity of subject in the final re-creation or consummation of men. The Acts of the Apostles (3:21) speaks even of the restoration of all things (*apokatastasis pantōn*). *Apokatastasis* means restoration, reestablishment, return to, or re-placement in, a former position (cf Liddell-Scott, *A Greek-English Lexicon*, Oxford, ⁹1961; W. Bauer, *Griechisch-Deutsches Wörterbuch*, Berlin, 1963: both *ad vocem*). The identity of subject would seem to be implied. Cf also very clearly St Jerome, *In Isaiam*, 1. 18, c. 65, 17–18: *Corpus Christianorum*, series latina, 73A, 760.

[75] II Cor 5:17–18, 20.

of the *eschaton*.⁷⁶ Witnessing to her saints in canonization she proclaims her present existence in the *eschaton*, she proclaims herself the 'Holy Church'. In her communion with these she acknowledges that 'we all, although in a different way and degree, partake in the same love for God and neighbour, sing the same hymn of glory to God, for all who belong to Christ, having His Spirit, form one Church and cleave together in him (cf Eph 4:16).'⁷⁷ But at the same time, in the same movement, she points upwards and forwards to a perfect realization of what she now is only imperfectly. Here and now she is the pilgrim Church, looking and moving forward with sighs and groans, towards what is to come. Her saints of the past point her upwards and forwards. They are the 'signs of his kingdom' who 'inspire us with a new reason for seeking the city which is to come (Heb 13:14; 11:10)'.⁷⁸

⁷⁶ Cf Vatican II, DCC, ch. 7, nn. 49–51; O. Semmelroth, in *Commentary on the Documents of Vatican II*, ed. by H. Vorgrimler, vol. I, pp. 282f; K. Rahner, 'The Church of the Saints' in *Theological Investigations*, vol. III, pp. 91–104.
⁷⁷ Vatican II, DCC, ch. 7, n. 49.
⁷⁸ *Ibid.*, n. 50.

Conclusion

IN concluding my two-volume study of Karl Barth's and Catholic ecclesiology I would like to point out briefly its basic results. The average pre-conciliar Catholic ecclesiological treatise would have very much to learn from Karl Barth. He brings out admirably the fact that the Church is primarily a *theological* and *spiritual* reality. It is the fundamental form of God's subjective creation of faith, love, hope and witness. Barth's insistence on the *theological aspect of ecclesiology* involves his converse insistence on the *ecclesiological aspect of theology*. The mystery of the Church is the whole Christian mystery. The Christian mystery is the mystery of the Church. Barth's ecclesiology is essentially christocentric, trinitarian, pneumatological, soteriological and eschatological. With few exceptions one would have to go back to the (pre-Tridentine) scholastics for a comparable ecclesiological profundity and breadth of vision. At the end of a study on 'the idea of the Church in St Thomas Aquinas', Fr Congar sums up in words which I reproduce here for their amazing aptness (*mutatis mutandis*, of course) to serve as a conclusion to a study of the idea of the Church in Karl Barth.

'The ecclesiological thought of St Thomas is so rich and there are in his works so many ecclesiological elements that, to fulfil our aim of studying his idea of the Church a whole treatise on the Church would have to be written. But it can hardly be too strongly emphasized that this treatise would be rather different from the treatises which are all descended from the *De regimine christiano* of James of Viterbo and the "Controversies" of Bellarmine. In reality everything in the thought of St Thomas has an ecclesiological reference and the author of an essay on his theology of the Mystical Body has gone so far as to say that this doctrine is the heart of his theology. The reason is that the Church is not a separate reality, but the very mystery—Christian, trinitarian, man-centred, Christ-centred, and sacramental—which is the subject of theology. So much is this true, that I am forced to ask myself if it be not a deliberate act on St Thomas' part that he has refused to write a separate treatise *De Ecclesia*, seeing that the Church pervaded his theology in all its parts. I am indeed inclined, personally, to think so. In any case, it must be obvious that if we are going to make up a treatise *De Ecclesia*, we must not concentrate on just those features of the Church which are *not theological*, but canonical, juridical and sociological. The more mystical approach of the Middle Ages needs to be supplemented by the insights of later times. But the chief task is to discover the ecclesiastical implications of all the other treatises: of the Trinity and the divine missions, anthropology and moral theology, christology and soteriology, the sacraments and the hierarchical ministry, etc. So we shall preserve, as St Thomas did, the full, large and undefiled Catholic tradition, the inspiration of the Fathers. That tradition can be characterized by three marks: the Church is contemplated as a Spirit-centred reality, as the body whose soul and principle of unity is the Holy Ghost. The Church is contemplated in Christ, as Christ is contemplated in the Church. And the inward Church is not separated from the outward Church, social, hierarchical and sacramental. I think no one will deny this to be the ecclesiology of the Fathers. And I hope that I may have proved it to be that of St Thomas Aquinas.'[1]

In the footsteps of St Thomas, Fr Congar's desires for the future Catholic ecclesiological treatise have been, to a great extent, repeated and programmed by Vatican II's Dogmatic Constitution on the Church. These also are the desires of Karl Barth. Vatican II has, therefore, in this respect, acknowledged and partly fulfilled the legitimate demands of Barth's ecclesiology. To put it another way: reflections on the ecclesiology of Karl Barth lead one naturally to the following trinitarian ecclesiological scheme outlined by Vatican II.

'All the elect, before time began, the *Father* "foreknew and *predestined* to be conformed to the image of his Son, in order that he might be the first-born among many brethren" (Rom 8:29). All those who believe in Christ, he planned to assemble in the holy *Church*, which already *prefigured* from the beginning of the world, *prepared* in a remarkable way in the history of the people of Israel and in the Old Testament, *established* in the last times, was *made manifest* in the outpouring of the Spirit, and at the end of time will be gloriously *consummated*. . . .

The *Son*, therefore, came on mission from the Father. . . . To carry out the will of the Father, Christ inaugurated the kingdom of heaven on earth, revealed to us his [the Father's] mystery, and by

[1] Congar, *The Mystery of the Church*, pp. 73-4 (*Esquisses* . . ., pp. 89-91).

his obedience brought about redemption. The Church, or the kingdom of God now present in mystery, by the power of God grows visibly in the world. . . . As often as the sacrifice of the cross in which "Christ, our paschal lamb, has been sacrificed" (I Cor 5:7) is celebrated on an altar, the work of redemption is carried on. At the same time, in the sacrament of the eucharistic bread, the unity of all believers who form one body in Christ (cf I Cor 10:17) is both expressed and brought about. All men are called to this union with Christ, who is the light of the world, from whom we proceed, through whom we live, towards whom we tend.

When the work which the Father had given the Son to do on earth (cf Jn 17:4) was accomplished, the *Holy Spirit* was sent on the day of Pentecost in order that he might for ever sanctify the Church, and thus all believers would have access to the Father through Christ in the one spirit (cf Eph 2:18). He is the Spirit of life, a fountain of water springing up to life eternal (cf Jn 4:14; 7:38-39). Through him the Father gives life to men who are dead from sin, till at last he revives in Christ even their mortal bodies (cf Rom 8:10-11). The Spirit dwells in the Church and in the hearts of the faithful as in a temple (cf I Cor 3:16; 6:19). In them he prays and bears witness to the fact that they are adopted sons (cf Gal 4:6; Rom 8:15-16, 26). The Spirit guides the Church into the fulness of truth (cf Jn 16:13) and gives her a unity of fellowship and service. He furnishes and directs her with various gifts, both hierarchical and charismatic, and adorns her with the fruits of his grace (cf Eph 4:11-12; I Cor 12:4; Gal 5:22). By the power of the Gospel he makes the Church grow, perpetually renews her, and leads her to perfect union with her spouse. The Spirit and the bride both say to the Lord Jesus, "Come!" (cf Rev 22:17).

Thus, the universal Church shines forth as "a people made one with the unity of the Father, the Son, and the Holy Spirit ".'[2]

This is Vatican II's essentially trinitarian programme for the future Catholic ecclesiological treatise. It still remains to be realized in the ecclesiological manuals. Despite their inadequateness, I hope that my reflections on the ecclesiology of Karl Barth may make some contribution, however small, to that more 'catholic' ecclesiological treatise desired by Vatican II. Any contribution made is, in the last analysis, the contribution of Karl Barth, for I only try to develop Catholic ecclesiology along the lines he suggests. Let this be the expression of my sincere admiration and gratitude to Barth for

[2] Vatican II, DCC, ch. I, nn. 2-4 (emphasis mine).

the truly spiritual, christological and trinitarian aspects of his thought.

In addition to the theological, christocentric and trinitarian aspects, Catholic ecclesiology can learn much from Karl Barth's dynamic-functional and response-witness ecclesiology. All these are intimately related. I have tried to satisfy his legitimate demands in this respect in the third section of my reflections. As the fundamental form of the participation in the divine triune *life*, and as the reality *sent* by Christ in continuation of his own mission from the Father to be his minister in the subjective actualization of the reconciliation of the whole world, the Church is essentially dynamic and functional. It (the *whole* Church) exists in the fulfilment of its threefold prophetic, priestly and kingly ministry. As Barth says: the Church is the living community of the living Lord Jesus Christ in the fulfilment of its existence.[3] Its existence is both a response to the Father's gift to it in Christ through his Spirit and the instrument of his gift to it and to the whole world. It is a response and a mediation, an acknowledgment of Christ's gift and the minister of his communication of his gift. It is the effective sign, the sacrament, of God's self-communication.

According to Karl Barth the Church is, essentially, the fundamental, that is, the communitarian, form of the subjective human response to, and reflection of, the direct act of the risen Christ through his Holy Spirit. I am in complete agreement with this statement as it stands—at least as the expression of one aspect of ecclesiology. But I insist that the response or reflection, despite its distance from that to which it is the response or reflection, takes place on the *basis of a participation in divine life and power*. In other words, the human Church is not a 'purely human' reflection of a 'divine Church'. It is intimately united in being and operation to the 'divine Church' so as to form one divine-human mystery. I do not think Barth safeguards this ontological and operational unity. This is my basic objection to his thought. It is but another way of saying that I think his ecclesiology manifests signs of both a 'Nestorianism' and a 'monophysitism'.

Despite profound agreements between Barth's and the Catholic Church's ecclesiologies there is this basic and all-pervading difference. While I have agreed with Barth that the Church is a creation from above, enjoys priority over the individual, is essentially missionary, functional and dynamic, I have had always to express misgivings with regard to this ontological participation of the human in the divine and the resultant salvific cooperation or sub-operation of the human under the divine in his theology. Everything in Barth's theology must be

[3] Cf *CTKB*, p. 251.

discussed on the level of christology, for his theology is christology, pure and simple. In fact it is too much so. I repeat my basic objection to his doctrine on the Church when I say that it is restricted or constricted, both ontologically and operatively, to Jesus Christ.

I have the same objection to make to his mariology, justification, doctrine of Scripture and theological method. According to him, the human Church *itself* does not participate in Christ's holiness and triple ministry so that it acts salvifically. The Mother of God is not ontologically sanctified so that she sub-operates in the work of reconciliation. The justified man does not receive the gift of God's grace so that he is intrinsically holy and can and must sub-operate in his own sanctification. The human word of Scripture is not in itself in some way the Word of God so that it mediates the Word of God. The light of faith does not become incarnate in the human mind and work through it so that the mind can grasp and express the knowledge of God.

Barth says all this because the Christ to whom he restricts all divine holiness and divine salvific operation is Christ as God. Barth himself clearly recognizes the intimate connection between the doctrine of christology and all the other aspects of theology. For the God-man is the basic incarnate factor, the basic sacrament of God's encounter with man. The nature of every encounter is determined by the nature of this encounter. In Barth's christology we meet the same divine monoactualism, or economic monophysitism, that we meet in his doctrine on the Church, our Lady, justification and Scripture. Barth's assertion of a *solely* divine salvific activity is the ultimate basis of all ecclesiological and other differences between his and Catholic theology.

It is not easy to determine the exact origin of this Barthian *solo Deo*. He himself would say that it owes its origin to the reality of the living person Jesus Christ, for he is the noetic basis of all theology. One wonders, however, whether the doctrine of justification is not its ultimate source. He himself acknowledges that the norm of true christology is justification.[4] Furthermore, he rejects the theology of 'and', not because of christology, but 'in view of the strong enough doctrine of justification'.[5] This would seem to be also the consistent application of his original interpretation of the relationship between God and man on the basis of an ultra-Calvinistic *soli Deo gloria*.

I certainly admit development in Barth's position on analogy, christology and justification. But I do not think (as von Balthasar and Küng do) that he has developed to such a Catholic position on

[4] Cf above, pp. 19-20, 238, 250.
[5] *C.D.* IV/3, I, p. 102 (=S. 113).

these points that his ecclesiological doctrine should be *logically* also Catholic. His development has been more on what God can do, and not on what he creates man to be, or on what he gifts to man. Barth's ecclesiological doctrine, and his consistency as a systematic theologian, bear me out in my interpretation. For his ecclesiology is not Catholic, and I would not like to accuse Barth of inconsistency! He has remained consistently faithful all through to the assertion of a solely divine salvific activity. His later all-pervading actualism is but the expression of this solely divine salvific activity and of his denial of a human salvific activity under God's action.

One could express the difference between the Barthian and Catholic conception of the economy of salvation by saying that the former is *solely theistic* while the latter is *theandric*. We should note that both are theistic. Catholicism, no less than Barth, rejects all Pelagianism and semi-Pelagianism in its doctrine on the Church, our Lady and justification. Barth's objections to it on this score (and they are his basic ones) do not actually touch it. I have tried to bring this out in my exposition of Catholic ecclesiology. Catholicism also asserts a *solo Deo, solo Christo, solo Spiritu, sola gratia*. But this *solo* does not exclude but includes the sub-operation of a human element through God's gift to it. The 'and' in God and man, grace and nature, Christ and the sacraments, faith and works, does not attribute an independent contribution to each, but asserts the divine incarnate *in*, and salvifically operative *through*, the human.

I am in wholehearted agreement with Karl Barth's recommendation for the resolution of the disunity of Christian Churches.[6] Jesus Christ must be placed in the centre, must be granted the power to reopen the problem of the one Church, and call in question the contrary plurality. He, the *living* Lord, must be allowed to speak to the Church of *today* in the witness of the prophets and apostles. The christocentric and biblical renewal in recent Catholic theology in general has led to a more 'complete' Catholic ecclesiology. The ecclesiology of Vatican II is an immense step forward in meeting the legitimate demands of a theologian like Karl Barth. The Church of Jesus Christ has nothing in common with pride, arrogance or triumphalism. It does not control its Lord, but exists solely in his service to the world.

On the other hand, a truly christocentric and biblical theology will have nothing to do with any preconceived idea of a *solely* divine salvific activity in the economy of salvation. I believe that Karl Barth (and he claims to give the consistent interpretation of Protestant

[6] Cf *CTKB*, pp. 270-1.

theology) neglects one aspect of revelation: the elevation of man and created reality to a participation in God's life and activity. His theology of 'response' and 'reflection' must be broadened to include a theology of participation, of 'sub-operation' and 'mediation'. It is not enough to insist on God's action in the man Jesus. One must insist also on the man Jesus' action in and under God. It is as man that Christ redeemed and redeems the world: the man for others. It is not enough to insist on Christ's act through his Spirit. One must insist also on the term of Christ's act, that is, on the gift of his free grace to man, on his creation of man to a participation in his own divine life and triple ministry. Then man's response is possible as the response *of man*. It is completely God's gift, and yet it is truly man's own holy and salvific act, because he participates in the life and activity of God. Insistence on both these aspects is necessary if Jesus Christ, the God-man, is really placed in the centre, and if he is to be allowed to question the plurality of Christian Churches.

We can say then that the Catholic Church can listen and has in great part already listened to the basic positive demands of Karl Barth. Its self-awareness as documented by its Second Vatican Council is trinitarian, christological, pneumatological, dynamic, open, joyous, charismatic, missionary, eschatological—all of which aspects are essentially Barthian. Karl Barth has not listened to the legitimate counter-demands made by the Catholic Church. He has refused and refuses to allow any real human participation in, and consequent salvific cooperation with and mediation of, divine life and salvation. In the case of Jesus Christ, our Lady, the Church and justification, God's presence and activity remain for him so transcendent that they never really become immanent as human life and action. This is due to a 'Christological constriction' or 'a divine economic mono-actualism', that is, the restriction or reduction of all salvific life and activity in the economy of salvation to Jesus Christ alone and as God. This in turn Barth considers to be the only logical, consistent and consequent position for a Protestant to adopt in the light of the original basic Lutheran principle of *sola fide* in conjunction with the original basic Calvinist principle of *soli Deo gloria*.

Modern Protestantism, as we have seen at various times in the course of this study, has gone beyond Barth to meet the demands of Catholicism in this regard, for example, in the questions of justification, Church ministry, apostolic succession, tradition, etc. The current 'death of God' and 'secularization' theologies are also, I believe, or will be, a step in this same direction. These imply or presuppose a certain immanence of God in man, human activity and created reality, which is foreign to pure Barthianism. May they not be regarded as a reaction to the otherness and transcendence of the Barthian God? I believe they may. It is interesting to note that the recent discussion in the 'death of God' and 'secularization' theologies has been mainly Protestant. They manifest more a problem of Protestantism than of Catholicism. The former, on the basis of the reformation principle of 'faith alone' (especially when this interpreted in the Barthian and Calvinist sense of 'by divine activity alone') always tended to detach religious reality from human and earthly activity, whereas there has always been a strong incarnational tendency in the Catholic doctrine of Jesus Christ, the Church and Christian life. Was it not to be expected that precisely because Barth represents the radical revival of the Protestantism of the reformers, there would be an incarnational and secular reaction?

Barth has contributed enormously to the recent renewal in Catholic theology, and especially in its theology of the Church. He epitomizes in fact many of the advances made by Vatican II. Its primary emphasis on Jesus Christ and the Holy Spirit in relation to the Church, its dynamic and joyful presentation of Christian life, etc, were already his. The Council, however, only barely outlined or intimated many of these aspects. For their full implementation in theory and practice in the post-conciliar Church we could have no better guide than Karl Barth. At the same time, post-Vatican II Catholic theology must go beyond Barth, especially in its development, in conjunction with modern Protestantism, of an evolutionary and secularized theology. But in doing so it, and all Protestant forms of secularized theology, would do well to begin from Barth and continually return to him, for then there will be no danger of theology's becoming once more a pure anthropology, humanism or cosmology. Barth's perennial service to theology, and especially in an age of secularization, will be his recall to the transcendence of God and the pure grace of his salvific action. In his footsteps transcendence will never be swallowed up in immanence. God must be allowed to become man, of course, but he must not be allowed to be substituted by man and the world.

Bibliography

A. OVERALL REFERENCE WORKS

Abbott, W. M.–Gallagher, J. (ed.), *The Documents of Vatican II*, New York–London–Dublin, 1966.
Barauna, G. (ed.), *La Chiesa del Vaticano II. Studi e commenti intorno alla Costituzione dogmatica 'Lumen Gentium'*, Florence, 1965.
Bäumer, R.–Dolch, H. (ed.), *Volk Gottes. Zum Kirchenverständnis der Katholischen, Evangelischen und Anglikanischen Theologie* (Festgabe für Josef Höfer), Freiburg–Basel–Vienna, 1967.
Burke, T. P. (ed.), *The Word in History*. The St Xavier Symposium, New York, 1966, London, 1968.
Butler, B. C., *The Idea of the Church*, London–Baltimore, 1962.
The Theology of Vatican II. The Sarum Lectures 1966, London, 1967.
Cerfaux, L., *La Théologie de l'Eglise suivant St Paul* (Coll. Unam Sanctam, 54), Paris, ³1965.
Congar, Y. M.-J., *The Mystery of the Church* (Translation by A. V. Littledale of *Esquisses du Mystère de l'Eglise* (Coll. Unam Sanctam, 8), Paris, ²1953, and of *La Pentecôte*, Chartres, Paris, 1956), London, 1965.
Sainte Eglise. Etudes et approches ecclésiologiques (Coll. Unam Sanctam, 41), Paris, 1963.
Cullmann, O., *Salvation in History*, London, 1967.
de Lubac, H., *The Splendour of the Church*, London–New York, 1956.
Catholicism. A Study of Dogma in Relation to the Corporate Destiny of Mankind, London–New York, 1950.
Dublanchy, E.–Hasseveldt, R., art. 'Eglise' in *DTC, IV*, 2108–24; Tables Générales, I, 1110–30.
Favale, A., et al., *La Costituzione Dogmatica sulla Chiesa*, Turin, 1965.
Feiner, J.–Löhrer, M. (ed.) *Mysterium Salutis. Grundriss Heilsgeschichtlicher Dogmatik*, 2 vols to date, Einsiedeln, 1966–67.
Flanagan, D. (ed.), *The Meaning of the Church*, Dublin, 1966.

Flannery, A. (ed.) *Vatican II: The Church Constitution*, Dublin, 1967.
Fries, H., *Aspects of the Church*, Dublin–Melbourne, 1965; Westminster, Md, 1966.
Hamer, J., *The Church is a Communion*, London, 1964.
Holböck, F.–Sartory, T. (ed.), *Mysterium Kirche in der Sicht der theologischen Disziplinen*, 2 vols, Salzburg, 1962.
Hordern, W. (ed.), *New Directions in Theology Today*, 7 vols, London, 1968.
Journet, C., *The Church of the Word Incarnate*, vol. I, New York, 1955; vol. II: *L'Eglise du Verbe incarné*, Paris, ²1962.
Küng, H., *Structures of the Church*, London, 1965.
The Church, London, 1967.
Le Guillou, M.-J.–Rahner, K.–Sauras, E., Art. 'Church' in *Sacramentum Mundi: An Encyclopedia of Theology*, vol. I, ed. by K. Rahner, C. Ernst and K. Smith, London–New York, 1968, 313–37.
McNamara, K. (ed.), *Vatican II: The Constitution on the Church. A Theological and Pastoral Commentary*, London–Dublin–Melbourne, 1968.
O'Rourke, J. J.–Lawlor, F. X., art. 'Church' in *New Catholic Encyclopedia*, vol. III, New York–London–Sydney, 1967, 678–93.
Peters, E. H. (ed.), *The Constitution on the Church of Vatican Council II*. Foreword by B. C. Butler, commentary by G. Baum, London, 1967.
Philips, G., *L'Eglise et son Mystère au deuxième concile du Vatican*, Tournai–Paris, 2 vols, 1968.
Rahner, K., *Theological Investigations*, 5 vols translated to date, Baltimore–London, 1961f.
Ratzinger, J., art. 'Kirche' in *LTK*, VI, 172–83.
Schillebeeckx, E., *Christ the Sacrament of Encounter with God*, London–New York, 1963.
Schlink, E., *The Coming Christ and the Coming Church*, New York–London, 1968.
Schmaus, M., *Katholische Dogmatik*, vol III/1, *Die Lehre von der Kirche*, Munich, 1958.
Schnackenburg, R., *The Church in the New Testament*, Freiburg–London, 1965.
Shook, L. K. (ed.), *Theology of Renewal*, Proceedings of the Canadian Centennial Theological Congress, 2 vols, New York–London, 1968.
Stanley, D. M., *The Catholic Church in the New Testament*, Westminster, Md, 1965.

Suenens, Card. L.-J., *Coresponsibility in the Church*, New York–London, 1968.
Sullivan, F. A., *De Ecclesia:* vol. I, *Quaestiones Theologiae Fundamentalis*, Rome, 1965.
Tavard, G., *The Pilgrim Church*, London–New York, 1967.
Vorgrimler, H. (ed.), *Commentary on the Documents of Vatican II*, vol. I, London–New York, 1967, 105–305: 'Dogmatic Constitution on the Church'.

B. CHAPTER ONE

Baum, G. (ed.), *The Future of Belief Debate*, New York, 1968.
Beumer, J., *Theologie als Glaubensvertändnis*, Würzburg, 1953.
Chenu, M.-D., *Is Theology a Science?* (Faith and Fact Books, 2), London, 1962.
Faith and Theology, Dublin, 1968.
Congar, Y. M.-J., art. 'Théologie' in *DTC*, XV, col. 341–502.
La Foi et la Théologie (Coll. Le Mystère Chrétien, Théologie Dogmatique I), Tournai–Paris, 1962.
Situation et tâches présents de la théologie, Paris, 1967.
Corcoran, P., 'The Influence of Existentialism on Contemporary Theology' in *IER*, 107 (1967) 105–113, 287–300; 108 (1967) 1–18.
Cox, H., *The Secular City. Secularization and Urbanization in Theological Perspective*, New York–London, 1965.
Dewart, L., *The Future of Belief. Theism in a World come of Age*, New York, 1966, London, 1967.
Lonergan, B., 'The Dehellenization of Dogma' in *Theol. Studies*, 28 (1967) 336–51.
MacQuarrie, J., *An Existentialist Theology*, London, 1965.
God-Talk. An Examination of the Language and Logic of Theology, London, 1967.
Maritain, J., *Existence and the Existent. An Essay on Christian Existentialism*, New York, 1961.
McHenry, F., 'Philosophy and the Renewal of Moral Theology' in *IER*, 107 (1967) 92–104.
'Philosophy and the Renewal of Dogmatic Theology' in *IER*, 108 (1967) 81–88, 214–226.
McLean, G. (ed.), *Christian Philosophy and Religious Renewal*, Washington, 1966.
Robinson, J. A. T., *Honest to God*, London, 1963.

Schillebeeckx, E., *Theological Soundings*: vol I/1, *Revelation and Theology*, London–Melbourne, 1967; vol I/2, *The Concept of Truth and Theological Renewal*, London–Melbourne, 1968.
Vatican II–A Struggle of Minds and other Essays, Dublin, 1963.
Van Buren, P.M., *The Secular Meaning of the Gospel*, London, 1963.

C. SECTION ONE: THE CHURCH OF THE FATHER

CHAPTER TWO

Beumer, J., 'Die altchristliche Idee einer präexistierenden Kirche und ihre theologische Auswertung' in *Wissenschaft und Weisheit*, 9 (1942) 13–22.
de Finance, J., 'La présence des choses à l'Eternité d'après les scolastiques' in *Archives de Phil.*, 19 (1956) 24–62.
Jocz, J., *A Theology of Election. Israel and the Church*, London, 1958.
Orbe, A., 'Cristo y la Iglesia en su Matrimonio anterior a los siglos' in *Estud. Eccles.*, 29 (1955) 299–344.
Rowley, H. H., *The Biblical Doctrine of Election*, London, 1964.
Schlier, H., 'Die Kirche als Geheimnis Christi (nach dem Epheserbrief)' in *Theolog. Quartalschrift*, 134 (1954) 385–96.

CHAPTER THREE

Barth, M., *Israel und die Kirche im Brief des Paulus an die Epheser* (Theol. Exist. heute, 75), Munich, 1959.
Baum, G., *The Jews and the Gospel: A Re-examination of the New Testament*, London, 1961.
Bover, J. M., 'La Reprobacion de Israel en Rom 9–11' in *Estud. Eccles.*, 25 (1961) 63–82.
Charue, A., *L'Incrédulité des Juifs dans le Nouveau Testament. Etude historique, exégétique et théologique*, Gembloux, 1929.
Demann, P., 'Israël et l'Eglise. Essais de Dialectique' in *Cahiers Sioniens*, 3 (1950) 1–16.
Les Juifs. Foi et Destinée, Paris, 1961.
Dinkler, E., 'The Historical and the Eschatological Israel in Romans chapters 9–11. A Contribution to the Problem of Predestination and individual Responsibility' in *Journal of Religion*, 36 (1956) 109–27.
Journet, C., *Destinées d'Israel. A propos du salut par les Juifs*, Paris, 1945.

Lyonnet, S., *Questiones in Epistulam ad Romanos. Series altera: De Predestinatione Israel et Theologia Historiae* (Rom 9–11), Rome, ²1962.
'De Doctrina predestinationis et reprobationis in Rom 9' in *Verbum Domini*, 34 (1956) 193–201, 257–71.
Munck, J., 'Israel and the Gentiles in the New Testament' in *Journal of Theological Studies*, new series, 11 (1951) 3–16.
Christ and Israel. An Interpretation of Romans 9–11, Philadelphia, 1967.
Peterson, E., *Die Kirche aus Juden und Heiden*, Salzburg, 1923.
Prat, F., *La Théologie de Saint Paul*, vol. I, Paris, ²1924, 300–21, 509–32.
Schlier, H., 'Das Mysterium Israels' in *Die Zeit der Kirche. Exegetische Aufsätze und Vorträge*, Frieburg i. Br., ²1958, 232–44.
Schmidt, K. L., *Die Judenfrage im Lichte der Kapitel 9–11 des Römerbriefs* (Theol. Stud., 13), Zurich, 1943.

CHAPTER FOUR

Beumer, J., 'Die Idee einer vorchristlichen Kirche bei Augustinus' in *Münchener Theol. Zeitschrift*, 3 (1952) 161–75.
Congar, Y. M.-J., 'Ecclesia ab Abel' in *Abhandlungen über Theologie und Kirche* (Festgabe für K. Adam), Düsseldorf, 1952, 79–110.
de Lubac, H., 'L'unité des deux Testaments' in *Exégèse Médiévale*, vol. I, 305-63.
Feuillet, A., 'Les ouvriers de la vigne et la théologie de l'Alliance' in *Rech. de Sc. Relig.*, 1947, 303–27.
Hofmann, A. M., 'Die Gnade der Gerechten des Alten Bundes nach Thomas von Aquin' in *Divus Thomas*, 29 (1951) 167-87.
Johnston, G., 'The Church and Israel. Continuity and Discontinuity in the New Testament's Doctrine of the Church' in *Journal of Religion*, 34 (1954) 26–36.
Philips, G., 'La grace des justes de l'Ancien Testament' in *Eph. Theol. Lov.*, 23 (1947) 521–56; 24 (1948) 23-58.
Pribilla, M., 'Die Kirche von Anbeginn' in *Stimmen der Zeit*, 117 (1929) 241–54.

CHAPTER FIVE

Baeck, L., *Das Wesen des Judentums*, Cologne, ⁶1960.
Baum, G., 'The Doctrinal Basis for Jewish-Christian Dialogue' in *The Ecumenist*, 6 (1968) 145–52.

Bea, Card. A., *The Church and the Jewish People: A Commentary on the Second Vatican Council's Declaration on the Relationship of the Church to non-Christian Religions*, London–Dublin, 1966.
de Quervain, A., *Das Judentum in der Lehre und Verkündigung der Kirche heute* (Theol. Exist. heute, 130), Munich, 1967.
Dix, G., *Jew and Greek. A Study in the Primitive Church*, London, 1955.
Eckert, W. P.–Ehrlich, E. L., *Judenhass—Schuld der Christen?*, Essen, 1964.
Foerster, F. W., *The Jews*, London, 1961–New York, 1962.
Gilbert, A., 'Jewish Resistance to Dialogue' in *Journal of Ecumenical Studies*, 4 (1967) 280–9.
Hedenquist, G., et al., *The Church and the Jewish People*, London–Edinburgh, 1954.
Kremers, H., *Das Verhältnis der Kirche zu Israel*, Düsseldorf, 1965.
Kummel, W. G., art. 'Judenchristentum' in *RGG*3, III, 967–72.
Lacoque, A., 'Israël, pierre de touche de l'oecuménisme' in *Verbum Caro*, 12 (1958) 331–43.
Lichtenberg, J.-P., 'Strength and Weakness of the Declaration on the Jews' in *Concilium*, 5 (1968), 69–74.
Louis-Gabriel, Sr, 'Jews and Christians after Vatican II' in N. Lash (ed.), *Doctrinal Development and Christian Unity*, London–Melbourne, 1967, 84–113.
Lousky, F., 'Remarques sur la notion de rejet par rapport au mystère d'Israël et l'unité de l'Eglise' in *Rev. d'Hist. et de Phil. Rel.*, 43 (1963) 32–47.
Marquardt, F.-W., *Die Entdeckung des Judentums für die christliche Theologie. Israel im Denken Karl Barths* (Abhandlungen zum christlich-jüdischen Dialog, ed. by H. Gollwitzer, I), Munich, 1967.
Marsch, W.-D.–Thieme, K. (ed.), *Christen und Juden. Ihr Gegenüber vom Apostelkonzil bis heute*, Mainz–Göttingen, 1961.
Richards, H. J.–De Rosa, P., 'The Crucifixion and the Jews' in *The Clergy Review*, 52 (1967) 257–75.
Schultz, H. J. (ed.), *Juden-Christen-Deutsche*, Stuttgart–Olten–Freiburg, 1961.
Studiorum Paulinorum Congressus Internationalis Catholicus, 1961 (*Anal. Bibl.*, 17–18), Rome, 1963.
Vogel, M. H., 'The problem of Dialogue between Judaism and Christianity' in *Journal of Ecumenical Studies*, 4 (1967) 684–99.
von Balthasar, H. U., *Martin Buber and Christianity: A Dialogue between Israel and the Church*, London–New York, 1962.

D. SECTION TWO: THE CHURCH IN THE SON

CHAPTERS SIX–SEVEN

Adam, K., *The Christ of Faith. The Christology of the Church*, London, 1957.
Benoit, P., *La Passion et la Résurrection de Jésus*, Paris, 1966.
Bertetto, D., *Gesù Redentore. Cristologia*, Florence, 1958.
Bonnefoy, J., *La primauté du Christ*, Rome, 1959.
Bouessé, H., 'Causalité efficiente et causalité méritoire de la Sainte Humanité du Christ' in *Rev. Thomiste*, 87 (1938) 256–98.
Bouessé, H.–Latour, J. J. (ed.), *Problèmes actuels de Christologie*, Paris, 1965.
Boyer, C., *De Verbo Incarnato*, Rome, 1948.
Brown, R., *Jesus God and Man*, London, 1968.
Carmody, J. M.–Clarke, T. E. (ed.), *Christ and His Mission. Christology and Soteriology* (Sources of Christian Theology, III, ed. by P. F. Palmer), Westminster, Md, 1966.
Catao, B., *Salut et Redemption chez Saint Thomas d'Aquin*, Paris, 1965.
Cerfaux, L., *Christ in the Theology of St Paul*, Freiburg, 1962.
Christus Victor Mortis (Terza Sett. Teolog., Greg. Univ., 23–7 Sept. 1957), in *Gregorianum*, 39 (1958) 201–524.
Comblin, J., *The Resurrection in the Plan of Salvation*, London, 1966.
Concilium, 1/2 (January 1966).
Congar, Y. M.-J.,*Jesus Christ*, London–Dublin–Melbourne, 1966.
'Considerations and Reflections on the Christology of Luther' in the same author's *Dialogue Between Christians. Catholic Contributions to Ecumenism*, London–Dublin, 1966, 372–406 (originally in *Das Konzil von Chalkedon*, vol. III., ed. by A. Grillmeier and H. Bacht, Würzburg, 1954, 457–86).
' "Dum visibiliter Deum cognoscimus..." Méditation théologique' in *Les Voies du Dieu Vivant*, Paris, 1962, 79–107.
Cullmann, O., *Christ and Time*, London, 1962.
The Christology of the New Testament, London, 1963.
Daniélou, J., *The Lord of History*, London, 1960.
Christ and Us, London, 1961.
De Rosa, P., *God Our Saviour. A Study in the Atonement*, London–Dublin–Melbourne, 1968.
Dupont, J., *La réconciliation dans la théologie de S. Paul*, Bruges–Paris, 1953.

Durrwell, F. X., *The Resurrection. A Biblical Study*, London–New York, 1960.
Feuillet, A., *Le Christ Sagesse de Dieu d'après les épîtres pauliniennes*, Paris, 1966.
Franzelin, J. B., *Tractatus de Verbo Incarnato*, Rome–Turin, 1869.
Galtier, P., *De Incarnatione ac Redemptione*, Paris, 1926.
Gogarten, F., *Jesus Christus, Wende der Welt*, Tübingen, 1966.
Grillmeier, A., *Christ in Christian Tradition*, London, 1965.
Gutwenger, E., 'Zur Ontologie der Hypostatischen Union' in *Zeit. für Kath. Theol.*, 76 (1954) 385–410.
Harl, M., *Origène et la fonction révélatrice du Verbe incarné*, Paris, 1958.
Henry, P., art. 'Kénose' in *DBS*, V, Paris, 1950, 7–161.
Holz, F., 'La valeur sotériologique de la résurrection du Christ' in *ETL*, 29 (1953) 609–45.
Kramer, W., *Christ, Lord, Son of God* (Studies in Biblical Theology, 50), London, 1966.
Latourelle, R., 'Révélation, Histoire et Incarnation' in *Gregorianum*, 44 (1963) 225–62.
Lécuyer, J., 'La causalité efficiente des mystères du Christ selon S. Thomas' in *Doctor Communis*, 1953, 91–120.
Lonergan, B., *De Verbo Incarnato*, Rome, 1960.
Malmberg, F., *Über den Gottmenschen* (Quaest. Disputatae, 9), Freiburg–Basel–Vienna, 1960.
Martin, R. P., *Carmen Christi. Philippians 2:5–11 in recent interpretation and in the setting of early Christian Worship*, Cambridge, Mass., 1967.
Mascall, E. L., *Christ, the Christian and the Church. A Study of the Incarnation and its Consequences*, London, 1946.
McIntyre, J., *The Shape of Christology*, Westminster, Md., 1966.
Mersch, E., *The Theology of the Mystical Body*, St. Louis–London, 1958.
Mooney, C. F., *Teilhard de Chardin and the Mystery of Christ*, London, 1966.
'New Thinking about Jesus Christ' in *Herder Correspondence*, 4 (1967), 213–21.
Pannenberg, W., *Jesus—God and Man*, London, 1968.
Rahner, K., 'Current Problems in Christology' in *Theological Investigations*, vol. 1, 149–200.
'The Eternal Significance of the Humanity of Jesus for our Relationship with God', *ibid.*, vol. 3, 35–46.

'Christology within an Evolutionary View of the World', *ibid.*, vol. 5, 157–92.
'Chalkedon—Ende oder Anfang?' in *Das Konzil von Chalkedon*, ed. by Grillmeier–Bacht, vol. III, 3–49.
Schmaus, M., art. 'Ämter Christi' in *LTK*, I, 457–9.
Gott der Erlöser (*Katholische Dogmatik*, II/2), Munich, ⁶1962.
Stanley, D. M., *Christ's Resurrection in Pauline Soteriology* (Anal. Bibl., 27), Rome, 1961.
Taylor, V., *The Person of Christ in New Testament Teaching*, London–New York, 1966.
Tschipke, T., *Die Menschheit Christi als Heilsorgan der Gottheit*, Freiburg im Br., 1940.
von Balthasar, H. U., *Word and Revelation and Word and Redemption* (Essays in Theology, vols 1 and 2), New York, 1964–65.
Vonier, A., *The Incarnation and Redemption* (The Collected Works of Abbot Vonier, I), London, 1952.
Witte, J. L., 'Die Christologie Calvins' in *Das Konzil von Chalkedon*, vol. III, ed. by Grillmeier–Bacht, 487–529.

CHAPTER EIGHT

Adam, K., *The Spirit of Catholicism*, London, 1939.
Alfaro, J., 'Cristo, Sacramento de Dios Padre: La Iglesia, Sacramento de Cristo Glorificado' in *Gregorianum*, 48 (1967) 5–27.
Congar, Y. M.-J., 'Dogme christologique et ecclésiologie: Vérité et limites d'un parallèle' in *Das Konzil von Chalkedon*, vol. III, ed. by Grillmeier–Bacht, Würzburg, 1954, 239–68 (also reproduced in Fr Congar's *Sainte Eglise: Etudes et approches ecclésiologiques* (Unam Sanctam, 41), Paris, 1963, 69–104).
Le Christ, Marie et l'Eglise, Bruges–Paris, 1952 (in English as *Christ, Our Lady and the Church*, London, 1956).
Geiselmann, R., 'Christus und die Kirche nach Thomas von Aquin' in *Theol. Quartal.*, 106–7 (1925–26) 198–222; 108 (1927) 233–55.
Mühlen, H., 'Das Verhältnis zwischen Inkarnation und Kirche in den Aussagen des Vatikanum II' in *Theologie und Glaube*, 55 (1965) 171–90.
Sartory, T., 'Die Gefahr der Kategorie des "Inkarnatorischen" für die Ekklesiologie' in *Ich glaube eine heilige Kirche* (Festschrift für D. H. Asmussen), ed. by W. Bauer, Stuttgart–Berlin–Hamburg, 1963, 64–79.

CHAPTER NINE

Coathelem, H., *Le parallélisme entre la Sainte Vierge et l'Eglise dans la tradition latine jusqu' à la fin du XIIe siècle* (Analecta Gregoriana, 74), Rome, 1954.
Congar, Y. M.-J., 'Marie et l'Eglise dans la pensée Patristique' in *Rev. des Sciences Phil. et Théol.*, 38 (1954) 3–38.
'Mary and the Church in Protestantism' in the same author's *Dialogue Between Christians. Catholic Contributions to Ecumenism*, London–Dublin, 1966, pp. 407–34 (originally in *Marie et l'Eglise* (cf below), 10 (1952) 87–106).
Edwall–Hayman–Maxwell (ed.), *Ways of Worship*. The Report of a Theological Commission of Faith and Order, London, 1951.
Flanagan, D., 'The Church and Our Lady' in D. Flanagan (ed.), *The Meaning of the Church*, Dublin, 1966, 144–64.
Hofmann, F., 'Mariens Stellung in der Erlösungsordnung nach dem Hl. Augustinus' in *Alma Socia Christi (Acta Congressus Mariani Romae anno sancto 1950 cel.)*, vol. V, Rome, 1952, 87–100.
Langemeyer, B., 'Konziliare Mariologie und biblische Typologie. Zum ökumenischen Gespräch über Maria nach dem Konzil' in *Catholica*, 21 (1967) 295–316.
Laurentin, R., *Court Traité sur la Vierge Marie*, 5e éd. réfondue à la suite du Concile, Paris, 1967.
Mary's Place in the Church, London, 1965.
Hémery, J. (ed.), *La Vierge Marie dans la Constitution sur l'Eglise* (Bulletin de la Société Française d'Etudes Mariales), Paris, 1965.
Maria et Ecclesia. Acta Congressus Mariologici-Mariani in civitate Lourdes anno 1958 cel., Rome, 1959, especially vols. II, III and VI.
Marie et l'Eglise. Bulletin de la Société Française d'Etudes Mariales, vols 9–11, Paris, 1951–53 (bibliography, *ibid.*, 9 (1951), 145–52, by R. Laurentin).
Müller, A., *Ecclesia-Maria. Die Einheit Marias und der Kirche* (Paradosis, 5), Fribourg in der Schw., ²1955.
Philips, G., 'Marie et l'Eglise. Un thème théologique renouvelé' in *Maria*, vol. 7, ed. by H. Manoir, Paris, 1964, 363–419 (cf bibliographical note, 418–19).
Rahner, H., *Our Lady and the Church*, London, 1961.
Sartory, T., 'Does Christ's Mother Divide Us?' in *Theology Digest*, Spring 1964, 14–18.
Schillebeeckx, E., *Mary, Mother of the Redemption: The Religious Bases of the Mystery of Mary*, London–New York, 1964.

Semmelroth, O., *Mary: Archetype of the Church*, New York, 1963.
Spiazzi, R., *Maria Vergine, Madre della Chiesa*, Assisi, 1966.
Thurian, M., *Mary, Mother of the Lord, Figure of the Church*, London, 1964.
Vollert, C., 'Mary and the Church' in J. Carol (ed.), *Mariology*, vol. 2, Milwaukee, 1957, 550–95.

E. SECTION THREE: THE CHURCH THROUGH THE HOLY SPIRIT

CHAPTER TEN

Betz, J., 'Die Gründung der Kirche durch den historischen Jesus' in *Theologische Quartalschrift*, 138 (1958) 152–83.
Braun, F. M., *Nuovi Aspetti del problema della Chiesa*, Brescia, 1943.
Coppens, J., 'L'Eglise, nouvelle alliance de Dieu avec son peuple' in *Aux origines de l'Eglise* (Recherches Bibliques, VII), Bruges, 1965, 13–22.
'L'Eucharistie, Sacrament et sacrifice de la nouvelle alliance, Fondement de l'Eglise', *ibid.*, 125–38.
Dupont, J., 'Jésus et las Païens' in *Rythmes du Monde*, 3 (1957) 76–88.
Feuillet, A., 'Les grandes étapes de la fondation de l'Eglise d'après les évangiles synoptiques' in *Sc. Ecclés.*, 11 (1959) 5–21.
'Le Regne de Dieu et la personne de Jésus d'après les evangiles synoptiques' in *Introd. à la Bible*, vol. II, ed. by Robert and Feuillet, Tournai, 1959, 771–818.
Grässer, E., *Das Problem der Parusieverzögerung in den synoptischen Evangelien und in der Apostelgeschichte*, Berlin, 1957.
Hahn, F. (ed.), *Die Anfänge der Kirche im Neuen Testament*, Göttingen, 1967.
Jeremias, J., *Jesus' Promise to the Nations*, London, 1958.
Kuss, O., 'Bemerkungen zu dem Fragenkreis: Jesus und die Kirche im Neuen Testament' in *Theol. Quart.*, 135 (1955) 28–55, 150–83.
Kümmel, W. G., 'Jesus und die Anfänge der Kirche' in *Studia Theologica*, 7 (1953) 1–27.
'Die Naherwartung in der Verkündigung Jesu' in *Zeit und Geschichte* (Festschrift für R. Bultmann), Tübingen, 1964, 31–46.
Promise and Fulfilment, London–Napier, Illinois, 1957.
Nepper-Christensen, P., *Wer hat die Kirche gestiftet?*, Uppsala, 1950.

Oepke, A., 'Der Herrenspruch über die Kirche in der neueren Forschung' in *Studia Theologica*, 2 (1948) 110–65.
Schlier, H., 'Die Entscheidung für die Heidenmission in der Urchristenheit' in *Die Zeit der Kirche*, Freiburg, ²1958, 90–107.
Schmid, J., *Das Evangelium nach Matthäus* (Regensburger N.T., 1), Regensburg, ⁴1959.
Das Evangelium nach Markus (Regensburger N.T., 2), Regensburg, ⁵1963.
Stanley, D. M., 'Kingdom to Church' in *Theological Studies*, 16 (1955) 1–29.
Vögtle, A., 'Der Einzelne und die Gemeinschaft in der Stufenfolge der Christusoffenbarung' in *Sentire Ecclesiam* (Festschrift für H. Rahner), Freiburg, 1961, 50–91.
'Jesus und die Kirche' in *Begegnung der Christen* (Festschrift für O. Karrer), Stuttgart–Frankfurt, ²1960, 54–81.
'Exegetische Erwägungen über das Wissen und Selbstbewusstsein Jesu' in *Gott in Welt* (Festschrift für K. Rahner), vol. I, Freiburg, 1964, 608–67.

CHAPTER ELEVEN

Asmussen, H. (ed.), *Die Kirche, Volk Gottes*, Stuttgart, 1961.
Baum, G., 'The Ecclesial Reality of Other Churches' in *Concilium*, 4 (1965) 34–46.
Bea, Card. A., *The Church and Mankind*, London, 1967.
Bläser, P., 'Die Kirche und die Kirchen' in *Catholica*, 18 (1964) 89–107.
Bright, L. (ed.), *The Committed Church*, London, 1966.
Congar, Y. M.-J., 'The Church: The People of God' in *Concilium*, 1 (1965) 7–19.
The Wide World My Parish, London, 1961.
Cornelis, E., *Valeurs chrétiennes des religions non-chrétiennes*, Paris, 1965.
Dahl, N. A., *Das Volk Gottes, Eine Untersuchung zum Kirchenbewusstsein des Urchristentums*, Oslo, 1941.
'The People of God' in *The Ecumenical Review*, 9 (1957) 154–61.
Delhaye, P., *Le dialogue de l'Eglise et du monde d'après Gaudium et Spes*, Gembloux, 1967.
Dietzfelbinger, W., 'Die Grenzen der Kirche nach der dogmatischen Konstitution "De Ecclesia"' *Kerygma und Dogma*, 11 (1965) 165–76.
Gribomont, J., 'Du sacrament de l'Eglise et de ses réalisations impar-

faites. Essai de théologie du schisme' in *Irenikon*, 22 (1949) 345-367.
Groot, J., 'The Church as Sacrament of the World' in *Concilium*, 1/4 (1968) 27–34.
Heislbetz, J., *Theologische Gründe der nichtchristlichen Religionen* (Quaest. Disp., 33), Freiburg, 1967.
Hillmann, E, *The Wider Ecumenism. Anonymous Christianity and the Church*, London–New York, 1967.
The Church as Mission, London–Melbourne, 1966.
Kasper, W., 'Der ekklesiologische Charakter der nichtkatholischen Kirchen' in *Theol. Quart.*, 145 (1965) 24–62.
Käsemann, E., *Das wandernde Gottesvolk. Eine Untersuchung zum Hebräerbrief*, Göttingen, 1961.
Laurentin, R.–Neuner, J., *Declaration on the Relation of the Church to Non-Christian Religions*, Glen Rock, N.J., 1966.
Lichtenberg, J.-P., *L'Eglise et les Religions non chrétiennes*, Mulhouse, 1967.
Mühlen, H., 'Der eine Geist Christi und die vielen Kirchen nach den Aussagen des Vaticanum II' in *Theol. und Glaube*, 55 (1965) 329–66.
Neuner, J. (ed.), *Christian Revelation and World Religions*, London, 1967.
Norris, F. B., *God's Own People: An Introductory Study of the Church*, Baltimore, 1962.
Nys, H., *Le Salut sans l'évangile. Etude historique et critique du problème du 'salut des infideles' dans la literature théologique récente* (1912–1964), Paris, 1966.
Oepke, A., *Das neue Gottesvolk*, Gütersloh, 1950.
Rahner, K., *The Church and the Sacraments* (Quaest. Disp., 9), London, 1963.
Art. 'Church and World' in *Sacramentum Mundi*, I, 346–57.
Ricken, F., 'Ecclesia ... Universale Salutis Sacramentum' in *Scholastik*, 40 (1965) 352–88.
Schillebeeckx, E., 'The Church and Mankind' in *Concilium*, 1/1 (1965) 34–50.
Schlette, H. R., *Towards a Theology of Religions*, London–New York, 1965.
Semmelroth, O., 'Die Kirche als "sichtbare Gestalt der unsichtbaren Gnade"' in *Scholastick*, 28 (1953) 23–39.
Church and Sacrament, Dublin–Sydney, 1965.
Valeske, U., *Votum Ecclesiae. I. Teil: Das Ringen um die Kirche in der neueren römisch-katholischen Theologie. Dargestellt auf dem*

Hintergrund der evangelischen und ökumenischen Parallel-Entwicklung. II. Teil: Interkonfessionelle ekklesiologische Bibliographie, Munich, 1962.
Willems, B., 'Who belongs to the Church?' in *Concilium*, 1/1 (1965) 62–71.

CHAPTER TWELVE

Adams, R. A., 'The Holy Spirit and the Real Presence' in *Theological Studies*, 29 (1968) 37–51.
Bardy, E., *Le Saint Esprit en nous et dans l'Eglise d'après le Nouveau Testament*, Albi, 1950.
Barrett, C. K., *The Holy Spirit and the Gospel Tradition*, London, 1947.
Berkhof, H., *The Doctrine of the Holy Spirit*, London–Richmond, 1964.
Collins, J. D., 'Discovering the Meaning of Pentecost' in *Scripture*, 20 (1968) 73–9.
Congar, Y. M.-J., 'The Holy Spirit and the Apostolic College, Promoters of the Work of Christ' in *The Mystery of the Church*, London, 1965, 105–45 (*Esquisses du Mystère de l'Eglise*, Paris, 1953, pp. 129–79.
'The Church and Pentecost', *ibid.*, 146–98 (transl. of *La Pentecôte, Chartres*, Paris, 1956).
de Letter, P., 'The Soul of the Mystical Body, in *Sciences Eccles.*, 14 (1962) 213–34.
Dewar, L., *The Holy Spirit in Modern Thought*, New York, 1959.
Dubarle, A., 'Les fondements bibliques du Filioque' in *Russie et Chrétienté*, 1950, 234–42.
Ertis, O., *Die Erneuerung der Gemeinde durch den Geist*, Kassel, 1960.
Flender, H., *St Luke, Theologian of Redemptive History*, London, 1967.
Gleason, R. W., *The Indwelling Spirit*, New York, 1961.
Gore, C., *The Holy Spirit and the Church*, London, 1924.
Hamilton, N. Q., *The Holy Spirit and Eschatology in Paul*, London, 1957.
Hamp, V.–Schmid, J.–Mussner, F., art. 'Pneuma' in *LTK*, 8, 568–576.
Haubst, R., art. 'Heiliger Geist', *ibid.*, 5, 108–13.
Hermann, I., art. 'Heiliger Geist' in *Handbuch der Theologischen Grundbegriffe*, vol. I, ed. by H. Fries, Munich, 1962, 642–7.

Kleinknecht, H.–Sjöberg, E.–Schweizer, E., art. 'Pneuma' in *TWNT*, VI, 330–449.
Lampe, G. W. H., 'The Holy Spirit in the Writings of St Luke' in *Studies in the Gospels: Essays in Memory of R. H. Lightfoot*, ed. by D. E. Nineham, Oxford, 1955, 159-200.
Lebreton, J., *Les origines du dogme de la trinité* (Bibl. de théol. hist.), vol. I, *Des origines à Saint Augustine*, Paris, ²1919; vol. II, *De Saint Clément à Saint Irénée*, Paris, 1928.
Leenhardt, F. J., et al., *Le Saint-Esprit, Genève*, 1963.
L'Huillier, P., 'Théologie de l'épiclèse, in *Verbum Caro*, (1960) 307–327.
Liégé, A., art. 'Ame de l'Eglise' in *Catholicisme*, vol I, 434–6.
McNamara, K., 'The Holy Spirit in the Church, in *ITQ*, 32 (1965) 281–94 (Reproduced in D. Flanagan (ed.), *The Meaning of the Church*, Dublin–Melbourne, 1966, 18–35).
Morenz, S.–Beck, N.-D., art. 'Geist' in ³*RGG*, 2, 1268–90.
Mühlen, H., *Una Persona Mystica. Die Kirche als das Mysterium der Identität des Heiligen Geistes in Christus und den Christen: Eine Person in vielen Personen*, Paderborn, 1964.
'Die Kirche als die geschictlich Erscheinung des übergeschichtlichen Geistes Christi' in *Theol. und Glaube*, 55 (1965) 270–89.
Nautin, P., *Je crois à l'Esprit-Saint dans la sainte Eglise pour la résurrection de la chair* (Unam Sanctam, 17), Paris, 1947.
Navone, J., 'The Holy Spirit' in *Scripture*, 20 (1968) 80–95.
Prümm, K., 'Die katholische Auslegung von 2 Cor 3:17 in den letzten vier Jahrzehnten nach ihren Hauptrichtungen' in *Biblica*, 31 (1950) 316–45, 459–82; 32 (1951) 1–24.
Schillebeeckx, E., 'Ascension and Pentecost' in *Worship*, 35 (1961) 336–64.
Schweizer, E., *Geist und Gemeinde im NT*, Munich, 1952.
Spicq, C., 'Le Sainte-Esprit, vie et force de l'Eglise primitive' in *Lumière et Vie*, 10 (1953) 9–28.
Swete, H. B., *The Holy Spirit in the New Testament*, London, 1909.
Tillard, J.-M. R., 'L'Eucharistie et le Saint-Esprit' in *NRT*, 90 (1968) 363–87.
Tromp, S., *De Spiritu Sancto anima corporis mystici:* vol. I, *Testimonia selecta ex Patribus graecis*, Rome, ²1948; vol. II, *Testimonia selecta ex Patribus latinis*, Rome, ²1952.
Corpus Christi quod est Ecclesia: vol. III, *De Spiritu Christi anima*, Rome, 1960.
Vauthier, E., 'Le Saint Esprit principe d'unité de l'Eglise d'après

S. Thomas d'Aquin' in *Mélanges de Sc. Rel.*, 5 (1948) pp. 175–196; 6 (1949) 57–80.
von Allmen, J. J., 'L'Esprit de vérité vous conduira dans toute la vérité' in *L'Infaillibilité de l'Eglise*, Chevetogne, 1962, 13–26.
von Balthasar, H. U., 'Le Saint-Esprit: l'Inconnu au-delà du Verbe' in *Lumière et Vie*, 67 (1964) 115–26.
Spiritus Creator. Skizzen zur Theologie, vol. III, Einsiedeln, 1967.
von Campenhausen, H., *Kirchliches Amt und geistliche Vollmacht in den ersten drei Jahrhunderten*, Tübingen, 1953.
Vonier, A., *L'Esprit et l'Epouse* (Unam Sanctam, 16), Paris, 1947 (*The Spirit and the Bride*, in *The Collected Works of Abbot Vonier*, vol. II, London, 1952).
Witte, J. L., 'Le Saint-Esprit dans les Eglises séparées' in *Dict. de Spiritualité*, vol. IV/2, 1961, 1318–33.

CHAPTER THIRTEEN

Anderson, G. H. (ed.), *The Theology of the Christian Mission*, London, 1962.
Arnold, F. X., *Grundsätzliches und Geschichtliches zur Theologie der Seelsorge*, Freiburg, 1949.
Barosse, T., 'The Mission Church—A New Testament View' in *Reappraisal: Prelude to Change*, ed. by W. J. Richardson, New York, 1965.
Blauw, J., *The Missionary Nature of the Church. A Survey of Biblical Theology of Mission*, London, 1962.
Chavasse, A.–Denis, H. et al., *Eglise et apostolat*, Paris–Tournai, 1954.
Couturier, C., *The Mission of the Church*, London–Baltimore, 1960.
Davies, J. G., 'The Meaning of Mission' in *Cross Currents*, 16 (1966) 416–28.
Worship and Mission, London, 1967.
de Lubac, H., *Le fondement théologique des missions*, Paris, 1946.
Dewailly, L. M., *Envoyés du Père. Mission et apostolicité*, Paris, 1960.
Hahn, F., *Mission in the New Testament*, London, 1965.
Henry, A., *A Mission Theology*, Indiana, 1962.
Hillmann, E., *The Church as Mission*, New York, 1965, London, 1966.
Hoekendijk, J. C., 'The Church in Missionary Thinking' in *The International Review of Missions*, 41 (1952) 324–36.
The Church Inside Out, London, 1967.

Le Guillou, M.-J., *Mission et Unité. Les exigences de la communion* (Unam Sanctam, 33), 2 vols, Paris, 1960.
'Mission as Ecclesiological Theme' in *Concilium*, 3/2 (1966) 43–67.
Masson, J., 'Fonction missionaire, fonction de l'Eglise' in *NRT*, 80 (1958) 1042–61; 81 (1959) 41–59.
Newbigin, L., *The Household of God. Lectures on the Nature of the Church*, London, 1953.
Rademakers, J., 'Mission et apostolat dans l'evangile Johannique' in *Stud. Evan.*, 2 (1964) 100–21.
Suenens, Card. L., *L'Eglise en état de mission*, Bruges, 1953. (Cf. also the bibliography to Chapters 11 and 24.)

CHAPTER FOURTEEN

Auer, A., *Open to the World. An Analysis of Lay Spirituality*, Dublin–Sydney, 1966.
Barrau, P., 'Le laïcat, signe d'Eglise', in *Masses Ouvrières*, 135 (1957) 130–88.
Brungs, R. A., *A Priestly People*, New York, 1968.
Buckley, J. C., 'Parish Councils' in *The Clergy Review*, 53 (1968) 264–74.
Callahan, D., *The Mind of the Catholic Layman*, New York, 1963.
Cerfaux, L., 'Regale Sacerdotium' in *Recueil L. Cerfaux*, vol. II, Gembloux, 1954 (reprint 1964), 283-315.
Colson, J., 'Prêtres et peuple sacerdotal' in *Vie Spirit.*, 117 (1967) 450–77.
Congar, Y. M.-J., *Lay People in the Church: A Study for a Theology of Laity*, London, 1959.
Laity, Church and World, London, 1960.
Priest and Layman, London, 1967.
'Laienstand' in *LTK*, 6, 733–40.
Dabin, P., *Le sacerdoce royal des fidèles dans l'Ecriture*, Louvain, 1942.
Le sacerdoce royal des fidèles dans la Tradition ancienne et moderne, Brussels–Paris, 1950.
Dejaifve, G., 'Laïcat et mission de l'Eglise' in *NRT*, 80 (1958) 23–38.
de la Potterie, I.–Lyonnet, S., *La vie selon l'Esprit. Condition du Chrétien* (Unam Sanctam, 55), Paris, 1965.
de Smedt, E. J., *Le sacerdoce des fidèles*, Bruges–Paris, 1961.
Ferro-Calvo, M., *et al.*, *The Christian and the World*, New York, 1965.

Friedrich, G., art. 'kērussō', in *TWNT*, III, 701–17.
art. 'euaggelizomai', *ibid.*, II, 703–35.
Gerken, J., *Toward a Theology of the Layman*, Indianapolis, 1961.
Glorieux, P., *Le laïc dans l'Eglise*, Paris, 1960.
Heimerl, H., *Laien im Dienst der Verkündigung. Laienmitwirkung an der Lehraufgabe der Kirche*, Vienna, 1958.
Kirche, Klerus und Laien—Unterscheidungen und Beziehungen, Vienna, 1961.
Ketter, P., 'Das allgemeine Priestertum der Gläubigen nach dem I. Petrusbrief' in *Trier. Theol. Zeitschrift*, 56 (1947) 43–51.
Krueger, A. F., *Synthesis of Sacrifice*, Mundelein, 1950.
Lécuyer, J., 'Essai sur de sacerdoce des fidèles chez les pères' in *La Maison Dieu*, 27 (1951–53) 7–50.
Lombardía, P., 'Lay People in Church Law' in *IER*, 109 (1968) 281–312.
Ministère et Laïcat (Sémaine de théologie pastorale), Taizé, 1964.
Moran, W. L., 'A Kingdom of Priests' in *The Bible in Current Catholic Thought*, ed. by J. L. McKenzie, New York, 1962, 7–20.
Newman, J. H., *On Consulting the Faithful on Matters of Doctrine*, ed. by J. Coulson, London, 1961.
Newman, J., *The Christian in Society: A Theological Investigation*, London, 1962.
Newman, J. (ed.), *Vatican II: The Christian Layman*, Dublin, 1967.
Oepke, A., art. 'Lampō', in *TWNT*, IV, 17–28.
Philips, G., *The role of the Laity in the Church*, Cork, 1956.
Etudes sur l'apostolat des laïcs, Brussels, 1960.
Rea, J. E., *The Common Priesthood*, Westminster, Md, 1947.
Reed, J. J., 'The Laity in Church Law' in *TS* 24 (1963) 602–25.
Rengstorf, K. H., art. *didaskō* in *TWNT*, II, 138–68.
Ryan, L., 'Vatican II and the Priesthood of the Laity' in *ITQ*, 32 (1965) 93–115.
Schelkle, K. H., *Die Petrusbriefe. Der Judasbrief* (Herders Theol. Komm. zum NT, III, 2), Freiburg, 1961.
A Priestly People (Theol. Meditations 4), London–Melbourne, 1965.
Schillebeeckx, E., 'The Layman in the Church' in *Doctrine and Life*, 11 (1961) 369–75; 397–408 (reproduced in *Vatican II: A Struggle of Minds and other Essays*, Dublin, 1963, 33–60).
Schnackenburg, R., 'Ihr seid das Salz der Erde, das Licht der Welt. Zu Matthäus 5:13–16' in *Mélanges E. Tisserant*, vol. I, Rome, 1964, pp. 364–87.
Schrenk, G., art. 'hieros' in *TWNT*, III, 221–84.

Selwyn, G., *The First Epistle of St Peter*, London, 1955.
Semmelroth, O., 'The Priestly People of God and its Official Ministers' in *Concilium*, 1/4 (1968) 45–51.
Strathman, H., art. 'martus', in *TWNT*, IV, 492–510.
Art. 'laos', *ibid.*, pp. 29–39.
Thils, G., *L'enseignement de S. Pierre*, Paris, 1943.
Thorman, D. J., *The Emerging Layman: The Role of the Catholic Layman in America*, New York, 1962.
Torrance, T. F., *Royal Priesthood*, Edinburgh, 1955.
van Balthasar, H. U., *Der Laie und der Ordenstand*, Einsiedeln, 1949.
'Der Laie und die Kirche' in *Viele Ämter, ein Geist*, ed. by H. Nüsse, Einsiedeln, 1954.

Chapter Fifteen

Barrett, C. K., 'The Apostles in and after the New Testament' in *Svenk Exegetisk Arsbok*, 21 (1957) 30–49.
Benoit, P. 'Les origines de l'épiscopat dans le N.T.' in *Exégèse et Théologie*, vol. II, Paris, 1961, 232–46.
'La primauté de Pierre dans le N.T.' in *Istina*, 2 (1955) 305–34 (=*Exégèse et Théologie*, vol. II, 250–84).
Baum, G., 'The Magisterium in a Changing Church' in *Concilium*, I, n. 3 (1967) 34–42.
Betz, O., 'Felsenmann und Felsengemeinde' in *Zeitschrift für die Neutest. Wissen.*, 48 (1957) 49–77.
Betz, J., 'Christus-Petra-Petros' in *Kirche und Überlieferung* (Festschrift R. Geiselmann), Freiburg i. Br., 1960, 1–20.
Beyer, H. W., art .'episkopos' in *TWNT*, II, 604–19.
Art. 'diakoneō', *ibid.*, 81–93.
Bläser, P., 'Zum Problem des urchristlichen Apostolats' in *Unio Christianorum* (Festschrift L. Jaeger), Paderborn, 1962, 92–107.
Bouësse, H.–Mandouze, A. (ed.), *L'Evêque dans l'Eglise du Christ*, Bruges–Paris, 1963.
Cerfaux, L., 'Pour l'histoire du titre "apostolos" dans le Nouveau Testament' in *Recueil L. Cerfaux*, vol. III, Gembloux, 1964, 185–200 (=*Rech. Sc. Rel.*, 48 (1960) 76–92).
'La mission apostolique des Douze et sa portée eschatologique' in *Mélanges E. Tisserant*, vol. I, Rome, 1964, 43–66.
Clavier, H., 'Petros-petra' in *Neutestamentliche Studien für R. Bultmann*, Berlin, 1954, 94–109.
Colson, J., *L'Evêque dans les communautés primitives*. Tradition

paulinienne et Tradition johannique de l'Episcopat des origines à saint Irénée (Unam Sanctam, 21), Paris, 1951.
Les fonctions ecclésiales aux deux premiers siècles, Paris, 1956.
Ministre de Jésus-Christ ou le sacerdoce de l'évangile, Paris, 1966.
Congar, Y. M.-J.–Dupuy, B.-D. (ed.), *L'Episcopat de l'Eglise universelle* (Unam Sanctam, 39), Paris, 1962.
Congar, Y. M.-J., *Power and Poverty in the Church*, London, 1964.
Crocker, J., 'The Apostolic Succession in the Light of the History of the Primitive Church' in *Anglican Theol. Rev.*, 18 (1936) 1–21.
Cullmann, O., *Peter Disciple—Apostle—Martyr*, London, ²1962.
Art. 'Petra—Petros—Kephas' in *TWNT*, VI, 94–112.
'L'Apôtre Pierre instrument du diable et instrument de Dieu: la place de Matt. 16:16–19 dans la tradition primitive' in *New Testament Essays. Studies in Memory of T. W. Manson*, ed. by A. J. B. Higgins, Manchester, 1959, 94–105.
Dalrymple, J., et. al., *Authority in a Changing Church*, London–Sydney, 1968.
de Albornoz, A. F. C., *Roman Catholicism and Religious Liberty*, Geneva, 1959.
Dupont, J., 'Le nom d'apôtre a-t-il été donné aux Douze par Jésus?' in *L'Orient Syrien*, I (1956) 267–90, 425–44.
'La révélation du Fils de Dieu en faveur de Pierre (Mt 16:17) et de Paul (Gal. 1:16)' in *Rech. Sc. Rel.*, 52 (1964) 411–20.
Ekström, R., 'Some Aspects of the Ministry in the New Testament' in *Biblical Theol.*, 15 (1965) 8–17.
Farrer, A. M., et al., *Infallibility in the Church. An Anglican–Catholic Dialogue*, London, 1968.
Freyne, S., *The Twelve: Disciples and Apostles*, London, 1968.
Frisque, J.–Congar, Y. M.-J. (ed.), *Les Prêtres: Formation, Ministère et Vie* (Unam Sanctam, 68), Paris, 1968.
Gaechter, P., *Petrus und seine Zeit*, Innsbruck, 1958.
Ganoczy, A., *Calvin théologien de l'Eglise et du ministère* (Unam Sanctam, 48), Paris, 1964.
Geweiss, J.–Jungmann, J. A.–Rahner, K., art. 'Der Diakon (in der Schrift, Geschichte und Dogmatik)' in *LTK*, 3, 318–22.
Gewiess, J., 'Die neutestamentliche Grundlagen der kirchlichen Hierarchie' in *Histor. Jahrb.*, 72 (1953) 1–24.
Giblet, J., 'Les promesses de l'Esprit et la mission des Apôtres dans les Evangiles', in *Irenikon*, 30 (1957) 5–43.
'Les Douze. Histoire et Théologie' in *Aux Origines de l'Eglise* (Rech Bibl. VII), Bruges, 1965, 51–64.

Gils, F., 'Pierre et la foi au Christ ressuscité, in *ELT*, 38 (1962) 5–43.
Grelot, P., 'La vocation ministérielle au service du Peuple de Dieu' in *Aux Origines de l'Eglise* (Rech. Bibl., VII), Bruges, 1965, 159–73.
Le ministère de la Nouvelle Alliance, Paris, 1967.
Grosche, R.–Asmussen, H., *Brauchen wir einen Papst? Ein Gespräch zwischen den Konfessionen*, Cologne–Olten, 1957.
Guerry, E., 'La sacramentalité de l'Episcopat' in *Docum. Cath.*, 61 (1964) 367–84.
Häring, B., *The Liberty of the Children of God*, London–Dublin–Melbourne, 1967.
Infallibility in the Church. An Anglican Dialogue, London, 1968.
Jeremias, J., art. 'poimen' in *TWNT*, VI, 484–501.
art. 'kleis', *ibid.*, III, 743–53.
Karrer, O., *Peter and the Church: An Examination of Cullmann's Thesis* (Quaest. Disp., 8), New York–London, 1963.
'Das Petrusamt in der Frühkirche' in *Festgabe für J. Lortz*, Baden-Baden, 1957, vol. I, 507–25.
Käsemann, E., 'Ministry and Community in the New Testament' in *Essays on New Testament Themes*, London–Napierville, Ill., 1964, 63–94.
Kirk, K. E., *The Apostolic Ministry*, London, 1946 (reprinted 1957).
Kredel, E. M., 'Der Apostelbegriff in der neueren Exegese' in *Zeitschrift für kath. Theol.*, 78 (1956) 169–93, 257–305.
La collégialité épiscopale. Histoire et théologie (Unam Sanctam, 52), Paris, 1965.
L'ecclésiologie au XIXe siècle (Unam Sanctam, 34), Paris, 1960.
L'Infaillibilité de l'Eglise, Chevetogne, 1962.
Lambert, G., 'Lier—Délier: L'expression de la totalité par opposition de deux contraires' in *Vivre et Penser*, 3 (1943–44) 98–9.
Lécuyer, J., 'Le sacrament de l'Episcopat' in *Divinitas*, 1 (1957) 221—51.
Le sacerdoce dans le mystère du Christ, Paris, 1957.
Légault, A., 'L'Authenticité de Mt 16:17–19 et le silence de Marc et de Luc' in *L'Eglise dans la Bible*, Paris, 1962.
Leenhardt, F.-J., 'Les fonctions constitutives de l'Eglise et l'Episcopé selon le Nouveau Testament' in *Rev. Hist. Phil. Rel.*, 47 (1967) 111–49.
Manson, T. W., *The Church's Ministry*, London, 1948.
Marchal, L., 'Evêques, origine divine des' in *DBS*, II, 1297–1333.
McKenzie, J. L., *Authority in the Church*, New York, 1966.
Art. 'Apostle' in *Dictionary of the Bible*, 1966, 46–8.

Menoud, P., *L'Eglise et les ministères selon le Nouveau Testament* (Cahiers théologiques de l'actualité protestante, 22), Neuchâtel–Paris, 1948.
Ministère et Laïcat (Verbum Caro 71–2), 1964.
Mosbech, H., 'Apostolos in the New Testament' in *Stud. Theol.*, 2 (1948) 166–200.
Müller, A., *Obedience in the Church*, Westminster, Md, 1966.
Munck, J., 'Paul, the Apostles and the Twelve' in *Stud. Theol.*, 3 (1949) 96–110.
Nowell, R., *The Ministry of Service. Deacons in the Contemporary Church*, London, 1968.
Obrist, F., *Echtheitsfragen und Deutung der Primatstelle Mt 16:18f in der deutschen protestantischen Theologie der letzten 30 Jahre*, Münster, 1961.
Refoulé, F., 'Primauté de Pierre dans les évangiles' in *Rev. des Sc. Rel.*, 38 (1964).
Rengstorf, K. H., art. 'apostellō', in *TWNT*, I, 397–448.
Art. 'doulos', *ibid.*, II, 264–83.
Richter, W., 'Das Petrusamt im Lichte des apostolischen Zeugnisses' in *Una Sancta*, 12 (1957) 201–13.
Rigaux, B., 'Die "Zwölf" in Geschichte und Kerygma' in *Der historische Jesus und der kerygmatische Christus*, ed. by H. Ristow and K. Matthiae, Berlin, 1960, 468–86.
'The Twelve Apostles' in *Concilium*, vol. 4, n. 4 (1968) 4–9.
Ringger, J., 'Das Felsenwort. Zur Sinndeutung von Mt 16:18, vor allem im Lichte der Symbolsgeschichte' in *Begegnung der Christen* (Festschrift für O. Karrer), Stuttgart–Frankfurt, 1959, 271–347.
Roloff, J., *Apostolat—Verkündigung—Kirche. Ursprung, Inhalt und Funktion des Apostelamts nach Paulus, Lukas und den Pastoralbriefen*, Gütersloh, 1965.
Ryan, S., 'Episcopal Consecration' in *ITQ*, 32 (1965) 295–324; 33 (1966) 3–38, 133–50, 208–41.
San Pietro. Atti della XIX Settimana Biblica, Assoc. Bibl. Italiana, Brescia, 1967.
Schelkle, K. H., *Discipleship and Priesthood. A Biblical Interpretation*, London, 1966.
Schmid, J., 'Petrus "der Fels" und die Petrusgestalt der Urgemeinde' in *Begegnung der Christen*, Stuttgart–Frankfurt, ed. by Roesle–Cullmann, ²1960, 347–59.
Schmithals, W., *Das kirchliche Apostelamt. Eine historische Untersuchung* (FRLANT, 79), Göttingen, 1961.
Schnackenburg, R., *The Truth will make you Free*, London, 1967.

Schweizer, E., *Church Order in the New Testament*, London, 1961.
Semmelroth, O., *Das geistliche Amt*, Frankfurt, 1958.
Stanley, D. M., 'Authority in the Church: A New Testament Reality' in *Cath. Bibl. Quart.*, 29 (1967) 555–73.
'The New Testament Basis for the Concept of Collegiality', in *Theological Studies*, 25 (1964) 197–216.
Sutcliffe, E. F., 'Et tu aliquando conversus, St Luke 22:32', in *Cath. Bibl. Quart.*, 15 (1953).
Tobin, W. J., 'The Petrine Primacy, Evidence of the Gospels' in *Lumen Vitae*, 23 (1968) 27–70.
Vögtle, A., 'Der Petrus der Verheissung und der Erfüllung: zum Petrusbuch von O. Cullmann in *Münch. Theol. Zeitschrift*, 4 (1954) 1–47.
'Messiasbekenntnis und Petrusverheissung: Zur Komposition Mt 16:13–23' in *Bibl. Zeits.*, 1 (1957) 257–72; 2 (1958) 85–103.
'Ekklesiologische Auftragsworte des Auferstandenen' in *Sacra Pagina*, vol. II, ed. by J. Coppens–A. Descamps–E. Massaux, Paris–Gembloux, 1959, 280–94.
art. 'Zwölf' in *LTK*, 10, 1443–5.
art. 'Binden und Lösen', *ibid.*, 2, 480–2.
van Balthasar, H. U., 'Office in the Church' in *Church and World*, New York, 1967, 44–111.
von Campenhausen, H., *Kirchliches Amt und geistliche Vollmacht in den ersten drei Jahrhunderten*, Tübingen, 1959.
Vorgrimler, H. (ed.), *Diaconia in Christo. Uber die Erneuerung des Diakonates* (Quaest. Disp. 14), Freiburg–Basel–Vienna, 1959.
Winninger, P.–Congar, Y. M.-J. (ed.), *Le Diacre dans l'Eglise et le monde d'aujourd'hui* (Unam Sanctam 59), Paris, 1966.

CHAPTER SIXTEEN

Amann, E., art. 'Pères (de l'Eglise)' in *DTC*, XII, 1192–1215.
Appel, N., *Kanon und Kirche. Die Kanonkrise im heutigen Protestantismus als kontroverstheologisches Problem*, Paderborn, 1964.
Baillie, J., *The Idea of Revelation in Recent Thought*, New York–London, 1960.
Barucq, A.–Cazelles, H., 'Les livres inspirés' in *Introd. à la Bible*, vol. I, ed. by Robert-Feuillet, Tournai, 1957, 3–68.
Baum, G., 'Vatican II's Constitution on Revelation' in *Theological Studies*, 28 (1967) 51–75.
Beumer, J., 'Katholisches und protestantisches Schriftprinzip im Urteil des Trienter Konzils' in *Scholastik*, 34 (1959) 249–58.

'Das katholische Traditionsprinzip in seiner heute neu erkannten Problematik', *ibid.*, 36 (1961) 217–40.

Die Mündliche Uberlieferung als Glaubensquelle (Handbuch der Dogmengeschichte, I, 4), Freibrug i. Br., 1962.

Benoit, P., *Aspects of Biblical Inspiration*, Chicago, 1965.

'Inspiration and Revelation', in *Concilium*, 10/1 (1965) 5–14.

Brinckmann, B., 'Inspiration und Kanonizität der Hl. Schrift in ihrem Verhältnis zur Kirche', in *Scholastik*, 73 (1958) 208–33.

Bulst, W., *Offenbarung, Biblischer und Theologischer Begriff*, Düsseldorf, 1960.

Condon, K., 'Word and Logos—Reflections on the Problem of Inspiration' in *ITQ*, 33 (1966) 114–32.

Congar, Y. M.-J., *Tradition and Traditions. An Historical and Theological Essay*, London, 1966.

The Revelation of God, London, 1968.

Concilium, 10/2 (1966): 'The Bible and Tradition.'

1/3 (1967): 'Revelation and Dogma.'

Courtade, G., art. 'Inspiration' in *DBS*, IV, 482–559.

Cullmann, O., 'The Tradition' in *The Early Church*, London, 1956, 59–99.

'Scripture and Tradition' in *Christianity Divided*, ed. by Callahan–Obermann–O'Hanlon, London–New York, 1961, 7–31.

Dejaifve, G., 'Bible, Tradition, Magistère dans la théologie catholique' in *NRT*, 78 (1956) 135–51.

'Bible et Tradition dans le luthéranisme contemporain' *ibid.*, 33–49.

De Vooght, P., 'Ecriture et Tradition d'après les études catholiques récentes' in *Istina*, 7 (1958) 183–96.

Dubarle, A.-M., 'Ecriture et Tradition à propos de publications protestantes récentes' in *Istina*, 5 (1956) 299–416; 6 (1957) 113–28.

Dupont, J., 'Ecriture et Tradition' in *NRT*, 85 (1963) 337–56, 449–468.

Ebeling, G., *The Word of God and Tradition*, London, 1968.

Flesseman-Van Leer, E., *Tradition and Scripture in the early Church*, Assen, 1954.

Franzelin, J. B., *Tractatus de Divina Traditione et Scriptura*, Rome, 1882.

Geiselmann, J. R., *The Meaning of Tradition* (Quaest. Disp. 18), London–New York, 1966.

'Die Tradition' in *Fragen der Theologie heute*, ed. by Feiner–Trütsch–Böckle, Einsiedeln–Zurich–Cologne, 1959, 69–108.

'Scripture, Tradition and the Church: An Ecumenical Problem' in *Christianity Divided*, London–New York, 1961, 39–70.

'Das Missverständnis über das Verhältnis von Schrift und Tradition und seine Überwindung in der katholischen Theologie' in *Una Sancta*, II (1956) 131–50.

(For additional works of Geiselmann on this subject, cf *Kirche und Überlieferung* (Festschrift für J. R. Geiselmann zum 70 Geburtstag), ed. by J. Betz and H. Fries, Freiburg–Basel–Vienna, 1960, pp. 367–71.)

Harrington, W.–Walsh, L., *Vatican II on Revelation*, Dublin, 1967.

Holmes, J. D.–Murray, R. (ed.), *On the Inspiration of Scripture* by J. H. Newman, London–Dublin–Melbourne, 1967.

Holstein, H., *La Tradition dans l'Eglise*, Paris, 1961.

Kasper, W., *Die Lehre von der Tradition in der römischen Schule* (G. Perrone, C. Passaglia, C. Schräder), Freiburg, 1962.

Latourelle, R., *Theology of Revelation. Including a commentary on the Constitution 'Dei Verbum' of Vatican II*, New York, 1966.

Lengsfeld, P., *Überlieferung, Tradition und Schrift in der evangelischen und katholischen Theologie der Gegenwart*, Paderborn, 1960.

Leuba, J.-L., 'Le rapport entre l'Esprit et la Tradition selon le Nouveau Testament' in *Verbum Caro*, 50 (1959) 133–50.

Levie, J., *The Bible. Word of God in Words of Men*, New York, 1962.

Mackey, J., *The Modern Theology of Tradition*, Dublin–New York, 1963.

Tradition and Change in the Church, Dublin–Sydney, 1967.

Moran, G., *Scripture and Tradition: A Survey of the Controversy*, New York, 1963.

Theology of Revelation, New York–London, 1967.

Murphy, J. L., *The Notion of Tradition in John Driedo*, Milwaukee, 1959.

Oepke, A., art. 'apokalupto' in *TWNT*, III, 565–97.

O'Flynn, J. A., 'The Constitution on Divine Revelation' in *ITQ*, 33 (1966) 254–65.

'The Inspiration of Scripture' in *IER*, 107 (1967) 362–72.

Ortigues, E., 'Ecritures et Traditions apostoliques au concile de Trente' in *Rech. Sc. Rel.*, 36 (1949) 271–99.

Rahner, K., *Inspiration in the Bible* (Quaest. Disp. I), New York–London, 1961.

Rahner, K.–Ratzinger, J., *Revelation and Tradition* (Quaest. Disp. 17), New York–London, 1966.

Schildenberger, J., 'Inspiration und Irrtumslosigkeit der Heiligen

Schrift' in *Fragen der Theol. heute*, Zürich–Köln, 1960, 109–122.
Schmaus, M. (ed.), *Die Mündliche Uberlieferung. Beiträge zum Begriff der Tradition*, Munich, 1957.
Schökel, A., *The Inspired Word. Scripture in the Light of Language and Literature*, New York–London, 1967.
Schutz, R.–Thurian, M., *Revelation: A Protestant View*, Westminster, Md., 1968.
Smulders, P., 'Le mot et le concept de tradition chez les Pères grecs' in *Rech. Sc. Rel.*, 40 (1952) 41–62.
Stramare, T., 'La trasmissione della rivelazione' in *Riv. Bibl.*, 15 (1967) 225–47.
Synave, P.–Benoit, P., *La Prophétie*, Paris, 1947 (French transl. and commentary of *Summa theol.*, II–II, qq. 171–8).
Tavard, G. H., *Holy Writ or Holy Church. The Crisis of the Protestant Reformation*, New York–London, 1960.
Taylor, V., *The Formation of the Gospel Tradition*, London, 1953.
Tromp, S., *De Sacrae Scripturae Inspiratione*, Rome, ⁵1953.
von Campenhausen, H., *Tradition and Life in the Church*, London, 1968.
Vosté, J.-M., *De Divina Inspiratione et Varitate Sacrae Scripturae*, Rome, ²1932.

CHAPTER SEVENTEEN

Alfaro, J., 'Persona y gracia' in *Gregorianum*, 41 (1960) 5–29.
'Justificacion Barthiana y Justificacion Catolica' in *Gregorianum*, 39 (1959) 757–69.
Bonnetain, P., art. 'Grâce' in *DBS*, III, 701–1319.
Brinkmann, B. R., 'Karl Barth and Justification' in *ITQ*, 25 (1958) 274–84.
Cerfaux, L.–Descamps, A., art. 'Justice, Justification' in *DBS*, IV, 1417–1510.
Chavaz, E., *Catholicisme romain et protestantisme. Pour la clarté du dialogue*, Tournai, 1958.
Conzelmann, H., 'Rechfertigung durch den Glauben' in *Luth. Monatshefte*, April, 1967.
Flick, M., *L'Attimo della giustificazione secondo S. Tommaso*, Rome, 1947.
Flick, M.–Alzeghy, Z., *Il Vangelo della grazia*, Florence, 1964.
Grosche, R., 'Simul peccator et iustus' in *Catholica*, 4 (1935) 132–9.

Groussouw, W., art. 'Rechtfertigung' in *Bibel-Lexikon* (ed. by Haag), 1403–9.
Hein, N. J.–Wurthwein, E.–Stählin, G.–Kähler, E.–Joest, W., art. 'Gnade Gottes' in *RGG*, II, 1630–45.
Journet, C., *The Meaning of Grace*, New York, 1960.
Klein, G.–Joest, W.–Kinder, E.–Hermann, R., art. 'Rechtfertigung' in *RGG*, V, 825–846.
Kösters, R., 'Die Lehre von der Rechtfertigung unter besonderer Berücksichtigung der Formel "simul iustus et peccator" ' in *Zeits. für kath. Theol.*, (1968) 309–24.
Küng, H., *Justification. The Doctrine of Karl Barth and a Catholic Reflection. With a Letter by Karl Barth*, New York–Toronto–London, 1964.
'Justification and Sanctification according to the New Testament' in *Christianity Divided*, ed. by Callahan–Obermann–O'Hanlon, New York–London, 1961, 309–34.
Lackmann, M., *Zum reformatorischen Rechtfertigungslehre*, Stuttgart, 1963.
Loosen, J., 'Ekklesiologische, christologische und trinitätstheologische Element im Gnadenberriff' in *Theologie in Geschichte und Gegenwart* (Festschrift Schmaus), Munich, 1957, 89–102.
Lyonnet, S., 'De justitia Dei in Epistola ad Romanos' in *Verbum Domini*, 25 (1947) 23–34, 118–21, 129–44, 193–203, 257–63.
'Justification, Judgement, Redemption, principalement dans l'Epître aux Romains' in *Littérature et théologie Pauliniennes* Rech. Bibl. V), Bruges, 1960, 166–84.
Michel, A., 'Foi, principe du salut' in *L'Ami du Clergé*, 16 Feb., 1967, 108–12.
Moeller, C., 'Théologie de la grâce et oecuménisme' in *Irenikon*, 28 (1955) 19–56.
Pesch, O. H., *Theologie der Rechfertigung bei Martin Luther und Thomas von Aquin*, Mainz, 1967.
Rahner, K., 'Some Implications of the Scholastic Concept of Uncreated Grace' in *Theol. Investig.*, I, 319–46.
'Questions of Controversial Theology on Justification' in *Theological Investigations*, IV (originally in *Tübing. Theol. Quart.*, 1958, 40–78).
'Concerning the Relationship between Nature and Grace' in *Theol. Investig.*, I, 297–317.
Nature and Grace, New York–London, 1964.
Rengsdorf, K. H., 'Rechtfertigung aus dem Glauben–heute' in *Lutherische Monatshefte*, Oct. 1967.

Rondet, H., *Gratia Christi. Essai d'histoire du dogme et de théologie dogmatique*, Paris, 1948.
Schreiber, G., *Das Weltkonzil von Trient*, Freiburg, 1951.
Schrenk, G., art. 'dikawsunē' in *TWNT*, II, 194–214.
Sheridan, F. L., *Newman on Justification*, New York, 1968.
Stakemeier, E., *Glaube und Rechtfertigung*, Frieburg i. Br., 1937.
Torrance, T. F., 'Justification: Its radical nature and place in Reformed doctrine and life' in *Christianity Divided*, New York–London, 1961, 283–304.
Villette, L., *Foi et sacrement* (Travaux de l'Instit. Cath., 5–6); vol. 1, *Du Nouveau Test. à Saint Augustin*, Paris, 1959; Vol. II, *De saint Thomas à Karl Barth*, Paris, 1964.
Volk, H., 'Gnade und Person' in *Theol. in Geschichte und Gegenwart* (Festschrift M. Schmaus), Munich, 1957, 219–36.
Witte, J. L., 'Is Barths Rechtfertigungslehre grundsätzlich katholisch?' in *Münch. Theol. Zeits.*, 1959, 38–48.

CHAPTER EIGHTEEN

Aubert, R., 'L'Institution et l'Evénement, à propos de l'ouvrage de M. le Pasteur Leuba' in *ETL*, 28 (1952) 683–93.
Beinert, W., 'Die Una Catholica und die Partikularkirchen' in *Theol. und. Phil.*, 42 (1967) 1–21.
Bertrams, W., 'De constitutione Ecclesiae simul charismatica et institutionali' in *Per. Mor. Can. Lit.*, 57 (1968) 281–330.
Brosch, H. J., *Charismen und Ämter in der Urkirche*, Bonn, 1951.
Casiano, F., *The Parish: Eucharistic Community*, London, 1965.
Chevallier, M.-A., *Esprit de Dieu. Paroles d'hommes. Le rôle de l'Esprit dans les ministères de la parole selon l'apôtre Paul*, Neuchâtel, 1966.
de Bovis, A., 'La fondation de l'Eglise' in *NRT*, 85 (1963) 3–18, 113–38.
de Lubac, H., *Corpus Mysticum. Eucharistie et l'Eglise au moyen age*, Paris, ²1949.
Eichholz, E., *Was heisst charismatische Gemeinde* (Theol. Ex. heute, 77), Munich, 1960.
Elert, W., *Eucharist and Church Fellowship in the First Four Centuries*, St Louis, Mo., 1966.
Emmet, C. W.–Riesenfeld, H., 'Spiritual Gifts' in *Dict. of the Bible*, Edinburgh, 1963.
Gardeil, A., 'Dons du Saint-Esprit' in *DTC*, IV, 1728–81.

Gewiess, J.–Rahner, K., 'Charisma' in *LTK*, II, 1025–30.
Hurley, M. (ed.), *Church and Eucharist*, Dublin–Melbourne, 1966.
Käsemann, E., 'Ministry and Community in the New Testament' in *Essays on New Testament Themes*, London–Napierville, Ill., 1964, 63–94.
'Geist und Geistesgaben im NT' in *RGG*, II, 1272–9.
Küng, H., 'The Charismatic Structure of the Church' in *Concilium*, 4/1 (1965) 23–33.
Lemonnyer, A., 'Charismes', in *DBS*, I, 1233–43.
Leuba, J.-L., *L'Institution et l'événement*, Paris–Neuchâtel, 1952 (Engl. transl., *New Testament Patterns*, London, 1953).
Maréchaux, B., *Les charismes du Saint Esprit*, Paris, 1921.
Rahner, K., 'The Charismatic Element in the Church' in *The Dynamic Element in the Church* (Quaest. Disp. 12) New York–Edinburgh, 1964, 42–83.
Rahner, K.–Ratzinger, J., *The Episcopate and the Primacy* (Quaest. Disp. 4), New York–Edinburgh, 1962.
Schmidt, K. L., art. *kaleō-ekklēsia* in *TWNT*, III, 488–539.
Semmelroth, O., 'Institution und Charisma' in *Geist und Leben*, 36 (1963) 433–54.
Suenens, Card. J., Speech to conciliar Fathers of Vatican II on 22 Oct. 1963, reproduced in *The Furrow*, Feb. 1964, 72–4.

CHAPTER NINETEEN

Chirico, P. F., 'Visibility of the Church' in *New Cath. Encyl.*, vol. 14, 715.
Congar, Y. M.-J., *Chrétiens Désunis. Principes d'un "oecuménisme" catholique* (Unam Sanctam I), Paris, 1937, 78–114.
Huarte, G., 'Quomodo ecclesia Christi, quae visibilis est, possit esse objectum fidei', in *Gregorianum*, 3 (1922) 78–98.
Olsson, H., 'The Church's Visibility and Invisibility according to Luther' in *This is the Church*, ed. by A. Nygren, Philadelphia, 1952, 226–42.
Rahner, H., 'Theologie der sichtbaren Kirche' in *Zwölf Vorlesungen über Kerygmatische Theologie*, Vienna, 1938, 90–106.
Salaverri, J., *De Ecclesia Christi* (Sac. Theol. Summa I), Madrid, 1950, nn. 1120–47.
Semmelroth, O., 'Die Kirche als "sichtbare Gestalt der unsichtbaren Gnade" ' in *Scholastik*, 28 (1953) 23–39.
Walz, J. B., *Die Sichtbarkeit der Kirche. Ein Beitrag zur Grundfrage des Katholizismus*, Würzburg, 1924.

CHAPTER TWENTY

Benoit, P., 'Corps, tête et plérome dans les Epitres de la captivité', in *Exégése et Théologie*, vol. II, Paris, 1961, 107–53 (originally in *Rev. Bibl.*, 56 (1956) 5–44).
Best, E., *One body in Christ: A Study in the Relationship of the Church to Christ in the Epistles of the Apostle Paul*, London, 1955.
Bouyer, L., 'Où en est la théologie du corps mystique?' in *Rev. Sc. Rel.*, 22 (1948) 313–33.
Colpe, C., 'Zur Leib-Christi Vorstellung im Epheserbrief' in *Judentum, Urchristentum, Kirche* (Festschrift J. Jeremias), 1960, 172–87.
Delling, G., 'Pleroma' in *TWNT*, VI, 297–304.
de Lubac, H., *Corpus Mysticum*, Paris, ²1949.
Feuillet, A., 'L'Eglise plérome du Christ d'après Eph 1:23' in *NRT*, 78 (1956) 499–72, 593–610.
Gewiess, J., 'Die Begriffe "pleroun" und "pleroma" im Kolosser— und Epheser-Brief' in *Vom Wort des Lebens* (Festschrift M. Meinertz), 1951, 128–41.
Havet, J., 'La doctrine paulinienne du "Corps du Christ". Essai de Mise au Point' in *Littérature et Théologie Pauliniennes* (Rech. Bibl. V), Bruges, 1960, 185–216.
Kearns, C., 'The Church the Body of Christ according to St Paul' in *IER*, 90 (1958) 1–11, 145–57; 91 (1959) 1–15, 313–27.
Lawlor, F. X., 'Mystical Body of Christ' in *New Cath. Eycycl.*, 10,166–70.
MacGregor, G., *Corpus Christi. The Nature of the Church according to the Reformed Tradition*, London, 1959.
Malavez, L., 'L'Eglise, corps du Christ: sens et provenance de l'expression chez saint Paul' in *Rech. Sc. Rel.*, 32 (1944) 27–94.
Mascall, E. L., *Corpus Christi*, London–New York, 1953.
Michalon, P., 'Eglise, corps mystique du Christ glorieux' in *NRT*, 74 (1952) 673–87.
Mussner, F., *Christus, das All und die Kirche*, Trier, 1955.
Percy, E., *Der Leib Christi in den paulinischen Homologoumena und Antilogoumena*, Lund-Leipzig, 1942.
Pius XII, 'Encyclicae Litterae: de Mystico Jesu Christi Corpore deque nostra in eo cum Christo coniunctione' in *AAS*, 35 (1943) 193-248.
Robinson, J. A. T., *The Body. A Study in Pauline Theology*, London–Chicago, 1952.

Schlier, H., 'Corpus Christi' in *Reallexikon für Antike und Christentum*, vol. III, 437–53.
Der Brief an die Epheser, Düsseldorf, ³1962: Excursus, 90–6.
Schweizer, E., 'Die Kirche als Leib Christi in den paulinischen Homologoumena und Antilogoumena' in *Neotestamentica*, 1963, 276–316.
Skydsgaard, K. E., *The Church and the Body of Christ*, Indiana, 1963.
Soiron, T., *Die Kirche als der Leib Christi. Nach der Lehre des heiligen Paulus exegetisch, systematisch und in der theologischen wie praktischen Bedeutung dargestellt*, Düsseldorf, 1951.
Tromp, S., *Corpus Christi quod est ecclesia:* Vol. II; *De Christo Capite Mystici Corporis*, Rome, 1960.
Wikenhauser, A., *Die Kirche als der mystische Leib Christi nach dem Apostel Paulus*, Münster in West., ²1940.
Will, R., 'La conception protestante de l'Eglise considerée comme le Corpus Christi' in *Rev. Hist. Phil. Rel.*, 12 (1932) 465–94.

CHAPTER TWENTY-ONE

de Lubac, 'Credo Ecclesiam' in *Sentire Ecclesiam* (Festschrift H. Rahner), ed. by J. Daniélou and H. Vorgrimler, Freiburg–Basel–Vienna, 1961, 13–16.
Kopling, A., 'Notae Ecclesiae' in *LTK*, VII, 1044–8.
Le Guillou, M.-J., *Christ and Church. A Theology of Mystery*, New York, 1966.
Malmberg, F., *Ein Leib—Ein Geist. Vom Mysterium der Kirche*, Freiburg–Basel–Vienna, 1960.
Montcheuil, Y., *Aspects de l'Eglise*, Paris, 1951.
Nautin, P., *Je crois à l'Esprit Saint dans la Sainte Eglise pour la résurrection de la chair. Etude sur l'histoire et la théologie du symbole* (Unam Sanctam 17), Paris, 1947.
Philips, G., *La Sainte Eglise Catholique*, Tournai–Paris, 1947.
Rahner, H., *Die Kirche. Gottes Kraft in menschlicher Schwäche*, Freiburg i. Br., 1957.
Salaverri, J., *De Ecclesia Christi*, Madrid, 1950, nn. 1149–1275.
Semmelroth, O., *Ich glaube an die Kirche*, Düsseldorf, 1959.
Thils, G., *Les notes de l'Eglise dans l'Apologétique dépuis la Réforme*, Gembloux, 1937.
Witte, J. L. 'Zu den vier Wesenszügen der Kirche' in *Gott in Welt* (Festgabe K. Rahner), vol. II, Freiburg–Basel–Vienna, 1964, 427–54.

Zapelena, T., *De Ecclesia Christi*, Pars Apologetica, Rome, 1955, 464–573.

Chapter Twenty-Two

Adam, K., *One and Holy*, London–New York, 1954.
Adams, M. (ed.), *Vatican II on Ecumenism*, Dublin–Chicago, 1967.
Baum, G., *That they may be one. A Study of Papal Doctrine* (Leo XIII–Pius XII), Westminster, Md–London, 1958.
Bea, Card. A., *The Way to Unity after the Council*, London–Dublin–Melbourne, 1967.
Beckmann, J.–Steck, K. G.–Viering, F., *Von Einheit und Wesen der Kirche*, Göttingen, 1960.
Cerfaux, L., 'L'Unité du corps apostolique dans le Nouveau Testament' in *Recueil L. Cerfaux*, vol. II, Gembloux, 1964, 227–37.
Chaillet, P., et al., *L'Eglise est une. Hommage à J. A. Möhler*, Paris, 1939.
Chirico, P., 'One Church: What does it Mean?' in *TS* (1967) 659–682.
Congar, Y. M.-J., *Chrétiens Désunis. Principes d'un 'oecuménisme' catholique* (Unam Sanctam I), Paris, 1937, re-issued 1964 (Engl. transl., *Divided Christendom*, London, 1939).
'The Church and its Unity' in *The Mystery of the Church*, London, 1965, 15–52.
Dialogue Between Christians. Catholic Contributions to Ecumenism, London–Dublin–Melbourne, 1966.
Fascher, E., 'Ökumenisch und katholisch. Zur Geschichte zweier, heute viel gebrauchte Begriffe' in *Theol. Literaturzeitung*, 85 (1960) 7–20.
Hanson, S., *The Unity of the Church in the New Testament. Colossians and Ephesians*, Uppsala, 1946.
Hastings, A., *One and Apostolic*, London–New York, 1963.
Jaeger, Card. L., *A Stand on Ecumenism. The Council's Decree*, London–Dublin, 1965.
Kaiser, M., *Die Einheit der Kirchengewalt nach dem Zeugnis des Neuen Testaments und der apostolischen Väter*, Munich, 1956.
Kasper, W., 'The Dialogue with Protestant Theology' in *Concilium*, 4 (1965) 76–87.
Kuss, O., 'Die Schrift und die Einheit der Kirche' in *Münch. Theol. Zeits.*, 18 (1967) 292–307.
Lambert, B., *Ecumenism. Theology and History*, 2 Vols, New York–London, 1967.

Leeming, B., *The Vatican Council and Christian Unity*, London, 1966.
Le Guillou, M.-J., *Mission et Unité. Les exigences de la communion* (Unam Sanctam 33), Paris, 1960.
Lengsfeld, P., 'Die Einheit der Kirche und die Wiedervereinigung der getrennten Christen in katholischer Sicht' in *Una Sancta,* 18 (1963) 1–12.
Lescrauwaet, J., *The Bible on Christian Unity*, London, 1965.
Lortz, J., 'Die Einheit des Christentums in katholischer Sicht' in *Trier. Theol. Zeits.*, 68 (1959) 8–29, 85–107.
Martin, F., 'Pauline Trinitarian Formulas and Church Unity' in *Cath. Bibl. Quart.*, 30 (1968) 199–219.
Marxsen, W. (ed.), *Einheit der Kirche?*, Witten, 1964.
McNamara, K. (ed.), *Christian Unity*, Dublin, 1962.
Möhler, J. A., *Die Einheit der Kirche oder das Prinzip des Katholizismus dargestellt im Geiste der Kirchenväter der drei ersten Jahrhunderte*, ed. by J. R. Geiselmann, Cologne, 1957.
Roesle, M.–Cullmann, O. (ed.), *Begegnung der Christen. Studien evangelischer und katholischer Theologen* (Festschrift O. Karrer), Stuttgart–Frankfurt, ²1960.
Sartory, T., *The Ecumenical Movement and the Unity of the Church*, Westminster, Md, 1963, Oxford, 1964.
Schiffers, M., *Die Einheit der Kirche nach J. H. Newman*, Düsseldorf, 1956.
Schlier, H., 'Die Einheit der Kirche im Denken des Apostels Paulus' in *Die Zeit der Kirche*, Freiburg, ²1958, 287–99.
'Einheit der Kirche' in *LTK*, III, 750–4.
'Die Einheit der Kirche nach den Neuen Testament' in *Catholica,* 14 (1960) 161–77.
Schütte, H., *Um die Wiedervereinigung im Glauben*, Essen, 1958.
Subilia, V., 'L'unité de l'Eglise selon le Nouveau Testament' in *Rev. Réf.*, 18 (1967) 1–30.
Sullivan, F. A., 'De unitate Ecclesiae: Doctrina Catholica et Doctrina quae praevalet in Concilio Mundiali Ecclesiarum' in *Gregorianum*, 43 (1962) 510–26.
Tavard, G. H., *Two Centuries of Ecumenism*, London, 1961.
Thils, G., *Histoire doctrinale du mouvement oecuménique*, Paris–Louvain, ²1963.
'Le decret conciliaire sur l'oecuménisme' in *NRT*, 87 (1965) 225–44.
Syncrétisme ou catholicité, Paris, 1967.
'Unity of the Church' in *New Cath. Encycl.*, 14, 450–1.
Thurian, M., 'The Visible Unity of Christians' in *Ecum. Rev.*, 13 (1960–1) 313–34.

Villain, M., *Vatican II et la dialogue oecuménique*, Paris, 1966.
'L'oecuménisme à l'aube d'une nouvelle periode' in *NRT*, 88 (1966) 561–80.
'La grâce de l'oecuménisme aujourd'hui', *ibid.*, 90 (1968) 513–30.
Volk, H., *Gott alles in allem*, Mainz, 1961.
Von Geusau, L. A. (ed.), *Ecumenism and the Roman Catholic Church*, London–Melbourne, 1966.

Chapter Twenty-Three

Burghardt, W. J., 'A Holy Church', in *The Way*, 3 (1963) 22–31.
Chirico, P., 'Holiness of the Church', in *New Cath. Encycl.*, 7, 54–5.
Congar, Y. M.-J., *Vraie et fausse Réforme dans l'Eglise* (Unam Sanctam 20), Paris, 1950.
Dejaifve, G., 'L'Eglise Catholique peut-elle entrer dans la répentance oecuménique?' in *NRT*, 84 (1962) 225–39.
Hislop, I. (ed.), *The Purification of the Church*, London, 1967.
Hofmann, F., 'Heiligkeit der Kirche' in *LTK*, V, 128–9.
Jungmann, J., 'The Holy Church' in *The Church: Readings in Theology*, New York, 1963, 30–9.
McGoldrick, P., 'Sin and the Holy Church' in *ITQ*, 32 (1965) 3–27.
Mörsdorf, K.–Rahner, K., 'Kirchengliedschaft' in *LTK*, VI, 221–5.
Rahner, K., *Die Kirche der Sünder*, Freiburg, 1948.
von Balthasar, H. U., 'Casta Meretrix' in *Sponsa Verbi. Skizzen zur Theologie*, II, Einsiedeln, 1961, 203–305.

Chapter Twenty-Four

Asmussen, H.–Stählin, W., *Die Katholizität der Kirche*, Stuttgart, 1957.
Beinert, W., *Um das dritte Kirchenattribut. Die Katholizität der kirche im Verständnis der evangel. luth. und röm kath. Theologie der Gegenwart*, 2 vols, Essen, 1964.
Congar, Y. M.-J., 'La catholicité de l'Eglise une' in *Chrétiens désunis* (Unam Sanctam I), Paris, 1937, 115–48.
'Catholicité' in *Catholicisme*, II, 722–5.
Dejaifve, G., 'Oecuménisme et Catholica' in *NRT*, 75 (1952) 1039–1052; 76 (1954) 24–43.
de Poulpiquet, A., *La notion de Catholicité*, Paris, 1910.
Garciadiégo, A., *Katholiké Ekklesia*, Mexico, 1953.
Lackmann, M., *Credo ecclesiam catholicam*, Graz, 1960.
Le Guillou, M. J., 'Plénitude de catholicité et oecuménisme' in *Istina*, 6 (1959) 237–56, 261–78.

McGarry, C., 'Collegiality and Catholicity' in *ITQ*, 32 (1965) 189–208.
Paquier, R., *Vers la catholicité evangélique*, Lausanne, 1935.
Przywara, E., 'Römische Katholizität—All-Christliche Ökumenizität' in *Gott in Welt* (Fest. K. Rahner), vol. II, 524–8.
Rétif, A., *Catholicité* (Je sais, Je crois 87), Paris, 1956.
Salaverri, J., 'Katholizität der Kirche' in *LTK*, VI, 90–2.
Sartory, T., *Mut zur Katholizität. Geistliche und theologische Erwägungen zur Eingung der Christen*, Salzburg, 1962.
Seckler, M., 'Katholisch als Konfessionsbezeichnung' in *Theol. Quart.*, 145 (1965) 401–31.
Tavard, G. H., *The Quest for Catholicity: A Study in Anglicanism*, New York, 1964.
Thils, G., 'La notion de catholicité de l'Eglise à l'epoque moderne' in *ETL*, 13 (1936) 5–73.
'Catholicity' in *New Cath. Encyclopedia*, vol. 3, 339–40.
Tomkins, O., *The Wholeness of the Church*, London, 1949.
Witte, J. L., 'Die Katholizität der Kirche. Eine neue Interpretation nach alter Tradition' in *Gregorianum*, 42 (1961) 193–241.

CHAPTER TWENTY-FIVE

Bainvel, J., 'Apostolicité' in *DTC*, I, 1618–31.
Concilium, 4/4 (1968): 'Apostolic by Succession?'.
Congar, Y. M.-J., 'Apostolicité' in *Catholicisme*, I, 728–30.
'L'Apostolicité de l'Eglise selon St Thomas d'Aquin' *Rev. de Sc. Phil. et Theol.*, 45 (1960) 209–24.
Ehrardt, A., *The Apostolic Succession in the First Two Centuries of the Church*, London, 1953.
Grivec, F., 'De Ecclesiae Mysterio et Successione Apostolica' in *Salmanticenses*, 19 (1957) 635–57.
Holstein, H., 'L'Evolution de mot "apostolique" au cours de l'histoire de l'Eglise' in A. Hamman *et al.*, *L'Apostolat*, Paris, 1957, 41–61.
Javierre, A., *El tema literario de la succesión. Prologomenos para el estudio de la sucésion apostolica*, Rome–Zurich, 1963.
Karrer, O., 'Apostolische Nachfolge und Primat' in *Fragen der Theologie heute*, ed. by Feiner–Trütsch–Böckle, Einsiedeln–Zurich–Cologne, ³1960, 175–206.
'Apostolizität der Kirche' in *LTK*, I, 765–6.
Lécuyer, J., 'Mystère de la Pentecôte et apostolicité de la mission de

l'Eglise' in *Etudes sur le sacrement de l'ordre*, Paris, 1957, 167–213.
Ratzinger, J., 'Primat, Episcopat und Successio Apostolica' in *Catholica*, 13 (1958) 260–77.
Salaverri, J., 'Sucésion apostolica y singularidad de la mision de "los Doce" ' in *Rev. Esp. Teol.*, 27 (1967) 245–69.
Schlink, E., 'La succession apostolique' in *Verbum Caro*, 69 (1964) 52–86.
'Die apostolische Sukzession' in *Der kommende Christus und die kirchlichen Traditionen*, Göttingen, 1961, 160–95.
Söhngen, G., 'Überlieferung und apostolische Verkündigung. Eine fundamentaltheologische Studie zum Begriff des Apostolischen' in *Episcopus*, Regensburg, 1949, 89–109.
Sullivan, F. A., 'Apostolic Succession' in *New Cath. Encycl.*, I, 695–6.
Thils, G., 'Apostolicity', *ibid.*, 699–700.
Turner, C. H., 'Apostolic Succession' in *Essays on the Early History of the Church and the Ministry*, ed. by H. B. Swete, London, 1921, 95–214.
XVI Semana Española de Teologia (17–22 Sept. 1956) Problemas de actualidad sobre la sucesion apostolica. Otros Estudios, Madrid, 1957, pp. 1–454.
(Cf also the bibliography to chapters 13–15).

CHAPTER TWENTY-SIX

Auvray, P., 'Eschatologie' in *Catholicisme*, IV, 410–14.
Beasley-Murray, G. R., *Jesus and the Future*, London–New York, 1954.
Besret, B., *Incarnation où Eschatologie?*, Paris, 1964.
Blank, J., *Krisis. Untersuchungen zur johanneischen Christologie und Eschatologie*, Freiburg, 1964.
Bonsirven, J., *Le Régne de Dieu*, Paris, 1957.
Bultmann, R. K., *History and Eschatology*, Edinburgh, 1957.
Cerfaux, L., 'L'Eglise et le Régne de Dieu d'après saint Paul' in *Recueil L. Cerfaux*, II, Gembloux, 1964, 365–87.
Ceroke, C. P.–Duffy, S. J., 'Parousia' in *New Cath. Encycl.*, 10, 1032–9.
Corell, A., *Consummatum est: Eschatology and Church in the Gospel of St John*, New York, 1958.
Daniélou, J., 'Christologie et eschatologie' in *Das Konzil von Chalkedon*, III, 269–86.

Dodd, C.H., *The Parables of the Kingdom*, rev. ed. New York, 1961.
Feuillet, A., 'Parousie' in *DBS*, VI, 1331–1419.
'Le temps de l'Eglise d'après le quatrième Evangile et l'Apocalypse' in *La Maison Dieu*, 65 (1961) 60–79.
Galot, J., 'Eschatologie' in *Dict. Spir. Asc. Myst.*, 4, 1020–59.
Haughey, J. C., 'Church and Kingdom: Ecclesiology in the Light of Eschatology' in *TS*, 29 (1968) 72–86.
Holwerda, D., *The Holy Spirit and Eschatology in the Gospel of John. A Critique of R. Bultmann's Present Eschatology*, Kampen, 1959.
Jeremias, J., *The Parables of Jesus*, rev. ed., New York, 1963.
Joest, W., 'Die Kirche und die Parousie Jesu Christi' in *Gott in Welt* (Festschrift K. Rahner), vol. I, Freiburg–Basel–Vienna, 1964, 536–50.
Kleinknecht, H.–Schmidt, K. L., *basileus, basileia* . . . in *TWNT*, I, 562–95.
Koch, R., 'L'aspect eschatologique de l'Esprit du Seigneur d'après S. Paul' in *Studia Paulina*, I (1963) 131–41.
Kümmel, W. G., 'Futuristic and Realized Eschatology in the Earliest Stages of Christianity' in *Journ. Relig.*, 43 (1963) 303–14.
Martin, F.–Williams, M. E., 'Eschatology' in *New Cath. Encycl.*, 5, 524–38.
McEvoy, J. A., 'Realized Eschatology and the Kingdom Parables' in *CBQ*, 9 (1947) 329–57.
Moltmann, J., *The Theology of Hope. On the Ground and the Implications of a Christian Eschatology*, New York–London, 1967.
Mouroux, J., *The Mystery of Time. A Theological Inquiry*, New York, 1964.
Murray, J. C.–Cantley, M. J., 'Kingdom of Christ, of God' in *New Cath. Encycl.*, 8, 188–95.
Oepke, A., 'Parousia' in *TWNT*, V, 856–69.
Piolanti, A., *La communione dei Santi de la vita eterna*, Florence, 1957.
Pautrel, R.–Mollat, D., 'Judgment dans l'Ancien Testament, dans le Nouveau Testament' in *DBS*, IV, 1321–94.
Rigaux, B., 'La seconde venue de Jésus' in *La Venue du Messie. Messianisme et Eschatologie* (Rech. Bibl. VI), Bruges, 1962, 173–216.
Robinson, J. A. T.,*Jesus and His Coming*, London–Nashville, 1958.
Schlier, H., 'Reich Gottes und Kirche' in *Studia Catholica*, 32 (1957) 178–89.

Schnackenburg, R., *God's Rule and Kingdom*, New York, 1963.
'Kirche und Parusie' in *Gott in Welt*, vol. I, 551–78.
Schuster, H., 'Die konsequente Eschatologie der Interpretation des NT kritisch betrachtet' in *ZTZ*, 47 (1956) 1–25.
Skydsgaard, K. E., 'The Kingdom of God and the Church' in *Scot. Journ. Theol.*, 4 (1951) 383–97.
von Balthasar, H. U., 'Eschatology' in *Theology Today*: Vol. I, *Renewal in Dogma*, ed. by J. Feiner, J. Trütsch and F. Böckle, Milwaukee, 1965, 222–44.
Winklhofer, A., *The Coming of His Kingdom*, Edinburgh–London–New York, 1963.

GENERAL INDEX

Abbott, W. M., 341
actualism, mono-actualism, 5, 14–16, 19, 64, 68–9, 76, 107, 215, 261, 271, 314, 326, 337–9
Adam, K., 65 n.7, 85 n.31, 202 n.152, 346, 349, 371
Adams, M., 102 n.19, 371
Adams, R. A., 210 n.174, 353
Adolfs, R., 120 n.83
Albert the Great, St, 84, 281 n.11
Alexandria, School of, 37ff.
Alfaro, J., 247 n.44, 349, 366
Amann, E., 234 n.64, 363
Ambrose, St, 39
Ambrosiaster, 36 n.2
Anabaptists, 216
analogy, 5, 7–9, 19, 57, 74, 80
Anderson, G. H., 355
anointing, 113
Anselm, St, 9 n.16
anthropology, Karl Barth's, 7ff.
Antioch, School of, 41
apokatastasis, 21, 27–34, 42, 324
Appel, N., 363
Aquinas, St Thomas, Thomism, 9 nn.16, 18, 10, 12, 13–14, 17, 36 n.3, 37 n.9, 39, 55 nn.4, 5, 56–7, 58 n.18, 59 nn.19–21, 60 nn.23–5, 61 n.28, 64 nn.2, 5, 71 n.3, 77, 101, 117, 129, 134–5, 145 n.7, 150 nn.2, 3, 152 n.9, 159, 179, n.34, 202, 205 n.162, 206 n.163, 209, 211, 213 n.184, 219, 245 n.28, 254 n.15, 281 n.11, 294 n.22, 297, 301 n.45, 333–4
Aristotle, Aristotelianism, 12–5
Arnold, F. X, 355
Asmussen, H., 352, 360, 373
Athanasius, St, 36 n.2
Aubert, R., 256 n.21, 367
Auer, A., 356
Augustine, St, 9, 28, 31, 36–9, 61 n.29, 83, 117, 141, 145 n.7, 152 n.9, 159, 165 n.64, 206 n.163, 211, 213 n.184, 247, 254 n.16, 280, 294 n.22, 297
Aulén, G., 69 n.22
Auvray, P., 375

Baeck, L., 345
Baillie, J., 220 n.20, 363
Bainvel, J., 374
baptism, 113–14, 119, 129, 149–52, 209–10, 291, 300–1
Barauna, G., 153 n.12, 297 n.29, 341
Bardy, E., 353
Barosse, T., 356
Barrau, D., 356
Barrett, C. K., 353, 358
Barth, M., 344
Bartmann, B., 328 n.60
Barucq, A., 363
Baum, G., 102 n.19, 342, 344–5, 352, 358, 363, 371
Bäumer, R., 341
Bea, Card. A., 345, 352, 371
Beasley-Murray, G. R., 375
Beckmann, J., 371
Bede, St, 293 n.16
Behm, J., 331 n.74
Beinert, W., 367, 374
Bellarmine, Card., 265 n.3, 333
Benoit, P., 268 n.4, 269 n.7, 272 n.20, 273 nn.28, 29, 274, 275 n.40, 276, 277 n.47, 346, 358, 363, 365, 369
Berkhof, H., 353
Berkouwer, G. C., 31 n.17, 32 n.18, 42
Bernard, St, 247 n.43
Bertetto, D., 346
Bertrams, W., 367
Besret, B., 375
Best, E., 369

Betz, J., 96 n.30, 350, 359
Betz, O., 359
Beumer, J., 342–3, 345, 363
Beyer, H. W., 359
Blank, J., 376
Bläser, P., 102 n.19, 352, 359
Blauw, J., 356
Blondel, H., 16 n.37
Bonaventure, St, 129
Bonnefoy, J., 346
Bonnetain, P., 366
Bonsirven, J., 376
Bosc, J., 64 n.5
Boston, Archbishop of, 103 n.24
Botte, B., 36 n.3
Bouessé, H., 346, 359
Bouillard, H., 8 n.12, 38 n.16, 64 n.2, 69 n.21, 248 n.45
Bouyer, L., 209 n.170, 369
Bover, J. M., 28 n.7, 344
Boyer, C., 55 n.5, 346
Braun, F. M., 40 n.21, 90 n.4, 92, 350
Bright, L., 160 n.44, 352
Brinckmann, B., 363, 366
Brosch, H. J., 367
Brown, R. E., 227 n.42
Brungs, R. A., 356
Brunner, E., 42, 213
Buckley, J. C., 356
Bulst, W., 363
Bultmann, R., 20 n.47, 227 n.42, 376
Burghardt, W. J., 373
Butler, B. C., 341

Cadoux, C. J., 93 n.17
Callaghan, D., 164 n.57
Callahan, D., 356
Calvin, Calvinism, 2, 19, 26, 28, 31, 64 n.5, 66, 70, 114, 171, 216, 218, 219 n.16, 228, 234–5
Carmody, J. M., 346
Carthage, Council of, 294–5
Casel, O., 208 n.168
Casiano, F., 367
Catao, B., 347
Catechismus Romanus, 64 n.5
Catherine of Siena, St, 170 n.85
Cazelles, H., 363
Cerfaux, L., 22 n.2, 28 nn.4, 7, 29 n.11, 41 n.28, 174 n.6, 268 n.3, 269, 272 nn.20, 24, 273 nn.28, 29, 274, 275 n.39, 276, 341, 347, 357, 366, 371, 376
Ceroke, O. P., 376
Chaillet, P., 371
Chalcedon, Council of, 52, 55 n.2, 56 n.8, 57
Charue, A., 344
Chavasse, A., 356
Chavaz, E., 366
Chenu, M.-D., 9 n.19, 11, 343
Chevallier, M. A., 368
Chirico, P. F., 368, 371, 373
christocentrism, 5, 19f., 52–3, 88, 148, 200, 238, 268, 338–9
christology, 11, 14–15, 19, 37–8, 51–70, 127, 171, 215, 238, 300, 307, 326, 337, 339
and ecclesiology and mariology, 71–86
and justification, 19–20, 70, 85, 238, 337ff.
Chrysologus, St Peter, 58 n.18
Chrysostom, St John, 36 n.2, 41 n.29, 100 n.13, 208 n.168
Church
God the Father and the eternal election of, 21–32
God the Son and the objective realization of, 51–70
God the Holy Spirit and the subjective realization of, 87, 123–142
trinitarian aspect of, 1–2, 51, 87, 304, 333–6
and Jews, 27–32, 43–50
before and after Christ, 35–42, 96–97, 131–2, 285–6, 290
foundation by Christ, 89–97
as people of God, 93–122
as community, 98–108
necessity for salvation, 99–122
and Roman Catholic Church, 102, 115, 287
and non-Roman Christian Churches, 102, 115, 287
and non-Christian religions, 103–107, 116–19
and world, 104, 108–11, 114, 116–122

GENERAL INDEX

semper reformanda, 17–18, 109, 120, 298, 305
missionary, 118–22, 143–8
charismatic, 139–40, 256–62
as institution/event, 38–9, 88, 138–40, 173, 177, 188, 251–62
of freedom, 140, 211–12, 291–2, 236–7
of joy, 140–2
dynamic nature of, 143–6, 268, 279, 288, 304, 336
functional nature of, 144–8, 267f., 336
of service, 144–6, 192–3
authority of the, 7, 172–87, 191, 200–1
and revelation, 194–9
law of, 212–13
as mystery of faith, 279–81
as visible and invisible, 92f., 108, 263–6, 282f.
as Body of Christ, 267–78
as universal sacrament of salvation, 18, 91–2, 71–8, 98–122
unity and disunity of, 282–8
holiness and sinfulness of, 289–301
catholicity of, 91–2, 103–9, 114–122, 302–9
apostolicity of, 143–8, 194–5, 210–211, 259, 261–2, 310–17
eschatological nature of, 90, 95, 299–300, 318–32
Clarke, T. E., 346
Clavier, H., 359
Clement of Alexandria, St, 9, 12, 170 n.85
Clement of Rome, St, 144, 191 n.108, 192
Clement, Second Epistle of, 24
Coathelem, H., 349
Collins, J. D., 130 n.22, 353
Colpe, C., 369
Colson, J., 357, 359
Comblin, J., 347
community, fundamental form of salvation, 98–108
Condon, K., 363
confession of faith, 235–6
confirmation, 113, 149–52
Congar, Y., 9 n.16, 11 n.21, 14, 36 n.6, 37 n.11, 39, 41 n.29, 52 n.4,
68 n.14, 69 n.22, 71 n.4, 72 nn.7, 8, 77 nn.14, 15, 83 nn.14, 24, 129 n.15, 135 n.35, 136, 154 nn.17, 18, 159, 197 n.136, 206 n.163, 213 n.184, 221 nn.21, 22, 225, 226 nn.38, 39, 40, 227 n.42, 232 n.58, 235 n.65, 260 n.26, 261 n.30, 274, 281 n.11, 304 n.11, 333–4, 341, 343, 345, 347, 349, 352–3, 357, 359–60, 363, 371, 374
Constantinople, Council of, 134
Conzelmann, H., 366
Cooperation, 8; see justification
Coppens, J., 350
Corcoran, P., 343
Corell, A., 376
Cornelis, E., 352
Courtade, G., 363
Courturier, C., 356
covenant, 12, 34, 93ff., 98ff.
Cox, H., 17, 121 n.91, 327 n.56, 343
creation, 7–8, 12, 24, 55, 64 n.2, 76
Creed, of Nicaea-Constantinople, 279–81, 302, 315
Crocker, J., 359
Cullmann, O., 96 n.30, 182 n.53, 194, 200, 320 n.16, 341, 347, 359, 363, 372
Cyprian, St, 110
Cyril of Alexandria, St, 59 n.20

Dabin, P., 357
Dahl, N. A., 352
Dalrymple, J., 359
Damarie, J., 36 n.3
Damascene, St John, 59 n.20
Damian, St Peter, 255 n.17
Daniélou, J., 347, 376
Davies, J. G., 356
Davis, C., 120 n.83, 135, 141
De Albornoz, C., 201, 359
de Bovis, A., 260 n.28, 368
de Chardin, Teilhard, 164
de Finance, J., 16 n.37, 343
de Fraine, J., 93 n.17
de Grandmaison, L., 320 n.14
Dejaifve, G., 357, 364, 373, 374
de la Potterie, I., 357
de Letter, P., 354
Delhaye, P., 352
Delling, G., 369

de Lubac, H., 40 n.23, 41 n.27, 83 n.15, 120, 129 n.16, 203 n.154, 254 nn.14, 15, 281, n.11, 293, 341, 345, 356, 368–70
Demann, P., 28 n.4, 344
Denis, H., 356
De Petter, 16 n.37
de Poulpiquet, A., 374
de Quervain, A., 345
De Rosa, P., 346–7
Descamps, A., 366
de Smedt, E. J., 357
De Vooght, P., 364
Dewailly, L. M., 65 n.5, 144 n.6, 356
Dewar, L., 354
Dewart, L., 17, 147 n.17, 343
diaconate, 192–4
Dibelius, O., 92 n.15
Dietzfelbinger, W., 352
Dinkler, E., 22 n.2, 28 n.4, 40 n.22, 344
Dix, G., 345
Dodd, C. H., 376
Dolch, H., 341
Dubarle, A., 354, 364
Duffy, S. J., 376
Dupont, J., 226 nn. 39, 40, 347, 351, 359, 364
Dupuy, B.-D., 359
Durrwell, F. X., 130 n.19, 347

Eagleton, T., 160 n.44
Ebeling, G., 364
ecclesiology, 3, 21ff., 37–8, 51–3, 63ff., 71–86, 177, 271, 307, 333–340
    see also Church
    and christology, 52–3, 71–8, 109–111, 267f., 336–7
    and mariology, 52–3, 83–6
    and justification, 52–3, 85–6, 105, 239
    trinitarian, 1–2, 51, 87, 333–6, 133
Eckert, W. P., 345
ecumenical movement, 16–17, 308–9
Ehrardt, A., 374
Ehrlich, E. L., 345
Eichholz, E., 368
Eichrodt, W., 319 n.4
Ekström, R., 360

election, 3, 21ff., 27ff.
    of the Church, 22ff.
Elert, W., 368
Emmet, C. W., 368
Ephesus, Council of, 81
Ertis, O., 354
eschatology, 88, 90
essentialism, 14–15
eucharist, 113, 128–9, 138, 252–4, 260, 209–10
Eusebius of Caesarea, 36 n.2, 64 n.5, 191 n.108
existentialism, 16–17

Fabro, C., 16 n.37
faith, 8f., 214, 280
    sola fide, see justification
Farrer, A. M., 360
Fathers, authority of, 233–4
Faustus of Riez, 281 n.11
Favale, A., 341
Feeney, Fr, 103 n.24
Feiner, J., 341
Ferro-Calvo, M., 357
Feuillet, A., 42 n.32, 96 n.30, 320 nn.15, 16, 329 n.61, 345, 347, 351, 369, 376
Fisher, D., 121 n.90
Flanagan, D., 341, 349
Flannery, A., 341
Flender, H., 354
Flesseman-Van Leer, E., 364
Flick, M., 366
Florence, Council of, 223
Florovsky, G., 234 n.65
Foerster, F. W., 345
Fransen, P., 117
Franzelin, J. B., 55 n.5, 179 n.34, 225 n.37, 266 n.7, 347, 364
Freyne, S., 360
Friedrich, G., 357
Fries, H., 235 n.68, 341
Frisque, J., 360
Fuchs, J., 64 n.5
Funk, F. X., 191 n.108, 192 nn.109, 110, 254 n.16

Gaechter, P., 360
Gallagher, J., 341
Galot, J., 376
Galtier, P., 55 n.5, 347

Ganoczy, A., 360
Gardeil, A., 368
Garciadiégo, A., 374
Geiselmann, J. R., 59 n.20, 227 n.42, 349, 364
Gewiess, J., 194 n.120, 360, 368–9
Giblet, J., 174 n.6, 360
Gilbert, A., 345
Gils, F., 360
Gilson, E., 16 n.37
Gloege, G., 93 n.16
Glorieux, P., 357
God
  'death' of, 339
  knowledge of, 8f.
  sole subjectivity of, 8–9, 19–20
  soli Deo gloria, *see* justification
Gogarten, F., 347
Goguel, M., 91 n.7, 98 n.2
Gore, C., 354
Grabmann, M., 59 n.20
grace, doctrine of, 1, 11, 15, 85, 103, 241ff., *see also* justification
Grässer, E., 91 n.6, 351
Gregory Nazianzen, St, 36 n.2
Grelot, P., 175 n.15, 360
Gribomont, J., 352
Grillmeier, A., 59–60, 68 n.14, 72 n.7, 102 n.19, 206 n.164, 347
Grivec, F., 375
Groot, J., 352
Grosche, R., 249 n.52, 360, 366
Grossouw, W., 366
Guerry, E., 360
Gutwenger, E., 347

Hahn, F., 351, 356
Hales, Alexander of, 129
Hamer, J., 6 n.3, 36 n.6, 153 n.12, 159 n.34, 169 n.81, 216 n.4, 219 n.16, 251 n.2, 265 n.3, 301 n.45, 341
Hamilton, N. Q., 354
Hamp, V., 354
Hanson, S., 372
Häring, B., 360
Harl, M., 347
Harrington, W., 364
Hastings, A., 372
Haubst, R., 354
Haughey, J. C., 376

Havet, J., 269 n.6, 369
Hebblethwaite, P., 121 n.90
Hedenquist, G., 345
Hegesippus, 191 n.108
Heimerl, H., 357
Hein, J., 366
Heislbetz, J., 352
Helz, F., 347
Hémery, J., 350
Hennig, J., 36 n.3
Henry, A., 356
Henry, P., 65 n.7, 347
Hermas, Shepherd of, 24
Herrmann, I., 354
Herrmann, R., 366
Herrmann, W., 280
Hillmann, E., 352, 356
Hislop, I., 373
Hoekendijk, J. C., 148 n.18, 327 n.56, 356
Hofmann, A. M., 345
Hofmann, F., 83 n.16, 349, 373
Holböck, F., 342
Holmes, J. D., 364
Holmström, F., 90 n.4
Holstein, H., 364, 375
Holwerda, D., 376
Holy Spirit, 6–8, 18, 79–81, 87–8, 123-142, 165-6, 228, 232, 257–8, 266, 280–1, 314, 326-32
Holtzmann, 91 n.7
Huarte, G., 369
Hurley, M., 368

Ignatius of Antioch, St, 191, 254 n.16
incarnation, *see* christology
inspiration, 217ff.
instrumentality, 12, 28, 58, 66, 74, 78, 107, 150, 206, 219
Irenaeus, St, 110, 191 n.108, 261 n.30
Isidore, St, 41

Jaeger, Card. L., 372
James of Viterbo, 333
Jansenius, 31
Javierre, A., 375
Jeremias, J., 91, 94 n.27, 96 n.31, 177 n.25, 180, 182 n.49, 183 n.56, 187 n.94 262, 351, 360, 376

Jerome, St, 36 n.2, 293 n.16, 331 n.74
Jesus Christ, see christology
Joest, W., 366, 376
Jocz, J., 343
John XXIII, Pope, 203–4
Johnston, G., 40 n.22, 345
Journet, Mgr C., 28 n.17, 40 n.21, 150 n.3, 159, 247 n.43, 301 n.45, 342, 344, 366
Judaism, the Church and, 43–50
Jungmann, J. A., 193 n.119, 360, 373
justification, 1–3, 52, 63, 88, 105, 128, 171, 215, 238–249, 339
   and christology, ecclesiology, mariology, 19–20, 52–3, 70–86, 238–9, 249–250, 171, 337–8
Justin, 64 n.5, 170 n.85

Kähler, E., 366
Kaiser, M., 372
Karrer, O., 91 n.9, 360, 375
Käsemann, E., 135, 188–90, 273 n.29, 352, 360, 368
Kasper, W., 126 n.8, 352, 364, 372
Kattenbusch, F., 93 nn.16–17
Kavanaugh, J. A., 120 n.83
Kearns, C., 369
Ketter, P., 357
Kinder, E., 366
Kirk, K. E., 360
Kittel, G., 69 n.20
Klein, G., 91 n.6, 174 n.6, 366
Kleinknecht, H., 354, 376
Klostermann, F., 151 n.7
Koch, R., 376
Kopling, A., 370
Koser, C., 153 n.12
Kösters, R., 366
Kredel, E. M., 360
Kremers, H., 345
Krueger, A. F., 357
Kümmel, W. G., 91 nn.6, 7, 10, 96 n.32, 351, 376
Küng, H., 17–18, 103 n.25, 106 n.39, 117, 126 n.8, 172–3, 184 n.62, 187 n.94, 188 nn.98, 99, 189, 190 nn.105, 106, 197 n.135, 202 n.153, 203–4, 238–9, 243, 244 n.25, 245

nn.29, 30, 246 n.36, 247 n.43, 248 n.51, 249 n.52, 251 n.2, 262, 297 n.28, 328 nn.58, 59, 329 n.66, 337, 342, 366, 368
Kuss, O., 351, 372

Lachenschmidt, R., 208 n.168
Lackmann, M., 366, 374
Lacoque, A., 345
Lambert, B., 372
Lambert, G., 361
Lampe, G. W. H., 354
Langemeyer, B., 350
Latour, J. J., 346
Latourelle, R., 347, 364
Laurentin, R., 350, 352
Lawlor, F. X., 342, 369
Lebreton, J., 354
Lécuyer, J., 347, 357, 361, 375
Leeming, B., 372
Leenhardt, F. J., 354, 361
Legault, A., 361
Le Guillou, M.-J., 342, 356, 370, 372, 374
Lemonnyer, A., 368
Lengsfeld, P., 364, 372
Leo the Great, St, 61 n.29, 69 n.20, 254 n.16
Leo XIII, Pope, 219 n.17
Lescrauwaet, J., 372
Leuba, M. J., 38 n.17, 256 n.21, 261, 364, 368
Levie, J., 365
L'Huillier, P., 354
Lichtenberg, J. P., 346, 352
Liégé, A., 354
Linton, O., 93 n.16
Löhrer, M., 341
Loisy, A., 90 n.3
Lombardía, P., 357
Lonergan, B., 16 n.37, 18 n.44, 55 n.5, 348
Loosen, J., 245 n.27, 366
Lortz, J., 372
Louis-Gabriel, Sr, 346
Lousky, F., 346
Luther, Lutheranism, 2, 10–11, 19, 28, 69–70, 114, 171, 188, 216, 234–5, 249, 277
Lyonnet, S., 27 n.2, 28 nn.4–6, 29 n.11, 344, 357, 366

GENERAL INDEX

MacGregor, G., 369
Mackey, J., 365
MacQuarrie, J., 343
Malevez, L., 272 n.24, 370
Malmberg, F., 348, 370
man, Barth's doctrine of, *see* anthropology
Mandouze, A., 359
manichaeism, 35
Manson, T. W., 93 n.17, 361
Marchal, L., 361
Marcionism, 35
Maréchal, 16 n.37
Maréchaux, B., 368
mariology, 52–3, 63, 79–86
 and justification, 52–3, 84–6
 and christology, 52–3, 79–83
 and ecclesiology, 52–3, 83–6
Maritain, J., 16 n.37–8, 343
Marquardt, F. W., 346
Marrou, H. I., 36 n.3
Marsch, W. D., 346
Marsh, T., 150 n.2
Martin, F., 372, 376
Martin, R. P., 348
Marxsen, W., 372
Mascall, E. L., 83 n.19, 348, 370
Masson, J., 356
matrimony, 113
McEvoy, J. A., 376
McGarry, C., 374
McGoldrick, P., 373
McHenry, F., 16 n.38, 343
McIntyre, J., 348
McKenzie, J. L., 361
McLean, G., 343
McNamara, K., 102 n.19, 112 n.60, 127 n.10, 157 n.23, 169 n.81, 342, 354, 372
McNamara, M., 133 n.32
Menoud, P., 315 n.19, 361
Mersch, E., 10, 55 n.5, 56–7, 71 n.4, 348
Meyer, 194 n.120
Michalon, P., 370
Michel, A., 367
ministry, 138, 149–213
 as service, 192–3, 202–3, 211
 institutional/charismatic, 138–40, 153, 188, 261–2
 lay, 138–9, 149–70

hierarchical, 138, 171–213
 of priesthood, 60–1, 64–5, 149–51, 157–61, 171–83, 185–6, 204–11
 of kingship, 60–1, 64–5, 149–51, 162–4, 171–83, 186–7, 211–13
 of prophecy, 60–1, 64–5, 149–51, 164–70, 171–83, 183–5, 195–204
 of diaconate, 192–4
mission, 104–5, 118–19, 143–213, 175, 312–17
Moeller, C., 367
Möhler, J. A., 126 n.8, 372
Mollat, D., 377
Moltmann, J., 376
'monophysitism', 66–70, 74, 76, 127, 219, 264–5, 336–7
Montanism, 35
Montcheuil, Y., 370
Mooney, C. F., 348
Moos, E., 209 n.173
Moran, G., 365
Moran, W. L., 357
Morenz, S., 354
Mörsdorf, K., 373
Mosbech, H., 361
Mouroux, J., 280 n.6, 285 n.15, 376
Mozarabic Prayer, the, 254 n.16
Mühlen, H., 310 n.2, 349, 352, 354
Müller, A., 83 n.17, 350, 361
Munck, J., 344, 361
Murphy, J. L., 365
Murray, R., 364
Mussner, F., 354, 370

natural theology, 11, 19, 105
nature and grace, 8, 12, 76
Nautin, P., 281 n.10, 355, 371
Navone, J., 355
Nédoncelle, M., 16 n.37
Nepper-Christensen, P., 351
Nestorius, nestorianism, 70, 81, 127, 264–5, 336
Neuner, J., 106 n.39, 117 n.74, 352–353
Newbigin, L., 356
Newman, J., 357
Newman, J. H. Card., 235 n.68, 298, 357
Nietzsche, 142
Norris, F. B., 353

Novak, M., 121 n.90
Nowell, R., 361
Nygren, A., 69 n.22
Nys, H., 353

Obrist, F., 361
O'Callaghan, D., 150 n.2
Oepke, O., 167 n.71, 168 n.77, 180 n.38, 351, 353, 357, 365, 377
O'Flynn, J. A., 365
Olsson, H., 369
Orange, Council of, 295 n.26
Orbe, A., 343
orders, 113, 149
Origen, 24–5, 36 n.2, 170 n.85, 319 n.11
O'Rourke, J. J., 342
Orthodoxy, Eastern, 129, 134, 234 n.65
Ortigues, E. 365
Outler, A. C., 227 n.42

Paquier, R., 374
Pannenberg, W., 348
Paul VI, Pope, 155 n.19
Pautrel, R., 377
Pelagius, Pelagianism, semi-Pelagianism, 105, 127–8, 200, 229, 241, 249
penance, 113
Percy, E., 273 n.29, 370
Pesch, O. H., 367
Peters, E. H., 342
Peterson, E., 6 n.3, 28 n.4, 344
Philips, G., 342, 345, 350, 358, 371
Philo, 39
philosophy, thought-forms of, 11–13, 17–18
Piolanti, A., 377
Pius XII, Pope, 116 n.71, 161 n.45, 208 n.168, 212, 370
Polycarp of Smyrna, 191 n.108
Prat, F., 27 n.1, 28 n.4, 30, 344
Pribilla, M., 345
Prümm, K., 355
Pryzwara, E., 8 n.12, 374

Quakers, 216
Quodvultdeus, 41

Rabanus Maurus, 293 n.16

Rademakers, J., 356
Rahner, H., 83 n.15, 91 n.9, 350, 369, 371
Rahner, K., 16 n.37, 71 n.5, 91 n.9, 112 n.59, 116–17, 131 n.24, 173 n.2, 174 n.6, 175 n.17, 194 nn.121, 124, 195 n.128, 209 n.170, 213 n.184, 217 n.7, 224, 226 n.38, 232 n.57, 236 n.72, 246 n.35, 247 n.42, 253 n.12, 255 n.17, 297 n.29, 301 n.45, 332 n.76, 342, 348, 353, 360, 365, 368, 373
Ratzinger, J., 173 n.2, 342, 365, 368, 375
Rea, J. E., 358
reason, 10, 12, 19, 76
redemption, 94, 205ff; see also reconciliation
reconciliation, 8, 14, 51–3, 65–9, 79–81, 86, 89, 99, 123, 205, 310, 331
Reed, J. J., 358
Reformers, Reformation, 1, 2, 19, 154, 216, 218, 219 n.16, 225–7, 229, 232, 243, 265 n.3, 340
Refoulé, F., 361
Reisner, E., 52 n.4
religion, 105
'natural religion', 107
Rengstorf, K. H., 175 n.12, 178 n.32, 179 n.35, 191 n.107, 358, 361, 367
resurrection, 14, 60–1, 130
Rétif, A., 374
revelation, 8–10, 68, 79–81, 86, 106–107, 195ff., 214–37, 339
Richards, H. J., 346
Richter, W., 361
Ricken, F., 353
Riesenfeld, H., 96, 368
Rigaux, B., 174 n.6, 322 n.29, 361, 377
Ringger, J., 362
Robinson, J. A. T., 370, 377
Roesle, M., 372
Rogues, J., 150 n.4
Roloff, J., 362
Rondet, H., 367
Rowley, H. H., 344
Rückert, H., 227 n.42
Ryan, L., 169 n.81, 358
Ryan, S., 362

sacraments, 110, 112–14, 138, 144–145, 152, 208–9
Salaverri, J., 369, 371, 374, 375
salvation, history of, 14–15
Sartory, T., 342, 349, 350, 372, 374
Sauras, E., 342
Scheeben, M. J., 84
Schelkle, K. H., 166 n.66, 193 n.114, 358, 362
Schildenberger, J., 365
Schillebeeckx, E., 15 n.35, 16 n.37, 39, 67 n.10, 68 n.12, 71 nn.1, 3, 72 nn.6, 8, 116 n.73 117, 121 n.90, 152 n.9, 204 n.160, 209 nn.170, 173, 210 n.174, 342–3, 350, 353, 355
Schiffers, M., 372
Schlatter, A., 93 n.16
Schlette, H. R., 353
Schlier, H., 92 n.11, 188–9, 304 n.8, 344, 351, 370, 372, 377
Schlink, E., 187 n.94, 262, 375
Schmaus, M., 36 n.5, 227 n.42, 235 n.68, 251 n.2, 252 n.9, 342, 348, 365
Schmid, J., 91 n.9, 95, 177 n.25, 351, 354, 362
Schmidt, K. L., 29 n.12, 93 n.16, 251 nn.2, 3, 252 n.8, 320 n.12, 344, 368, 376
Schmithals, W., 91 n.6, 174 n.6, 362
Schnackenburg, R., 96 nn. 32, 34, 129, 167 n.73, 174 n.7, 182 nn.52, 53, 266 n.5, 268 n.4, 270, 273 n.29, 304 n.12, 320 nn.12, 13, 18, 328 nn. 57, 60, 342, 358, 362, 377
Schökel, A., 365
Schreiber, G., 367
Schrenk, G., 162 n.51, 165 n.60, 245 n.29, 358, 367
Schultz, H. J., 346
Schuster, H., 377
Schütte, H., 372
Schutz, R., 365
Schweizer, E., 131 n.24, 354, 355, 362, 370
Scripture
  and the Word of God, 6–7, 215, 217f.
  and justification, 215–16
  and christology, 215–16
  and tradition, 196–200, 222–37
  inspiration of, 217–25
  authority of, 6–7, 222
  canon of, 189–90, 223–5
Seckler, M., 374
Selwyn, E. G., 159, 358
Semmelroth, O., 246 n.36, 258 n.24, 330 n.70, 332 n.76, 350, 353, 358, 362, 368–9, 371
Sheridan, F. C., 367
Sjöberg, E., 354
Skydsgaard, K. E., 370, 377
Smulders, P., 365
Sohm, R., 213
Söhngen, G., 8 n.12, 375
Soiron, T., 370
soteriology, 37–8
Spiazzi, R., 350
Spicq, C., 355
Stählin, G., 245 n.29, 366
Stählin, W., 373
Stakemeier, E., 367
Stramare, T., 365
Stanley, D. M., 342, 348, 351, 362
Steck, K. G., 371
Strathman, H., 358
Subilia, V., 373
Suenens, Card. L., 356, 368
Sullivan, F. A., 3, 180 n.38, 181 nn. 41, 45, 342, 373, 375
Sutcliffe, E. F., 362
Swete, H. B., 355
Synave, P., 219 n.17, 220 n.19, 365
synergism, 32, 85–6, 249

Tavard, G. H., 342, 365, 373–4
Taylor, V., 93 n.17, 348, 365
Ternus, 69 n.22
Tertullian, 170 n.85, 191 n.108
theology
  nature and method of, as *fides quaerens intellectum*, 5–20
  and philosophy, 11f.
  and sociology, 17
Thérèse of Lisieux, St, 285 n.15
Thieme, K., 346
Thierry, William of, 254
Thils, G., 358, 371, 373–5
Thorman, D. J., 358
Thurian, M., 350, 365, 373
Tillard, J.-M. R., 254 n.14, 355

Tobin, W. J., 362
Toledo, Council of, 55 n.2
Tomkins, O., 374
Torrance, T. F., 358, 367
Tradition, 196–200, 222–237
Trent, Council of, 194 n.125, 223, 226, 231, 238, 240 nn.9–13, 242–244, 246 nn.37, 39–40, 248, 249 n.52, 295 n.26, 296 n.27, 301 n.45
Trinity, 1, 2, 101, 123, 128, 134, 245, 280, 287, 302, 310, 334ff.
Tromp, S., 36 n.6, 197 n.135, 218 n.15, 294 n.22, 355, 365, 370
truth
 double order of, 12
 historical, 15 n.35, 17
Tschipke, T., 348
Turner, C. H., 375

universalism, 91–2

Valeske, U., 353
van der Linde, H., 308 n.28
Vatican Council I, 12 n.28, 197, 315–16
Vatican Council II, 2, 3, 17, 18 n.43, 21, 25, 34 n.30, 37–8, 43–7, 50 n.22, 59–60, 65 n.5, 7, 74, 81 n.9, 83 n.13, 84, 97–9, 102–3, 108–22, 123, 127, 136–9, 144–7, 149 n.1, 150–4, 155 n.19, 161 n.45, 163, 166, 174 n.6, 193, 194 n.125, 198, 200 n.146, 206 n.164, 207 n.165, 208 n.168, 210–13, 214 n.1, 228, 235 n.67, 253 n.12, 254, 257, 260, 266 n.5, 272 n.23, 287, 291, 296, 299, 301, 302 n.2, 316, 328, 329 n.65, 330 nn.67–71, 332 nn.76–8, 334–5, 338–40
Vauthier, E., 355
Viering, F., 371
Villain, M., 262 n.34, 373
Villette, L., 367

virgin birth, 79–80
Vogel, M. H., 346
Vögtle, A., 91, 93 n.17, 174 n.6, 178 n.28, 326 n.42, 351, 362
Volk, H., 245 n.27, 367, 373
Vollert, C., 350
von Allmen, J. J., 355
von Balthasar, H. U., 16 n.37, 20 n.47, 31 n.17, 42, 249 n.52, 285 n.15, 337, 46, 348, 355, 358, 362, 373, 377
von Campenhausen, H., 355, 363, 365
von Geusau, A., 308 n.28, 373
von Harnack, A., 91 n.7, 188
Vonier, A., 60 n.24, 140, 348, 355
von Rad, G., 167 n.71, 319 n.5
Vorgrimler, H., 60 n.22, 102 n.19, 131 n.24, 151 n.7, 174 n.6, 207 n.164, 213 n.184, 330 n.70, 332 n.76, 342, 363
Vosté, J.-M., 219 n.17, 220 n.19, 365

Walsh, L., 364
Walter, E., 328 n.60
Walz, J. B., 369
Wendland, H. D., 93 n.16
Wheeler Robinson, H., 93 n.17
Wikenhauser, A., 370
Will, R., 370
Willems, B., 353
Williams, M. E., 376
Winklhofer, A., 377
Winninger, P., 363
Witte, J. L., 3, 65 n.7, 70 n.23, 243 n.24, 277 n.47, 304 n.11, 308 n.28, 348, 355, 367, 371, 374
Word of God, 5ff., 11, 14, 18, 71 215ff.
Wurthwein, E., 366

Zapalena, T., 371

INDEX TO THE WORKS OF KARL BARTH
(References are to mentions in the text and longer quotations)
1. Church Dogmatics
 I/2, 6, 82, 85–6, 105–6
 II/1, 19–20
 II/2, 13, 32, 33
 III/2, 13, 33

 III/4, 33 n.22
 IV/1, 242–3, 250
 IV/2, 16, 242

2. Credo, 79